Lauderdale County Tennessee

COURT MINUTES

VOLUME 1

1836–1844

WPA RECORDS

Heritage Books
2024

HERITAGE BOOKS
AN IMPRINT OF HERITAGE BOOKS, INC.

Books, CDs, and more—Worldwide

For our listing of thousands of titles see our website
at
www.HeritageBooks.com

A Facsimile Reprint
Published 2024 by
HERITAGE BOOKS, INC.
Publishing Division
5810 Ruatan Street
Berwyn Heights, MD 20740

Originally published 1936

International Standard Book Number
Paperbound: 978-0-7884-9077-4

WPA RECORDS

The WPA Records are, for the most part, carbon copies of the original that was typed on onion skin paper during the Depression. Since these records were typed on poor machines by people who did not type well either and read by persons not always sure of the older handwritten material, the results are often less that perfect.

We have made every attempt to make as good a copy as can be made from these older papers. Sometimes there are water stains and burned edges around the paper.. This is the results of a fire at the home of one of the workers, Mrs. Penelope Allen, who was over most of the project.

The WPA Records are now very scattered between the State Archives, various Public and Private Libraries and other collections. Some day, there is a hope that all of these can be collected and stored in one place. In spite of their many mistakes and problems, these are still the most complete collection of Tennessee records found anywhere.

Minute Book A - 1836 - 1844 - No. pages 711

Minute Book A - Index -

A

B

B-cont.

C

D

F

H

J

J-cont.

Lauderdale County
Minute Book 1836-1844
Vol. A

Pg. 1 Be it remembered that at Lauderdale county court began and held for
a county of Lauderdale agreeable to an act of the assembly passed on the
third day of December, eighteen hundred and thirty five at the house of
Samuel Lusk on the first Monday in May in the year of our Lord one thousand
eight hundred and thirty six it being the day of said month present
Robert C. Campbell, Ben F. Jordan Esqs. acting Justices of the peace for
the County of Tipton in that part now Lauderdale. Whereupon the following
gentlemen produced here in Court Commissions from the governor of the
State of Tennessee authorizing and inpowering them to fulfill and discharge
the duties of Justices of the peace for said County of Lauderdale for the
term of six years from the first Saturday in March eighteen hundred and
thirty six, To Wit, Jerimiah Penick, Milton G. Turner, John H. Maxwell,
Able H. Pope, William Strain, Elijah B. Foster, Henry Crihfield, Christopher
G. Titsworth, Henry P. Crawford and Henry R. Chambers, whereupon they took
the oath of office as the law directs and took their seats accordingly and
proceeded to business. Robert C. Campbell and Benjamin F. Jordan was
qualified as Justices of the Peace for said County of Lauderdale and took
their seats as such. The court proceeded to elect chairman of their body
whereupon, R. C. Campbell was elected. William Carrigan who was elected by
the people of the County of Lauderdale on the first Saturday in March 1836
Pg. 2 Clerk of the County Court of said County of Lauderdale presented here in
court a certificate from the proper officer of his election whereupon he
took the oath of office and intered in to bond conditioned and payable as
the law directs.

This day Guy Smith who was elected by the people of the County of Lauderdale on the first Saturday in March 1836, high sheriff for said County for the ensuing two years from said election was qualified as the Law directs and intered into bond conditioned and payable as the law directs.

This day Harry L. Williams proved the killing of two wolves in the County of Lauderdale over the age of four months which is ordered to be certified to the Treasurer their being a majority of the Justices for said County present.

This day William Mathews proved the killing of two wolves in the County of Lauderdale over the age of four months which is ordered to be certified to the Treasurer their being a majority of Justices for said County present.

This day the court proceeded to elect a coroner for the County of Lauderdale for the two succeeding years, whereupon on counting out the votes given it is ascertained that Isaac Braden was duly elected whereupon he came into Court and took the oath and intered into bond, conditioned and
Pg. 3 payable as the law directs.

This day the court proceeded to elect a ranger for the County of Lauderdale whereupon on counting out the votes given it is ascertained that Samuel Lusk was duly and constitutionally elected. Whereupon Samuel Lusk came into Court and took the oath as such and intered into bond conditioned and payable as the law directs.

Ordered by the Court a majority of the Justices for said County being present that Milton G. Turner Esq. be appointed a Revenue Commissioner to take in a list of taxable property and polls in Dist. No. one for the year 1836 and that he return the same here in Court as the law directs.

Ordered by the Court majority being present that John H. Maxwell be appointed a Revenue Commissioner to take in a list of taxable property and polls in Lauderdale County in Dist. No. Second for the year 1836 and that he return the same here in Court as the law directs.

Ordered by the Court a majority being present that Able H. Pope Esq. be appointed Revenue Commissioner to take in a list of taxable property and polls for the County of Lauderdale for the year 1836 and that he return the

Pg. 3 Cont. same here into Court as the law directs.

Pg. 4 Ordered by the Court that a majority being present John Passor Esq. be appointed a Revenue Commissioner to take in a list of taxable property and polls in the County of Lauderdale for the year 1836 for district no. fourth and that he return the same here into Court as the law directs.

Ordered by the Court a majority being present that Robert C. Campbell Esq. be appointed a Revenue Commissioner to take in a list of taxable property and polls in the County of Lauderdale for the year 1836 for district No. fifth and that he return the same here into Court as the law directs.

Ordered by the Court a majority being present that Isaac M. Steele be appointed a Revenue Commissioner to take in a list of taxable property and polls for District no. sixth for the year 1836 and that he return the same here into Court as the law directs.

Ordered by the Court that Christopher G. Titsworth Esq. be appointed Revenue Commissioner to take in a list of taxable property and polls for the year 1836 in District no. seventh and that he return the same into Court as the law directs.

Ordered by the Court that Henry R. Crawford Esq. be appointed Revenue Commissioner for the year 1836 for District no. eighth to take in a list of taxable property and polls liable to taxation in said district and that he return the same here into Court as the law directs.

Ordered by the Court that the following named persons be appointed Commissioners for the Town of Ripley in said County of Lauderdale to sell the lots in the same, to let out the public buildings and superintend the same, to wit, Griffith L. Rutherford, Rezin L. Byron, Hiram C. Keller, Henry R. Crawford and Robert C. Campbell.

This day William L. Moorehead who was elected by the people of the County of Lauderdale on the first Saturday in March 1836 for Trustee for the two ensuing years came into Court and took the oaths required by Law and entered into bond conditioned and payable as the law directs.

Ordered by the Court that Court be adjorned until tomorrow morning.

R. C. Campbell, Chm.

Tuesday morning May the 1836.

Court met pursuant to adjornment present Robert C. Campbell Chairman and Pope, Strain, Penick, Turner, Maxwell, Foster, Crihfield, Titsworth, Chambers and Crawford associate Justices, William Carrigan, Clerk and Guy Smith Sheriff, the Court proceeded to business.

This day Samuel V. Gilliland produced here in Court a commission from the Governor of the State of Tennessee authorizing and impowering him to discharge the duties of a justice of the peace for the County Lauderdale for six years from the first Saturday in March 1836 whereupon S. V. Gilliland took the oath of office required by Law and took his seat accordingly.

Pg. 6 The Court then proceeded to appoint a venire for the next Circuit Court for the County of Lauderdale,,To Wit; for District no. one Thomas Fitzpatrick, Archy Phillips and William Turner, District no. second John H. Maxwell, James Whitson, Isaac Maxwell and William Calhoon, District no. third Hiram C. Keller, W. P. Gaines, Levi Gardner, District no. fourth John Vassor, Samuel Givins and James Tompkins, District no. fifth Hugh Smith, Benjamin F. Jordan and John Holliman, District no. sixth Bird L. Jones, Issac M. Steele and Armstead Wood, District no. seventh Christopher G. Titsworth, Henry Crihfield and G. L. Rutherford, District no. eighth James P. Purcell, James Buck and James J.

Pg.
6 Crawford and that the states Wit of Venire Facious issue accordingly.
Cont. Ordered by the Court that William Braden be appointed overseer of the Ashport road from William P. Gaines to the Cane Creek bridge and that he have all the hands north of the Fulton road belonging to the third district to work under him.

Ordered by the Court that James Crook be appointed Overseer of the Fulton road from William P. Gaines to the Cane Creek bridge and that he have all the hands south of said road in the third district to work under him.

Ordered by the Court that Carey Alsobrook be appointed Overseer of the Dyersburg road commencing at the old county line and that he work to bridge on Cane Creek and that he have the following hands to work under him, To wit, Henry Sumrow, John Smith, Thomas Pruit, Capt. Lee's hands, George Fisher's hands, Carter Ellis, Soloman D. Spain, Isaac D. Maxwell, M. G. Maxwell, Anderson Jordan, J. H. Maxwell's hands, A Vickory, V. Williams and L. Byler's hands.

Pg.
7 Ordered by the Court that Dickinson Jennings be appointed Overseer of the road leading from Buck's Ferry to Stokes Landing, commencing at the Haywood County line and that he work to Blackwell's and that he have the following hands to work under him, To wit; all north of Cane Creek and west of Byler's Fork and east of H. Meadow's Spring Branch and with the path from Meadows to Blackwells, Meadows excluded from Blackwells along the road to Kirbies on the bluff on Forkeddeer River to Cob Creek. Thence up said Creek to the path from Lusk's to H. Sumrow's thence a direct line to the bridge on Byler's Fork of Cane Creek and to include the hands of Jacob Byler's Plantation and the hands of Carooth's and Nelson's places.

Ordered by the Court that John Holliman be appointed Overseer of the road from Ashport to the Cole Creek Bridge and that he have all the hands in the bounds of Cole Creek.

Ordered by the Court that Jerimiah Cheek be Overseer of the Ashport road commencing at the bridge on Cole Creek and that he work to the Hurricane Branch and all the hands between the Fulton road including the Hogsettes, except Lain G. Hogsette, the Jones and May Smith hands.

Ordered by the Court that James Braden be appointed Overseer of the road from Blackwells to Stokes landing and that he have all the hands west of Kirby's road and all west of Jennings boundary and east of the road from Hogsett to the Byler tract road so as to exclude the Hogsetts and Birds L. Jones.

Pg.
8 Ordered by the Court that Jacob Jones be appointed Overseer on the Covington road from the center of the bridge on Rutherford Mill Creek to the old county line and that all the hands west of said road and as far east of the same as to Henry Crihfield, Stephen M. Sullivan and James Rutherford work under him.

Ordered by the Court that Claiborn Ronnsaville be appointed Overseer of the road leading from the Key Corner to Buck Ferry and that he have all the hands East of said road and all west of the same within a half mile of Covington road except Stephen M. Sullivan and Jacob Jones hands to work under him beginning at the bridge on Mill Creek and to work to the dividing ridge between Rutherford Creek and Rounsaville Creek.

Ordered by the Court that Samuel Stricklin be appointed Overseer of the road from the Key Corner to Rutherford's old mill and that he have the following hands to work under him, To wit, H. F. Rutherfors's hands, Benjamin Porter hands, Peschal W. Sanders and hands, James J. Crawford and hands, Malcom Gwinn and John Lee Witter.

Ordered by the Court that William Jordan be appointed Overseer of the

Pg. 8 Cont. Pg. 9 Dyersburg road commencing at the center of the bridge on Mill Creek and that he work to the Dyer County line and he have the following hands under him, To Wit, William Ball and hands, John Cannon, James N. Buck and hands, James P. and John N. Purcells and hands, E. Kennelly, William Miskelly, Saban Jones, John Soward and hands, Mrs. E. Jordan's hands, John Jordan, C. Cowel, H. R. Chambers hands, James Ring, Jesse Goodman hands, Henry Rutherford hands.

Ordered by the Court that Martin R. Hatcher be appointed Overseer of the road leading from Durhamville to Williams Ferry on Hatchey and that he have all the hands east of said road and west of the Haywood County line except Lancy Graves and David Walker and to have all the hands at J. Bradfords, Barfields, G. S. Johnston, H. S. Williams, also, all the hands that L. D. Fisher has at his residence.

Ordered by the Court that Jefferson Brown be appointed Overseer of the road leading from Canton to Buck's Ferry commencing at the end of John Mitchells road and that he work to the County line and that he have all the hands on the south east side of Rutherford Creek to the County line to run up the Creek so as to take the Walpoles.

Ordered by the Court that Samuel Rudder be appointed Overseer of the road leading from Brownsville to Hurricane Hill beginning at the County line and that he work to the west boundary line of district no.one including Lancy Graves and David Walker on the south side of said road and all the hands on the north belonging to said district no. one.

Pg. 10 Ordered that John Byron be appointed Overseer of the Dyersburg road from Hurricane Hill to Cane Creek bridge and that he have the following hands to work under him, To Wit, six or half of the hands belonging to Mrs. Anthony, John Stone and hands, Robert West, Joseph Taylor, John Rudder, Rudder B. Griffy, Lawson Murry, W. H. Stone, W. H. McCarrol, William Laird, John Land, David Reynolds, David Lofton, S. Malone, J. Peterson, J. Reaves, W. Reaves, Roger L. Byron hands and James Morman and hands.

Ordered that James L. Lovelace be appointed Overseer of the road leading from Durhamville to the Dyersburg road and that the following hands work under him, To Wit, Carry Hays, James Price, Claibourn Hutton, Thomas Fitzpatrick and hands, Joseph Wardlow and hands, R. Goldin, I. Roberson, Elisha Robison, Right Koonce, Glidwell and Son, William Hiram, Edward Harris, D. P. Phillips and boarder and all other hands that may move in said bounds.

Ordered by the Court that Pendleton Gaines be appointed Overseer of the road leading from Dyersburg Fullen's Ferry from the intersection of the Durhamville road to the ferry and that he have the following hands to work under him, To Wit, P. Gaines hands, W. Fullens Son, J. Holmes, Mrs. Foster's hands, Coleman Hall and hands, J. Cleancy, H. Davis, I. Albirson, I. Chandler, B. Mosely, J. Fullen, I. Linville, P. G. Davenport and all other hands that may move in said bounds shall be subject to said order.

Pg. 11 Ordered that David Russell be appointed Overseer of the Dyersburg road from its intersection with the Durhamville road to Hurricane Hill and that he have the following hands to work under him, To Wit, I. R. Stone, H. T. Chislim, R. Moore, David P. Posey and hands, Z. Norman, S. V. Gilliland and hands, also all the hands that may move into said bounds shall be subject to said order.

Ordered that William Calhoon be appointed Overseer of the Fulton road leading from R. P. Russell to William P. Gaines and that he have the following hands to work under him, Robert P. Russell, Ezekial Smith, W. J. Connerly, C. Watson, S. J. Blackwell hands, W. Watkins, C. Whitson, John Blackwell, James Whitson,and hands, E. Stringer, W. McClellan, I. Keller, Griggs, I. McCall, I. P. Fuller, and all the hands that may move in said bounds are subject to work under him.

Lauderdale County
Minute Book 1836-1844
Vol. A

Pg. 11 cont. The Court then proceeded to the nomination of the place at which the next term of this Court should be held, a majority of all the justices for said County being present and voted. There was three places nominated, To Wit, Hurricane Hill, the former residence of Col. Jacob Byler, and Samuel Lusk, and after several ballotings it was decided that the Court should be held at Bylers.

Pg. 12 Ordered by the Court the following good and lawful men be appointed a jury of men to straighten the road leading from Buck's Ferry to Stokes Landing, To Wit, Isaac D. Maxwell, Samuel Lusk, Eluathan H. Condry, William R. Ledbetter, Alfred L. Byler and Dickinson Jennings.

Court then adjorned until tomorrow morning ten o'clock A. M.

Wednesday Morning, May the 1836.

Court met pursuant to adjornment present, Robert C. Campbell Esq. Chairman and Esqs. Maxwell, Titeworth, Crawford and S. V. Gilliland, William Carnigan Clerk, and Guy Smith Esq. High Sheriff, the Court proceeded to business.

This day Rezin L. Byron, Robert C. Campbell, Henry R. Crawford and Hiram C. Keller, the Commissioner for the town of Ripley, came into Court and entered to bonds and took oath accordingly.

There being no other business before the Court, ordered by the Court that Court be adjorned until Court in course.

R. C. Campbell, Chairman

Pg. 13 Know all men by these presents that we, Pleasant C. Dyal are all of the County of Lauderdale are held and firmly bound unto Samuel V. Gilliland Chairman of the County Court of said County and his successor in office in the sum of dollars for the payment of which will and truly to be made, we bind ourselves and each of ourselves, jointly, firmly and severally by these presents sealed with our seals and dated this second day of July 1838.

The condition of the above obligation is such that when as the above bounded, Pleasant C. Dyal has this day been appointed guardian of Matilda Dyal a minor of about three years now if the above bounden Pleasant Dyal shall will and truly discharge the duties of guardian in all things agreeable to Law then the above obligation to be void.

(Seal)
(Seal)
(Seal)

Pg. 14 Be it remembered that at a County Court began and held for the County of Lauderdale and State of Tennessee at the house of Col. Jacob Byler on the first Monday in June in the year of our Lord one thousand eight hundred and thirty six being the sixth day of said month present Esqs. Samuel V. Gilliland, Able H. Pope, William Strain, Maxwell, Crawford, Chambers, Crihfield, Titsworth, Justices, sitting and holding the County Court of Lauderdale and Guy Smith Esq. high sheriff.

The Court proceeded to business, whereupon Samuel V. Gilliland was elected Chairman protem.

The Court then proceeded to elect a clerk protem whereupon Griffith L. Rutherford was elected and took the oath of such.

This day Lewis Huchison, John Vassor and John Lackard produced here in Court commissions from the Governor of the State of Tennessee bearing date

Pg. 14 cont. from the eighth day of April 1836 authorizing and impowering each of them to fulfill the duties of Justices of the peace in and for said County agreeable to the constitution and laws for the term of six years from the first Monday in May 1836. Whereupon they severally took the oaths of office as such and took their seats accordingly.

The court then proceeded to elect a clerk for the County Court of Lauderdale County to fill the vacancy accasioned by the death of William Carmigan, Esq.,to serve until the next election in March eighteen hundred and thirty eight, whereupon Griffith L. Rutherford was duly and constitutionally elected.

Pg. 15 Whereupon he came into court with Henry R. Crawford and Samuel V. Gilliland, his securities and entered into bond, conditioned and payable as the law directs and took the several oaths of office.

The court then proceeded to elect a County Surveyor for Lauderdale County and upon counting out the votes, Able H. Pope received the highest number of votes, whereupon he came into court with John C. Bain, Rezin L. Byron, Samuel V. Gilliland, Thomas D. Fisher and Hiram C. Keller, his securities and entered into bond conditioned and payable as the law directs and took the oaths of office.

This day the court proceeded to elect an Entry Taker for the County of Lauderdale and upon counting the votes given, Henry Rutherford had received the highest humber of votes and was constitutionally elected Entry Taker for said County for the ensuing four years and until his successor is elected and qualified whereupon Henry Rutherford came into court with Henry R. Crawford and Christpoher G. Titsworth, his securities and entered into bond conditioned and payable as the law directs and took the oath prescribed by law.

This day Thomas D. Fisher who was elected by the people of the County of Lauderdale on the first Saturday in March last for the ensuing four years from the first Saturday of March 1836, register for said County, came into Court with John C. Bain, Martin R. Hatcher and Hiram C. Keller, his securities and entered into bond conditioned and payable as the law directs and took the oaths of office.

Pg. 16 State of Tennessee)
Lauderdale County Court)
Hennis Champ)
Administrator of)
George W. Childrys)

Whereas it appearing to the satisfaction of the court that George W. Childrys has departed this life having a last will and testament which was made without the United States. It is therefore ordered by the court that Hennis Champ be appointed Administrator of said estate with the will annexed and that letters testamentary issue accordingly he having entered into bond conditioned and payable as the law directs and took the oath of Administrator.

Delphy Byler &)
Davis Gilliland)
Administratrix &)
Administrator of)
W. L. Byler)

Whereas it appearing to the satisfaction of the court that William L. Byler hath departed this life leaving no last will or testament it is therefore ordered by the court that Delphy Byler be appointed Administratrix and David Gilliland Administrator on said estate and that letters testamentary issue accordingly they having entered into bond conditioned and payable as the law directs and took the oaths as such.

The court then adjourned for half an hour.

Court met pursuant to adjournment and proceeded to business.

Ordered by the court that Leonard Dunavant's hands be taken from the Bucks Ferry road and that they work on the Covington road leading from Dyersburg under Jacob Jones, Overseer on said road.

Pg. 17 David Gilliland) Whereas it appearing to the satisfaction of Administrator of) the Court that Jehugh Innman had departed this life Jehugh Innman) having no last will and testament it is therefore ordered by the Court that David Gilliland be appointed Administrator on the estate of said decedant whereupon David Gilliland came into Court with Samuel V. Gilliland and Hiram C. Keller, his securities and entered into bond, conditioned and payable as the law directs and took the oath as such.

John Blackwell) This day it appearing to the satisfaction of the Court that Stephen J. Blackwell Administrator of Estate) is dead and that he left no last will or Stephen J. Blackwell) testament, it is therefore ordered by the Court that John Blackwell be appointed Administrator on the estate of said decedant whereupon the said John Blackwell came into Court with David Gilliland and John C. Bains, his securities and entered into bond conditioned and payable as the law directs and took the oath as such.

This day the Court proceeded to lay a tax for the year eighteen hundred and thirty six, a motion being made to lay the following rates (VIZ) on every hundred dollars worth of property, five cents jury tax, four cents county contingent expenses, one cent poor tax, on each free poll twelve and a half cents jury tax, ten cents contingent expenses, two and one half cents poor tax. The vote was taken, those that voted for said rates were Esqs. Gilliland, Pope, Strain, Maxwell, Crawford, Chambers, Crihfield, Titsworth, Huchison, Vassor, and Lockard a majority of the Justices in said County so said rates were laid, State tax, five and one half cents on the one hundred dollars, twelve and one half cents on each free poll.

Pg. 18 The Court then proceeded to make an appropriation to build a temporary court house in the town of Ripley of following dimensions (to wit) good hewed logs 22 ft. by 21, seventeen feet high, two doors and windows, to be covered with rafters and sheeting, with three feet boards, to be built on a reserve lot in said town to be designated by the town commissions. On a motion being made to allow the undertaker of said job two hundred dollars out of any money in the hands of the Treasurer not otherwise appropriated. The votes was taken and those that had voted for said allowance were Esqs. Gilliland, Pope, Strain, Maxwell, Crawford, Chambers, Crihfield, Titsworth, Huchison, Vassor, and Lockard, a majority of the Justices in said county so said so said allowance was made.

This day a deed of conveyance from Henry Rutherford to John Oliver was produced in open court and acknowledged and is ordered to be so certified for registration.

A deed of conveyance from Henry Rutherford to John Lee Witter was produced in open court and acknowledged which is ordered to be so certified for registration.

A deed of conveyance from Henry F. Rutherford and Sarah Rutherford was produced in open court and proved by the oaths of Henry Rutherford and Henry R. Crawford the subscribing witnesses then to which is ordered to be so certified for registration.

It is ordered by the court that court be adjorned until tomorrow at ten o'clock A. M.

Sameul V. Gilliland, Chairman protem
H. R. Crawford, J. P.
J. H. Maxwell, J. P.

Lauderdale County
Minute Book 1836-1844
Vol. A.

Pg. 19 State of Tennessee Lauderdale County Court. The worshipful county court for said county met pursuant to adjournment, present Esqs. Gilliland, Chairman, Maxwell, Huchison, Vassor, H. R. Crawford associate Justices, Griffith, L. Rutherford, Clerk and Guy Smith, high sheriff.

The Court proceeded to business.

The Court proceeded to appoint commissioners to let out and superintend the building of a temporary court house in the town of Ripley, whereupon the following gentlemen were appointed (to wit) Milton Turner, Rezin L. Byron, Hiram C. Keller, Jacob Jones and Henry R. Crawford.

Ordered by the court that the following good and lawful men be appointed a jury of view to lay off and mark out the nearest and best way for a road leading from Ripley to intersect the road leading from Hurricane Hill to Fulton, the nearest and best route and that they report to the next term of this court the conveniences and inconveniences resulting from the same (to wit) Hiram C. Keller, John Chapman, Isaac Braden, James B. Crook, Ellison P. Fuller, William Braden and Landay Shumake, a majority can act.

Ordered by the court that the following good and lawful men be appointed a jury of view to lay off and mark out the nearest and best way for a road from Ripley towards Dyersburg to intersect the Covington road near the old county line of Dyer and that they report to the next term of this court (to wit) Thomas McG. Rutherford, Stephen M. Sullivan, John Linneths, Henry Sumroe, John Flippin, A. Vickory and Alfred G. Byler.

Pg. 20 Ordered by the Court that the following good and lawful men be appointed a jury of view to lay off and mark out the nearest and best route for a road leading from Ripley to the Haywood county line in a direction to Brownsville and that they report to the next term of this court (to wit) Rezin L. Byron, Isaac D. Maxwell, Richard Reaves, James A. Morris, Robert Walker, Claton Harris and John F. Burks, a majority can act.

Ordered by the court that the following good and lawful men be appointed a jury of view to lay off and mark out the nearest and best way for a road leading from Ripley to Fullen's Ferry on Hatchy in a direction to Covington and that they report to the next term of this court (to wit) Robert P. Russell, Joseph Carry, Pendleton G. Gaines, James Whitson, William Wardlaw, Esq., Thomas Fitzpatrick and David P. Posey, a majority can act.

There being no further business before the court it is ordered that court be adjourned until court in course.

Samuel V. Gilliland, Chairman
John H. Maxwell, J. P.
H. R. Crawford, J. P.

Pg. 21 State of Tennessee Lauderdale County Court

Be it remembered that a county court began and held for the county of Lauderdale and State of Tennessee at the house of Col. Jacob Byler on the first Monday in July in the Year of our Lord, one thousand eight hundred and thirty six being the fourth day of said month. Present, the worshipful Samuel V. Gilliland, Able H. Pope, Milton Turner, Hichison, Lockard, Foster, Maxwell, Crihfield, Crawford, Esqs. and Justices sitting and holding the county court of Lauderdale and Griffith L. Rutherford, Clerk and Guy Smith, high sheriff, the court proceeded to business whereupon Jerimiah Penick was appointed Chairman protem.

The jury of view appointed at the last time of this court to lay out the nearest and best route for a road from Ripley in a direction to Dyersburg to intersect the old road near the old county line of Dyer make report to this court which is in the following words (to wit) we the undersigned met

Pg. 21 cont. agreeable to an order of the court at the June term 1836 and being sworn as the law directs commencing at the north east corner of Ripley turning down the ridge north to the fork of the creek thence to John Maxwell's, thence to J. Byler's, thence to A. J. Byler's, then to intersect the Dyersburg road where the old Byler trace intersects, the same reviewed and marked, Alfred S. Byler, John Flippin, Thomas McG. Rutherford, Henry S. Sumrow, Absolum Vickory, and John J. Smith.

This day James Salsberry proved the killing of two wolves in the County of Lauderdale over the age of four months it is therefore ordered by
Pg. 22 court that the same be so certified Treasurer a majority of the Justices of said county being present.

This day William Wardlow Esq. proved the killing of seven wolves in the County of Lauderdale over the age of four months it is therefore ordered by the court that the same be so certified to the Treasurer a majority of the Justices of said county being present.

This day the jury of view appointed at the last term of this court to view, mark and lay off the nearest and best way for a road leading from Ripley to Fullen's Ferry on Hatchy in a direction to Covington present here in court a report the result of said review which report is in the following words (to wit) that they could not agree about the route and therefore marked no way out---A motion was then made to appoint another jury of view. The vote was then taken, those that voted for said jury of view was Pope, Huchison, and Turner; those against, Gilliland, Lockard, Foster, Maxwell, Crihfield, Crawford and Penick.

This day the jury of view appointed at the last time of this court to view mark and lay off the nearest and best way for a road leading from Ripley to the County line in a direction of Brownsville, present here in court a peport the result of said view which report is in the following words (to wit) July the 1, 1836, it being ordered by the court of Lauderdale at the June term that we should view and mark a road the nearest and best way from Ripley the county seat of Lauderdale to the Haywood line is a direction to Brownsville being summoned and sworn according to law have viewed several ways and report as follows: beginning at Ripley passing by the widow Innmans the corner of Mrs. Pain's field, through John Stone's lot and past Dials and
Pg. 23 intersect the Brownsville road at Graves. Given under our hands the date above written, Rezin L. Byron, Claton C. Harris, John F. Burk, I. A. Morris, Isaac D. Maxwell.

This day the jury of view appointed at the last term of this court to lay off and mark out the nearest and vest way for a road leading from Ripley to intersect the old Fulton road made and presented here in court a report of the result of said review, which report is in the following words (to wit) Tennessee State, Lauderdale County agreeable to an order of the County Court of Lauderdale we the undersigned met on the first inst. and after being duly sworn as the law directs proceeded to view and mark out a road from Ripley to intersect the Fulton road west of William Strains in the direction of Fulton, we report to said court that we have the location at the south west boundary line near the southwest corner of the same, thence west to Bates Fork, thence taking a ridge and going through J. Chapman's grass lot, thence to the Ashport road between Chapmans and William Bradens, thence following the Ashport road about thirty poles west of Bradens field leaving the Ashport road and going in a west direction and intersecting the Fulton Road about half a mile west of Strains and C. William Bradens, James B. Crook, Landy Shumaker, John H. Chapman, Isaac Braden, and E. P. Fuller, which report is received by the court and ordered to be recorded.

Lauderdale County
Minute Book 1836-1844
Vol. A

Pg.
23 This day the Court pwoceeded to bind two orphan children of Thomas
cont. Robison dec'd (to wit) Amandy Jane Robison and Elijah W. Robison whereupon
Jemima Chisum a connection came into court and prayed that the said children
Pg. be bound to her it therefore ordered by the court that the said Amandy Jane
24 Robison be bound unto this Jemima Chisum until she arrives the age of eighteen years and that the said Elijah W. Robison be bound as the above until
he arrives to the age of twenty-one years and that the said Jemima Chisum is
hereby bound to school the above bound children.

Whereupon Jemima Chisum came into court with William Chisum her security and entered into bond conditioned and payable as the law directs.

This day a petition for a jury of view to be appointed to review the road from Ripley to the county line towards Brownsville was presented here into court which was rejected.

Ordered by the 6ourt that William Timm be and he is hereby appointed Overseer of the road leading from Durhamville to Williams Ferry on Hatchy River in the place of Martin R. Hatcher who was appointed at the May term of this Court.

Whereas it appearing to the satisfaction of the Court that William Lovell has departed this life having no will or testament and widow relinquishing her right to administer on the estate of the said decedant whereupon it is ordered by the court that Moses Pain be appointed administrator on said estate that letters testamentory be issued accordingly whereupon Moses Pain came into court with Thomas B. Stokes and Jordan G. Stokes his securities and entered into a bond conditioned and payable as the law directs and took the oath as such.

Ordered by the Court that the following persons be and they hereby
appointed Commissioners to lay of the widow Sorrell's dower (to wit) Elijah
Pg. B. Foster, Samuel Lusk and Isaac D. Maxwell and that they report to the next
25 term of this court.

Ordered by the Court David Gilliland be and is hereby appointed Administrator on the estate of Ruben A. Braden dec'd whereupon the said David Gilliland came into court with Able H. Pope his security and entered into bond conditioned and payable as the law directs and took the oath as such.

Ordered by the Court that Rezin L. Byron, Nicky Reaves and Samuel Land be and they are hereby appointed Commissioners to lay off Jehugh Innman's widow her dower and that report to this court.

This day the Court proceeded to appoint Commissioners to lay off William Byler's widow dower whereupon Soloman D. Spain, Alfred S. Byler, and Isaac D. Maxwell was appointed for purpose specified above.

William Turn records his stock mark (to wit) an under half-crop in each ear.

The Court proceeded to lay a county tax on all privileges whereupon it was proposed to lay on each privilege over half the amount of State tax, those voting in favor of said rates were Penick, Huchison, Foster, Pope, Gilliland, Lockard, Crawford and Maxwell. Those voting against were Turner and Cribfield.

Ordered by the Court that Soloman D. Spain be and he is hereby appointed Overseer to cut out the road from Ripley towards Dyersburg to Covington road and that he have all the hands in Capt. Nun's company to work under him and that he put the same in repair as second class road.

Pg. Ordered by the Court a majority being present and voting in the affirma-
26 tive that the following good and lawful men be appointed a jury of view to
lay off and work out the nearest and best route for a orad from Ripley to

Pg. 26 cont. Stoke's Ferry on the Forkeddeer River (to wit) William Deason, Joshua Wright, Samuel Hogsett, Armstead Wood, Jordan G. Stokes, Bird L Jones and Robison Meadows and that they report to the next term of this Court.

This day the last will and testament of Benjamin Jordan was produced in open court and the execution thereof duly proven by the oaths of Pascal W. Saunders and James Soward the subscribing witnesses thereto. Thereupon William Jordan one of the executors named thereon came into open court and took upon himself the burden and execution of said last will and testament. It is therefore ordered by the court that letters testamentary with the will annexed issue to the said executor, whereupon he together with Pascal W. Saunders and James Soward his securities entered into and acknowledged bond in the penal sum of fourteen thousand dollars conditioned and payable as the law directs.

This day Griffith L. Rutherford who was appointed one of the Commissioners for the town of Ripley at the May term of this court, came into court and entered into bond conditioned and payable as the law directs and took the oath accordingly.

Ordered by the court that James Braden be and he is hereby appointed Overseer of the road from Blackwell's to Stokes landing and that they have all the hands west of Kirbies road and west of Jennings boundary, and east of the

Pg. 27 road from Hogsetts to Bylers so as to include Hogsett and Bird L. Jones and that he keep the same in repair as a third class road.

Ordered by the court that the following good and lawful men be appointed Jurors for the next Circuit Court (to wit) for district No. one; H. L. Williams, Sampson Smith, Joseph Wardlow and Milton Turner; District no. two; John H. Maxwell, John Stone, Joseph Taylor, Robert Walker; third district; Isaac Braden, E. P. Fuller, A. H. Pope, John Chapman; fourth district; Lewis Huchison; sixth district; E. B. Foster, John Lockard, Samuel Lisk, Isaac Moore, James Braden; district seven; Henry Crihfield, Esq., C. G. Titsworth, James Salsberry, John H. Mitchell; district eight; William Jordan, William Miskelly, William Ball, Ivy Chandler and Amos H. Rounsaville. Constables to wait on the court and jury and that venire facious issue accordingly.

Whereas it appears to the satisfaction of the court here that according to law the sheriff and clerks bonds which have been taken herein court should have been spread upon the records. But for the want of a knowledge of the same it was not done, therefore it is ordered by the court that the same now be done which bonds are in following words (to wit) sheriff bond.

State of Tennessee) Know all men by these present that we, Guy Smith,
Lauderdale County) Robert C, Campbell, James Whitson, Elijah Wright, James Braden, and James Blair and John C. Bains are held and firmly bound unto Newton Carmon, Governor over said State ofer said state and his successors in office in the penal sum of ten thousand dollars for which payment will and truly to be made to said Governor and his successors in office, we bind ourselves our heirs, executors and administrators, jointly and severally,

Pg. 28 firmly by these presents signed with our seals and dated this second day of May 1836.

The condition of the above obligation is such that whereas the above bounder Guy Smith was on the first Saturday in March last duly and constitutionally elected by the people of said county and state, sheriff of said county. Now therefore if the said Guy Smith shall, will and truly execute and return make of all proceps and preceps to him directed and satisfy all fees and sums of money by him received or levied by virtue of any proceps into the proper office by which the same by the tenor thereof ought to be

Pg. 28 cont. paid or to the person or persons to whom the same may be due his or their executors, attorneys or agents and in all other things will and truly, and faithfully execute the said office of sheriff during his continuance therein then the above obligation to be void otherwise to remain in full force and effect this day and date above written.

Guy Smith (seal)
R. C. Campbell (seal)
James Whitson (seal)
Elijah Wright (seal)
James Braden (seal)
John C. Bains (seal)
James Blair (seal)

County Court Clerk's bond

Know all men by these present that we, Griffith L. Rutherford, Henry R. Crawford, and Samuel V. Gilliland all of the County of Lauderdale and State of Tennessee are held and firmly bound unto Newton Carmon Esq., Governor of the State of Tennessee, and his successors in office in the penal sum of ten thousand dollars for the payment of which will and truly to be made we do
Pg. 29 bind ourselves, our heirs, executors and administrators jointly, severally and firmly by these presents sealed with our seal and dated this seventh day of June.

The condition of the above obligation is such that whereas the above bound Griffith L. Rutherford was this day duly and constitutionally elected Clerk of the County Court of Lauderdale County until the next general election in March eighteen hundred and thirty eight. Now if the said Griffith L. Rutherford shall, will and truly discharge the duties of his office according to law and safely keep the books and records of this office and shall pay and satisfy all sums of money that shall come to his hands by virtue of his office and shall do and perform all the duties enjoined on him by law then this obligation to be void.

Griffith L. Rutherford (seal)
Henry P. Crawford (seal)
Samuel V. Gilliland (seal)

Ordered by the Court that Nicholas Rummass Esq. and Carey Alsobrook be fined five dollars each for contempt of the Court.

This day the Court proceeded to regulate the ferry keepers in the County of Lauderdale. It was proposed that the following rate and no other be allowed and no other (to wit) that all ferry keepers on Hatchy be allowed fifty cents for long ferrage, twelve and a half cents in low water, and Forkeddeer that they have twelve and one half cents in all stages. The Justices voting for said rates were Penick, Gilliland, Pope, Huchison, Turner, Foster, Lockard, Crihfield, Crawford, Maxwell, a majority of whole.

Pg. 30 Ordered by the Court that James Tompkins be and he is hereby appointed Overseer of road from Fulton to the bridge on Cane Creek and that he have all the hands in the fourth district to work under him and that he keep the same in repairs as a third class road.

This day the Court proceeded to make an appropriation for the support of John Williams a pauper in this county the next ensuing twelve months. Whereupon it was ordered by the Court that Sarah Coleman be allowed at the rates of six dollars and twenty-five cents per month to be paid out of any money in the hands of the County Trustee arising from the poor tax not otherwise appropriated which is to be under the instruction of Henry Crihfield, Esq.

Pg. 30 cont. Ordered by the Court that Court be adjourned until tomorrow morning at nine o'clock.

Jeremiah Penick, Chairman protem
J. H. Maxwell, J. P.
Lewis Hutcheson, J. P.
John Packard, J. P.

Tuesday July the 5th, 1836.

Court met pursuant to adjournment present Esqs. Penick, Maxwell, Huchison, Lockard, Griffith L. Rutherford, Clerk and Guy Smith Esq., high sheriff.

The Court proceeded to business ordered by the Court that the fines assessed here on yesterday against Rummass and Alsobrooks be remitted.

Ordered by the Court that Dickoson Jennings be and he is hereby appointed Overseer of the road from Stokes in a direction to Bucks Ferry from the
Pg. 31 County line of Haywood to Blackwells and that all the hands east of Lusk Creek and east of Kirby road to Cole Creek from thence in a direct line to the Haywood line as to include the Widow Wilson's hands and the Caroothe from thence so as to include all the hands on Col. Buler's plamtation thence from Byler's Mill down Cane Creek to the mouth of Lusk Creek and that he keep the same in repairs as a third class road.

Griffith L. Rutherford records his stock mark (to wit) a crop of right ear and under slope of the left. There being no further business before the Court it is ordered that the Court be ajourned until Court in course.

Jeremiah Penick, Chairman Protem
John Packard, J. P.
Lewis Hucheson, J. P.
J. H. Maxwell, J. P.

Pg. 32 State of Tennessee, Lauderdale County.
Court Minute Docket, August Term 1836.

Be it remembered that at a County Court began and held for the County of Lauderdale and State of Tennessee at the house of Col. Jacob Byler on the first Monday in August in the year of our Lord one thousand eight hundred and thirty six, it being the first day of said month. Present the worshipful Samuel V. Gilliland, Pope, Crihfield, Lockard, Titsworth, Chambers, Strain, Maxwell, Vassor, Justices sitting and holding a county court for said county, Griffith L. Rutherford, Clerk and Guy Smith, Esq., high sheriff, the court proceeded to business.

Whereupon Esq. Lockard was elected Chairman protem for this term.

Ordered by the court a majority being present that the following good and lawful men be appointed a jury of view to lay off and mark out the nearest best route for a road from Ripley in a direction to Covington to Fullen's Ferry on Hatchy River and that they report to the next term of this court the convenience and inconveince resulting from the same (to wit) Thomas D. Fisher, Thomas Durham, Thomas Fitzpatrick, William Turner, Jeremiah Penick, Milton Turners and Michael Cleaves.

Ordered by the Court that E. P. Fuller be appointed Overseer from Ripley toward Fulton to intersect to the road from Hurricane Hill to Fulton west of Mrs. Strains, and that he have all the hands in the third district to cut the same and put it in repairs as a second class road.

Pg. 33 This day Asa Pate proves the killing of three wolves in the County of Lauderdale two of them under the age of four months the other over the age of four months which is ordered to be so certified to the Treasurer their

Pg. 33 cont. being a majority of the Justices for said county present.

Ordered by the Court that the Bakers be taken from the Ashport road and that they work on the Fulton road under James Crook.

This day Benjamin F. Boilston proved the killing of one wolf in the County of Lauderdale over the age of four months which is ordered to be so certified to the Treasurer their being a majority of the Justices of said county present.

This day Nickolas Reynolds proved the killing of one wolf in the County of Lauderdale over the age of four months which is ordered to be so certified to the Treasurer, there being a majority of the Justices in said county present.

This day John New proved the killing of one wolf in the County of Lauderdale over the age of four months which is ordered to be so certified to the Treasurer there being a majority of the Justices in said County present.

This day the last will and testament of George W. Childrys was produced in open Court and duly proven by the oaths of John C. Baines and J. P. Holliway and is ordered to be recorded.

Pg. 34 State of Tennessee, Lauderdale County Court Minute Docket.
August Term, 1836.

This day a jury of view that was appointed at the last term of this Court to view, lay off and mark a road the nearest and best route from Ripley to Stokes Landing on the Forkeddeer river, make a report to this court the result of said view which is in the words and figures following (to wit) We the undersigned Jurors of view to mark and lay off a road from Ripley to Stokes Landing and Forkeddeer River, report to the worshipful court of Lauderdale that we commenced at Ripley and run a direct ridge to Graves old mill seat from thence to Mr. Acuffs from thence to intersect the road leading from Bucks Ferry to Stokes landing near Thomas J. Smiths from thence a direct course to Stokes Landing. Given under our hands this 26th day of July, 1836, William Deason, Armstead Wood, Bird L. Jones, Samuel L. Hogsett, and J. G. Stokes. Whereupon Elijah Wright came into Court and pray the court that they would not receive said report stating that it was not the nearest and best route, but that there was a better route, one that would be more advantageous to the community. The vote was then taken whether said report should be received by the Court. Those that voted for the report being received were Esqs. Pope, Foster, Vassor, Turner, Crawford, Crihfield, Titsworth, Chambers and Maxwell, Lockard voting against said report. So said report was received by the court and recorded. Whereupon Elijah Wright prayed the court that he may have a jury appointed to assess the damages that he sustain by said road running through his land and it is therefore ordered by the court that the following men be appointed (to wit) L. D. Spain, Esaac Moore, Dickinson,Jennings, Samuel Lusk, Benjamin Nunn,

Pg. 35 James Braden and Angle Rennels and that they report to the next term of this Court.

Ordered by the Court there being a majority present and voting in the affirmative that the following good and lawful men be appointed a jury of view to lay off and mark out the nearest and best route for a road from Canton to intersect the road from Dyersburg to Ripley somewhere near Henry Sumrows and that they report to the October term of this court the result of said view (to wit) Alen F. Goodman, Robert Crihfield, Henry Crihfield, Jim James, J. Crawford, Pascal W. Saunders, Henry F. Rutherford and John Flippin.

This day the Court proceeded to bind the orphan children of Thomas Robison dec'd whereupon William T. Robison of the age of eleven years unto Henry L. Chisum to the art of planter and farmer until he come to the age of

Pg. twenty-one years, whereupon the said Henry T. Chisum came into court with
35 Moses B. Chisum and Ivy Cjandler, his securities and entered into bond con-
cont. ditioned and payable as the law directs.

This day the court placed and bound unto William Chisum, Anna A. Robison the daughter of Thomas Robison dec'd of the age of thirteen years until she arrives to the age of eighteen years, whereupon William Chisum came into court with Moses B. Chisum and Henry T. Chisum, his securities and entered into bond conditioned and payable as the law directs.

Ordered by the court that court be adjourned for half an hour.

Pg. Court met pursuant to adjournment.

36 James H. Cleaves records his stock mark (to wit) a half crop and slit in the right ear and half crop of the left.

This day Angle Rennels records his stock mark (to wit) a swallow fork in the left ear and an under bit in right ear.

Armstead Wood records his stock mark (to wit) a crop and slit in each ear.

John Lockard records his stock mark (to wit) a crop and under bit in the left ear and an under bit in the right.

John C. Barnes records his stock mark (to wit) a swallow fork in each ear and a hole in the right.

Whereas it appearing to the satisfaction of the court that William Carnigan has died intestate and application being made by Adolphus Carnigan that letters of administration be granted him on the estate of said decedent it is therefore ordered by the court that letters of administration be granted unto the said Adolphus Carnigan he having taken the oath and entered into bond conditioned as the law directs with Milton Turner and John H. Maxwell, his securities.

This day the commissions that was appointed at the last term of this court to lay off to the widow of William L. Byler dec'd, her dower presented here in court a report which is received by the court and is ordered to be recorded.

Pg. Ordered by the court a majority being present that Joseph Taylor be
37 appointed Overseer to cut out the road from Ripley to the county line in a direction to Brownsville as far as the west part of John Stone's farm and that he have all the hands that work under John Byron to cut out the same and put it in repair as a second class road.

Ordered by the court a majority being present that John T. Burks be appointed Overseer to cut out the road leading from Ripley to the county line in a direction to Brownsville from the west part of John Stone's plantation to where it intersects the Brownsville road near Lancy Graves and that he have all the hands that work under Rudder and William Gunner to cut out said road and put it in repair as a second class road.

This day the commissions that was appointed at the last term of the court to lay off to the widow of Jehugh Innman dec'd, her dower presents here in court a report which is received by the court and is ordered to be recorded.

Ordered by the court that Fi Facious be issued against the widow of Stephen J. Blackwell dec'd that she appear at the next term of this court and show cause if any she has why the continuation of John Blackwell, Administrator of her deceased husband should not be continued.

Pg. This day Milton Turner the revenue commissioner for district no. one
38 return here in court a list of taxable property and polls taken in by him for said district which is received by the court and is ordered to be recorded.

Pg. 38 cont. This day John H. Maxwell the revenue commissioner for district no, two returned here into court a list of taxable property and polls taken by him for said district for the year 1836 which is received by the court and is ordered to be recorded.

Able H. Pope revenue commissioner for district no. third for the year 1836 returned here into court a list of taxable property and polls by him taken for said district which is received by the court and is ordered to be recorded.

This day John Vassor the revenue commissioner for the year 1836 for district no. fourth returned here into court a list of taxable property and polls by him taken for said district which is received by the court and is ordered to be recorded.

This day Isaac M. Steele the revenue commissioner for the year 1836 for district no. sixth returned here into court a list of taxable property and polls by him taken for said district which is received by the court and is ordered to be recorded.

This day Christppher G. Titsworth who was appointed a revenue commissioner for the year 1836 for district no. seventh returned here into court a list of taxable property and polls by him taken for said district which is received by the court and is ordered to be recorded.

Pg. 39 This day Henry R. Crawford the revenue commissioner for the year 1836 for district no. eight returned here into court a list of taxable property and polls by him taken for said district which is received by the court and is ordered to be recorded.

This day Rezin L. Byron one of town commissioners for the town of Ripley returned here to court a plan of said town which is received by the court and ordered to be filed in the Clerk's office. Ordered by the court this day there being a majority present and voting in the affirmative that the revenue commissioners be allowed five dollars each for their services. Ordered by the court that court be adjourned until tomorrow morning, nine o'clock A. M.

John Lockard, J. P., Chairman
Benjamin F. Jordan, J. P.
J. H. Maxwell, J. P.

Tuesday, August the second, 1836.

Court met pursuant to adjournment, present the worshipful John Lockard, Chairman pro tempore, Benjamin F. Jordan and John Maxwell, associate justices sitting and hold a county court for Lauderdale County, Griffith L. Rutherford, Clerk and Guy Smith, Esq. high sheriff.

The court then proceeded to business.

Ordered by the court that Benjamin F. Jordan be appointed a revenue commissioner to take in a list of taxable property and polls in district no. five and that he make due return here to court according to law.

Pg. 40 Ordered by the court that Robert C. Campbell who was appointed at the May term of this court as revenue commissioner for said County in district no. five be fined fifty dollars for neglecting his duty as a revenue commissioner for said district no. five. Ordered by the court that Moses B. Chisum who is charged with double tax for not listing his poll tax be released from said double tax by paying single tax. There being no further business before the court it is ordered by the court that court be adjourned until court in course to meet in Ripley.

John Packard, Chairman J. P.
J. H. Maxwell, J. P
Benjamin F. Jordan, J. P.

Lauderdale County
Minute Book 1836-1844
Vol. A

Pg. Be it remembered that at a county court began and held for the County
41 of Lauderdale and State of Tennessee in the town of Ripley on the first
Monday in September in the year of our Lord one thousand eight hundred and thirty six it being the fifth day of said month. Present, Robert C. Campbell, Chairman, Pope, Gilliland, Jordan and Strain Esq., associate Justices sitting and holding a county court for said county, C. L. Rutherford, Clerk and Guy Smith, Esq., high sheriff,

The court proceeded to business.

Then a copy of the last will and testament of Alexander G. Park properly authenticated upon the records of Indale County, State of North Carolina was presented in open court by the parties interested in said will and upon examination it is ordered by the court that the same be recorded according to the provisions of the act of assembly in such cases made and provided.

This day a deed of conveyance from Alexander Jefferson work for one third part of an undivided five thousand acre tract of land lying in the County of Lauderdale to Alexander W. Brandon and William B. McCorkle of the State of North Carolina properly authenticated from said State and registered in the County of Dyer was examined by the Court and ordered to be registered.

Ordered by the court that the report made at the last term of this court for a road from Ripley in a direction to Fulton be recended and that a new jury of review be appointed.

Pg. This day David Gilliland, Administrator of Jehugh Innman dec'd returned
42 here in court an inventory of said estate and an account sale which is
received by the court and ordered to be recorded.

This day David Gilliland and Delphy Byler, Administrator and Administratrix on the estate of William L. Byler presented here in court an inventory and account of sale of said estate which is received by the court and ordered to be recorded.

Joseph Taylor who was appointed at the last term of this court to cut out the road leading from Ripley in a direction to Brownsville commencing at Ripley and to work to the west part of John Stone's plantation return here into court his order and wishes Claton C. Harris appointed in his stead.

Ordered by the court that Claton C. Harris be appointed Overseer of the road leading from Ripley in a direction to Brownsville road of Joseph Taylor.

Whereas it appearing to the satisfaction of the court that Stephen J. Blackwell has died intestate and Samuel V. Gilliland and Maria Blackwell applying for letters of administration on said estate is is ordered by the court that letters testamentary issue accordingly they having taken the oath and entered into bond conditioned payable as the law directs.

Pg. This day Robert C. Campbell, Esq., who was fined at the last term of
43 this court fifty dollars for neglecting his duties as a revenue commissioner
for district no. five (Viz) for not returning his tax list, came into court with his list of taxable property and polls taken by him for said district no. five which list is received by the court and is ordered to be recorded. It is also ordered by the court that R. C. Campbell, Esq. be released from said fine of fifty dollars.

Hennis Champ, Administrator of George W. Childry dec'd returned here into court an inventory of said estate which is received by the court and ordered by the court to be recorded.

Ordered by the court that E. P. Fuller and Isaac Braden be appointed commissioners to settle with Hennis Champ, Administrator of G. W. Childrys dec'd and that report to the next term of this court.

Ordered that court be adjourned for half an hour.

Court met pursuant to adjournment.

William Jordan, Executor of the last will and testament of Benjamin

Pg.
43 Jordan deceased returned here into court an inventory and account of sale
cont. which is received by the court and ordered to be recorded.

Ordered by the court that Joseph Gwinn be released from the payment of double tax by the payment of single tax and the Clerk's fees.

Ordered by the court that Robert Maxwell be released from double tax on 100 acres of land by the payment of single tax & the Clerk's fees.

Ordered by the court that Dickeson Jennings open the road leading from Buck's Ferry to Stoke's Landing sufficiently wide for waggons to pass and that he keep it in repairs.

Ordered by the court that the following good and lawful men be appointed Jurors of review to lay off and mark out a road from Ripley to intersect the Ashport road at or near John Chapman's and that they report to the next term of this coutt (to wit) William Braden, John Chapman, Ezekial Farmer, William P. Gains, James Sherman, William Nash and Lewis Mathews.

Ordered by the court that the following good and lawful men be appointed Jurors of review to lay off and mark out the nearest and best way for a road from Ripley in a direction to Fulton and that they report to the next term of this court (to wit) Rezin L. Byron, Hiram C. Keller, James Whitson, James Sherman, A. B. Gaines, Levi Gardner and Lewis Mathews.

Ordered by the court that Robert P. Russell be appointed Overseer of the Fulton Road from the eastern boundary line of the second civil division to the western boundary of the same and that he have all the hands to work under him that Calhoon was entitled to.

Ordered by the court that the following good and lawful men be appointed Jurors of view to lay off and mark out the nearest and best way for a road from Ripley to Fullen's Ferry towards Covington and they report to the next term of this court (to wit) Rezin L. Byron, Thomas Fitzpatrick, David C. Russell, Emri Keller, Johseph Wardlow, Milton Turner and John Fullen.
Ordered by the court that John Stone, Rezin L. Byron and Robert P. Russell be appointed commissioners to lay off to the widow of Stephen J. Blackwell dec'd a years provisions and that they report to the next term of this court.

Pg. Ordered by the court that court be adjourned until tomorrow morning at
46 nine o'clock.

R. C. Campbell, Chairman L.C.C.
Sam V. Gilliland, J.P.
William Strain, J.P.

Tuesday morning, September 6, 1836.

The County Court of Lauderdale County met pursuant to adjournment, present R. C. Campbell, Chairman and Esqs. Gilliland, Strain and Maxwell, Associate Justices and G. L. Rutherford, Clerk.

Ordered by the court that Rezin L. Byron, Hiram C. Keller and James Whitson be appointed commissioners for the year 1836 to settle with the officers of Lauderdale County.

This day Levina Linnville came into court and pray the court that Pleasant G. Davenport be appointed her guardian which granted he having entered into bond conditioned and payable as the law directs.

Isaac D. Maxwell records his stock mark (to wit) crop of the left ear and under bit in the right ear.

Pg. John H. Maxwell records his stock mark (to wit) smooth crop of the
47 right ear and hole and split in the left.

John Land recodds his stock mark (to wit) crop of right ear and crop and half crop on the under side of the left ear.

Pg. 47 cont. William Strain records his stock mark (to wit) split and under bit in the right ear and slit in the left.

Ordered by the court that Lewis Hucheson, John Vassor and James Crook be appointed commissioners to examine the bridges on the Fulton rpad and report to the next term of this court the condition of said bridges.

Ordered by the court that Ivy Chandler, David Russell and William Fullen be appointed commissioners to examine the bridges in the County of Lauderdale on the Covington road and that they report to the next term of this court.

Ordered by the court that Bartus Alford, Henry Murry and Jerry Cheek be appointed commissioners to examine the bridges in this county on the Ashport road and that they report to the next term of this court.

Isabella Wilson records her stock mark (to wit) a swallow fork in each ear.

Pg. 48 James Whitson records his stock mark (to wit) swallow fork in each ear and under bit in the right and an under nick in the left ear.

R. C. Campbell Esq. records his stock mark (to wit) crpp and slit in the left ear and under bit in the right.

Ordered by the court that court be adjourned until court in course.

R. C. Campbell, Chairman L.C.C.
Samuel V. Gilliland, J.P.
William Strain, J.P.

Pg. 49 State of Tennessee) Be it remembered that at a County Court began and held Lauderdale County) for the County of Lauderdale and State of Tennessee in the Town of Ripley on the first Monday in October in the year of our Lord, one thousand eight hundred and thirty six, it being the third day of said month, present R. C. Campbell, Esq., Chairman, Penick, Strain, Vassor, Maxwell, Gilliland, Titsworth, Cribfield, Turner and Pope, Associate Justices, sitting and holding a county court for said county, G. L. Rutherford, Clerk and Guy Smith, Esq., high sheriff.

The court then proceeded to business.

Moses Parr, Administrator of William Terrell dec'd returned here in open court an inventory and account of sale of the property belonging to said estate which is received by the court and ordered to be recorded.

The commissioners that was appointed at the July term of this court to lay to the widow of William Terrell dec'd her dower returns here in open court a report which is received by the court and ordered to be recorded.

Pg. 50 Ordered by the court a majority of all the Justices of said county being present and voting in the affirmative that Griffith L. Rutherford, Clerk of the county court be allowed twenty dollars for making out the tax list for the collector for the year 1836 to be paid out of any money in the hands of Trustee not otherwise appropriated.

It is ordered by the court a majority being present that John W. Campbell be allowed to establish a ferry on the Mississippe River at Ashport and that he have until the next term of this court to give bond and that he be allowed the following rates (viz) in low water for man and horse one dollar in high water two dollars and fifty cents, single man fifty cents in low water, in high water seventy five cents,for each head of cattle fifty cents in low water and in high water seventy five cents, waggon and team three dollars in low water and in high water five dollars, hogs a sow and pigs to count two,twelve and a half cents in low water in high water twenty five cents.

Lauderdale County
Minute Book 1836-1844
Vol. A

Pg. 50 cont. The commissioners that was appointed at the last term of this court to lay off to the widow of Stephen J. Blackwell dec'd her year's provisions made a report to court which is received by the court and ordered to be recorded.

Pg. 51 Ordered by the court a majority being present and voting in the affirmative that G. L. Rutherford, Clerk of the county court be allowed eighteen dollars for book bought by him for the use of the county out of any money in the hands of the Trustee not otherwise appropriated.

John McCall records his stock mark (to wit) a crop off of each ear and two slits in each.

S. V. Gilliland records his stock mark (to wit) two under slopes.

The jury of view that was appointed at the September term of this court to lay off and mark out a road from Ripley to Fullen's Ferry on Hatchie River report here into open court which is received by the court and is ordered to be established.

Ordered by the court that William Calhoon be appointed Overseer to cut out the road leading from Ripley to Fullen's Ferry and that he have all the hands that work under James Lovelass, D. C. Russell and Robert P. Russell except the hands south of the Dyersburg road to Bates Fork of Cane Creek and that he put the same in repairs as a first class road.

Pg. 52 Ordered by the court that the following good and lawful men be appointed a jury of view to lay off and mark out the nearest and best way for a road leading from the bridge on Cane Creek to the most suitable point on the Mississippi River and that they report to the next term of this court (to wit) Samuel A. Givens, A. C. Kidd, C. Hutcherson, James B. Hutcherson, Wiley Garvin, James Tompkins and John Vassor.

This day Harry Williams proves the killing of one wolf in the County of Lauderdale under the age of four months and is ordered to be so certified to the Treasurer their being a majority of the Justices in the county present.

This day Jeremiah Penick proved the killing of one wolf in the County of Lauderdale under the age of four months and ordered to be certified to the Treasurer their being more than five Justices present.

Ordered by the court that the following good and lawful men be appointed a jury of view to lay off and mark out a road from Ripley to intersect the Ashport road east of Whitson bridge on Cane Creek and that they report to the next term of this court (to wit) R. L. Pyron, Isaac Braden, William P. Gaines, William Nash and Ellison P. Fuller.

Pg. 53 This day the jury of view that was appointed at the September term of this court to lay off and mark out the nearest and best route for a road leading from Ripley to Fulton report to court which is received by the court and is ordered to be established.

Ordered by the court that James Whitson be appointed Overseer to cut out the road leading from Ripley in a direction to Fulton and that he have the following hands to cut out the same (to wit) Nancy Childress hands, Elijah Lake and hands, John C. Barnes, Levi Gardner, Hennis Champ, Mabra Hunter and hands, Alex Warlow, Thomas Wardlow, Ira Gaines, Richard Gaines, A. B. Gaines, W. P. Gaines and hands, John D. Edney, William Prescott, Benjamin F. Childrys, Nathaniel Barnes, Laundy Shumake and all the hands west of the Dyersburg road to Fullen's Ferry as far as McClellans and that he put the same in repair as a second class road.

Ordered by the court that the following good and lawful men be appointed a jury to assess the damage to Elijah Right for the road leading from Ripley to Stokes landing passing through his land or change the road and that they report to the next term of this court (to wit) William Braden, Ellison P. Fuller, Armstead Wood, Isaac D. Maxwell, Absalum Vickory, Alfred L. Byler, and John Hogsette.

Lauderdale County
Minute Book 1836-1844
Vol. A

Pg. This day Edward Kennelly who was elected Constable by the people for
54 the eighth civil division on the first Saturday in March last came into court and tendered his resignation which is received by the court.

This day Samuel Lusk who was elected Ranger in the County of Lauderdale came into court and tendered his resignation which is received by the court. The court then proceeded to elect a Ranger for the County of Lauderdale to fill vacancy occasioned by the resignation of Samuel Lusk to serve until the next general election in March in the year 1838 whereupon John H. Maxwell was duly and constitutionally elected.

This day Guy Smith, Sheriff and Collector for Lauderdale County for the year 1836 came into court and entered in bond conditioned and payable as the law directs and took the oaths accordingly.

Ordered that court be adjourned until tomorrow morning at eleven o'clock.

R. C. Campbell, Chairman
A. H. Pope, J.P.
J. H. Maxwell, J.P.

Pg. Tuesday morning, October [illegible], 1836.
55 Court met pursuant to adjournment present John H. Maxwell, Esq., A. H. Pope, and R. C. Campbell, Chairman, G. L. Rutherford, Clerk and Guy Smith, Esq., high Sheriff.

The court then proceeded to business.

Ordered by the court that William Calhoon shall be exempt from working on the road under James Whitson.

This day John H. Maxwell who was elected Ranger on yesterday came into court and entered into bond conditioned and payable as the law directs and took the oath of office.

Ordered by the court that Rebecca Roswell, a pauper in this county be allowed the balance of the poor tax if there should be any after supporting John Williams.

There being no further business before the court it is ordered that court be adjourned until court in course.

R. C. Campbell, Chairman
A. H. Pope, J.P.
J. H. Maxwell, J.P.

Pg. Be it remembered that at a county court began and held for the County
56 of Lauderdale and State of Tennessee in the Town of Ripley on the first Monday in November in the year of our Lord, one thousand eight hundred and thirty six it being the seventh day of said month. Present Robert C. Campbell, Chairman, Esqs., Gilliland, Turner, Maxwell, Strain, Lockard, Titsworth and Crawford Associate Justices sitting and holding a county court for said county, G. L. Rutherford, Clerk and Guy Smith, Esq., high sheriff, proclamation being made the court proceeded to business.

On motion of Thomas Fitzpatrick to be released from the payment of taxes on lands improperly charged through mistake on nine hundred and forty acres of land and mistake in the valuation the sum of five dollars and fifty three cents the vote was then taken, those that voted for said release were, Esqs. Campbell, Gilliland, Maxwell, Strain, Turner, Titsworth, Crawford and Lockard, so said release was made and is ordered that Guy Smith, Esq., the Collector for said county be released from the payment of said amount of five dollars and fifty three cents and is ordered to be so certified to the

Pg. Comptroller of the Treasury and the County Trustee.
56 On motion Col. Sampson to have Guy Smith, Esq. sheriff and collector
cont. for said county a credit for thirty one dollars and twenty cents the taxes
on two thousand and eighty acres of land twice charged in the name of Calvin
Pg. Jones valued at ten dollars per acre which is ordered to be so certified to
57 the Comptroller of the Treasurer and County Trustee.

This day Joseph Gwinn proved the killing of one wolf in the County of Lauderdale over the age of four months which is ordered to be certified to the Treasurer there being more than five Justices present.

On a motion to allow David Gilliland, Clerk of the circuit court for said county sixteen dollars and forty cents for books bought by him for the Clerk's office, the vote was taken those that voted for said allowance were, Esqs. Campbell, Strain, Maxwell, Turner, Crawford, Lockard and Titsworth. So said allowance was made and is ordered to be paid out of any money in the hands of the Trustee not otherwise appropriated.

On a motion to allow Robert Walker eight dollars and twenty cents for a
table and chairs for the use of the county the vote was taken, those that
voted for said allowance were Esqs. Gilliland, Campbell, Turner, Lockard,
Pg. Strain, Maxwell, Crawford and Titsworth so said allowance was made and order-
58 ed to be paid out of any money in the hands of the Trustee not otherwise
appropriated.

Ordered by the court that Malcum Gwinn be appointed Overseer of road from Rutherfords old mill to the key corner in room of Samuel Stricklin and that he have the hands that worked under Stricklin to work under him.

This day the Jury of review that was appointed at the last term of this court to assess the damage to Elijah Right for the road leading from Ripley to Stokes Landing passing through his land or turn the road, make report here into court which is received by the court and is ordered to be established.

Ordered by the court that Thomas Hazlewood be appointed Overseer to cut out the road leading from Ripley to Stokes Landing and that he have all the hands that belong to Capt. Nunn's Company to cut out the same and put it in repair as a second class road.

This day the Jury of view that was appointed at the last term of this court to lay off and mark out a road from Ripley to Ashport present here in court a report which is received by the court and is ordered that the road be established and that Isaac Braden be appointed Overseer to cut out the same as marked by the jury and put it in repair as a second class road and that he have all the hands in the third district to work under him.

Pg. Ordered by the court that W. T. Moorehead, Trustee of Lauderdale County
59 call on the county courts of Tipton and Dyer Counties to pay back to him the
amount of tax by them collected from the County of Lauderdale for the year
eighteen hundred and thirty five.

This day the Jury of view that was appointed at the last term of this court to lay off and mark out a road from the bridge on Cane Creek to the most suitable point on the Mississippi River report here in court which is received by the court and is ordered to be established.

Ordered by the court that James Tompkins be appointed Overseer to cut out the road from the bridge on Cane Creek to the mouth of Cole Creek and that he have all the hands in fourth district to work under him and that he put the same in repair as a second class road.

Christopher G. Watson records his stock mark (to wit) a swallow fork in each ear and an under bit in the right ear.

A. U. Kidd records his stock mark (to wit) an under half crop in each ear.

Pg. This day Samuel V. Gilliland, Administrator and Mariah Blackwell,
59 Administratrix of the Stephen J. Blackwell dec'd, present here ih court an
cont. inventory and account of sale which is received by the court and ordered to
be recorded.

Pg. Ordered by the court that James Whitson be appointed Overseer of the
60 road leading from Ripley in a direction to Fulton and that he keep the same
in repair as a second class road.

This day Adolphus Carrigan, Administrator of William Carrigan dec'd, returned into court an inventory and account of sale which is received by the court and is ordered to be recorded.

Ordered by the court that William Calhoon be appointed Overseer of road leading from Ripley in a direction to Fullen's Ferry on Hatchey and that he keep the same in repair.

Ordered by the court that the following good and lawful men be appointed Jurors for the next circuit court to be held for the County of Lauderdale in the town of Ripley on the third Monday in Fefruary in the year eighteen hundred and thirty seven (to wit) Milton G. Turner, Thomas Fitzpatrick, Archer Phillips, William Turner for the first district; William Strain, Levi Gardner, James Crook and John Champman for the third district; John H. Maxwell, A. Vicory, James Whitson, David P. Posey for the second district; Benjamin F. Jordan for the fifth district; Elijah Right, Dickerson Jennings, Soloman D. Spain and Alfred S. Byler for the sixth district; Henry Crihfield Sr., Thomas McG. Rutherford, Lawson H. Dunaway and Stephen M. Sullivan for the seventh;
Pg. Henry R. Chambers, Malcom Gwinn, John C. Crinshaw and Sabon Jones for the
61 eighth district; Ivy Chandler and Hiram Meadows, Constables to wait on the
court and jury and venira facious issue accordingly.

It is ordered by the court that R. C. Campbell Esq. be released from the payment of the fees of revenue commissioner of the fifth district on seventeen tracts of land.

This day Robert C. Campbell, Chairman of the county court hath place and put under the care of Soloman D. Spain a minor pauper as an apprentice, the daughter of Soloman D. Spain dec'd of the age of eleven years until she arrives to the age of eighteen years to be instructed in the arts and mysteries of house wifery and spinster, to be taught to read and write and at the expiration of her apprentice-ship is to have a good feather bed and clothing. Whereupon the said Soloman D. Spain entered into bond conditioned and payable as the law directs.

Ordered that court be adjourned until tomorrow morning, eight o'clock.

R. C. Campbell, Chairman
Sam V. Gilliland, J.P.
William Strain, J.P.

Pg. Tuesday morning November the eighth, 1836.
62 Court met pursuant to adjournment, presnet, R. C. Campbell, Chairman,
and Esqs. Gilliland and Strain, G. L. Rutherford, Clerk and Guy Smith, Esq., high sheriff proclamation being made the court proceeded to business. On motion of R. C. Campbell their being no further business before the court it is ordered that court be adjourned until court in course.

R. C. Campbell, Chairman

Pg. Be it remembered that at a county court began and held for the County
63 of Lauderdale County and State of Tennessee in the Town of Ripley on the
first Monday in December in the year of our Lord, one thousand eight hundred and thirty six, it being the fifth day of said month, present the worshipful Able H. Pope, Esq. and Gilliland, Maxwell, Strain, Crihfielf, Penick, Esqs.,

Lauderdale County
Minute Book 1836-1844
Vol. A

Pg. 63 cont. Associate Justices sitting and holding a county court for said county, G. L. Rutherford, Clerk and Guy Smith, Esq., high sheriff, proclamation being made the court proceeded to business, whereupon Able H. Pope was elected Chairman protem for the present term.

Ordered by the court that Benjamin Porter, James Blair and Hugh Smith, be appointed commissioners to settle with Griffith L. Rutherford, Administrator of Oliver Crenshaw dec'd and with Henry F. Rutherford, Guardian for the heirs said Oliver Crenshaw and to divide said estate equally between John C. Crenshaw, Charles D. Crenshaw, Laura Jane Crenshaw and Oliver Crenshaw.

Ordered by the court that the following good and lawful men be appointed a jury of view to lay off and mark a road leaving the Fulton road near A. B. Gaines leading to some convenient point on Hatchy River and that they report

Pg. 64 to the next term of this court (to wit) William Wardlow, Levi Gardner, I. D. Edney, E lijah Lake and Hennis Champ.

Ordered by the court that John C. Barnes be appointed Overseer to cut out the road from A. B. Gaines to some point on Hatchy River to be marked by the jury of view and that he have the following hands to work under him (to wit) Nancy Childrys hands, Hennis Champ, John D. Edney, Levi Gardner, Jackson Gardner, Natheniel Barnes, Thomas Wardlow, Alex Wardlow, Ira Gaines, Churchwell, Elijah Lake, Gilly Hunter, James Silvertooth, Martin Kelly, W. P. Gaines, Green Baker, Noah Baker, James Crook, and A. B. Gaines.

Ordered by the court that the heirs of William Bogsette dec'd be releas- from the payment of the tax on one black poll improperly charged for double tax valued at four hundred dollars tax sixty cents and is ordered to be certified to the Comptroller and County Trustee.

On a motion to allow Able H. Pope twenty two dollars for services rendered for surveying the lots in the town of Ripley, those that voted for said allowance were Esqs. Maxwell, Strain, Penick, Gilliland, Crihfield, so said allowance was made and is ordered to be paid out of any money in the hands of the Trustee not otherwise appropriated.

Pg. 65 This day on a motion to allow John C. Barnes four dollars for two days services crying off the lots in the town of Ripley the vote was taken, those that voted for said allowance were Esqs. Pope, Gilliland, Maxwell, Strain, Penick and Crihfield one third of the Justices for said county so said allowance was made and ordered to be paid out of any money in the hands of the Trustee not otherwise appropriated.

On a motion be made to allow Rezin L. Byron nine dollars for money expended by him for advertising the sale of the lots in the town of Ripley, for three benches for the use of the court and a lock and key for the Clerk's table the vote was taken, those that voted for said allowance were Esqs. Pope, Gilliland, Penick, Strain, Maxwell, and Crihfield one third of all the Justices for said county, so said allowance was made and ordered to be paid out of any money in the hands of the Trustee not otherwise appropriated.

A motion being made to allow Guy Smith, Esq., high sheriff his exofficio fee fpr the year 1836, a motion being made to allow him fifty dollars, the vote was taken, those that voted for said allowance were Esqs. Pope, Penick, Gilliland, Strain, Maxwell and Crihfield, one third of all the Justices in said county so said allowance was made for fifty dollars and ordered to be

Pg. 66 paid out of any money in the hands of the Trustee not otherwise appropriated.

On motion of G. L. Rutherford, Clerk of the County Court of said county for his allowance for his exofficio services for the year 1836 there being a motion for to allow forty dollars and one for fifty dollars, the vote was taken, those that voted for allowing fifty dollars were Esqs. Maxwell, Pope, Strain, Penick, Gilliland and Crihfield, one third of all the Justices in

Pg. 66 cont. said county so said allowance of fifty dollars was made and is ordered to be paid out of any money in the hands of the Trustee not otherwise appropriated.

Jeremiah Penick records his stock mark (to wit) a split in each ear.

Henry Crihfield Esq. records his stock mark (to wit) a crop and under bit in the right ear and slit in the left ear.

Ordered by the court that all the Overseers of roads in the county of Lauderdale except Thomas Hazlewood report to the next term of this court their roads in good order.

Ordered by the court there being one third of all the Justices in said county present and voting in the affirmative that Milton G. Turner, Esq., be appointed a revenue commissioner to take in list of taxable property and polls in Lauderdale County in district no.first for the year 1837 and that he return the same here into court as the law directs.

Pg. 67 Ordered by the court there being one third of all the Justices in said county present that John H. Maxwell, Esq., be appointed a revenue commissioner to take in a list of taxable property and polls in Lauderdale County in district no.second for the year 1837 and that he return the same here into court as the law directs.

Ordered by the court there being one third of all the Justices in said county present that Able H. Pope, Esq., be appointed a revenue commissioner to take in a list of taxable property and polls in Lauderdale County in district no. third for the year 1837 and that he return the same here into court as the law directs.

Ordered by the court there being one third of all the Justices in said county present that Lewis Hutcherson, Esq., be appointed a revenue commissioner to take in a list of taxable property and polls in Lauderdale County in District no. fourth for the year 1837 and that he return the same here into court as the law directs.

Ordered by the court there being one third of all the Justices in said county present that Robert C. Campbell, Esq., be appointed a revenue commissioner to take in a list of taxable property and polls in Lauderdale County in district no. fifth for the year 1837 and that he return the same here into court as the law directs.

Pg. 68 Ordered by the court there being one third of all the Justices in said county present that John Lockard, Esq., be appointed a revenue commissioner to take in a list of taxable property and polls in Lauderdale County for district no. sixth for the year 1837 and that he return the same here into court as the law directs.

Ordered by the court there being one third of all the Justices in said county present that Christopher G. Titsworth, Esq., be appointed a revenue commissioner to take in a list of taxable property and polls in Lauderdale County for district No. seventh for the year 1837 and that he return the same here into court as the law directs.

Ordered by the court there being one third of all the Justices in said county present that Henry R. Crawford, Esq., be appointed a revenue commisioner to take in a list of taxable property and polls in Lauderdale County for district no. eighth for the year 1837 and that he return the same here into court as the law directs.

Ordered that court be adjourned until tomorrow morning at ten o'clock.

A. H. Pope, Chairman Protem
J. H. Maxwell, J.P.
William Strain, J.P.

Pg. 69 Tuesday morning, December the sixth, 1836.

Lauderdale County
Minute Book 1836-1844
Vol. A

Pg. Court met pursuant to adjournment, present Able H. Pope, Esq., Chairman
69 protem and John H. Maxwell, William Strain, Esq., G. L. Rutherford, Clerk
cont. and Guy Smith, Esq., high sheriff, proclamation being made the court proceeded to business.

Whereas it appearing to the satisfaction of the court that Mabra Hunter has departed this life intestate and Ellison P. Fullen applying for letters of administration issue accordingly he having entered into bond conditioned and payable as the law directs and took the oath as directed by law.

Ordered by the court that Able H. Pope, William Strain, William P. Gains be appointed commissioners to lay off to the widow of Mabra Hunter her years provisions and report to court. There being no further business before the court, it is ordered that court be adjourned until court in course.

A. H. Pope, Chairman Protem
J. H. Maxwell, J.P.
William Strain, J.P.

Pg. State of Tennessee, Lauderdale County.
70 Be it remembered that a county cort began and held in and for the county of Lauderdale and State of Tennessee in the town of Ripley on the first Monday in January in the year of our Lord one thousand eight hundred and thirty seven it being the second day of said month, present the worshipful Able H. Pope, Esqs. Maxwell, Jordan, Gilliland, Crawford, Lockard, Titsworth, Turner, Strain, Penick and Foster, Associate Justices sitting and holding a county court for said county, Griffith L. Rutherford, Clerk and Guy Smith, Esq., high sheriff, proclamation being made the court proceeded to business.

The court proceeded to elect a Chairman for the county court of said county for the year 1837, whereupon Able H. Pope was elected Chairman for the present year.

This day James Blair, Benjamin Porter and Hugh Smith, who was appointed at the last term of this court commissioner to settle with G. L. Rutherford, Administrator of Oliver Crenshaw, dec'd and Henry F. Rutherford, Guardian for John C. Crenshaw, Louiza Jane Crenshaw, Charles D. Crenshaw and Oliver B. Crenshaw and to divide the property belonging to said estate equally between John C, Crenshaw, Louiza Jane Crenshaw, Charles D. Crenshaw and Oliver B. Crenshaw report here into court the result of said settlement which is receiv-
Pg. ed by the court and is ordered to be recorded.
71 On a motion being made by James Blair for an allowance being made to himself, Benjamin Porter and Hugh Smith Commissioners to divide the estate of Oliver Crenshaw dec'd between the Legatees of said estate a proposition being made to them one dollar and fifty cents per day the vote was taken, those that voted for said allowance were Esqs. Pope, Strain, Maxwell, Gilliland, Penick, Turner, Titsworth, so said allowance was made to Benjamin Porter and Hugh Smith for two days services at one dollar and fifty cents per day., and James Blair for three days at one dollar & fifty cents per day.

This day Henry Rutherford, Entry Taker for said county presented here in court a plan of said county by him made and motioned that the court should make him an allowance for said services and for three books bought by himself at one dollar and seventy five cents and for four days and a half traveling to Covington and returning one dollar and a half per day, the whole account amounting in all to one hundred and one dollars and ninty cents. The vote was taken, those that voted for said allowance were Esqs. Pope, Maxwell, Jordan, Gilliland, Crawford, Lockard, Titsworth, Turner, Strain, Penick and Foster, a majority of all the Justices in said county so said allowance was made for one
Pg. hundred and one dollars and ninety cents and is ordered to be paid out of any
72

Pg. 72 cont. money in the hands of the trustee not otherwise appropriated.

Ordered by the court there being a majority of the Justices in said county present and voting in the affirmative that Hiram C. Keller be allowed out of any money in the hands of the trustee not otherwise appropriated the sum of twelve dollars it being the amount of money advanced by him as commissioner for the town of Ripley in advertising the sale of the lots for commissioner's bond and for a book bought for the use of the county.

This day Rezin L. Byron, Hiram C. Keller, Henry R. Crawford and Griffith L. Rutherford, Commissioners for the town of Ripley, presents here in court an account of the sale of the lots in said town which is received by the court and is ordered to be recorded.

John Russell records his stock mark (to wit) a swallow fork and under bit in each ear.

Ordered by the court that Thomas Durham, Robert P. Russell and Christopher Watson be appointed commissioners to lay off to the widow of William Carrigan dec'd her years provisions and report to the next term of this court.

Pg. 73 Ordered by the court a majority of all the Justices in said county being present and voting in the affirmative that Rebecca Boswell a pauper in this county be allowed for her support for the year eighteen hundred and thirty seven the sum of fifty dollars out of any money in the hands of the Trustee not otherwise appropriated.

Ordered by the court Christopher G. Titsworth be appointed Overseer of the road leading from Ripley in a direction to Dyersburg in place of Jacob Jones and that he have the same hands to work under him.

Ordered by the court that Able H. Pope be appointed Trustee for the pauper, Rebecca Boswell this county.

Ordered that court be adjourned until tomorrow morning at eleven o'clock.

A. H. Pope, Chairman
Sam V. Gilliland, J.P.
William Strain, J.P.

Pg. 74 Tuesday morning, January the third, 1837.

Court met pursuant to adjournment, present and presiding the worshipful Able H. Pope, Chairman, Samuel V. Gilliland and William Strain, G. L. Rutherford, Clerk and Guy Smith, Esq., high sheriff, proclamation being made the court proceeded to business.

Ordered by the court that the following good and lawful men be appointed a jury of view to lay off and mark out a road from Durhamville to Ripley the nearest and best way and to as little prejudice to inclosure as possible and report to the next term of this court (to wit) Robert P. Russell, John Watson, Thomas Durham, Samuel Hammel, William Calhoon, William Turner, William McCleland.

Ordered by the court that Dabney P. Phillips be appointed Overseer of the road leading from Durhamville in a direction to Fullen's Ferry as far as the Ripley road in the place of Lovelass and that the same hands work under him.

There being no further business before the court it is ordered that court be adjourned until court in course.

A. H. Pope, Chairman
Sam V. Gilliland, J.P.
William Strain, J.P.

Lauderdale County
Minute Book 1836-1844
Vol. A

Pg. 75 Be it remembered that at a county court began and held for the County of Lauderdale and State of Tennessee in the town of Ripley on the first Monday in February in the year of our Lord one thousand eight hundred and thirty seven it being the sixth day of said month, present and presiding the worshipful Able H. Pope, Chairman and Esqs. Gilliland, Strain, Maxwell, Titsworth, Crihfield, Lockard, Turner and Chambers, Associate Justices sitting and holding a county court for said county, G. L. Rutherford, Clerk and Guy Smith, Esq., high sheriff, proclamation being made the court proceeded to business.

Henry R. Crawford, Esq. one of the acting Justices of the peace in and for said county presented here in court his resignation as a Justice of the peace which is received by the court.

Ordered by the court that James J. Crawford be appointed a revenue commissioner to take in a list of taxable property and polls in Lauderdale County for the year 1837 in district no. eight and then he return the same here into court as the law directs in the room of Henry R. Crawford.

This day Michael Salsberry proved the killing of four wolves in the County of Lauderdale over the age of four months and is ordered to be certified to the Treasurer there being more than five Justices present.

Pg. 76 Ordered by the court that Howard J. Anderdon be released from the payment of the state and county tax on two hundred and twenty five acres of land improperly charged tax for double tax. Tax two dollars and is ordered to be ordered to be certified to the treasurer and trustee.

The court proceeded to lay tax for the year 1837 a proposition being made to lay the following rates (to wit) on each hundred dollars worth of property five cents jury tax, county contigent expenses five cents, road and bridge tax two and one half cents, poor tax two and one half cents, on each white poll twelve and a half cents, county tax on same twelve and one half cents, jury tax on same twelve and one half cents, state tax on each hundred dollars five cents, on each white poll twelve and one half cents. The votes were taken those that voted for said rates were Esqs. Pope, Gilliland, Strain, Maxwell, Titsworth, Chrifield, Lockard, Turner and Chambers a majority of all the Justices in said county so said rates for said year. County tax on all privileges equal to the state tax.

James McElyea records his stock mark (to wit) a smooth crop each ear and an under bit in the same.

Benjamin Nearn records his stock mark (to wit) a swallow fork and under bit in the right ear and an under half crop of the left.

Pg. 77 Phillip F. Crihfield records his stock mark (to wit) a swallow fork in each ear and under bit in the right.

Rezin L. Byron, Hiram C. Keller and Milton G. Turner, Esqs., Commissiones to let out and superintend the building of a court house in the town of Ripley report here in court that they have received said house from the undertaken.

It is ordered by the court there being a majority of all the Justices in said county present that John and William Land be allowed one hundred and seventy four dollars and ninety three and three fourths cents for building the court house in the Town of Ripley out of any money in the hands of the Trustee not otherwise appropriated.

David Runnels records his stock mark (to wit) swallow fork in the left ear and a crop and under bit in right ear.

Adolphus Carrigan, Administrator on the estate of William Carrigan dec'd returned here in court an additional inventory of property sold by him as administrator on said estate which is received by the court and ordered to be recorded.

Pg. Whereas it appearing to the satisfaction of the court that Westly Keller
77 died intestate and Hiram C. Keller applying for letters of administration on
cont. said estate it is ordered that letters issue accordingly he having taken the
Pg. oath and entered into bond conditioned and payable as the law directs.
78 It is ordered by the court that Rezin L. Byron, Hiram C. Keller and James Price be appointed commissioners to let out and superintend the running up a pair of stairs in the court house putting up a ban jury box and a seat for the court in the same.

Ordered by the court there being a majority of all the Justices in said county present that the following good and lawful men be appointed a jury of view to lay off and mark out the nearest and best way for a road from Stokes landing on the Forkeddeer river to Ross Haws on the Missispippi and that they report to the next term of this court (to wit) Blow, Ross, Haw, Elijah B. Foster, Jordan G. Stokes, William C. Cowin and James Braden.

Ordered by the court there being a majority of all the Justices in said county present that the following men be appointed a jury of view to lay off and mark out the nearest and best way for a road from Durhamville to Ripley and that they report to the next term of this court (to wit) Robert P. Russell, John Watson, Thomas Durham, Samuel H. Hammel, William Calhoon, William Turner and William McClelland.

Pg. Ordered that court be adjourned for half an hour.
79 Court met pursuant to adjournment, Hiram C. Keller records stock mark (to wit) a split in the right ear and under bit in the left.

Imy Keller records his stock mark (to wit) crop and split in the right ear.

Ordered by the court there being one third of all the Justices in said county present that Henry Sumrow be appointed Overseer of the road leading from Ripley to Dyersburg from the old county line of Dyer to the forks of road where the Covington road leaves the Ripley road and that he have the following hands to work under him (to wit) Capt. Lee's son and hands, Boling Fisher's hands, George Fisher, Benjamin Fisher, Thomas Pewitt, John Smith, Onesemus Fudge and the Hoopers.

Ordered by the court that Samuel King be released from the payment of the state and county tax on nine hundred acres of land in the county of Lauderdale improperly charged and that the same be certified to the Comptroller and County Trustee tax two dollars and sixteen cents.

Ordered by the court that John H. Maxwell, Esq. be allowed to turn the road leading from Ripley to Dyersburg around a small piece of new ground
Pg. cleared by him, that he run the road along with L. D. Spain's fence til it gets
80 to Spain's gate, thence to run nearly south until it gets to the old road again.

This day Ivy Chandler a constable in the county of Lauderdale tendered to the court his resignation which is received by the court.

Ordered by the court that court be adjourned until tomorrow morning at ten o'clock.

A. H. Pope, Chairman
John Lockard, J.P.
William Spain, J.P.

Tuesday morning, February the seventh, 1837.

Court met pursuant to adjournment, present Able H. Pope, Chairman, William Strain, John Lockard, Samuel V. Gilliland, G. L. Rutherford, Clerk and Guy Smith, Esq., high sheriff, proclamation being made the court proceeded to business.

Pg. 80 cont. This day William Strain, one of the acting Justices of the peace in and for said county tendered here in court his resignation as a Justice of the peace in and for said county which is received by the court.

Ordered by the court that the following boundaries shall contain the hands to work on and keep in repair the road from Fullen to John Fullen's field (Viz) beginning at the south boundary line of the second civil district on Hatchy river thence with the line of the same to Amy Fisher's field thence Pg. 81 east so as to include Albison V. Davenport thence south to include all the hands on Wardlaw and Nesmunger plantation.

Ordered by the court that Coleman Hall be appointed Overseer of the road from Fullen's Ferry to John Fullen's field and that he have all the hands in the following bounds (to wit) beginning on Hatchy river at the southern boundary line of the second civil division thence with said line to Mrs. Fishers thence east so as to include Albison and Davenpart thence south to include all the hands on Wardlow and Nesmunger plantation and that he keep the same in repair as a first class road.

Ordered by the court that David Russell be appointed Overseer of the road from John Fullen's field to the north end of the lane at Bates Fork of Cane Creek and that he have all the hands in the second civil division north of Mrs. Fisher's and Davenport's to a supposed line one half mile north of David P. Posey and that he keep the same in repair as a first class road.

Rezin L. Byron records his stock mark (to wit) an under bit in each ear.

There being no further business before the court it is ordered by the Pg. 82 court that court be adjourned until court in course.

A. H. Pope, Chairman
Sam V. Gilland, J.P.
John Lockard, J.P.

Be it remembered that at a county court began and held for the county of Lauderdale and State of Tennessee in the town of Ripley on the first Monday in March in the year of our Lord one thousand eight hundred and thirty seven it being the sixth day of said month, present and presiding, the worshipful Able H. Pope, Esq., Chairman and Esqs, Gilliland, Lockard Turner, Titsworth, Crthfield, and Hutcherson, Associate Justices sitting and holding a county court for said county, Guy Smith Esq., high sheriff by deputy and G. L. Rutherford, Clerk, proclamation being made the court proceeded to business.

Able H. Pope, Esq., revenue commissioner for the third civil district in said county returned here into court a list of taxable property and polls by him taken for said district for the year 1837 which is recieved by the court and is ordered to be recorded.

John Lockard, Esq., revenue commissioner for district no. sixth in said county returned here into court a list of taxable property and polls by him taken for said district for the year 1837 which is received by the court and is ordered to be recorded.

Milton G. Turner Esq., revenue commissioner for distrcit no. one in Pg. 85 said county to take in a list of taxable property and for said district returned here into court a list of taxable property and polls by him taken for said district for the year 1837 which is received by the court and is ordered to be recorded.

C. G. Titsworth, Esq., a revenue commissioner for district no. seven in said county returned here into court a list of taxable property and polls by him taken for said district for the year 1837 which is received by the court and is ordered to be recorded.

Pg. 85 cont. John H. Maxwell, Esq., a revenue commissioner to take in a list of taxable property and polls in civil district no. second for said county for the year 1837, returns here into court a list of taxable property and polls by him taken for said district which is received by the court and is ordered to be recorded.

James J. Crawford, the revenue commissioner to take in a list of taxable property and polls in civil district no. eight for the year 1837, returned here in court a list of taxable property and polls by him taken for said district which is received by the court and is ordered to be recorded.

This day the jury of view appointed at the last term of the court to view, lay off and mark out a road from Stoke's Landing on the Forkeddeer river to Ross Haws on the Mississippi river reports here into court the result of said view which is received by the court and it is further ordered that the petitioners for said road cut out and keep up the same.

Pg. 86 This day the jury appointed to lay off and mark a road from Durhamville to Ripley and report to this court makes report here into court the result of said view, which is received by the court. Whereupon Mary Lee petitioned the court to appoint a jury to assess damage to her for the roads running through her land or turn the road. It is ordered by the court that the following good and lawful men be appointed a jury to view the road as marked from Durhamville to Ripley and assess the damage to Mary Lee for the roads running through her land or turn the road to the most convenient place taking into view the good as well as the injury the said Mary Lee may sustain and that they report to the next term of this court (to wit) John Stone, John Bradford, Thomas Fitzpatrick, Christopher G. Watson, Pleasant Dial, Lancy Graves and Robert Walker.

It is ordered by the court that all persons that are subject to double tax on account of mot listing their property within the time directed by law that will come in at the present term of this court or at the next term of the court be released from double tax.

Ordered by the court there being a majority of all the justices in said county present that Samuel H. Hammel be appointed Overseer of the Fulton road from the Haywood county line to the western boundary of the first civil division in Lauderdale county and that he have the following hahds (to wit) David Walker and all the hahds north of said road that belong to the first civil district first class road.

Pg. 87 Ordered by the court that Robert P. Russell be continued Overseer of the Fulton road from the eastern boundary line of the second civil division of said county to the western boundary of the same and to have all the hands that live within the following described bounds (to wit) to commence where the eastern boundary line of the second civil division crosses the road then south to William P. Gaines spring branch thence down the same unti it strikes a line drawn for David C. Russell's north line for his hands thence east with said line till it strikes the line between the first and second civil division thence north with said line to where it crosses Morphis line near W. H. Stone then west with said line to Nelly Woods south-west corner thence north with her line to Bates Creek thence down the smae to a line drawn for James Whitson thence south and west with said line to the beginning.

This day Jemima F. Chism was appointed Guardian for the orphan minor children of Elijah Chism dec'd (to wit) George W. Chism, Jemima E. Chism, Elijah G. Chism, Fanny H. Chism, and Amanda Chism and entered in bond conditioned and payable as the law directs with William R. Chism and John Lockard her security.

Pg. 88 It is ordered that court be adjourned for half an hour.

Court met pursuant to adjournment.

Pg. It is ordered that Jerry Cheek be appointed Overseer of the Ripley road
88 from the north end of the lane at Rezin L. Byron's old place and work to the
cont. Brownsville road at John F. Burks and that he have all the hands that live
in the following described bounds to work under him and that he keep the same
in repair as a first class road, commencing at John F. Burks run down the
Brownsville road to the one mile tree thence south with a line drawn for the
Whitson road to Bates Creek thence up the creek to where Nelly Woods line
Crosses the same thence south with her line to her corner thence east with
her line to her corner thence north with her line to Burks to the beginning.

It is ordered by the court that Joseph Taylor be appointed Overseer of
the road from Ripley in a direction to Brownsville commencing at Ripley and
that he work to the eastern boundary of the second civil division and that
he have all the hands that live in the following bounds to work under him
(to wit) beginning on the Haywood County line where it crosses Walker's branch
thence south with said county line to where the divison line between the
first and second civil division hits the same thence with said division line
Pg. until it passes William H. Stones thence with the Morphis line to Milly Woods
89 south-east corner thence north with her line to the Brownsville road thence
east with said road to the Dyersburg road thence with said road north-east to
a branch in Mrs. Panes lane thence down said lane to the creek thence up the
creek to the mouth of Walker's branch thence up the branch to the beginning.

It is ordered by the court that Lancy Graves be appointed Overseer of
the old Dyersburg road from where it leaves the Ripley road to where it
intersects the key corner road and that he keep the same in repair as a second
class road and that he have all the hands that live in the following described
bounds (to wit) beginning on Cane Creek at the mouth of Gilbert's branch
thence up the same to the Brownsville road thence east with said road to the
Dyersburg road thence north-east with said road to a branch in the lane between Mrs. Pane and C. C. Harriss thence down said branch to the creek thence
up the creek to the mouth of Walker's creek thence up the same to the Haywood
County line thence north of said line to the Buck's Ferry road thence with
said road to where the new key corner road intersects the same thence south
through A. Vickory's plantation to the beginning on the creek.

It is ordered by the court that Isaac D. Maxwell be appointed Overseer
of the road leading from Ripley in a direction to Dyersburg commencing on
Pg. Washing Street where the line dividing the second and third civil districts
90 crosses the same and that he work to the north boundary of the second civil
district that he keep the same in repair as a first class road and that he
have all the hands that live in the following described bounds (to wit)
commencing on Washington Street in the town of Ripley where the division line
between the second and third districts crosses the same running north-east
with said line to the mouth of Byler's Creek thence up said creek to the
Buck's Ferry road thence east with said road to where the new key corner road
intersects the same thence south passing through A. Vickory's plantation to
the mouth of Gilbert's branch on Cane Creek thence up said branch to the
Brownsville road east of Neddy Reames thence down said road to Wardlows line
thence north with his line and the east line of Ripley to Washington Street
thence with said street to the beginning.

It is ordered by the court that James Whitson be appointed Overseer of
the road leading from Ripley toward Fulton from Ripley to the old Fulton
road from Hurricane Hill that he keep the same in repair as a second class
road and that he have all the hands that live in following described bounds
(to wit) commencing in the town of Ripley where the division line between the
second and third civil districts crosses Washington Street, thence south-west
Pg. with said line to the old Fulton road thence up said road to the head of a
91

Pg. 91 cont. Hollow that runs east of Emry Kellers thence down the branch of said hollow to Bates Creek thence a north course to the one mile tree on the Brownsville road thence down said road to Joseph Wardlow's line thence north with his line to the east boundary line of Ripley to Washington Street thence west with said street to the beginning.

J. M. C. Robison records his stock mark (to wit) crop and under bit in left ear and a swallow fork in the right.

William R. Ledbetter records his stock mark (to wit) a swallow fork and over bit in the left ear.

It is ordered by the court that Levi Gardner be appointed Overseer of the road leading from Hatchy river in a direction to Ripley to intersect the old Fulton road near W. P. Gains.

Ordered that court be adjourned until tomorrow morning at eleven o'clock.

A. H. Pope, Chairman
Sam V. Gilliland, J.P.
Lewis Hutcherson, J.P.

Pg. 92 Tuesday Morning court met pursuant to adjournment, present and presiding the worshipful Able H. Pope, Esq.,Chairman and Esqs. Gilliland, and Hutcherson, Guy Smith, Esq.,high sheriff by deputy and G. L. Rutherford, Clerk proclamation being made the court proceeded to business. Lewis Hutcherson, Esq., the revenue commissioner for district no fourth in said county to take in a list of taxable property and polls returned here in court a list of taxable property and polls by him taken for said district for the year 1837 which is received by the court and is ordered to be recorded.

Ordered by the court that the following good and lawful men be appointed a jury for the next term of the circuit court to be held for the county of Lauderdale on the third Monday of June next (to wit) first distrcit, Milton G. Turner, Jeremiah Penick, James Anthony, Sampson Smith; second district, William Calhoon, John Land, Henry T. Chism, Robert P. Russell; third district, James Sherman, Elijah Lake, Sandy Shumake, A. H. Pope; fourth district, Lewis Hucherson, Andrew U. Kidd, Abraham Moss; fifth district, John Fletcher, sixth, Armstead Wood, Sam Lusk, Moses Roberson, E. B. Foster; seventh, Leonard Dunavant, C. G. Titsworth, Henry Crihfield; eighth, James J. Crawford, James N. Buck and David C. Russell and James Hucherson, constable to wait on the
Pg. 93 court and jury.

Lewis Hutcherson records his stock mark (to wit) swallow fork and under bit in the ear.

A. H. P. records his stock mark (to wit) a crop of each ear an under bit in the left and upper in the left.

There being no further business before the court it is ordered that court be adjourned until court in course.

A. H. Pope, Chairman
Lewis Hutcherson, J.P.
Sam V. Gilliland, J.P.

Pg. 94 Be it remembered that at a county court began and held for the County of Lauderdale and State of Tennessee in the town of Ripley on the first Monday in April in the year of our Lord one thousand eight hundred and thirty seven it being the third day of said month, present and presiding the worshipful Able H. Pope, Esq.,Chairman and Esqs. Gilliland, Maxwell, Campbell, Lockard and Crihfield associate Justices sitting and holding a county court for said county, Guy Smith, Esq.,high sheriff and G. L. Rutherford, Clerk,

Pg. proclamation being made the court proceeded to business.
94 Robert C. Campbell, Esq., the revenue commissioner for district no.
cont. five in Lauderdale County for the year 1837 returned here in court a list of taxable property and polls by him taken for said district which is received by the court and is ordered tobe recorded.

This day John Lockard, Esq., proved the killing of one wolf in County of Lauderdale by his own oath over the age of four months which is ordered to be so certified to the Treasurer there being five Justices present.

Ordered by the court that the following good and lawful men be appointed a jury of view to view the road leading from Ripley to Dyersburg near Boling Fisher and that they report to the next term of this court the convenience or
Pg. inconvenience that may result from changing said road (to wit) Henry Turner,
95 Edmond P. See, John Smith, Jim Thomas, McG. Rutherford, Samuel Hooper.

Ordered by the court that Armstead Wood be appointed Overseer of road leading from Ripley to Stokes Landing on the Forkeddeer river in place of Thomas Hazlewood and that he have all the hands in Capt. Nearns Company to work under him to cut out said road.

The jury of view appointed at the last term of this court to view the road leading from Ripley to Durhamville and assess the damage to Mary J. Lee for said road running through her land makes the following report (to wit) we, the Jury have met agreeable to the order of court and have examined the land and we give Mrs. Mary J. Lee, eighteen dollars, Thomas Fitzpatrick, John Stone, John Bradford, P. C. Dual, Robert Walker, Christopher Watson, Lancy Graves, the vote was then taken whither said road should be established, those against said road were Esq. Pope, Gilliland, Maxwell, Lockard and Crifield, so said road was voted down.

Hiram C. Kelier, Administrator of Westley Keller dec'd returned here into court an inventory and account of sale which is received by the court and is ordered to be recorded.

Pg. Ordered by the court that the following good and lawful men be appointed
96 a jury of view to change the old road leading from Covington to Dyersburg beginning at the Mounds share at Whites old place and to intersect the road from Ripley to Dyersburg where the same crosses the Bucks Ferry road and that they report to the next term of this court (to wit) Lancy Graves, James Morris, R. G. Byron, Absolum Vicory, Isaac D. Maxwell, Anderdon Jordan, Isaac Smith.

Ordered that the following good and lawful men be appointed a jury of review to view the road leading from Ripley to Durhamville and that they assess the damage to Fosit for said road running through his land or turn the road to the most convenient place taking into consideration the public good as well as the injury the said Fosit may sustain and that they report to the June term of this court, John Stone, C. M. Roberson, T. P. Russell, Milton G. Turner, William Turner, C. C. Harris and A. Phillips.

Ordered that the commissioners for the town of Ripley (to wit) R. L. Byron, H. R. Crawford, Robert C. Campbell, Hiram C. Keller and G. L. Rutherford be allowed one dollar and fifty cents per day for each day that they were employed in laying off and selling the lots in said town to be paid out of any money in the hands of the Trustee.

Ordered that Rezin L. Byron, Dabney P. Phillips and James J. Crawford be appointed commissioners of the internal improvement fund for the County of Lauderdale and they ask for, demand and received from the county of Dyer and
Pg. Tipton that part of said fund that belongs to Lauderdale County.
97 There being no further business before the court it is ordered that court be adjourned until court in course.

A. H. Pope, Chairman
John Packard, J.P.
J. H. Maxwell, J.P.

Pg. Be it remembered that at a county court began and held for the county
98 of Lauderdale and State of Tennessee in the town of Ripley on the first Monday in May in the year of our Lord one thousand eight hundred and thirty
seven, it being the first day of said month present and presiding the worshipful Able H. Pope, Esq.,Chairman and Esqs. Maxwell, Turner, Titsworth, Crihfield, Lockard, and Chambers, associate Justices sitting and holding a county
court for said county Guy Smith, Esq.,high sheriff by deputy and G. L. Rutherford, Clerk of said court proclamation being made the court proceeded to
business.

Whereas it appearing to the satisfaction of the court that Henry L. Williams, administrator of the estate of Phereba Williams hath departed this life and Henry B. L. Williams applying for letters of administrator de bonis non on said estate he having taken the oath and entered into bond as the law directs it is ordered that letters testamentary issue to the said Henry B. L. Williams accordingly.

Whereas it appearing to the satisfaction of this court that Henry L.
Pg. Williams hath departed this life leaving no last will or testament and Henry
99 B. L. Williams applying for letters of administration on said estate and
suggest in wrighting the insolvency of said estate it is ordered that letters
testamentary issue to the said Henry B. L. Williams accordingly.

This day the court proceeded to appoint a collector of the public taxes for the County of Lauderdale for the year 1837, whereupon John C. Barnes was appointed Collector for said county and took the oath accordingly and entered into bond which bonds are in the words and figures following (to wit) Know all men by these presents that we, John C. Barnes, Able H. Pope and John H. Maxwell, all of the county of Lauderdale and State of Tennessee are held and firmly bound unto his excellency Newton Cannon, Esq., Governor of the State of Tennessee for the time being and his successors in office in the penal sum of eight hundred and forty eight dollars for the payment of which will and truly to be made, we do bind ourselves and each of our heirs, executors or administrators, jointly, severally and firmly by these presents sealed with our seals and dated this tenth day of May 1837.

The condition of the above obligation is such that where as the above
bounden John C. Barns, Collector of the public taxes for the County of Lauderdale and State of Tennessee for the year eighteen hundred and thirty seven
Pg. now if the above bound, John C. Barnes does collect the state tax for said
100 year and pay over the same to the proper person agreeable to law then this
obligation to be void otherwise to remain in full force and virtue according
to law.

John C. Barnes (Seal)
A. H. Pope (Seal)
J. H. Maxwell (Seal)

Know all men by these presents that we, John C. Barnes, David C. Russell and John H. Maxwell, all of the County of Lauderdale and State of Tennessee are held and firmly bound unto Able H. Pope, Esq. Chairman of the county court of said County of Lauderdale for the time being and his successors in office in the penal sum of two thousand five hundred dollars for the payment of which will and truly to be made we do bind ourselves, our heirs, executors or administrators jointly, severally and firmly by these presents sealed with our seals and dated this first day of May 1837.

The condition of the above obligation is such that whereas the above bound John C. Barnes, Collector of the public taxes for the County of Lauderdale

Pg. 100 cont. for the year eighteen hundred and thirty seven, now if the above bound John C. Barnes does collect the county tax for said county for said year and pay over the same to the county trustee agreeable to law, then this obligation to be void otherwise to remain in full force and effect according to law.

John C. Barnes (Seal)
D. C. Russell (Seal)
J. H. Maxwell (Seal)

Pg. 101 Ordered by the court that the following good and lawful men be appointed a jury of view to review the road leading from Ripley to Dyersburg as it now runs near Boling Fishers and that they report to the next term of this court the convenience or inconvenience that may result from changing said road, (to wit) Henry Sumrow, Edmond P. Lee, John Smith,Jr., Thomas McG. Rutherford, and Samuel Hooper.

Ordered by the court that Armstead Wood Overseer of the road leading from Ripley to Stokes landing have until the September term of this court to cut out said road and put it in repair.

This day the jury that was appointed at the last term of this court to view the road leading from Covington to Dyersburg and turn the same near A. White's old place report to court which report is in the following words and and figures (to wit) April 22, 1837. We being ordered by the county court of Lauderdale at their April term to view and turn the road leading from Covington to Dyersburg that part of said road from A. White's old place to where the new road from Ripley to Dyersburg intersects the same to change it so as to intersect said Ripley road near the Bucks ferry road being summoned and sworn, report as follows, we have viewed and marked and do believe it save the work of one mile and a much better way given under our hands the date above written.

A. Vicory
L. Jordan
Isaac Smith
James A. Morris

Pg. 102 Ordered that Lancy Graves cut out the above road as marked with his hands.

David P. Russell records his stock mark (to wit) crop of the left ear and upper slope of the right.

John Stone records his stock mark (to wit) swallow fork in each ear and under bit in the right.

Ordered that court be adjourned for one hour.

Court met pursuant to adjournment.

Ordered by the court that Pleasant C. Dial be appointed Overseer of the road leading from Ripley towards Brownsville commencing at the division line between the first and second civil dividion and to work to the county line, that he have the followinghands to work under him, Smith, Kent, Hafford and hands, John Watson, George W. Tatum, Joseph Glossen, Sam Dunlap, first class road.

Arch Phillips records his stock mark (to wit) crop and under bit in the right ear, swallow fork and under bit in the left.

Pleasant C. Dial records his stock mark (to wit) crop off the left ear and slit in the right.

Smith Kent records his stock mark (to wit) a crop and under nick in each ear.

Lauderdale County
Minute Book 1836-1844
Vol. A

Pg. 103 Henry R. Chambers records his stock mark (to wit) crop and under half crop of the left ear and under half crop of the right.

Court adjourned until court in course.

A. H. Pope, Chairman
J. H. Maxwell, J.P.
C. P. Titsworth, J.P.

Pg. 104 Be it remembered that at a county court began and held for the county of Lauderdale and State of Tennessee in the town of Ripley on the first Monday in June in the year of our Lord one thousand eight hundred and thirty seven it being the fifth day of said month present and presiding the worshipful, John Lockard, Esq., Esqs. Gilliland, Maxwell, Vassor, Turner, Crihfield, associate Justices sitting and holding a county court for said county, Guy Smith, Esq.,high sheriff and G. L. Rutherford, Clerk. Proclamation being made the court proceeded to business, whereupon the court proceeded to appoint a Chairman protem for the present time whereupon John Lockard was appointed Chairman protem.

This day Thomas J. Childress came into court and produced a commission from Newton Cannon, Esq., Governor of the State of Tennessee, authorizing and commissioning him to serve as Justice of the peace in and for said county was qualified as the law directs and took his seat accordingly.

This day the jury of view that appointed at the last term of this court to view the road Boling Fishers in said county and report the expediency of changing said road for where it now runs makes report here in cort which is received by the court and is ordered to be established as marked out by said Jury.

Pg. 105 This day Samuel V Gilliland was appointed by the court, Guardian for the minor children of Labert Wood dec'd (to wit) William A. Wood, Betsy Ann Wood, Robert T. Wood, Levin R. Wood, Handy Wood, Labert Wood and Mary E. Wood, whereupon Samuel V. Gilliland entered into bond conditioned and payable as the law directs and took the oath accordingly.

Ordered by the court that Samuel Lusk be appointed Overseer of the road leading from Bucks ferry to Stokes landing in the place of Dickerson Jennings and that he have the same hands to work under him.

On a motion being made for the court to reconsider a vote given by them at the April term of said court in relation to the establishing of a road from Ripley to Durhamville through Mary Lee's lands, the ayes and noes being called for those that voted for considering said vote were Esqs. Turner, those that voted against reconsideration were Esqs. Gilliland, Maxwell, Childress, Lockard, Vassor and Crihfield, so said motion for reconsideration was overruled.

This day the jury of view to assess damages to Fossett for the road that
Pg. 106 leads from Ripley to Durhamville passing through H. Fossetts lands made
report here in court which is received by the court and is ordered cut out as
marked.

This day the court proceeded to make an allowance to the revenue comissioners for said county for the year 1837 compensations for their services for taking in a list of taxable property and polls for said year (to wit) Milton Turner, Esq., John H. Maxwell, Esq., A. H. Pope, Esq., Lewis Hutcherson, Esq., Robert C. Campbell, Esq., John Lockard, Esq., C. G. Titsworth, Esq., James J. Crawford, be allowed seven dollars and fifty cents to be paid out of any money in the hands of the Trustee not otherwise appropriated.

Thomas I. Smith records his stock mark (to wit) a smooth crop of the right ear.

Pg. 106 cont. Ordered that court be adjourned for one hour.

Court met pursuant to adjournment.

Whereas it appearing to the satisfaction of the court that Lewis Mathews has departed this life intestate and Reitha Mathews and Bozzile Billingsly applying for letters of administration on said estate they having entered into bond and taken the oath according to law.

Ordered that John C. Barnes, Collector of the public taxes for said county for the year 1837 be released from the payment of sixty cents that amount being improperly charged to William Turner. Pg. 107

There being no further business before the court it is ordered that court be adjourned until court in course.

John Lockard, Chairman Protem
Thomas J. Childress, J.P.
J. H. Maxwell, J.P.

Pg. 108 Be it remembered that at a county court began and held for the county of Lauderdale and State of Tennessee in the town of Ripley on the first Monday in July in the year of our Lord one thousand eight hundred and thirty seven it being the third day of said month presented and presiding the worshipful Able H. Pope, Esq.,Chairman and Esqs. John H. Maxwell, Lockard, Titsworth, Thomas Childress and Esq. Penick, Hutcheson and Campbell associate Justices sitting and holding a county court for said conty, Guy Smith, Esq.,high sheriff and G. L. Rutherford, Clerk. Proclamation being made the court proceeded to business.

Whereas it appearing to the satisfaction of the court that Richard Allison hath died intestate and Dickerson Jennings applying for letters of administration on said estate it is ordered that he have letters accordingly he having taken the oath and entered into bond conditioned and payable as the law directs.

This day Richard Right proved by his own oath the killing of one wolf in the county of Lauderdale over the age of four months which is ordered to be certified to the Treasurer there being five Justices present.

Ordered by the court that the following good and lawful men be appointed a jury of view to view, lay off and mark out a road leading from Ripley in direction to Fulton to the greatest advantage of the inhabitants and as little as may be to the prejudice of inclosures commencing in Ripley and view as far as to Cane Creek and that they report to the next term of this court (to wit) Hiram C. Keller, Joseph Wardlow, Ezekial Farmer, James Whitson, Elijah Lake, William Wardlow and James Sherman. Pg. 109

Ordered that the following good and lawful men be appointed a jury of view to lay off and mark out a road from Fulton in a direction to Ripley as far as to Cane Creek and then to meet the road viewed from Ripley towards Fulton to be laid off to the greatest advantage to the inhabitants and as little as may be to the prejudice of enclosure (to wit) John Vassor, James Garvin, Jesse Hutcherson, Samuel A. Givins, Abraham Moss, John C. Barnes and James Crook and that they report to the next term of this court.

Ordered by the court that the following good and lawful men be appointed a jury of view to lay off and mark out a road from the public square in the town of Ripley passing Hazelwood's mill and to intersect the Ashport Turnpike road on Cole Creek Bluff (to wit) Moses Roberson, Elijah B. Foster, Thomas Hazlewood, Isaac Braden, John Hogsette and Thomas T. Smith and that they report to the next term of this court.

Pg. 112 Ordered by the court that John Williams a pauper in this county be allowed the sum of thirty seven dollars and fifty cents from this term until

Pg. 112 cont. the first day of January 1838 to be paid out of any money in the hands of the Trustee not otherwise appropriated which is to be under the control of Henry Crihfield, Esq.

Ordered by the court that the following good and lawful men be appointed a venira for the next circuit court to be held for the county of Lauderdale on third Monday in October next and that States writ of veniri facious accordingly (to wit) William Turner; James Barfield, Thomas Fitzpatrick, John Watson for the first district; R. L. Byron, Isaac D. Maxwell, William McClelland, D. Posey, John H. Maxwell for the second district; Thomas J. Childress, A. B. Gaines, John D. Edney, Nathaniel Barnes for the third district; James Tompkins for the fourth district; Green B. Temple for the fifth district; Dickerson Jennings, Henry Sumrow, Joshua Wright, Robertson Meadows for the sixth; William Moore, John Mitchell, Claiborne Rounsaville for the seventh; William Jordan, James J. Crawford for the eighth district; Martin R. Hatcher and Hiram Meadows, Constables to wait on the court and jury.

Joseph Taylor records his stock mark (to wit) crop of the left ear and a hole in the right.

Ordered that court be adjourned for one hour.

Pg. 113 Court met pursuant to adjournment then proceeded to appoint a Chairman protem for the present term whereupon John Lockard, Esq., was appointed Chairman protem.

The court proceeded to business.

Ordered by the court that the following good and lawful men be appointed a jury of view to lay off and mark out a road from the Haywood County line where a road has lately been marked by the citizens of Haywood County and that the same intersect the Brownsville road from Ripley where the old Hurricane Hill road crosses the same and that they report to the next term of this court (to wit) Joseph Taylor, Walter Glawson, Robert Walker, Lancy Graves and R. L. Byron.

This day the commissioners of the county revenue came into court and reports of settlement with the county trustee which is received by the court and ordered to be recorded.

Ordered by the court that R. L. Byron, John Stone, J. M. C. Robison, be appointed commissioners to lay off Rutha Mathews, widow of Lewis Mathews dec'd her years provisions and that they report to the next term of this court.

Ordered by the court that Howel Taylor,Jr., N. T. Perkins and David Hays be paid out of any money in the hands of the Trustee not otherwise appropriated, the following sum of money for their services as commissioners to locate the county seat of Lauderdale County (to wit) Howel Taylor and N. T. Perkins twelve dollars each and David Hays nine dollars.

Pg. 114 Ordered by the court that the following good and lawful men be appointed a jury of view for the purpose of viewing and marking out a road commencing where the Brownsville road intersects the county line near Champs corner field and to run through James A. Morris lane and on to the Dyersburg road (to wit) Joseph Taylor, Walter Glawson, Robert Walker, Lancy Graves and Rezin L. Byron and that they report to the next term of this court.

Ordered by the court that court be adjourned until court in course.

John Lockard, Chairman Protem
Henry Crihfield, J.P.
R. C. Campbell, J.P.

Pg. 115 Be it remembered that at a county court began and held for the County of Lauderdale and State of Tennessee in the court house in the town of Ripley on the first Monday in August in the year of our Lord one thousand eight hundred and thirty seven it being the seventh day of said month, present and presiding the worshipful Able H. Pope, Esq., Chairman, John H. Maxwell, Titsworth, Vassor, Hutcherson, Penick, Lockard, Turner and Childress associate Justices sitting and holding a county court for said county, G. L. Rutherford, Clerk and Guy Smith, Sheriff, proclamation being made the court proceeded to business.

This day Dickerson Jennings administrator on the estate of Richard Allison, returned here into court an inventory and acp't sale which is received by the court and ordered to be recorded.

Ordered by the court that Charles I. Love be presented to list one thousand acres of land in the fifth district by paying the single tax.

This day the jury of view that was appointed at the last term of this court to view, lay off and mark out a road commencing at the county line near Champs corner field and to run through James A. Morris land and on to the Dyersburg road report to the court that they have marked the same which is received by the court.

Pg. 116 Ordered by the court that the following good and lawful men be appointed a jury of view to lay off and mark out the nearest and best way for a road commencing on the old Dyersburg road near Rezin L. Byron where a road has been viewed from Champs corner to Ripley and that they report to the next term of this court (to wit) R. L. Byron, Joseph Taylor, Walter Glawson, Robert Walker and Luncy Graves.

This day the jury of view that was appointed at the last term of this court for the purpose of laying off a road from Fulton to come through to meet a road marked from Ripley reports that they have complyed with said order which is received by the court.

This day Rezin L. Byron, John Stone and J. M. C. Roberson the commissioners that was appointed at the last term of this court to lay off to the widow of Lewis Mathews dec'd a years provisions report to2court which is received by the court and is ordered to be recorded.

James A. Morris records his stock mark (to wit) under bit and swallow fork in the right ear under bit and split in the left ear.

Ordered by the court the clerk record the special inventory returned by Henry B. Williams, administrator de bonis non on the estate of Pheraby Williams deceased which was returned at the June term of this court and was not recorded.

Pg. 117 Whereas it appearing to the satisfaction of the court that Samuel Hogsette has departed this life leaving no last will or testament and Isaac Braden and W. T. Moorehead applying to the court for letters of administration on said estate they having taken the oath and entered into bond conditioned and payable as the law directs it is ordered that letters issue accordingly.

Ordered by the court there being a majority of all the Justices in said county present and voting in the affirmative that Thomas D. Fisher be paid out of any money in the hands of the Trustee not otherwise appropriated the sum of ten dollars and fifty cents for a book bought for the registers office.

Ordered that Rezin L. Byron, George Williams, and G. L. Rutherford be appointed to draft a plan for building a bridge accross Cane Creek on the Fulton road and received proposals for building the same and that they report the same to the next term of this court.

Ordered that court be adjourned for one hour.

Court met pursuant to adjournment.

Pg. This day Ellison P. Fuller, Administrator on the estate of Mabry Hunter
117 dec'd returned here in court an inventory acp't of sale of the property
cont. belonging to said estate which is received by the court and ordered to be
Pg. recorded.
118 On a motion being made to allow Thomas Hazlewood the sum of eighty dollars for running up a pair of stairs in the court house, putting up a bar in the same and a bench for the court the vote was taken those that voted for said allowance were Esqs. Pope, Maxwell, Turner, Penick, Turner, Titsworth, Vassor, Childress, a majority of all the Justices in said county so said allowance was made for eighty dollars and ordered to be paid out of any money in the hands of the Trustee not otherwise appropriated.

Ordered by the court that John C. Barnes, Collector for the County of Lauderdale be released from the collecting of the tax on 953 in Charles Mc. Dowell valued 3342 the same having been twice listed. Tax 1.67.

Ordered by the court that A. Bledsoe be released from the payment of double tax on 560 acres of land lying in the third district by the payment of the single tax the same having been reported for double tax by the revenue commissioner through mistake.

Ordered by the court that John C. Barnes, Collector of the public taxes for the County of Lauderdale for the year 1837 be released from the collecting of the double tax on 800 acres of land valued at $3200 dollars charged double that he only collect the single tax.

Pg. This day Jeremiah Penick a Justice of the peace for said county handed
119 in his resignation as a Justice in said county which is received by the court.

This day Christopher G. Titsworth Esq., a Justice of the peace for said county tendered to the court his resignation as a Justice in said county which is received by the court.

This day the jury of view appointed to view the road from Ripley in a direction to Fulton as far as to Cane Creek report to court that they have marked out said road which is received by the court.

Ordered that court be adjourned until court in course.

A. H. Pope, Chairman
Lewis Hutcherson, J.P.
John Vassor, J.P.

Pg. Be it remembered that at a county court began and held for the County of
120 Lauderdale and State of Tennessee in the town of Ripley on the first Monday in September in the year of our Lord one thousand eight hundred and thirty seven it being the fourth day of said month present and presiding the worship-Able H. Pope, Esq., Chairman of the county court for said county, John H. Maxwell, Campbell, Crihfield, Lockard, Foster, Chambers, associate Justices sitting and holding a county court for said county, G. L. Rutherford, Clerk and Guy Smith, Esq., high sheriff, proclamation being made the court proceeded to business.

This day it appearing to the satisfaction of the court that Lawson A. Henry has departed this life intestate and Able H. Pope applying for letters of administration on said estate he having entered into bond conditioned and payable as the law directs and the oath it is ordered that letters issue accordingly.

Ordered by the court that James G. Anthony be appointed Overseer of the road in the place of Samuel Hammel and that he have in addition to the hands that belong to Hammel, Asa Pate and Thomas Durham work under him.

Pg. 121 This day Armstead Wood, Overseer that was appointed to cut out the road leading from Ripley to Stokes landing reports that he has cut out said road which is received by the court.

This day the jury of view that was appointed at the last term of this court to view and mark the road from Ripley to R. L. Byrons and then meet a road extended from the county line report that they have marked out said road which is received by the court and is ordered to be established.

Ordered by the court that James A. Morris be appointed Overseer to cut out the road from Ripley to the county line in a direction to Brownsville, known by the name of the corner road and that he have all the hands that work under Lancy Graves and Joseph Taylor to work under him and that he report to the next term of this court.

Ordered by the court that William Baxter be appointed Overseer of the road leading from Ripley to Dyersburg in the place of C. G. Titsworth and that he have the same hands to work under him.

Ordered by the court that Hiram C. Keller, Isaac Braden and John Chapman be appointed commissioners to lay off to the widow of Lawson A. Henry dec'd her years provisions and that they report to the next term of this court.

Pg. 122 Ordered by the court there being a majority of all the Justices in said county present and voting in the affirmative that G. L. Rutherford be allowed the sum of five dollars and seventy five cents for issuing jury tickets from the organization of this county upto the present term to be paid out of any money in the hands of the Trustee not otherwise appropriated.

On a motion being made to allow Guy Smith, sheriff for said county his exofficio fee for the year 1837 on a motion to allow him fifty dollars the vote was taken those that voted for said allowance were Esqs. Pope, Maxwell, Campbell, Chrifield, Lockard and Foster a majority of all the Justices in said county so said allowance was made and ordered to be paid out of any money in the hands of the Trustee.

On a motion being made to allow G. L. Rutherford, Clerkof the county court for said county for his exofficio fee for the year 1837 on a motion to allow him fifty dollars those that voted for said allowance were Esqs. Pope, Maxwell, Lockard, Campbell, Foster, Crihfield, a majority of all the Justices in said county so said allowance was made for fifty dollars and ordered to be paid out of any money in the hands of the trustee not otherwise appropriated.

Pg. 123 On a motion to allow G. L. Rutherford, Clerk of the county court for said county twenty dollars for amking out the tax list for the year 1837, those that voted for said allowance were Esqs. Pope, Maxwell, Campbell, Lockard, Crihfield and Foster so said allowance was made and ordered to be paid out of any money in the hands of the trustee not otherwise appropriated.

Ordered that the town commissioners for the town of Ripley draft a plan for a jail in the town of Ripley and that they report to the next term of court.

Henry Willard records his stock mark (to wit) a crop and slit in each ear.

This day John Flippin came into court with a certificate of his election as a constable in the seventh civil district in said county and entered into bond conditioned and payable as the law directs and took the oath of office.

Boyle Billingly, Administrator on the estate of Lewis Mathews dec'd returned into court and acp't of sale of property belonging to said estate which is received by the court and ordered to be recorded.

Ordered that Edmond H. Rudder be appointed Overseer of road from Hatchey

Pg. 124 in the place of Coleman Hall and that he have the same hands to work under him.

Ordered by the court that Benjamin Fisher be appointed Overseer of the road leading from Brownsville towards the key corner from the county line to the forks of the road near Benjamin Fisher and that he have the widow Nelson's hands to work under him.

Ross Howe records his stock mark (to wit) over bit out of each ear.

Ordered by the court that R. L. Byron, George Williams and G. L. Rutherford, the commissioners appointed at the last term of this court to draft a plan and receive proposals for building a bridge across Cane Creek take the bonds of Walter Glawson and John N. Byron in the sum of three hundred and eighty eight dollars and bind them to keep the bridge up five years and return the same in good order at the expiration of the term.

Ordered by the court that the following good and lawful men be appointed a jury of view to assess damage to the heirs of Tisdale for a road leading from Ripley in a direction to Brownsville passing through a tract of 640 acres of land or change the road taking into consideration the public good as well as the injury the individuals may sustain and that they report to the next term of this court (to wit) Robert Walker, Joseph Taylor, Isaac D. Maxwell, Absolum Vickory, Joseph Wardlow.

Pg. 125 Ordered by the court that court be adjourned until court in course.

A. H. Pope, Chairman
Henry Crihfield, J.P.
R. C. Campbell, J.P.

Pg. 126 Be it remembered that at a county court began and held for the county of Lauderdale and State of Tennessee in the town of Ripley on the first Monday in October in the year of our Lord one thousand eight hundred and thirty seven it being the second day of said month present and presiding the worshipful John Lockard, A. H. Pope, Chairman, Elijah B. Foster and Esqs. John H. Maxwell, R. C. Campbell, Thomas J. Childress, Guy Smith, Esq., high sheriff and G. L. Rutherford, Clerk of said court proclamation being made the court proceeded to business.

This day the Jury that was appointed at the last term of this court to assess damage to the heirs of James Tisdale for the road leading from Ripley towards Brownsville running through a six hundred and forty acre tract of land belonging to said heirs or change the road reports to this court which is in the following words and figures (to wit)

We the undersigned Jurors to assess damages for a road leading through the land of James Tisdale's heirs agreeable to the writters do report no damage found, September 30, 1837.

James Taylor
Robert Walker
A. Vickory

Pg. 127 Whereas it appearing to the satisfaction of the court that Francis Nunn hath departed this life intestate and David Nunn applying for letters of administration on said estate it is ordered by the court that he have letters accordingly he having taken the oath of administration and entered into bond with approved security conditioned and payable as the law directs.

Ordered by the court that James Braden be appointed Overseer of the Bucks Ferry road leading fowards Stokes landing commencing at Blackwells and that he work to Thomas I. Smith and that he have the following hands to work under

Pg. him and that he keep the same in repair as a second class road (to wit)
127 Joshua Wright, B. Weems and Read.
cont. Ordered by the court there being a majority present that Malcolm Gwinn
have in addition to the hands that he mow has all that live west of the
Dyersburg road in the eight district to work under him.

Ordered by the court that John Nearn be appointed Overseer of the road
from Blackwells to the county line and that he have the following hands to
Pg. work under him (to wit) Nicholas Reynolds, Arcell Reynolds, James Sanders,
128 Henry Reynolds, Isaac Reynolds, Dickerson Jennings and William Jennings and
that he keep the same in repair as a second class road.

Ordered by the court that Armstead Wood be appointed Overseer of the road leading from Ripley to Stokes landing commencing at Cane Creek and that he have all the hands south and west of the Buck's ferry road and north of Cane Creek to work under him and that he keep the same in repair as a second class road.

Ordered by the court that Thomas Turner be appointed Overseer of the Ashport road from Hurricane Creek to Burtis Alfords and that he have John King, John Jordan, Charles Black, Ely Graves to work under him and that he keep the same in repair as a first class road.

Ordered by the court that Hiram C. Keller be appointed Overseer of the road from Ripley towards Ashport that he work to the old Ashport road near William Bradens and that he have the following hands (to wit) A. B. Gaines, W. P. Gaines, James Wardlow, Jackson Barnes, Isom Roberson, William Brim and Alex Henry and that he keep the same in repair as a second class road.

Ordered that Levi Gardner, Overseer of the road from W. P. Gaines to
Titsworths landing on Hatchey River have the following hands to work under
him (to wit) John C. Barnes, Nancy Childress hands, L. Roberson, John D.
Pg. Edney, Ira Gaines, Blankinship, W. Prescott, Jackson Gardner, N. Barnes,
129 Mrs. Hunter's hands, James Titsworth and that he keep the same in repair as
a third class road.

Ordered by the court that Sandy Shumake be appointed Overseer of the Ashport road from the Fulton road to Hurricane creek and that he have the following hands (to wit) Richard Golden, Chapman, James Sherman, William Braden, James Braden, William Nash, E. P. Fuller and hands, George Riddle and Jerry Riddle, E. Farmer and W. Vauss and that he keep the same in repair as a first class road.

Ordered by the court that James B. Crook be appointed Overseer of the Fulton road from W. P. Gaines to Cane Creek bridge and that he have the following hands to work under him (to wit) all the Williams, Greens, Baker, N. Baker, R. Baker, M. Kelly, Ralph L. Inman, E. Lake and hands, J. D. Karlton, and Milton Strain and that he keep the same in repair as a second class road.

Ordered that James G. Anthony have in addition to the hands that he has to work under him, have the following hands (to wit) J. Bradford, Hatcher and hands, Chandler Golden and Thompson.

Pg. Ordered by the court that the following good and lawful men be appointed
130 a jury of view to examine the Brownsville road near Durhamville and report
to the next term of this court the convenience and inconvenience that may
result in the changing the same (to wit) P. G. Dyal, John Watson, Jim William,
Turner, Sampson Smith and John Bradford.

Ordered that court be adjourned for one hour.

Court met pursuant to adjournment this day James M. Scott came into court with a certificate of his election as a town constable for the town of Ripley and took the oath of office and entered into bond conditioned and payable as the law directs.

Pg. 130 cont. Ordered that court be adjourned until court in course.

A. H. Pope, Chairman
Elijah B. Foster, J.P.
J. H. Maxwell, J.P.

Pg. 131 Be it remembered that at a county court began and held for the county of Lauderdale and State of Tennessee in the Town of Ripley on the first Monday in November in the year of our Lord one thousand eight hundred and thirty seven, it being the sixth day of said month present and presiding the worshipful Able H. Pope, Esq., Chairman and Esqs. Maxwell and Foster associate Justices sitting and holding a county court for said county, R. L. Rutherford, Clerk and Guy Smith, Esq., high sheriff, proclamation being made as usual the court proceeded to business.

This day James Rrice, John L. Atkinson and Stith Richardson came into court and presented commission from Newton Cannon, Esq., Governor of the State of Tennessee commissioning and authorizing them to discharge the duties of Justices in the county of Lauderdale and took the several oaths of office and took their seats.

This day James M. Scott who was elected constable for the town of Ripley came into court and tendered his resignation as constable which is received by the court.

Pg. 132 David Nunn administrator on the estate of Francis Nunn dec'd returned into court an inventory of the property belonging to said estate which is received by the court and ordered to be recorded.

Whereas it appearing to the satisfaction of the court that Moses Parr, administrator on the estate of William Terrell has also died leaving a part of the property belonging to the estate of Terrell unsold and Thomas B. Stokes applying for letters of administration on said estate he having taken the oath of administrator and entered into bond conditioned and payable as the law directs it is therefore ordered that he have letters accordingly.

George W. Tatum records his stock mark (to wit) crop and under bit in the right ear and swallow fork and over bit in the left.

Ordered by the court that the following good and lawful men of the body of the county of Lauderdale be summoned as a venira for the next circuit court to be held for the county of Lauderdale on the third Monday in Bebruary next (to wit) John Bradford, Milton G. Turner, Ivy Chandler and Archer
Pg. 133 Phillips for the first district; James Price, John H. Maxwell, Robert P. Russell, Richard Wright and John Buckhannon for second district; Able H. Pope James B. Crook, Ezekial Farmer and Ellison P. Fuller for the third district; Samuel A. Given for the fourth district; John Fletcher for the fifth district; Elijah B. Foster, William Deason, John A. Hogsette, Robison Meadows, and Elijah Wright for the sixth district; John Walpole, Henry Crihfield, Sr., Lawson H. Dunaway for the sevenrh district; Henry F. Rutherford and William Espy for the eighth district; Hiram Meadows and Martin R. Hatcher, constables to wait on the court and jury.

Moses B. Chism recorded his stock mark (to wit) a crop and split in the left ear and swallow fork in the right.

Elizabeth Boilston records her stock mark (to wit) crop and split in the left ear and half crop in the right.

Ordered that court be adjourned for half an hour.

Court met pursuant to adjournment.

There being no further business before the court it is ordered that court

Pg. 133 cont. be adjourned until court in course.

A. H. Pope, Chairman
Stith Richardson, J.P.
James Price, J.P.

Pg. 134 Be it remembered that at a county court began and held for the county of Lauderdale and State of Tennessee in the town of Ripley on the first Monday in December in the year of our Lord, one thousand eight hundred and thirty seven, it being the fourth day of said month, present the worshipful Able H. Pope, Esq., Chairman, Maxwell, Price, Richardson, Crihfield, Campbell, Chambers, Lockard, associate Justices setting and holding a county court for said county, Guy Smith, Esq., high sheriff and G. L. Rutherford, Clerk, proclamation being made the court proceeded to business.

David Nunn, Administrator on the estate of Francis Nunn dec'd returned into court an account of sale of the property belonging to said estate which is received by the court and is ordered to be recorded.

Ordered by the court that Isaac Moore be appointed Overseer of the road from the county line of Haywood to Blackwells and that he have the following hands (to wit) Nicholas Reynolds, Ancell Reynolds, James Sanders, Henry Reynolds, Isaac Reynolds, Dickerson Jennings, William Jennings, Samuel Lusk, R. Canady, James Reynolds, Elnathon H. Condry and J. W. Nearn and that he keep the same in repair as a second class road.

This day Thomas B. Stokes, Administrator on the estate of William Terrell dec'd returned into court an account of sale of the perishable property belonging to said estate which is received by the court and ordered to be recorded.

Pg. 135 Ordered by the court that Henry Sumrow, Overseer of the road work in addition to the road that he has formerly worked to the Bucks ferry road.

Ordered by the court that Isaac D. Maxwell, Overseer of the road from Ripley towards Dyersburg work from the town of Ripley to where the Bucks ferry road crosses the same.

On a motion being made to allow Walter Glawson and John Byron one hundred and ninety four dollars for building a bridge across Cane Creek the vote was taken those that voted for said allowance were Esqs. Pope, Maxwell, Childress, Price, Turner, Richardson, Lockard, Chambers, Crihfield, a majority of all the Justices in said county so said allowance was made for one hundred and ninety four dollars and is ordered to be paid out of any money in the hands of the Trustee not otherwise appropriated.

Ordered by the court that the plan that was drafted by the commissioners for the building of a jail in Lauderdale county and was presented to the court at the last term of the court and was received by the court and was not put on record be put on the record book.

Ordered that Archer Phillips hands work under James Anthony Overseer of the road.

Pg. 136 Ordered by the court that Stith Richardson, Edmond Lee, Benjamin Porter, Henry R. Chambers and Henry Sumrow be appointed commissioners to divide the tract of land that belonged to Benjamin Jordan in his life time agreeable to the will of the said Benjamin and to give the legatees of the said Jordan their respective shares according to the will and report to the next term of this court.

Ordered that this court be adjourned for half an hour.

Court met pursuant to adjournment.

Whereas it appearing to the satisfaction of the court that James Curtis has departed this life intestate and Sarah Ann Curtis, the wife of the dec'd

Pg. applying for letters of administration on said estate and having entered
136 into bond conditioned and payable as the law directs and took the oath
cont. of administration it is ordered she have letters accordingly.

This day the commissioners that was appointed to lay off to the widow of Lauson A. Henry dec'd a years provisions reported to this court which is received by the court and ordered to be recorded.

It is ordered by the court that Armstead Wood, Overseer of the road leading to Stokes landing have all the hands that live in the bounds of the six district to build a bridge across Cole creek.

Pg. This day the court proceeded to the election of a Register for said
137 county to fill the vacancy occasioned by the removal of Thomas D. Fisher,
whereas James Price was constitutionally elected and entered into bond conditioned and payable as the law directs and took the several oaths of office.

Ordered by the court that James A. Morris be appointed Overseer of the road from Ripley leading towards Brownsville by Champs corner and that he have the following hands (to wit) R. L. Byron, John Byrons, Lancy Graves, David Walker, Bennit Griffith, David Reynolds, William Laird, John Laird and that he keep the same in repair as a second class road.

Ordered by the court that H. C. Keller, Isaac Braden, Rezin L. Byron, Isaac D. Maxwell and Burtis Alford be appointed a jury to examine the road leading towards Ashport from the old Fulton road and report to the next term of this court what amount of money they think it will take to make said road a first class road.

Ordered by the court that Erasmus D. Thurmond be appointed Overseer of the road in the place of Claiborne Raunsaville and that he keep the same in repair as a second class road.

Ordered by the court that the following good and lawful men be appointed a jury of view to examine the road leading from Durhamville towards Browns-
Pg. ville near the corner and report to the next term of this court the conven-
138 ience that may result from changing the same taking into consideration the
public good as well as the interest of individuals (to wit) P. G. Dyal, John Watson, Jr., William Turner, Sampson Smith and John Bradford.

Ordered by the court that Milton G. Turner, Esq., be appointed revenue commissioner to take in a list of taxable property and polls for the year 1838 for district no. one in Lauderdale county and that he return the same here in court as the law directs.

Ordered by the court that James Price, Esq. be appointed revenue commissioner to take in a list of taxable property and polls for the year 1838 for district no. second and that he return he same here in court as the law directs.

Ordered by the court that Thomas J. Childress, Esq. be appointed revenue commissioner to take in a list of taxable property and polls for the year 1838 for district no. third and that he return the same here in court as the law directs.

Ordered by the court that John Vassor, Esq. be appointed revenue comissioner to takein a list of taxable property and polls for the year 1838 for district no. fourth and that he return the same here in court as the law directs.

Ordered by the court that R. C. Campbell, Esq. be appointed a revenue commissioner to take in a list of taxable property and polls for the year 1838 for district no. fifth and that he return the same into court as the law
Pg. directs.
139 Ordered by the court that E. B. Foster, Esq. be appointed a revenue
commissioner to take in a list of taxable property and polls for the year 1838 for district no. sixth and that he return same here into court as the law directs.

Pg. 139 cont. Ordered by the court that Stith Richardson, Esq., be appointed a revenue commissioner to take in a list of taxable property and polls for the year 1838 and for district no. seventh and that he return the same here into court as the law directs.

Ordered by the court that Henry R. Chambers, Esq., be appointed a revenue commissioner to take in a list of taxable property and polls for the year 1838 for district no. eighth and that he return the same here into court as the law directs.

Ordered that court be adjourned until tomorrow morning ten o'clock.

A. H. Pope, Chairman
J. H. Maxwell, J.P.
James Price, J.P.

Pg. 140 Tuesday morning court met pursuant to adjournment.

There being no further business before the court it is ordered that court be adjourned until court in course.

A. H. Pope, Chairman
J. H. Maxwell, J.P.
James Price, J.P.

Pg. 141 Be it remembered that a county court began and held for the county of Lauderdale and State of Tennessee in the town of Ripley on the first Monday in January in the year of our Lord one thousand eight hundred and thirty eight it being the first day of said month, present and presiding the worshipful Able H. Pope, Esq., Chairman and Esqs. Price, Childress, Gilliland, Richardson, Chambers, Crihfield, Lockard, Atkinson, Turner, associate Justices sitting and holding a county court for said county, Guy Smith, Esq., high sheriff and G. L. Rutherford, Clerk, proclamation being made as the form is the court proceeded to business.

The court proceeded to elect a Chairman of their own body for the year eithteen hundred and thirty eight, whereupon Samuel V. Gilliland was elected Chairman for said year.

Whereas it appearing to the satisfaction of the court that Samuel Rudder hath departed this life intestate and Elizabeth Rudder and John Thompson applying for letters of administration granted them on said estate it is ordered that letters issue to them accordingly they having entered into bond conditioned and payable as the law directs and took the oaths of administratrix and administrator.

Pg. 142 Whereas it appearing to the satisfaction of the court that Andrew U. Kidd hath departed this life intestate and Nancy Kidd applying for letters of Administration on said estate it is ordered that she have letters accordingly she having taken the oath of administratrix and entered into bond conditioned and payable as the law directs.

Whereas it appearing to the satisfaction of the court that Sarah W. Johnson hath departed this life intestate and James H. Givins applying for letters of administration on said estate it is ordered that letters issue to him accordingly he having entered into bond conditioned and payable as the law directs and took the oath of administrator.

This day the court proceeded to lay a tax for the year eighteen hundred and thirty eight there being a majority of all the Justices in the county present the following proposition being made (towit) five cents jury tax, two and one half cents county contingent expenses, two and one half cents road and bridge tax, five cents poor tax, on each hundred dollars worth of

Pg. 142 cont. property, poor tax on each white poll twelve and one half eents, county tax on the same twelve and one half cents, jury tax on the same twelve and one half cents, state tax on each white poll twelve and one half cents, twelve and one half cents state tax on each hundred dollars worth of property, the vote being called for those that voted for said rates were Esqs. Gilliland, Pope, Chambers, Childress, Lockard, Richardson, Crihfield, Turner, Atkerson, and Price a majority of all the Justices in said county so said rates were laid.

Pg. 143

Ordered that Joseph Currie, P. G. Davenport and David C. Russell be appointed commissioners to draft a plan for to build a bridge across a slue in Hatchey bottom called Thompson Slue and let the building of the same sometime between this and the first Monday in May next and report to this court.

Whereas it appearing to the satisfaction of the court that James Cheek hath departed this life intestate and P. G. Davenport applying for letters of administration on said estate he having entered into bond conditioned and payable as the law directs and took the oath of administrator it is ordered that he have letters accordingly.

It is ordered that Abraham Moss, James Givin, James Hutcherson, Willy Garvin and James Thompkins be appointed commissioners to lay off to the widow of James Curtis dec'd a years provisions and that they report to the next term of this court.

It is ordered that Samuel Givin, John Garvin, Jessie Hutcherson, Coleman Hutcherson and John Vassor be appointed commissioners to lay off to the widow of Andrew U. Kidd a years provisions and report to the next term of the court..

Pg. 144 It is ordered that Becy Boswell a pauper in theis county be allowed forty dollars for her support for the year 1838 a majority of all the Justices in said county being present and voting for said allowance.

It is ordered that Sarah Coleman who has the care of John Williams a pauper in this county be allowed seventy five dollars for the support of the said pauper for the year 1838 or that she bring up the said Williams to the next term of this court.

Ordered that the following good and lawful men be appointed a jury of view to view and mark out the nearest and best way for a road leaving the present road at or near the place where the old Byler road leaves the present road about half a mile south of Height Smith thence along the ridge with or near the Bylers road to the house of Henry Sumrow and that the Jury examine the present Dyersburg road between said points and report as to the necesity of opening the new road proposed and also the propriety of keeping up both roads taking into consideration the public good as well as the interest of particular individuals and report to the next term of this court (to wit) Henry Rutherford, Henry Sumroe, James Salsberry, Henry Crihfield and S. M. Sullivan.

Pg. 145 This day Stith Richardson Esq., H. Sumroe, Edmond Lee, Henry R. Chambers Benjamin Porter, the commissioners that were appointed at the last term of this court to divide the tract of land that belonged to Benjamin Jordan in his life time amongst the legatees report to court which is received by the court and ordered to be recorded.

It is ordered that the following good and lawful men be appointed a jury of view to view and mark out the nearest and best way for a road from the Ashport road near William Bradens or between that and J. Chapman and run a southern direction to intersect the Fulton road one half mile west of William Strains and that they report to the next term of this court (to wit) James

Pg. 145 cont. Whitson, William Strain, James B. Crook, E. P. Fuller, Isaac Braden.
There being no further business before the court it is ordered that that court be adjourned until court in course.

Sam V. Gilliland, Chairman
Henry Crihfield, J.P.
Thomas J. Childress, J.P.

Pg. 146 Be it remembered that at a county court began and held for the county of Lauderdale and State of Tennessee in the town of Ripley on the first Monday in February in the year of our Lord one thousand eight hundred and thirty eight it being the fifth day of said month, Present and presiding the worshipful Samuel V. Gilliland, Esq., Chairman of said court and Esqs. Pope, Maxwell, Richardson, Lockard, Thomas J. Childress and Crihfield associate Justices sitting and holding a county court for said county Guy Smith, Esq., high sheriff by deputy and G. L. Rutherford, Clerk, proclamation being made the court proceeded tq business.

Able H. Pope, Administrator on the estate of Lawson A. Henry dec'd returned into court an inventory and account of sale which is received by the court and ordered to be recorded.

This day Abraham Moss, James Givin, James Hutcherson, Wesley Garvin, and James Thompkins, the commissioners that were appointed at the last term of the court to lay off to the widow of James Curtis dec'd a years provision reported to court which is received by the court and ordered to be recorded.

This day Samuel Givin, Coleman Hutcherson, Jessie R. Hutcherson and John Vassor the commissioners that was appointed at the last term of the court to lay off to the widow of A. U. Kidd her years provision reported to court which is received by the court and ordered to be recorded.

Pg. 147 David Nunn, Administrator on the estate of Francis Nunn dec'd returned here into court an additional account of sale of the property belonging to said estate which is received and ordered to be recorded.

Ordered by the court William T. Moorehead be allowed forty two dollars and seventeen cents for a stove furnished by him for the court house to be paid out of any money in the hands of the Trustee not otherwise appropriated.

Ordered by the court that the following good and lawful men be appointed a jury of view to view, lay off and mark out a road from Ripley to intersect the Buck ferry road at some point that will be most convenient to the community and report to the next term of court (to wit) Elnathan H. Condry, Isaac Moore, Samuel Lusk, John W. Hearn, Ancell Reynolds, James Reynolds and Reuben Cannady.

Ordered that Joshua Wright be appointed Overseer of the Buck ferry road in the place of James Braden, commencing at Blackwells and that he work to Thomas I. Smiths and that he have the following hands to work under him (to wit) Benjamin Weems, Read, Mr. Dillard's hands and that he keep the same in repair as a second class road.

Ordered that John Thompson be appointed Overseer of the road in the place of Jerry Cheek and that he have the same hands.

Pg. 148 This day James Gimins, Administrator on the estate of Sarah Johnson dec'd returned here in court an inventory of the personal property belonging to said estate which is received by the court and ordered to be recorded.

Ordered that the following good and lawful men be appointed a jury of view to view and mark out the nearest and best way for a road leaving the present Dyersburg road at or near where the Byler road leaves the same, thence along the ridge with the Byler road to the house of Henry Sumrow and that

Pg. 148 cont. they examine the present Dyersburg road between said points and report as to the necessity of opening the new road proposed and also the propriety of keeping up both roads taking into consideration the publiw good as well as the interest of individuals and report to the next term of this court (to wit) Henry Sumrow, Henry Rutherford, Henry Crihfield, James Salsberry, and Stephen M. Sullivan.

Ordered that John Holmes be appointed Overseer of the road in the place of Dabney P. Phillips and that he have the same hands to work under him.

Ordered that Joseph Currie be appointed Overseer of the road from the north end of the lane at Bates Fork of Cane Creek and work to John Fullen's field in the place of David C. Russell and that he have the same hands to work under him.

Pg. 149 Ordered by the court that there be the additional sum of twenty five dollars appropriated for the support of John Williams a pauper for the year 1838 to be paid out of any money in the hands of the Trustee not otherwise appropriated.

It is ordered that Hiram C. Keller, Overseer of the Ashport road have the following hands in addition to his former hands for the purpose of repairing the bridge across Bates fork of Cane creek (to wit) Isaac Braden, James Sherman, Sandy Shumake, E. P. Fullen, Benjamin Whetson, E. Farmer, Willy Voss, Williams, the jury of view that was appointed at the last term of this court for to view the road from the Ashport road near W. Bradens and to intersect the Fulton road half a mile west of William Strains, reports to this court which is not received by the court.

Ordered that court be adjourned for one hour.

Court met pursuant to adjournment. There being no further business before the court it is ordered that court be adjourned until court in course.

Sam V. Gilliland, Chairman
Thomas J. Childress, J.P.
J. H. Maxwell, J.P.

Pg. 150 Be it remembered that at a county court began and held for the county of Lauderdale and state of Tennessee in the town of Ripley on the first Monday in March in the year of our Lord one thousand eight hundred and thirty eight it being the fifth day of said month present and presiding the worshipful S. V. Gilliland, Chairman, Maxwell, Dockard, Richardson, Crihfield, Price, Turner, and Childress, Esqs., associate Justices sitting and holding a county court for said county and G. L. Rutherford, Clerk and Guy Smith, Esq., high sheriff, proclamation being made the court proceeded to business.

This day G. L. Rutherford produced here in open court a certificate from Guy Smith of said county of Lauderdale of his election to the office clerk of the county, who took the several oaths of office agreeable to law and entered into bond which is in the words and figures following (to wit)

Know all men by these presents that we, Griffith L. Rutherford, William T. Moorehead, Joseph Wardlow all of the county of Lauderdale and State of Tennessee are held and firmly bound unto his excellency, Newton Cannon, Esq., Governor of the state of Tennessee for the time being and his successors in office in the penal sum of five thousand dollars for the pay, whereof will and truly to be made we bind ourselves and each of our heirs, executors or administrators jointly, severally and firmly by these presents sealed with our seals and dated this fifth day of March 1838.

The condition of the above obligation is such that whereas the above bounden Griffith L. Rutherford was elected by the qualified votes of the county of Lauderdale on the first Saturday in March, 1838 to the office of

Pg. 151 cont. Clerk of the county court for said county. Now if the above bounden G. L. Rutherford shall safely keep the records of said county court and pay over all moneys by him collected by virtue of said office into the proper office or to those who are entitled thereto by law and in all things will and truly discharge the duties of clerk of said court so long as he may continue in office then the above obligation to be void otherwise to remain in full force and effect according to law.

G. L. Rutherford (Seal)
W. T. Moorehead (Seal)
Joseph Wardlow (Seal)

John C. Barnes produced here in court a certificate of his election from Guy Smith, Esq., sheriff of said county to the office of sheriff for said county of Lauderdale who took the several oaths of office agreeable to law and entered into bond which isin the words and figures following (to wit) Know all men by these presents that we John C. Barnes, William T. Moorehead, Hiram C. Keller and John H. Maxwell all of the county of Lauderdale and state of Tennessee are held and firmly bound unto his Excellency Newton Cannon, Esq., Governor of the state of Tennessee for the time being and his successors in office in the penal sum of twelve thousand five hundred dollars for the payment of which will and truly to be made we bind ourselves

Pg. 152 and each of our heirs, executors, or administrators jointly, severally and firmly by these presents sealed with our seals and dated this fifth day of March 1838.

The condition of the above obligation is such that whereas the above bounden, John C. Barnes having been elected by the qualified voters of said county on the first Saturday in March 1838 to the office of Sheriff for said county for the two ensuing years from the first Saturday in March 1838 now therefore if the said John C. Barnes shall, will and truly execute and due return make of process and precepts to him directed and pay and satisfy all fees and sums of money by him received or levied by virtue of any process into the proper office by which the same by tenor thereof ought to be paid or to the person or persons to whom the same may be due or to their executors or administrators attorney or agent and in all things will and truly execute the office of sheriff during his continuance therein then the above obligation is to be void otherwise to remain in full force and effect.

J. C. Barnes (Seal)
William T. Moorehead (Seal)
H. C. Keller (Seal)
J. H. Maxwell

This day William T. Moorehead presented here in open court a certificate from Guy Smith, Sheriff of Lauderdale County of his election to the office of Trustee for said county of Lauderdale entered into bond conditioned and payable as the law directs and took the several oaths of office agreeable to the laws of the state.

Pg. 153 James Price presented here in open court a certificate from Guy Smith, Sheriff of the county of Lauderdale of his election to the office of Register for said county who entered into bond conditioned and payable as the law directs and took the several oaths of office agreeable to the laws of the state.

This day H. G. W. Byron, Joshua Stone, Thomas J. Childress, Robertson Meadows, Green B. Temples, William S. Read, presented here in open court

Pg. 153 cont. certificates of their election to the office of constable for said county from Guy Smith, sheriff, who entered into bonds conditioned and payable as the law directs and took the several oaths of office agreeable to the laws of the state.

It is ordered that Moses E. Stone be appointed Overseer of the Brownsville road in the place of Joseph Taylor commencing at Ripley and work to the eastern boundary of the second civil district and that he have all the hands that live in the following bounds (to wit) commencing at the Haywood county line where it crosses Walker's branch thence south with said county line to where the division line between the first and second civil division line hits the same thence with said division line until it passeth W, H. Stones thence with the Morphis line to Nelly Woods south-east corner thence north with her line to the Brownsville road thence east with said road to the Dyersburg road thence with said road north-east to a branch in Mrs. Pane's lane thence down said branch to the creek thence up the creek to the mouth of Walker's branch thence up the branch to the beginning.

Pg. 154 This day Thomas J. Childress, Esq., presented here in court his resignation as a Justice of the peace for said court which is received by the court.

Ordered that John C. Barnes, Collector of the public taxes for the year 1837 be released from the payment of the taxes on one hundred acres of land improperly charged valued at - dollars and that the same be certified to the Treasurer and county Trustee.

Whereas it appearing to the satisfaction to court that Imry Keller hath departed this life intestate and Hiram C. Keller applying for letters of administration on said estate it is ordered that he have letters accordingly he having entered into bond conditioned and payable as the law directs and took the oath of Administrator.

Ordered that all persons that have been reported for double tax for the year 1838 that may apply to the clerk any time between this and the next term of the court be released from double tax by the payment of the single tax.

It is ordered that the county tax on all privileges for the year 1838 be equal to that of the state there being a majority of all the Justices present on the bench.

Pg. 155 Ordered by the court the following good and lawful men be appointed a jury of view to examine the road from Durhamville towards Brownsville near Mrs. Anthony 's field and report to the next term of this court the convenience or inconvenience that may result from changing the same taking into consideration the public good as well as the interest of particular individuals, P. G. Dyal, S. Smith, J. C. Lovelass, Smith Kent, G. W. Tatum, M. G. Turner and William Mathews.

Ordered the following good and lawful men be appointed jurors for the next term of the circuit court for Lauderdale county to be held on the third Monday in June next (to wit) Archer Phillips, Thomas Fitzpatrick, Smith Kent, James G. Anthony for the first district; David C. Russell, Isaac J. Penson, William McClelland, James Price and John H. Maxwell for the third district; Able H. Pope, Hiram C. Keller, Elijah Lake and William P. Gaines for the third district; James Thompkins for the fourth district; Robert C. Campbell, for the fifth district; William R. Ledbetter, Elnathan H. Condry, Dickerson Jennings and John Lockard for the sixth district; Claibourn Rounsaville, William B. Sawyers and John Russell for the seventh district; Henry R. Chambers, Saban Jones and Pascal W. Saunders for the eighth district; Joshua Stone and Thomas J. Childress, constables to wait on the court and jury.

Ordered that William Laird be appointed Overseer of the road in the place of Lancy Graves.

Pg. 156 Ordered that William Calhoon be appointed Overseer of the road in the place of Robert P. Russell resigned.

It is ordered that court be adjourned until court in course.

Sam V. Gilliland, Chairman
J. H. Maxwell, J.P.
James Price, J.P.

Pg. 157 Bd it remembered that at a county court began and held for the county of Lauderdale and state of Tennessee in the court house in the town of Ripley on the first Monday in April in the year of our Lord one thousand eight hundred and thirty eight it being the second day of said month present and presiding the worshipful Samuel V. Gilliland, Chairman and Esqs. Maxwell, Pope, Richardson, Turner, Chambers, associate Justices sitting and holding a county court for said county, John C. Barnes, high sheriff and G. L. Rutherford, Clerk, proclamation being made the court proceeded to business.

Richard Moore records his stock mark (to wit) swallow fork in the right ear and under bit in the left.

Stephen M. Sullivan records his stock mark (to wit) crop and slit in the left ear and swallow fork in the right.

This day Nancy Kidd, Administratrix on the estate of Andrew U. Kidd dec'd returned here in court an inventory and account of sale of the perishable property belonging to said estate which is received and ordered to be recorded.

This day William Cleaves who was elected constable for the first district in said county came into court entered into bonds conditioned and payable as the law directs and took the several oaths of office.

This day William Walpole who was elected constable in the seventh district came into court entered into bond conditioned and payable as the law directs and took the several oaths of office.

Pg. 158 It is ordered that William S. Read be released from the payment of double tax for the year 1838 by the payment of single tax.

It is ordered that the following good and lawful men be appointed a jury of view for the purpose of viewing the road that leads from Durhamville to Williams Ferry on Hatchey river that part of said road where it runs through the lands of Samuel Owen and report to the July term of this court the convenience or inconvenience that may result from changing the same (to wit) Sampson Smith, Jeremiah Penick, John Bradford, James Lovelass and William Turner.

Ordered by the court that the following good and lawful men be appointed a jury of view to examine the Dyersburg road from Ripley adjourning the town of Ripley and report tbe convenience or inconvenience that may result from changing the same and report to the July term of this court (to wit) Isaac D. Maxwell, I. J. Pinon, Joseph Wardlow, A. Vickory and Anderson Jordan.

Ordered that court be adjourned for one hour.

Court met pursuant to adjournment.

It is ordered that John Holmes Overseer of the road from Durhamville have the following hands to work under him (to wit) commencing at Williams Ferry on Hatchey river to include all the hands west of the road leading from said landing to Durhamville and south of the road leading to Covington in the first civil division except H. Chism, C. Whitson, William Flime and all hands on Wardlow's plantation and that he keep the same in repair as a first class road.

Pg. 159 Ordered that Edmond Rudder Overseer of the road have in addition to his former hands, Henry T. Chism, Carter Whitson, William Flime, the hands on Wardlow's plantation and thence in line south to Hatchey river including all west of said line in the first civil division including his former bounds and that he keep the same in repair as a first class road.

Ordered that Moses E. Stone Overseer of the road leading towards Brownsville have the following hands to work under him (to wit) William H. Stone, John Stone's hands, Lee H. Burks, George W. Elkins, R. C. Campbell's hands, Walter Glawson, John Taylor, Joseph Glawson and that he keep the same in repair as a first class road.

Ordered that John Thompson Overseer of road from the mouth of the lane at Byron's old place to Mathew's creek have his own hands, M. C. Hamer, Bennet Griffith and I. Balderson, that he keep the same in repair as a second class road.

Ordered that Rezin L. Byron Overseer to build a bridge across Mathew's creek and to work from said creek to Cane creek have his own hands and that he keep the same in repair as a second class road.

Ordered that A. Vickory be appointed Overseer of the old Dyersburg road from the south side of Cane creek to where the same intersects the Ripley road, have Isaac Smith and Curtis Elis and that he keep the same in repair as a second class road.

Pg. 160 Ordered that James A. Morris Overseer of the road from Ripley to the Haywood county line have the following hands to work under him (to wit) John B. Byron, William Hafford, David Walker, Lancy Graves, John Laird, Isaac Pittman, Jerry Cheek, David Reynolds and William Laird and that he keep the same in repair as a second class road.

It is ordered that I. J. Pinion be appointed Overseer to put the road from Ripley to Stokes landing in repair that part of said road that was not cut by the former Overseer and that he have the following hands (to wit) Mark Watson, John Chapman, Charles Prim, Thomas Gardner, W. K. Dolryus, Marshal Posey, William Cooper, John Holliman, Parham, Joseph Wardlow, A. Benton, John McCall, G. L. Rutherford and hand, Alfred Rutherford, John Blackwell, and hand, Marion Chapman, I. K. Goodwin, W. T. Moorehead, F. Goodwin, Thomas Hazelwood, Willis Wright, R. A. Braden, William Weddle, William P. Gaines and hand, James Wardlow and Ezekial Smith.

Ordered that Able H. Pope have the care of Becky Boswell, a pauper in this county.

Ordered that James Chambers be appointed Overseer of the road from the key corner to the center of the bridge across milcreek and that he have all the hands west of Dyersburg road in the eighth district except the Brandons and Kennelly to work under him and that he keep the same in repair as first class road.

Pg. 161 Ordered that Jefferson Brown Overseer of the road leading from the key corner towards Bucks ferry commencing at the end of John Mitchell order and that he work to the forks of the road near A. Rounsaville and that he have all the hands that live on the south-east side of Rutherford's creek.

Ordered that William O. Mohundra be appointed Overseer of the road in the place of Isaac D. Maxwell and that he work to Bylers fork of Cane creek and that he have the same hands to work under him and that he keep the same in repair as a first class road.

Ordered that Curtis Ellis be released from the payment of double tax for the year 1838 by the payment of the single tax.

This day Martin Alexander, who was elected for the fourth district of Lauderdale county came into court entered into bond conditioned and payable as the law directs and took the several oaths of office.

This day the court proceeded to appoint three of their body as a quorum

Pg. 161 cont. to transact the business for the year 1838 whereupon S. V. Gilliland, Richardson and Turner Esqs. was appointed for said quorum.

On motion of John C. Barnes, sheriff of said county to have Thomas J. Childress qualified as deputy sheriff for said county who came into court and took the several oaths of office.

Pg. 162 It is ordered that Henry Rutherford, entry taker for said county be notified to come into court at the next term of the court and give counter security.

There being no further business before the court it is ordered that court be adjourned until court in course.

Sam V. Gilliland, Chairman
Stith Richardson, J.P.
J. H. Maxwell, J.P.

Pg. 163 Be it remembered that at a county court began and held for the county of Lauderdale and State of Tennessee in the court house in the town of Ripley on the first Monday in May in the year of our Lord one thousand eight hundred and thirty eight, it being the seventh day of said month, present and presiding the worshipful Samuel V. Gilliland, Esq., Chairman and Esqs. Richardson, and Turner associate Justices sitting and holding a county court for said county, John C. Barnes, Sheriff and G. L. Rutherford, Clerk proclamation being made the court proceeded to business.

This day John C. Barnes, Sheriff and Collector of the public taxes for the county of Lauderdale came in court and entered into bond conditioned and payable and as the law directs which is in the words and figures following (to wit) State of Tennessee, Lauderdale County. Know all men by these present that we John C. Barnes, Hiram C. Keller, Milton G. Turner all of the state and county aforesaid are held and firmly bound unto his excellency Newton Cannon, Governor of the state of Tennessee for the time being and his successor in office for the use of the said state in the sum of sixteen hundred dollars to the payment of which will and truly to be made we bind ourselves, our heirs executors and administrators jointly and severally firmly by these presents sealed with our seals and dated this seventh day in May 1838. The condition
Pg. 164 of the above obligation on this that whereas the above bound John C. Barnes has been duly and constitutionally elected sheriff and collector of the public taxes of said countyof Lauderdale for two years from the first Saturday in March, 1838. Now if the said John C. Barnes shall, will and truly collect all state taxes and also all taxes on school lands within the said county which by law he ought to collect and will and truly account for and pay over all taxes by him collected or which ought to be collected on the first day of December 1838 and 1839 respectively then the above obligation to be void otherwise to remain in full force and virtue.

J. C. Barnes (Seal)
H. C. Keller (Seal)
Milton G. Turner (Seal)

State of Tennessee, Lauderdale County. Know all men by these presents that we, John C. Barnes, John Vassor, H. C. Keller and Milton G. Turner all of the state and county aforesaid are held and firmly bound unto Samuel V. Gilliland, Chairman of the county court of said county or his successors in office for the use of the county in the sum of five thousand five hundred dollars to the payment of which will and truly to be made we bind ourselves, our heirs, executors and administrators jointly and severally and firmly by

Pg. these presents sealed with our seals and dated this seventh day of May 1838.
165 The conditions of the above obligation are these that whereas the above bound John C. Barnes has been duly and constitutionally elected sheriff and collector of the public taxes of said county of Lauderdale for two years from the first Saturday in March 1838. Now if the said John C. Barnes shall, will and truly collect all county taxes and also all taxes on school land within said county which by law he ought to collect and will and truly account for and pay over all taxes by him collected or which ought to be collected on the first day of December 1838 and 1839 respectively then the above obligation to be void.

J. C. Barnes (Seal)
John Vassor (Seal)
H. C. Keller (Seal)
Milton G. Turner (Seal)

This day John C. Barnes, sheriff and collector of the taxes for Lauderdale county took the several oaths of collector.

Whereas it appearing to the satisfaction of the court that David Pitchford has departed this life entestate and Jessie R. Hutcherson applying for letters of administration on said estate and they being satisfied with his claim to the right of administration on said estate it is ordered that he have letters accordingly he having entered into bond conditioned as the law directs and took the oath of administrator.

Pg. This day Pascal W. Saunders, James Barfield and Henry Willard produced
166 here in court commissioners for Newton Cannon, Esq., Governor of the state empowering them to discharge the duties of Justices of the peace in said county who took the oaths of office agreeable to law.

It is ordered that court be adjourned for one hour.

Court met pursuant to adjournment.

This day Hiram C. Keller, administrator on the estate of Emry Keller dec'd returned here in court an inventory of the estate of said Emry dec'd which is received by the court and is ordered to be recorded.

Ordered by the court that J. A. Morris be appointed Overseer of the Fulton road from Fulton to Sammel Givins and that he have the following hands to work under him (to wit) Alexander, R. P. Thompson, Thomas C. Lewis, Miles Wakefield, Wakefield, James Thompkins, Dr. Lee's hands, Sugar Evans, Riley Hooten and that he keep the same in repair as a first class road.

Ordered by the court that James Givin be appointed Overseer of the Fulton road from Sam Givins to Cane creek and that he have the following
Pg. hands (to wit) T. W. Garvin, I. Garvin, Hugh Super, John Givin, T. Givin,
167 John Moss, Jackson, Hutcherson, Jesse Hutcherson, James Hutcherson, John King, James Gillespie and all hands that live between Cane and Cole creek below McConnels plantation, that he keep the same in repair as a first class road.

This day Henry Rutherford, entry taker for said county came into court entered into bond conditioned and payable as the law directs with John C. Barnes and Henry R. Chambers his security.

This day the court proceeded to elect a coroner for the county of Lauderdale for ensuing two years whereupon Isaac Braden was duly elected, came into court entered into bond conditioned and payable as the law directs and took the several oaths of office.

This day the court proceeded to elect a ranger for said county for the ensuing two years whereupon John H. Maxwell was duly and constitutionally elected and came into court entered into cond conditioned and payable as the

Pg. 167 cont. law directs and took the several oaths of office.

It is ordered by the court that Joseph Currie, P. G. Davenport and David Russell to be appointed commissioners to receive the bridge to be built across Thompsons Slue in Hatchey botton and report to the October term of this court and that the undertaker keep the same in repair five years.

Pg. 168 Ordered by the court there being a majority of all the Justices in said county being present and voting in the affirmative that Rezin L. Byron, William Turner, Able H. Pope, Henry Rutherford, and R. C. Campbell be appointed commissioners to reorganize the civil districts in said county and report to the July term of the court.

This day the Samuel V. Gilliland, Chairman of the county court of said county put under the care of Samuel Hooper, William Davis of the age of between thirteen and fourteen until he comes to the age of twenty one years to learn the blacksmith trade. The above named Hooper is to school the said William Davis Viz to read, write and cipher through the single rule of three and at the expiration of his time he is to give him a good decent suit of clothes and ten dollars in cash.

Whereas it appearing to the satisfaction of the court that Lewis Williams hath departed this life intestate and Pleasant G. Davenport applying for letters of administration on same estate and the court being satisfied as to the right of his administration it is ordered he have letters accordingly he having entered into bond conditioned and payable as the law directs and took the oath as such.

It is ordered that court be adjourned until court in course.

Sam V. Gilliland, Chairman
Milton G. Turner, J.P.
Stith Richardson, J.P.

Pg. 169 Be it remembered that at a county court began and held for the county of Lauderdale and state of Tennessee in the court house in the town of Ripley on the first Monday in June in the year of our Lord one thousand eight hundred and thirty eight it being the fourth day of said month present and presiding the worshipful Samuel V. Gilliland, Chairman of said county court and Esqs. Richardson and Turner the quorum court for said county sitting and holding a county court for said county, John C. Barnes, high sheriff and G. L. Rutherford, Clerk, proclamation being made the court proceeded to business.

It is ordered that John Garvin, Samuel A. Givin and Henry Willard be appointed commissioners to lay off to the widow of David Pitchford dec'd a years provision and report to the next term of this court.

It is ordered that Thomas Wardlow, David Russell and Joseph Currie be appointed commissioners to lay off to the widow of Lewis Williams dec'd a years provision and report to the next term of this court.

This day David Gilliland, administrator on the estate of Jehue Inman returned here in court an additional inventory of the property belonging to said estate which is received by the court and ordered to be recorded.

Pg. 170 Ordered that Abraham Moss be appointed Overseer of the road from Fulton towards Ripley to Cane creek and that he have all the hands in the fourth district north and west of Cane creek and all in the fifth district below McConnel's plantation and that he keep the same in repair as a second class road.

It is ordered that court be adjourned until court in course.

Sam V. Gilliland, Chairman
Milton G. Turner, J.P.
Stith Richardson, J.P.

Pg. 171 Be it remembered that at a county court began and held for the county of Lauderdale and state of Tennessee in the court house in the town of Ripley on the first Monday in July in the year of our Lord one thousand eight hundred and thirty eight it being the second day of said month present and presiding S. V. Gilliland, Chairman, Esqs. Maxwell, Campbell, Price, Lockard, Pope, Crihfield, Barfield, Richardson, Turner, Sanders, Atkison, associate Justices sitting and holding a county court for said county, G. L. Rutherford, Clerk, John C. Barnes, high sheriff proclamation being made the court proceeded to business.

This day G. L. Rutherford, Clerk of the county court of Lauderdale county presented here in open court a settlement made by him on the twenty eighth day of June 1838 with David Gilliland, administrator of Jehue Inman which is received by the court and ordered to be recorded.

Ordered by the court that Milton G. Turner, Esq., the revenue commissioner for district no. one for the year 1838 to take in a list of taxable property and polls for said year be allowed seven dollars and fifty cents to be paid out of any money in the hands of the Trustee not otherwise appropriated.

Ordered by the court that James Price, Esq., the revenue commissioner for district no. second for the year 1838 to take in a list of taxable property and polls for said year be paid out of any money in the hands of the Trustee not otherwise appropriated, the sum of seven dollars and fifty cents.

Pg. 172 It is ordered that Thomas J. Childress the revenue commissioner to take in a list of taxable property and polls for the third civil district of Lauderdale county for the year 1838 be paid out of any money in the hands of tho Trustee not otherwise appropriated, seven dollars and fifty cents.

It is ordered that John Vassor, Esq., the revenue commissioner to take in a list of taxable property,polls for the year 1838 in civil district no. four be paid seven dollars and fifty cents out of any money in the hands of the Trustee not otherwise appropriated.

It is ordered that Robert C. Campbell the revenue commissioner for the year 1838 to take in a list of taxable property and polls in the fifth civil district for said year be paid seven dollars and fifty cents out of any money in the hands of the Trustee not otherwise appropriated.

It is ordered that Elijah B. Foster, the revenue commissioner for the year 1838 to take in a list of taxable property and polls for said year in district no. sixth be paid seven and one half dollars out of any money in the hands of the Trustee not otherwise appropriated.

It is ordered that Stith Richardson, Esq., the revenue commissioner for the year 1838 for district no. seven be paid seven and one half dollars out of any money in the hands of the Trustee not otherwise appropriated.

It is ordered that Henry R. Chambers the revenue commissioner to take in a list of taxable property and polls for the year 1838 in district no. eight be paid seven and one half dollars out of any money in the hands of the Trustee not otherwise apporpriated.

Pg. 173 It is ordered by the court that the following good and lawful men be appointed a jury of view to examine the road leading from Ripley to Dyersburg commencing at or near Andersons and that they examine as far north as the branch that crosses said road running out of Nelson's field and that they report to the October term of this court the propriety or impropriety that may result from changing the same (to wit) Dickerson Jennings, Isaac D. Maxwell, A. Vickory, Isaac M. Steele and Anderson Jordan.

It is ordered that the following good and lawful men be appointed a jury of view for the purpose of viewing and marking the nearest and best way for a road commencing on the Forkeddeer bluf where the Ashport Trunpike strikes

Pg. 173 cont. the same and to intersect the old Ashport road east of Thomas Turner and that they report to the October term of this court, (to wit) Able H. Pope, Elison P. Fuller, Benjamin Whitson, Bentis Alford and R. C. Campbell.

This day Benjamin Weems proved in open court by his own oath the killing of one wolf in the county of Lauderdale over the age of six months and is ordered to be certified to the treasurer there being five Justices present. Ordered that William W. Lea be presented to list lot no.   in the town of Ripley value $80.00 by the payment of the single tax.

It is ordered that Rezin L. Byron, John H. Maxwell and Isaac D. Maxwell be appointed commissioners to let the building of a bridge across Cane creek
Pg. 174 on the road leading from Ripley to Dyersburg and that they receive the same when built and that they report to the October term of this court the undertaker is to keep up the same five years and return it in good.

It is ordered that Deberry P. Phillips and Thomas Fitzpatrick and William Turner be appointed commissioners to let out the building of a bridge across the branch west of Durhamville on the road leading from Durhamville to Fullens ferry and receive the same when done and bind the undertaker to keep the same in repair five years.

This day the jury of view that was appointed at the April term 1838 to view and report the propriety or impropriety of changing the road leading from Durhamville to Williams ferry on Hatchey river that part of said road near Samuel Owen report that if said road is changed the community will be injured which report is received by the court and it is ordered the road remain on the same ground where it has formerly run.

It is ordered that the following good and lawful men be appointed a jury of view for the purpose of examining the road leading from Ripley to Dyersburg commencing at the eastern boundary of Ripley and view as far northeast as one fourth of a mile from said point of beginning and report to the October term 1838 the propriety or impropriety that may result from changing the same (to wit) Isaac D. Maxwell, Isaac J. Pierson, Joseph Wardlow, A. Vickory and Anderson Jordan.

This day David Gilliland, Administrator on the estate of W. L. Byler returned into open court an additional account of sale which is received by the court and ordered to be recorded.

Pg. 175 Ordered by the court that the following good and lawful men be appointed a jury of view to lay off and mark out a road commencing at the termination of the Forkeddeer Turnpike and view to the Haywood county line and report to the October term of this court (to wit) John Russell, Amos Rounsaville, Z. Mitchell, James Salsberry and John Walpole.

This day Samuel V. Gilliland by and with the consent of the court have put and placed Mary Jane Dyal a minor child of the age of three years until she arrive to the age of eighteen years to Pleasant G. Dyal with him to live and serve as an apprentice to the full age of eighteen years.

It is ordered by the court that the clerk of this court give to Samuel Hooper a bond that he gave this court at the April or May term of this for William Davis an apprentice who this day they have give up to the mother of the boy.

This day the commissioners that was appointed at the April term of this court to reorganize the civil districts in Lauderdale county makes report here in open court the result of said labor which is received by the court and ordered to be recorded.

It is ordered by the court there being a majority present and voting in the affirmative that G. L. Rutherford be allowed twenty-dollars for making out the tax list for the year 1838 out of any money in the hands of the Trustee

Pg. not otherwise appropriated.
176 It is ordered by the court there being a majority of all the Justices in said county present that Able H. Pope be allowed five dollars for making out a plan of the civil districts in said county to be paid out of any money in the hands of the Trustee not otherwise appropriated.

It is ordered by the court there being a majority present that the following good and lawful men be appointed a jury of view to lay off and mark out the nearest and best way for a road from Ripley to intersect the Buck Ferry road at some point that will best suit the convenience of the neighborhood taking into consideration the public good and report to the October term of this court (to wit) E. H. Condray, Isaac Moore, Samuel Lusk, Ancel Reynolds, James Reynolds and Isaac M. Steel.

It is ordered that the following good and lawful men of the body of the county of Lauderdale be summoned as jurors for the next term of the circuit court for Lauderdale county and venire facias issued accordingly (to wit) William Turner, Sampson Smith, John S. Atkinson and Samuel V. Gilliland for the first district; William McClelland, John Thompson, Rezin L. Byron, Isaac D. Maxwell, James Price and Isaac J. Pinion for the second district; James Sherman, Thomas Wardlow, Edward H. Rudder and George Thumb for the third district; Henry Willard for the fourth district; Robert C. Campbell, for the fifth district; Samuel Lusk, Elijah B. Foster and John Lockard for the sixth district; William Baxter, Dickerson Jennings and Boling Fisher for the seventh
Pg. district;John Soward, William Espey and William Jordan for the eighth district
177 and that A. G. W. Byron and William Cleaver be appointed constables to wait on the court and jury.

It is ordered that court be adjourned until court in course.

Sam V. Gilliland, Chairman
John L. Atkinson, J.P.
J. H. Maxwell, J.P.

Pg. Be it remembered that at a county court began and held for the county
178 of Lauderdale and state of Tennessee in the town of Ripley on the first Monday in August in the year of our Lord one thousand eight hundred and thirty eight it being the sixth day of said month present and presiding the worshipful Samuel V. Gilliland, Esq.,Chairman and Esq. Richardson and Turner the quorum holding the county court for said county, G. L. Rutherford, Clerk and John C. Barnes, High Sheriff, proclamation being made the court proceeded to business.

This day Jessie R. Hutcherson, Administrator on the estate of David Pitchford dec'd returned here in open court an account of sale of the perishable property belonging to said estate which is received by the court and is ordered to be recorded.

This day the commissioners of the county revenue reported a settlement made by them with the county Trustee for the year 1837 which is received by the court and ordered to be recorded.

This d ay Benjamin M. Flippin a minor over the age of fourteen years came into open court and prayed the court to appoint Griffith L. Rutherford his Guardian to take possession of his property to which the court assented whereupon G. L. Rutherford came into court and entered in bond and took the oath of Guardian which is in the words and figures following (to wit) Know
Pg. all men be these presents that we Griffith L. Rutherford, Henry F. Rutherford
179 and John C. Barnes all of the county of Lauderdale and State of Tennessee are held and firmly bound unto Samuel V. Gilliland, Esq., Chairman of the

Pg. 179 cont. county court of said county and his successors in office in trust for the use and benefit of Benjamin M. Flippin in the sum of two thousand dollars for the payment of which will and truly to be made we bind ourselves, each of our heirs, executors and administrators jointly, severally and firmly by these presents sealed with our seals and dated this six day of August 1838.

The condition of the above obligation is such that whereas the above bounden Griffith L. Rutherford has this day been appointed Guardian to Benjamin M. Flippin a minor now if the said Griffith L. Rutherford shall faithfully execute his guardianship by securing and improving all the estate of the said Benjamin M. Flipin that shall come into his possession for the benefit of the said minor until he shall arrive at full age and shall also at the next county court held for the county of Lauderdale exhibit an account upon oath of all the estate of said minor which he shall have received into his hands or possession and shall thereafter exhibit annually before the Justices of said court his account and state the profits and disbursements of the estate of said minor upon oath as required by law then this obligation to be void otherwise to remain in full force and virtue.

Pg. 180 It is ordered by the court that H. C. Keller and Rezin L. Byron the commissioners of the county revenue be paid out of any money in the hands of the Trustee not otherwise appropriated the sum of ten dollars for sitting with the trustee of said county for the year 1836 and 1837.

This day John Holms proved by his own oath the killing of one wolf in the county of Lauderdale over the age of four months and is ordered to be certified to the treasurer there being five Justices present.

It is ordered that Smith Kent be appointed Overseer of the road from Ripley in a direction to Brownsville commencing at the old division line between the first and second civil division and that he work to the county line that he have the hands that live in the following bounds (to wit) all the hands north and south of the road leading from Durhamville towards Brownsville east of Turner's creek in the first district and that he keep the same in repair as a first class road.

Pg. 181 This day Henry T. Chism came into court and with the assent of the court gave up an orphan by the name of William T. Roberson of the age of thirteen years that was bound an apprentice to him to serve until he should attain the age of twenty one years.

I, Samuel V. Gilliland, Chairman of the county court of Lauderdale county by the direction of the court and in their behalf do hereby bind William T. Roberson an orphan of the age of thirteen years to Nathaniel Barnes with him to live and work as an apprentice until he attains the age of twenty one years during which time the said William T. Roberson shall obey the lawful commands and faithfully serve the Nathaniel Barnes and be in all respects subject to his authority and control according to law and his duty as an apprentice.

And the said Nathaniel W. Barnes on his part covenants that he will teach and instruct the said William T. Roberson in the trade and occupation of farming and give him two years schooling, a good farm horse, a saddle and bridle and at the expiration of his services a good suit of cloth clothes or cause the same to be done and he will also constantly find for the said William T. Roberson sufficient diet, lodging, washing and apparel and other necessities suited to an apprentice both in sickness and in health and take care of his morals and treat him with humanity, this sixth day of August 1838.

Pg. 182

N. W. Barnes (Seal)
J. C. Barnes (Seal)
Isham Roberson (Seal)

Pg. 182 cont. State of Tennessee) To Hiram C. Keller a citizen of county, it appearing Lauderdale County) to the county court now in session that Joel J. Reynolds has died leaving no will and that the court being satisfied as to your claim to the administration and you having given bond and qualified as directed by law and the court having ordered that letters of administration be issued to you.

These are therefore to authorize and empower you to take into your possession and control all goods, chattels, claims and papers of the said intestate and return a true and perfect inventory thereof to our next county court to collect and pay all debts and do transact all the duties in relation to said estate which lawfully devolve on you as Administrator and after having settled up said estate to deliver renderer thereof to those who are by law entitled. Witness G. L. Rutherford, Clerk of said court at office this sixth day of August 1838. G. L. Rutherford, Clerk.

Ordered by the court that the trustee pay to Thomas J. Childress two
Pg. 183 dollars out of any money in his hands not otherwise appropriated, it being the amount of cost for serving warrants in favor of Isaac J. Pierson, Overseer of a road.

On motion of John C. Barnes it is ordered that William A. Cleaves a constable in said county of Lauderdale came into court and given countersecurity whereupon William A. Cleaves came into court and gave additional security which is received by the court.

Ordered that court be adjourned until court in course.

Sam V. Gilliland, Chairman
Stith Richardson, J.P.
Milton G. Turner, J.P.

Pg. 184 Be it remembered that at a county court began and held for the county of Lauderdale and State of Tennessee in the court house in the town of Ripley on the first Monday in September in the year of our Lord one thousand eight hundred and thirty eight it being the third day of said month present and presiding the worshipful Samuel V. Gilliland, Chairman and Esqs. Richardson, Campbell, Maxwell, Lockard, G. L. Rutherford, Clerk and John C. Barnes, high sheriff, proclamation being made the court proceeded to business.

This day G. L. Rutherford, Clerk of the county court of said county presented here in open court a settlement made by him with David Gilliland, Administrator of the estate of William L. Byler dec'd which is received by the court and ordered to be recorded.

It is ordered that E. P. Fuller be appointed Overseer of the Ashport road in the place of Sandy Shumake commencing at William P. Gaines old place and work to Hurricane creek and that he have the following hands (to wit) E. Farmer, Wiley Voss, Asa Williams, James Braden, William Nash, Thomas J. Childress, James H. Johnson, James Sherman, J. M. Scott, Benjamin Whitson and E. P. Fuller's hand and that he keep the same in repair as a first class road.

It is ordered that Saban Jones be appointed Overseer of Dyersburg road from Mill Creek to the county line and that he have all the hands east of
Pg. 185 said road and north of Mill Creek and that he keep the same in repair as a first class road.

Whereas it appearing to the satisfaction of the court that William Jordan hath departed this life intestate and Robert Jordan applying for letters of administration and the court being satisfied as to his claim it is ordered that he have letters accordingly he having taken the oath and entered into

Pg. 185 bond conditioned and payable as the law directs.

This day Hiram C. Keller, Administrator on the estate of Joel J. Reynolds dec'd returned an inventory of the goods and chattels belonging to said estate which is received by the court and ordered to be recorded.

It is ordered that John Lockard, Samuel Lusk and Elanthan H. Condry be appointed to commissioners to lay off to the widow of Joel J. Reynolds dec'd her years provisions and report to the next term of this court.

It is ordered that court be adjourned until court in course.

Sam V. Gilliland, Chairman
Stith Richardson, J.P.
John Lockard, J.P.

Pg. 186 Be it remembered that at a county court began and held for the county of Lauderdale and state of Tennessee at the court house in the town of Ripley on the first Monday in October in the year of our Lord, one thousand eight hundred and thirty eight it being the first day of said month present and presiding the worshipful Samuel V. Gilliland, Esq., Chairman and Esqs. Richardson, Maxwell, Atkinson, Barfield, Pope, Price, Sanders, Turner, Chambers, Willard, associate Justices sitting and holding a county court of said county, G. L. Rutherford, Clerk and John C. Barnes, sheriff, proclamation being made the court proceeded to business.

It is ordered by the court that John L. Flippin be appointed Overseer of Dyersburg road in the place of William Baxter commencing at the bridge on Mill creek and he work to the forks of the road near Henry Sumroe and that he have all the hands west of said road and far enough east to take in Henry Crihfield taking all that live within the old district line and that he keep the same in repair as a first class road.

It is ordered that the following good and lawful men be appointed a jury of view to examine the Bucks ferry road leading from the key corner near Claibourne Rounsaville and report the propriety of impropriety that may result from changing said road (to wit) Henry F. Rutherford, Stith Richardson,

Pg. 187 Henry Crihfield, Sr., John Russell, Zacheriah Mitchell, and that they report to the January term of this court.

This day the jury of view that was appointed at the July term of this court to view and mark out a road commencing at the top of the bluff where the Ashport turnpike strikes the same and to intersect the Ashport road east of Thomas Turner presented here in court the result of said view which is received by the court and ordered to be established.

This day the jury of view that was appointed at the July term of this court to examine the Dyersburg road near the town of Ripley and report the propriety of changing said road which is received by the court and ordered to be established as marked by the jury.

This day Hiram C. Keller, Administrator on the estate of Joel J. Reynolds returns here in court an account of sale of perishable property belonging to said estate which is received by the court and ordered to be recorded.

It is ordered that Josiah Blankenship be appointed Overseer of the road from W. P. Gaines old place to Silvertooth landing on Hatchey river and that he have the following hands (to wit) James Silvertooth, John D. Edney, Mrs. Hunter's hands, William Hulme, William McFarlin, R. Moore, F. Barfield, Henry Barfield, C. C. Dyer, J. C. Barnes, Mrs. Childress' hands, Thomas J. Gardner and Lewis Gardner and that he keep the same in repair as a third class road.

Pg. 188 It is ordered by the court that William T. Moorehead, Trustee for the county of Lauderdale come into court and enter into counter security.

Pg. 188 cont. It is ordered by the court that the following good and lawful men be appointed a jury to condemn one acre of land belonging to the heirs of Samuel Wealy dec'd adjoining John C. Crenshall will and say what said land is worth James Salsberry, Z Mitchell, Claibourne Rounsaville, B. Porter and report to the next term of this court.

It is ordered by the court that the following good and lawful men (to wit) Sampson Smith, John Bradford, Thomas Rice, and Jeremiah Penick be appointed a jury to examine the lands of Malett adjoining the lands of Sam Owens where he is about to build a grist mill and lay off and value one acre of said land and report to the next term of this court.

It is ordered that Thomas Turner be appointed Overseer of road marked out by a jury lately commencing at the bluff on Cole creek and intersect the old road east of Thomas Turner and that he have the hands that he had on the old road.

Ordered by the court that the following good and lawful men be appointed a jury of view to lay off and mark out a road commencing at the termination of the Forkeddeer turnpike and view to the Haywood county line as established by A. H. Pope and report to the January term of this court (to wit) John Russell, Amos Rounsaville, Zacheriah Mitchell, James Salsberry, and John Walpole.

Pg. 189 It is ordered by the court that the following good and lawful men be appointed commissioners to draft a plan for a bridge across Mill creek on the Dyersburg road and let out the building of the same and report to the January term of the court (to wit) H. R. Chambers, Benjamin Porter and H. F. Rutherford.

It is ordered by the court there being a majority of the court there being a majority of all the Justices in the county present and voting in the affirmative that G. L. Rutherford be paid the sum of fifty dollars for his ex-officio services for the year 1838 out of any money in the hands of the Trustee not otherwise appropriated.

It is ordered by the court there being a majority of all the Justices in said county present and voting in the affirmative that G. L. Rutherford be paid out of any money in the hands of the Trustee not otherwise appropriated thirty dollars for making a duplicate tax list for books bought for the office and for road orders.

Ordered that John C. Barnes be paid the sum of twenty dollars for furnishing the court with wood, water, etc., to be paid out of any money in the hands of the trustee not otherwise appropriated for the year 1838.

Pg. 190 This day John C. Barnes presented here in open court the following insolvent tax list for which he is chargeable for 1839 (to wit)James M. Barbee, 50 one poll tax, William Carroll 50, John Blackwell 1.70, John Alberson 50, John Fullen 50, Jesse P. Fullen 50, B. Griffith double, J. K. Goodwin 50, Thomas Gossage 50, James Wakefield 50, R. Hooten 50, H. Corkin 50, Thomas S. Read 50, George Mizels 20, Shalle Black 50, William Braden 1.30, R. Gaines 50, Sandy Shumake 90, Turner Williams 50, D. Safland 50, James Parker 50, E. Smith 50, C.Black white poll, B. F. Parham one white poll, John Carlton poll, B. F. Childress white poll, John Holliman, T. B. Stokes white poll, W. D. Willard white poll, John Hogsette, G. Hogsette white poll, William Crihfield poll tax, David Forehand poll tax, which is received by the court and ordered to be certified to the Treasurer and county Trustee.

It is ordered there being a majority of all the Justices present and voting in the affirmative that Mark Glidwell be paid out of any money in the hands of the Trustee not otherwise appropriated fifty eight dollars for building a bridge across the branch near Durhamville.

This day Thomas J. Childress a constable in said county came into court and tendered his resignation which is received by the court.

Pg. 190 cont. On motion of John C. Barnes, Henry F. Rutherford came into court and took the several oaths of office as deputy sheriff for Lauderdale County.

John Homes proved by his own oath the killing of one wolf in the county
Pg. 191 of Lauderdale over the age of four months which is ordered to be certified to the Treasurer there being five Justices present.

It is ordered that court be adjourned until court in course.

Sam V. Gilliland, Chairman
James Price, J.P.
Henry Willard

Pg. 192 Be it remembered that at a county court began and held for the county of Lauderdale and State of Tennessee at the court house in the town of Ripley on the first Monday in November in the year of our Lord one thousand eight hundred and thirty eight it being the fifth day of said month present and presiding the worshipful Samuel V. Gilliland, Esq., Chairman and Esqs. Turner, Lockard, Atkinson, Barfield associate Justices sitting and holding a county court for said county, G. L. Rutherford, Clerk and John C. Barnes, high sheriff proclamation being made the court proceeded to business.

This day the commissioners that was appointed at the October term of this court to view, lay off and value one acre of land belonging to the estate of Samuel Weakley dec'd on the opposite side of the road adjoining John C. Crenshaw's mill reported to court which is in the words and figures following (to wit)

Scale ten poles per inch. State of Tennessee, Lauderdale County.

Agreeable to an order of the worshipful court of said county at October term 1838 to us directed to lay off and value one acre of land the property of the heirs of Samuel Wealey deceased have caused the same to be laid off in the following manner (to wit) Beginning at a point in the center of the creek opposite a forked sugar tree thence west eighteen poles to a point in the center of the creek opposite a mulberry thence down the meanders of the center of the channel of the creek to the beginning all of which is
Pg. 193 respectfully subscribed. The above plot pepresents the survey and we have valued at five dollars.

Commissioners (James Salsberry
(Zacheriah Mitchell
(Claibourne Rounsaville
(Benjamin Porter

Which is received and ordered to be recorded.

This day the jury that was appointed at the last term of this court to lay off and value one acre of land belonging to Maltell adjoining Samuel Owen reports to court which is received by the court and ordered to be recorded, which is in the words and figures following - Agreeable to the order of October term of Lauderdale county we have met being duly sworn and have layed out one acre of land from the Malet track adjoining Mr. Samuel Owen where he purposes puting up a mill lying as follows. Commencing on the said Samuel Owen west boundary at a black ash tree running north with the said Samuel Owens line one hundred yards to stake thence west forty nine yards to a sugar tree thence south to stake one hundred yards thence east forty nine yards to the beginning and have valued the same at three dollars October 27, 1838.

Thomas G. Rice
Jeremiah Penick

Pg. 193 cont.

John Bradford
Sampson Smith

Whereupon Samuel Owen came into court and paid the valuation so assessed.

Pg. 194 It is ordered that R. Parks & Co. be allowed to list 200 acres of land in the sixth district by the payment of the single tax.

This day the last will and testament of Edmond P. Lee dec'd was produced in open court and proven by the oath of Leonard Dunavant and Henry Sumroe the subscribing witness thereto and is ordered to be recorded.

This day William T. Moorehead, County Trustee came into court and entered into bond with Pleasant G. Davenport, A. H. Pope, William Calhoon, I. R. Stone, R. C. Campbell and John C. Barnes additional security for his performance as trustee for said county.

It is ordered that the following good and lawful men be appointed jurors for the next circuit court of Lauderdale county to be held on the third Monday in February next (to wit) Thomas Fitzpatrick, Samuel Owen, Robert P. Russell and Thomas Durham for the first diatrict; Lancy Graves, John H. Maxwell, Joseph Wardlow, John Stone, Sr. for the second district; Elijah Lake, James Crook, J. R. Williams, William Strain for the third district; James B. Hutcherson for the fourth district; William R. Howe for the fifth district; Ancell Reynolds, Joshua Wright, Hiram Meadows and Isaac Moore for the sixth district; Stith Richardson, Hehry Crihfield, Sr., Zacheriah Mitchell, -- Sawyers for the seventh district; Pascal W. Sanders, Henry B. Chambers and John C. Crenshaw for the eighth district; A. G. W. Byron and Roberson Meadows constables to wait on the court and jury and that venire facias issue accord-

Pg. 195 ingly.

It is ordered that court be adjourned until court in course

Sam V. Gilliland, Chairman
M. G. Turner, J.P.
James Barfield, J.P.

Pg. 196 Be it remembered that at a county court began and held for the county of Lauderdale and state of Tennessee in the town of Ripley on the first Monday in December in the year of our Lord one thousand eight hundred and thirty eight it being the third day of said month present and presiding the worshipful Samuel V. Gilliland, Esq., Chairman and Esqs. Richardson, Maxwell, Barfield, Saunders, Turner associate Justices sitting and holding a county court for said county, G. L. Rutherford, Clerk and John C. Barnes, Sheriff, proclamation being made the court proceeded to business.

This day Gilly Hunter came into court and was appointed guardian of William Hunter a minor orphan of the age of five years and entered into bond conditioned and payable as the law directs and took the oath of guardian.

This day Susan C. Morley came into open court and was appointed guardian of Josiah A. Morley and Malvina A. Morley minor orphans and entered into bond conditioned and payable as the law directs and took the oath of guardian.

This day Ezekel Farmer proved by his own oath the killing of one wolf

Pg. 197 in the county of Lauderdale over the age of four months and is ordered to be certified to the Treasurer there being five Justices present.

It is ordered by the court that Stith Richardson, Pascal W. Sanders and Leonard Dunavant be appointed commissioners to divide the perishable property that belonged to William Jordan in his life time held jointly between the said William and his mother, Elizabeth Jordan and report to the next term of this court.

Pg. 197 cont. This day John C. Crenshaw came into court and paid unto the clerk five dollars it being the value of one acre of land belonging to the estate of Samuel Weakley dec'd reported to the last term of this court opposite said Crenshaw's mill.

Ordered that court be adjourned until court in course.

Sam V. Gilliland, Chairman
S. Richardson, J.P.
James Barfield, J.P.

Pg. 198 Be it remembered that at a county court began and held for the county of Lauderdale and state of Tennessee in the court house in the town of Ripley on the first Monday in January in the year of our Lord one thousand eight hundred and thirty nine, it being the seventh day of said month, present and presiding Samuel V. Gilliland, Esq., Chairman and Esqs. Richardson, Pope, Price, Barfield, Campbell, Lockard, Crihfield, Chambers, Saunders associate Justices sitting and holding a county court for said county, G. L. Rutherford, Clerk and John C. Barnes, Sheriff, proclamation being made the court proceeded to business.

The court proceeded to elect a Chairman for the year 1839 whereupon Stith Richardson, Esq., was elected Chairman for said year 1839.

This day the court proceeded to elect from their own body a quorum to hold the county courts for said county of Lauderdale for the year eighteen hundred and thirty nine whereupon Esqs. Maxwell, Crihfield, and Barfield were elected for said purpose.

It is ordered that Milton G. Turner, Esq. be appointed a revenue commissioner to take in a list of taxable property and polls in the first civil district of Lauderdale county for the year 1839 and return the same as the law directs.

It is ordered that John H. Maxwell, Esq. be appointed a revenue commissioner to take in a list of taxable property and polls in the second civil district of Lauderdale county for the year 1839 and return the same as the law directs.

Pg. 199 It is ordered that Able H. Pope, Esq., be appointed a revenue commissioner to take in a list of taxable property and polls in the third civil district of Lauderdale county for the year 1839 and return the same as the law directs.

It is ordered that Henry Willard, Esq., be appointed a revenue commissioner to take in a list of taxable property and polls in the fourth civil district of Lauderdale county for the year 1839 and return the same as the law directs.

It is ordered that Robert C, Campbell, Esq., be appointed a revenue commissioner to take in a list of taxable property and polls in the fifth district of Lauderdale county for the year 1839 and return the same as the law directs.

It is ordered that John Lockard, Esq., be appointed a revenue commisseioner to take in a list of taxable property and polls in the sixth civil district of Lauderdale county for the year 1839 and return the same as the law directs.

It is ordered that E. G. Hinton be appointed a revenue commissioner to take in a list of taxable property and polls in the seventh civil district of Lauderdale for the year 1839 and return the same as the law directs.

Pg. 200 It is ordered that Pascal W. Saunders be appointed a revenue commissionto take in a list of taxable property and polls in the eighth civil district of Lauderdale county and return the same as the law directs.

Pg. 200 cont. This day the court proceeded to lay a county tax for county purposes for the year 1839 on a motion lay the following rates (to wit) contingent tax one and a half cents on each hundred dollars, jury tax one and a half cents on each hundred dollars, six cents on each white poll, six cents poor tax on the same, county tax on all privileges equal to the state tax, state tax five cents on the hundred dollars, state tax on each poll twelve and a half cents, the vote was taken those that voted for said rates were Esqs. Richardson, Gilliland, Price, Barfield, Pope, Lockard, Crihfield, Chambers, Sanders, and Robert C. Campbell, a majority of the Justices in said county so said rates were laid.

This day Margaret Buck and Sampson Smith came into court and was appointed guardians for William T. Buck, Mary J. Buck, Eleanor A. Buck, Robert A. Buck and Caledonia T. Buck, minor orphans and took the oaths of guradian and entered into bond conditioned and payable as the law directs.

It is ordered that Samuel Owen, Jeremiah Penick, John Bradford, Smith Kent, Milton G. Turner be appointed commissioners to lay off to Margaret
Pg. 201 Buck, widow of Arnold Buck dec'd her legacy in the said estate and report to the next term of this court.

This day John C. Crenshaw came into court and was appointed guardian for Oliver B. Crenshaw, a minor and took the oath of guardian and entered into bond conditioned and payable as the law directs.

Whereas it appearing to the satisfaction of the court that Amos Rounsaville has died intestate and the court being satisfied as to the claim of William Rounsaville's right of administration on said estate he having entered into bond conditioned and payable as the law directs and took the oath it is ordered that letters issue accordingly.

This day James Price a Justice of the peace for said county court came into court and tendered his resignation as a Justice of the peace which is received by the court.

It is ordered by the court there being a majority of the Justices in said county present and voting in the affirmative that Able H. Pope be allowed the sum of two hundred and twenty two dollars for surveying the county of Haywood to be paid out of any money in the hands of the Trustee not otherwise appropriated.

Pg. 202 It is ordered that G. L. Rutherford be paid out of any money in the hands of the Trustee not otherwise appropriated thirty dollars for paper box for the use of the county.

It is ordered there being a majority present and voting in the affirmative that John Russell be paid one hundred dollars out of any money in the hands of the Trustee not otherwise appropriated for the support of John Williams, a pauper, to be paid quarterly for the year 1839

Ordered that Henry Crihfield, Leonard Dunavant and John Russell be appointed commissioners to lay off to the widow of Amos Rounsaville,Sr., dec'd a years provision and report to the next term of this court.

Ordered that James C. Fullen be paid eight dollars for making a coffin and burying a stranger by the name of Thompson to be paid out of any money in the hands of the Trustee not otherwise appropriated.

It is ordered that John C. Barnes be paid six dollars and eight cents for window shutters for the court house to be paid out of any money in the hands of the Trustee not otherwise appropriated.

This day Robert Jordan, Administrator of William Jordan presented here in court an inventory and account of sale which is received and ordered to be recorded.

Pg. 203 This day the jury of view that was appointed at the October term 1838 to view the road near Claibourne Rounsaville reports to court which is received and ordered to be recorded.

This day the commissioners that was appointed at the October term 1838 to let the building of bridge across Cane creek on the road from Ripley to Dyersburg reports to court that they have complied with said order and that Absalum Vickory has completed said bridge and entered into bond to keep up said bridge five years.

It is ordered there being a majority of all the Justices in said county present and voting in the affirmative that Absalum Vickory be paid eighty seven dollars, sixty two and one half cents out of any money in the hands of Trustee not otherwise appropriated for building a bridge across Cane creek on the road from Ripley to Dyersburg.

This day Pleasant G. Davenport, Administrator of Lewis Williams dec'd returned into court an account of sale of the perishable property belonging to said estate which is received by the court and ordered to be recorded.

Pg. 204 Hiram Meadows records his stock mark (to wit) crop of the left ear and split in the same and crop off the right ear.

John Lockard records his stock mark (to wit) upper half crop of each ear.

It is ordered by the court there being a majority of all the Justices in said county present that the following good and lawful men be appointed a jury of view to examine the road leading from Ripley towards Brownsville near William McClelland and report the convenience or inconvenience that might result from changing the same taking into consideration the public good as well as the interest of individuals and report to the April term of this court (to wit) Jery Cheek, Joseph Wardlow, R. S. Byron, J. M. C. Robertson and John Chapman.

It is ordered there being a majority present and voting in the affirmative that Joshua R. Stone be paid ninety three dollars and fifty cents for building a bridge across Thompson's Slew in Hatchey bottom to be paid out of any money in the hands of the Trustee not otherwise appropriated.

It is ordered that Isaac Braden be paid ten dollars for holding two
Pg. 205 juries of inquest to be paid out of any money in the hands of the Trustee not otherwise appropriated.

It is ordered that court be adjourned until court in course.

Stith Richardson, Chairman
James Barfield, J.P.
H. R. Chambers, J.P.

Pg. 206 Be it remembered that at a county court began and held for the county of Lauderdale and state of Tennessee in the court house in the town of Ripley on the first Monday in February in the year of our Lord one thousand eight hundred and thirty nine it being the fourth day of said month present and presiding the worshipful John H. Maxwell, Henry Crihfield, and James Barfield, Esqs. appointed the quorum to hold the monthly courts for said county, G. L. Rutherford, Clerk and John C. Barnes, Sheriff, proclamation being made the court proceeded to business.

This day the commissioner that was appointed at the last term of the court to lay off to the widow of Amos Rounsaville dec'd a years provision, reports to court which report is received and ordered to be recorded.

It is ordered that Hiram Meadows be appointed Overseer of the road leading from Ripley to Stokes landing commencing at Cane creek and that he have all the hands west of the Buck's ferry road and north of Cane creek to work under him and that he keep the same in repair as a second class road.

It is ordered that Samuel Lusk be appointed Overseer of the Bucks road in the place of Isaac Moore commencing at the county line and work to Blackwells and he have Nicholas Reynolds, Ancell Reynolds, James Sanders, Henry Reynolds, Isaac Reynolds, James Reynolds, John Nearn and E. H. Condry to work under him and that he keep the same in repair as a second class road.

Pg. 207 It is ordered that Isaac Smith be appointed Overseer of the old Dyersburg road towards Covington commencing at Cane creek and that he work to where it intersects the present road from Ripley and that he have Anderson Jordan, Camel Jordan and Curtis Ellis and that he keep the same in repair as a second class road.

It is ordered that Stith Richardson, Pascal W. Sanders and Henry Crihfield, Esqs. be appointed commissioners to settle with Griffith L. Rutherford administrator on the estate of Oliver Crenshaw dec'd and report to the next term of this court.

This day Able H. Pope, one of the Justices of the peace for said county presented here in court his resignation as a magistrate which is received by the court.

Ordered that Joshua R. Stone be appointed Overseer of the road leading from Ripley to Covington in the place of Joseph Currie commencing at Bates fork of Cane creek and work to John Fullen's field and that he have all the hands that formerly worked under Joseph Curie and that he keep the same in repair as a first class road.

It is ordered that Isaac Braden be paid out of any money in the hands of the Trustee not otherwise appropriated five dollars for services rendered in case of the State of Tennessee vs John C. Barnes.

Pg. 208 This day the commissioners that was appointed at the last term of the court to lay off to Margaret Buck, widow of Arnold Buck dec'd her legacy in said estate reported to court which is received and ordered to be recorded.

Gideon Olds records his stock mark (to wit) crop of the left ear and under bit in the same and a swallow fork in the left ear.

Court adjourned for one hour.

Court met pursuant to adjournment.

This day Pleasant G. Davenport, guardian for Sevina Linvelle returned into court the amount of money received by him for said ward which is received and ordered to be recorded.

This day William G. Rounsaville, administrator on the estate of Amos Rounsaville dec'd returned here in court an account of sale of the property belonging to said estate which is received by the court and ordered to be recorded.

On the petition of Samuel Hawkins and it appearing to the court here that Benjamin Smith late of the State of North Carolina has departed this life intestate leaving no relations in the State of Tennessee and it further appear-
Pg. ing to the court here that the said Benjamin Smith dec'd seized and possessed
209 of lands in the State of Tennessee in the county of Lauderdale and it further appearing to the court that the said Samuel Hawkins is the largest creditor of the said Benjamin Smith dec'd it is therefore ordered by the court that the said Samuel Hawkins have letters of administration on all and singular the goods and chattel rights and credits and land and tenements which the said Benjamin Smith dec'd seized and possessed within the State of Tennessee and therefore the said Samuel Hawkins together with Isaac Sampson, John Barnes and G. L. Rutherford, his securities entered into and acknowledged bond in the penal sum of forty thousand dollars conditioned and payable as the law directs and thereupon the said Samuel Hawkins was duly sworn as administrator aforesaid.

It is ordered that John Nelson be appointed Overseer of road from Ripley towards Dyersburg in the place of W. A. Mohundra and that he have the same hands to work under him with the addition of Thomas Baker and hands.

Ordered that court be adjourned until court in course.

J. H. Maxwell, J.P.
Henry Crihfielf, J.P.
James Barfield, J.P.

Pg. 210 Be it remembered that at a county court began and held for the county of Lauderdale and State of Tennessee in the court house in the town of Ripley on the first Monday in March in the year of our Lord, one thousand eight hundred

Pg. 210 cont. and thirty nine it being the fourth day of said month present and presiding the worshipful John H. Maxwell, James Barfield and Henry Crifield, Esq. the quorum elected the county courts for said county G. L. Rutherford, Clerk and J. C. Barnes, Sheriff.

This day Stith Richardson and Henry Crihfield, the commissioners that was appointed at the last term of the court to settle with G. L. Rutherford, administrator of Oliver Crenshaw dec'd reported to court said settlement which is received by the court and ordered to be recorded.

This day G. L. Rutherford, Clerk of the county court of said county presented to court a settlement made by him with Samuel V. Gilliland and Mariah Blackwell, administrator and administratrix on the estate of Stephen J. Blackwell dec'd which is received by the court and ordered to be recorded.

This day G. L. Rutherford, Clerk of the county court of said county presented to court a settlement made by him with Henry F. Rutherford, guardian
Pg. 211 of the minor heirs of Oliver Crenshaw dec'd which is received by the court and ordered to be recorded.

John Davis recorded his stock mark (to wit) smooth crop of each ear and slit in the left ear.

Elnathan H. Condry records his stock mark (to wit) smooth crop split and under bit in the left ear and under half crop in the right.

It is ordered that Izabela Wilson be released from the payment of double tax by the payment of the single tax for the year 1839.

It is ordered that John Smith be appointed Overseer of the Ripley road towards Dyersburg from the north branch of Cane creek to old county line near Henry Sumrow in the place of Sumrow resigned and that he have the same hands and O. Fudge to work under him and that he keep the same in repair as a first class road.

Ordered that Lauson H. Dunaway be appointed Overseer of the Bucks ferry road in the place of Erasmus D. Thurmond and that he have the same hands to work under him commencing at the bridge on Mill creek and to work to the dividing ridge between Rutherford creek and Rounsavilles creek and that he keep the same in repair as a second class road.

Pg. 212 It is ordered that Elnathan H. Condry be appointed a revenue commissioner to take in a list of taxable property and polls in the sixth civil district of Lauderdale county in the place of John Lockard for the year 1839 and that he return the same by the next term of the court.

It is ordered that Isaac Braden, Coroner of Lauderdale county be paid two dollars for serving a state warrant on J. C. Barnes also for 4 spa to be paid out of any money in the hands of the Trustee not otherwise appropriated.

Whereas it appearing to the satisfaction of the court that John Lockard hath departed this life intestate and Leroy Lockard having applied for letters of administration on said estate and the court being satisfied with his claim to rites of administration it is ordered that he have letters according on all and singular the goods and chattel rites and credits belonging to said estate and therefore the said Leroy Lockard together with Hiram Meadows, William Weddle and Hiram C. Keller, his securities entered into and acknowledged bond in the penal sum of four thousand dollars payable as the law directs and thereupon the said Lockard took the oath of administration.

Pg. 213 This day Robert West came into court and was appointed guardian of the minor heirs of Robert Millen dec'd (to wit) Francis Marion and Rachel Caroline, Virginia Millen and entered into bond conditioned and payable as the law directs and took the oath of guardian.

Ordered by the court that William Campbell be released from the payment of the double tax on one thousand acres of land in the seventh civil district of Lauderdale county by the payment of the single tax valued at twenty hundred and six dollars.

Ordered that A. S. Martin and Ranson H. Byron be released from the payment of the double tax on 640 acres of land in the seventh civil district of Lauderdale county for the year 1839.

Ordered by the court that John C. Barnes, Sheriff and tax collector for the county of Lauderdale for the year 1838 be released from the payment of

Pg. 213 cont. taxes on the following tracts of land for said year the same having been twice listed (to wit) one tract of 955 acres listed in the name of Charles M. C. Dowell valued at $3342, tax $13.36, one tract of 200 acres listed in the name of William I. Russell valued at $1000, tax $4.00, it having been listed in the name of Joseph Wardlow.

Pg. 214 One tract of 640 acres listed in the name of Thomas Crutcher in the third civil district valued at $2000, tax $4.00 one tract of 2000 acres listed in the name of Samuel Haukins in the seventh district he having paid the double tax in the eight one tract of 200 acres listed in the six district in the name of R. C. Campbell which is ordered to be certified to the Treasurer and county trustee.

This day J. M. C. Robertson came into court with a commissioner from the Governor of the state of Tennessee authorizing him to discharge the duties of a Justice of the peace for said county and took the several oaths directed by law.

Ordered that the clerk of this court issue a Sciri facias against Sarah Curtis, Administratratrix of James Curtis requiring her to appear at the next term of this court and give Counter Security for said administration.

Ordered that court be adjourned until court in course.

J. H. Maxwell, J.P.
H. Crihfield, J.P.
James Barfield, J.P.

Pg. 215 Be it remembered that at a county court began and held for the county of Lauderdale and state of Tennessee in the court house in the town of Ripley on the first Monday in April in the year of our Lord one thousand eight hundred and thirty nine it being the first day of said month present the worshipful Stith Richardson, Esq., Chairman and Esqs. Gilliland, Maxwell, Barfield, Crihfield, J. M. C. Robertson, Chambers, associate Justices sitting and holding a county court for said county, G. L. Rutherford, Clerk and John C. Barnes, Sheriff, the court proceeded to business.

It is ordered that G. L. Rutherford be released from the payment of the double taxes on 128 acres of land listed in the eighth district for double tax for the year 1839.

It is ordered by the court Robert C. Campbell, Esq. the revenue commissioner appointed to take in a list of taxable property and polls in the fifth civil district of Lauderdale county be fined fifty dollars for failing to return his tax list within the time prescribed by law.

It is ordered that Henry Willard, Esq. the revenue commissioner that was appointed to take in a list of taxable property and polls for district no. 4 for the year 1839 be fined fifty dollars for failing to return his tax list agreeable to law.

Pg. 216 This day James Givins, Administrator on estate of Sarah Johnson returned into court an additional inventory of the good and chattel rights and credits that has come into his hands which is received by the court and is ordered to be recorded.

It is ordered by the court that Joseph Taylor be appointed Overseer of the road from Ripley towards Brownsville in the place of Moses E. Stone commencing in the town of Ripley and to work to cross road near Hennis Champ and that he have the following hands to work under him. (to wit) William H. Stone, John Stones hands, Lee.H. Buck, R. C. Campbells hands, Walter Clawson, Joseph Clawson, William McClelland and hands, Hennis Champ and hands and Samuel Dunlap and that he keep the same in repair as a first class road.

It is ordered that the following good and lawful men be appointed a jury of view to examine the road leading from Ripley towards Brownsville near William McClelland and report the convenience or inconvenience that might result from changing said road taking into condideration the public good as well as the interest of individuals and report to July term of this court(to wit) Joseph Wardlow, R. S. Byron, J. M. Robertson, John Chapman, Jerry Cheek.

Pg. Whereas it appearing to the satisfaction of the court that James Curtis
217 has departed this life and Sarah Curtis having taken out letters of administration on said estate and on petition of Hiram C. Keller one of her securities a Sciero facias was issued at that last term of this court requiring the
said Sarah Curtis to come into court at the April term and give counter
security and upon which the sheriff makes to following return came to hand
the 18 day of March 1839 J. C. Barnes, Sheriff Sarah Curtis is not to be
found in my county this 29th of March 1839, J. C. Barnes, Sheriff of Lauderdale County. It is therefore ordered that Hiram C. Keller have letters of
administration issued to him he having entered into bond conditioned and payable as the law directs and took the oath of administration.

Whereas it appearing to the satisfaction of the court that Joseph H.
Adams has departed this life intestate, it is ordered that Henry Crihfield,
Esq. have letters of administration issued unto him he having entered into
bond conditioned and payable as the law directs.

It is ordered by the court that all persons subject to double tax for
the year 1839 that will come to Clerks table and apply during this term shall
be released from double tax by the payment of the single tax.

Pg. It is ordered by the court there being a majority of all the Justices
218 present that G. L. Rutherford be paid fifty dollars for making out eight
plots and certificates of the civil district in Lauderdale county to be paid
out of any money in the hands of the Trustee not otherwise appropriated.

This day William G. Rounsaville, administrator on the estate of Amos
Rounsaville dec'd returned into court an additional inventory of the goods
and chattel rights and credits belonging to said estate which is received by
the court and ordered to be recorded.

This day Gilly Hunter, guardian of William Hunter returned into court
the amount that had come into her hands as guardian which is received by the
court and is ordered to be recorded.

It is ordered that Samuel Gilliland, Archer Phillips, Samuel Owen,
George Young and Smith Kent be appointed to divide the negroes belonging to
estate of Robert K. Millen amongst the legatees of R. K. Millen and report to
the next term of this court.

It is ordered that the following good and lawful men be appointed a jury
Pg. of view to lay off and mark out the nearest and best way for a road from Lee
219 bridge on the Forkeddeer river to the Haywood county line in a direction to
Ripley and report to July term of this court (to wit) John Russell, Zacheriah
Mitchell, John Walpole, James Salsberry and Henry Crihfield, Sr.

It is ordered by the court that the following good and lawful men be
appointed to lay off to the widow of Joseph H. Adams dec'd her years provision
(to wit) Benjamin Porter, Henry Crihfield, Jr. and Henry Sumrow and report to
the next term of this court.

This day Frederick Barfield a constable elected in the third civil district of Lauderdale came into court entered into bond conditioned and payable
as the law directs and took the oaths of office.

It is ordered that the following good and lawful men be appointed jurors
for the nest term of the circuit court to be holden for the county court of
Lauderdale county on the third Monday in June next (to wit) Sampson Smith,
James C. Lovelass, John Bradford and Samuel Goss for the first district;
James L. Green, John H. Maxwell, Isaac J. Pierson and James Witson, David C.
Russell, Nathaniel Barnes and James Barfield for the third;;Green B. Holland
for the fourth; William R. Howe for the fifth district; E. H. Condry, Elijah
Wright, E. B. Foster and W. R. Ledbetter for the sixth; D. Leonard Dunavant,
Pg. Edwin H. Hinton, Henry Summow and Edmond Wright for the seventh district;
220 Lawson H. Dunaway, William O. Mohundra, Sr. and John Soward for the eighth;
A. G. W. Byron and Frederick Barfield constables to wait on the court and jury.

It is ordered that Samuel V. Gilliland, John H. Maxwell, J. M. C. Robertson, R. L. Byron and A. H. Pope be appointed commissioners to draft a plan
for log jail in said county and report to the June term of this court and if
said plan is received let out the building of the same.

It is ordered that Becy Boswell a pauper in said county be paid twenty

Pg. 220 cont. dollars for her support for ensuing twelve months to be paid out of any money in the hands of the Trustee not otherwise appropriated under the control of A. H. Pope.

It is ordered that Milton G. Turner, the revenue commissioner for the first civil district be paid seven dollars and fifty cents for taking in a list of taxable property and polls in said district for the year 1839 out of any money in the hands of.

It is ordered that John H. Maxwell be paid seven dollars and fifty cents

Pg. 221 for taking in a list of taxable property and polls in the second civil district for the year 1839 out of any money in the hands of the Trustee not otherwise appropriated.

It is ordered that Able H. Pope be paid out of any money inthe hands of the Trustee not otherwise appropriated seven dollars and fifty cents for taking in a list of taxable proprty and polls in the third civil district for the year 1839.

It is ordered that Elnathan H. Condry be paid seven dollars and fifty cents out of any money in the hands of the Trustee not otherwise appropriated for taking in a list of taxable property and polls in the sixth civil district for the year 1839.

It is ordered that Edwin H. Hinton be paid seven dollars and fifty cents out of any money in the hands of the Trustee not otherwise appropriated for taking in a list of taxable property and polls for seventh district for the year 1839.

It is ordered that Pascal W. Sanders be paid seven dollars and fifty cents out of any money in the hands of the Trustee not otherwise appropriated for taking in a list of taxable property and polls in the eighth district for the year 1839.

It is ordered that court be adjourned until court in course.

Stith Richardson, Chairman
J. H. Maxwell, J.P.
J. M. C. Robertson, J.P.

Pg. 222 Be it remembered that a county court began and held for the county of Lauderdale and state of Tennessee in the court house in the town of Ripley on the first Monday in May in the year of our Lord one thousand eight hundred and thirty nine it being the sixth day of said month present the worshipful Henry Crihfield, James Barfield, two of the quorum appointed to hold the county courts for said county and Esqs. Chambers and Robertson, G. L. Rutherford, Clerk and J. C. Barnes, Sheriff proclamation being made the court proceeded to business.

This day Henry Crihfield, Esq., Administrator of Joseph H. Adams returned in open court an inventory of the goods and chattel rights and credits that has come into his hands as administrator on said estate which is received by the court and ordered to be recorded.

This day Samuel Haukins, administrator of all and singular the goods and chattel rights and credits of Benjamin Smith dec'd presented in open court an inventory which is received by the court and ordered to be recorded.

It is ordered that Samuel Lusk, Overseer of Bucks ferry road have in addition to his former hands John Hodge, Isaac Moore, P. F. Crihfield, H. Reynolds, Roland Ledbetter, I. M. Steele, Waly Voss.

Pg. 223 This day the commissioners that was appointed at the last term of this court to lay off to the widow of Joseph H. Adams dec'd a years provision reported to court which is received by the court and ordered to be recorded.

This day William T. Moorehead, County Trustee for Lauderdale county came into court with H. C. Keller, Isaac J. Finson and Richard G. McGaughy, his securities and entered into bond conditioned and payable as the law directs for his faithfully pay out of all money received on account of common schools for said county.

It is ordered that Isaac Moore, Elijah Wright and Hiram Meadows be

Pg. 223 cont. appointed commissioners to lay off to the widow of John Lockard dec'd a years provision and report to the next term of the court.

This day Hiram C. Keller, administrator of James Curtis dec'd returned into court an inventory of the goods and chattels, rights and credits belonging to said estate which is received by the court and ordered to be recorded.

This day G. L. Rutherford, Clerk of the county court of said county reported a settlement made by him with H. C. Keller, administrator on the estate of Wesley Keller dec'd which is received by the court and ordered to be recorded.

Pg. 224 This day G. L. Rutherford, Clerk of the county court of said county produced here in court a settlement made by him with Ellison P. Fuller, administrator of Mabry Hunter dec'd which is received by the court and ordered to be recorded.

It is ordered that William Hafford be appointed Overseer of the road from Ripley to the county line near Champ Conner in the place of James A. Morris and that he have the following hands to work under him (to wit) James A. Morris, John B. Byron, David Walker, Lancy Graves, John Laird, Jerry Cheek, David Reynolds and that he keep the same in repair as a second class road.

It is ordered that Henry R. Chambers be paid out of any money in the hands of the Trustee not otherwise appropriated for his services as a commissioner for building a bridge across Mill creek the sum of five dollars.

It is ordered that Benjamin Porter be paid the sum of five dollars for services as a commissioner for drafting a plan for a bridge across Mill creek to be paid out of any money in the hands of the Trustee not otherwise appropriated.

It is ordered that Henry F. Rutherford be paid the sum of five dollars out of any money in the hands of the Trustee not otherwise appropriated for serving as a commissioner and superintending the building of a bridge across Mill creek.

Pg. 225 It is ordered that Henry R. Chambers, Esq. be paid out of any money in the hands of the Trustee not otherwise appropriated for holding inquest over the dead body of a negro man found dead in the Forkeddeer river in the year 1837 the sum of five dollars.

This day Robert C. Campbell, a justice of the peace in said county came into court and tendered his resignation as a majistrate which is received by the court.

This day William G. Rounsaville, administrator of Amos Rounsaville dec'd came into court with Zacheriah Mitchell and Claiborne Rounsaville, his securities and entered into bond for his faithful performance of the duties of administrator on said estate.

It is ordered that court be adjourned unti court in course.

Henry Crihfield, J.P.
James Barfield, J.P.
J. M. C. Robertson, J.P.

Pg. 226 Be it remembered that at a county court began and held for the county of Lauderdale in the court house in the town of Ripley on the first Monday in June in the year of our Lord one thousand eight hundred and thirty nine it being the third day of said month present and presiding the worshipful John H. Maxwell, Esq. and Esqs. Crihfield and Barfield the quorum elected to hold the monthly courts for said county G. L. Rutherford, Clerk and John C. Barnes, Sheriff proclamation being made the court proceeded to business.

It is ordered that Samuel V. Gilliland, John Bradford, Samuel Owen, George Young and Smith Kent be and they are hereby appointed commissioners to divide the negros belonging to the estate of Robert K. Millen dec'd amongst the Legatees of Robert K. Millen and report to the next term of the court.

This day John C. Barnes, sheriff and collector of the public taxes for the county of Lauderdale for the year 1839 came into court and acknowledged himself indebted unto Stith Richardson, Chairman of the county court of said

Pg. 226 cont. county and his seccessors in office in the penal sum of four hundred dollars and Henry F. Rutherford and Robert West his securities acknowledged themselves to be indebted in the sum of two hundred dollars each but to be void on condition that John C. Barnes sheriff and collector as aforesaid shall

Pg. 227 will and truly collected the county tax for said county for the year 1839 and pay over the same agreeable to law, if not, to remain in full force and virtue whereupon John C. Barnes took the oath of collector.

It is ordered by the court that G. L. Rutherford be paid twenty dollars out of any money in the hands of the Trustee not otherwise appropriated for making out the collectors book for the year 1839.

This day David A. Posey came into open court and was appointed guardian for his grand-daughter, Virginia Hill Keller and entered into bond conditioned and payable as the law directs and took the oath of guardian.

This day Bozle Billingsley, administrator of Lewis Mathews dec'd returned here in open court an additional inventory of the goods and chattels, rights and credits of said Mathews which is received by the court and ordered to be recorded.

It is ordered that court be adjourned until court in course.

J. H. Maxwell, J.P.
James Barfield, J.P.
Henry Crihfield, J.P.

Pg. 228 Be it remembered that at a quarterly court began and held for the county of Lauderdale and state of Tennessee in the court house in the town of Ripley on the first Monday in July in the year of our Lord one thousand eight hundred and thirty nine it being the first day of said month present the worshipful Stith Richardson, Esq., Chairman of said county court and Esqs. Robertson, Barfield, Crihfield, Maxwell, Willard, associate Justices sitting and holding the county courts for said county, G. L. Rutherford, Clerk and John C. Barnes sheriff proclamation being made the court proceeded to business.

Ordered that Epharin H. Foster be presented to list one trace of land containing 910 acres of land for the taxes of 1839 by the payment of the single taxes.

This day J. M. Alexander a constable in said county tendered to the court his resignation as constable which is received by the court.

This day Thomas Pewit proved by his own oath the killing of one wolf in the county of Lauderdale under the age of four months and is ordered to be certified to the Treasurer there being five Justices present.

This day G. L. Rutherford, Clerk of the county court of said county presents to court a settlement made by him with Pleasant G. Gavenport, guardian

Pg. 229 of Lavina Linville which is received by the court and order to be recorded.

This day G. L. Rutherford, Clerk of said county court presented into court a settlement made by him with Bozle Billingsly, administrator of Lewis Mathews dec'd which is received by the court and is ordered to be recorded.

Ordered that James Jackson be appointed overseer of the Bucks ferry road from the key corner in the place of Thomas J. Brown commencing at the dividing ridge between Rutherfords creek and Rounsavilles creek and that he work to the forks of the road near Amos Rounsavilles old place and that he have all the hands on the east side of Rutherfords creek to work under him and that he keep the same in repair as a second class road.

This day the commissioners that was appointed to lay off for the widow of Joel R. Reynolds dec'd a years provision reported to court which is received by the court and ordered to be recorded.

This day Shadwick Black proved by his own oath the killing of one wolf in the county of Lauderdale over the age of four months which is ordered to be certified to the Treasurer there being five Justices present.

Pg. 230 Ordered that E. P. Fullen, Overseer of a road have in addition to his former hands James Gillespie, Isaiah Connelly, James Hodge, Harris Hodge, A. H. Pope to work under him.

Pg. 230 cont. It is ordered that the following good and lawful men of the body of the county of Lauderdale be summoned as jurors for the next circuit court to be holden for the county of Lauderdale on the third Monday in October next (to wit) Milton G. Turner, Archer Phillips, George Young and Thomas Fitzpatrick, for the first district; John Stone, Joseph Taylor, Thompson and Isaac D. Maxwell for the second district; Able H. Pope, David P. Posey, James B. Crook and George Williams for the third district; Samuel A. Givin for the fourth district; Benjamin F. Jordan for the fifth district; Armstead Wood, William Deason, Isaac Moore and Samuel Lusk for the sixth district; Isaac M. Steel, Boling Fisher, Zacheriah Mitchell and John Russell for the seventh district; Richard Parr, Henry R. Chambers and William B. Sawyers for the eighth; A. G. W. Byron and Frederick Barfield, constables to wait on the court and jury.

Ordered by the court that Henry Willard, Esq. be released from the payment of a fine of fifty dollars that was entered against him at the April term of this court for neglecting to return his list of taxable property taken by him for the year 1839.

It is ordered by the court that Robert C. Campbell be released from the
Pg. 231 payment of a fine of fifty dollars that was entered against him at the April term of this court for neglecting to comply with the act of assembly in returning a list of taxable property and polls taken by him for the year 1839.

It is ordered by the court there being a majority of all the Justices in said county present and voting in the affirmative that Samuel Stricklin be paid the sum of one hundred and fifty nine dollars and fifty cents for building a bridge across Mill creek on the road from Ripley to Dyersburg to be paid out of any money in the hands of the Trustee not otherwise appropriated.

It is ordered by the court there being a majority of all the Justices in said county present and voting in the affirmative that the following good and lawful men be appointed a jury of view to examine the road leading from Ripley to Dyersburg near H. A. G. Lea and report to the October term of this court the conveniences or inconveniences that might result from changing the same taking into consideration the public good as well as the interest of individuals (to wit) Henry F. Rutherford, James Salsberry, Henry Crihfield, E. H. Hinton and Samuel Hooper.

Ordered that Samuel Stricklin be appointed overseer of the road fromthe bridge on Mill creek on the Dyersburg road to the key corner and that he have
Pg. 232 all the hands west of the Dyersburg road except Mathew Bradon and William O. Mohumdra and that he keep the same in repair as a second class road.

It is ordered that David Hay be presented to list a 2100 acre tract of land for the tax of 1839.

It is ordered there being a majority of all the Justices in said county present and voting in the affirmative that John C. Barnes be paid fifty dollars for his ex-officio services for the year 1838 to be paid out of any money in the hands of the Trustee not otherwise appropriated.

This day the jury of view that was appointed to view and mark a road from Lee bridge on the south fork of Forkeddeer river to the Haywood county line reported to court which is received by the court.

This day the commissioners that was appointed at the April term of this court to draft a plan for a jail for said county presented to court said plan which is received it is therefore ordered that the commissioners for the town of Ripley let out and superintend the building of the same.

It is ordered that Samuel Gilliland one of the quorum appointed to hold the monthly courts for the county of Lauderdale for the year 1838 be paid out of any money in the hands of the Trustee not otherwise appropriated the sum of twelve dollars.

Pg. 233 It is ordered that Stith Richardson, Esq. one of the quorum elected to hold the monthly courts for said county for the year 1838 be paid ten dollars out of any money in the hands of the Trustee not otherwise appropriated.

It is ordered that Milton G. Turner, Esq. one ot the quorum elected to hold the monthly courts for said county for the year 1838 be paid ten dollars out of any money in the hands of the Trustee not otherwise appropriated.

Pg. It is ordered that Henry Willard be paid the sum of seven dollars and
233 fifty cents for taking in a list of taxable property and polls in the fourth
cont. district for the year 1839 to be paid but of any money in the hands of the
Trustee not otherwise appropriated.

It is ordered that Robert C. Campbell be paid the sum of seven dollars and fifty cents for taking in a list of taxable property and polls in the fifth district from the year 1839 to be paid out of any money in the hands of the Trustee not otherwise appropriated.

Pg. It is ordered that court adjourn until court in course.
234

Stith Richardson, Chairman
James Barfield, J.P.
J. M. C. Robertson, J.P.

Pg. Be it remembered that at a county court began and held for the county of
235 Lauderdale and State of Tennessee in the court house in the town of Ripley on
the first Monday in August in the year of our Lord one thousand eight hundred and thirty nine it being the fifth day of said month present John H. Maxwell and James Barfield, Esq. two of the Justices elected to hold the monthly courts for said county and J. M. C. Robertson, Esq. sitting and holding a county court for said county, G. L. Rutherford, Clerk and John C. Barnes, Sheriff.

Proclamation being madê the court proceeded to business.

This day Leroy Lockard, administrator of John Lockard dec'd returned in open court an account of sale of the perishable property belonging to said estate which is received by the court and is ordered to be recorded.

It is ordered that Isaac Moore, Hiram Meadows and Armstead be appointed commissioners to lay off to the widow of John Lockard dec'd a years provision and report to the next term of the court.

It is ordered that Caleb Arnold be appointed Overseer of the road from Durhamville toward Covington as far as Joseph Curies in the place of John Holmes and that he have all the hands west of the road from Williams ferry to
Pg. Durhamville and south of the road leading from Durhamville to Fullens ferry
236 on Hatchie except H. Chism, C. Whitson, W. Flinn and the hands on Wardlow's
plantation and that he keep the same in repair as a first class road.

Ordered by the court that Robert Walker be permitted to list his taxable property for the year 1839 by the payment of the single tax.

Ordered that Sugar T. Evans be appointed Overseer of the road from Fulton to Samuel A. Givins in the place of Abraham Moss and that he have the following hands to work under him (to wit) Martin Alexander, R. P. Thompson, Miles Wakefield, Ezekiel Wakefield, William W. Lea's hands and that he keep the same in repair as a first class road.

It is ordered that James H. Gimin be appointed Overseer of the Fulton road from Samuel A. Givin to Cane creek and that he have H. Willard, all the hands west of Willard and east of Samuel A. Givins to work under him and that he keep the same in repair as a first class road.

This day Margaret Burke, one of the guardians for the minor heirs of Arnold Burke dec'd came into court and surrendered to the court her guardianship which is received by the court.

This day Sampson Smith came into court and was appointed guardian for William T. Burke, Caladonia T. Burke, Mary J. Burke, Elinor Burke, Robert A.
Pg. Burke, minor heirs of Arnold Burke dec'd whereupon Sampson Smith came into
237 court and entered into bond conditioned and payable as the law directs and
took the oath ofguardian.

This day Jesse R. Hutcherson came into court and presented a certificate from John C. Barnes, Sheriff of said county of his election to the office of Constable in said county, whereupon Jesse R. Hutcherson came into open court and acknowledged himself indebted to the Governor of the State of Tennessee and his successors in office in the sum of four thousand dollars and

Pg. John C. Barnes, Hiram C. Keller and G. L. Rutherford his security came into
237 court and acknowledged themselves each to be indebted in the sum of thirteen
cont. hundred and thirty three dollars but to be void on condition that Jesse R. Hutcherson will and truly discharge the duties of constable agreeable to law whereon Jesse R. Hutcherson took the several oaths of office.

Ordered by the court that the clerk of the county court of said county issue a warrant directed to Stith Richardson, Benjamin Porter and Henry Crihfield, Esq., commissioners for the purpose of examining a two thousand acre tract of land granted by the state of North Carolina to Henry F. Rutherford by grant no. 34 lying within said county and to endeavor to establish
Pg. the north-east corner of said tract of land and return into the October term
238 of this court a plot of said tract of land.

E. P. Fullen records his stock mark, crop of the left ear swallow fork and under bit in the right.

James B. Crook records his stock mark, under bit in the ear and splitin the left.

M. A. Posey records his stock mark, smooth crop of the right ear and swallow fork and under bit in the left.

A. G. W. Byron records his stock mark, under bit and swallow fork in the left and split in the right.

Ordered that James E. Street be appointed Overseer of the Fulton road from Durhamville commencing at Durhamville and to work to where the Ripley road intersects said road and that he have the following hands to work under him (to wit) M. G. Turner, and hands, Robert West, Thomas Durham and hands, Rufus Inman, C. Watson, R. P. Russell, John Davis, Clement Grigs, A. Phillips and hands, Thomas R. Cousins, Joseph Hays and hands, Edwin Fitzpatrick and hands.

Ordered by the court that James G. Anthony be appointed Overseer of road
Pg. from Durhamville towards Brownsville to the county line that he keep the same
239 in repair as a first class road with the hands on the Durhamville farm.

Ordered that Nathaniel W. Barnes be appointed Overseer of the road from Joseph Curries to Silvertooth ferry on Hatchie and that he have the following hands (to wit) James Wardlow, William H. Fisher, Nancy Fisher's hands, Alex Wardlow, A. J. Fullen, John Fullen, Judge B. Mosely, Isaac Fullen, Henry T. Chism, P. G. Gaines and hands, James Watson, P. G. Davenport, Martin Norman, Z. Norman, Richard Golden, William Flinn, John Albison and son, George S. Johnson and hands, Jacob Linville and Jonathan Osment and that he keep the same in repair as a first class road.

It is ordered that court be adjourned until court in course.

J. H. Maxwell, J.P.
James Barfield, J.P.
J. M. C. Robertson, J.P.

Pg. Be it remembered that at a county court began and held for the county of
240 Lauderdale and State of Tennessee in the court house in town of Ripley on the first Monday in September in the year of Our Lord one thousand eight hundred thirty nine it being the second day of said month present the worshipful John H. Maxwell, Esq. and Esqs. Barfield, and Foster associate Justices sitting and holding a county court for said county, G. L. Rutherford, Clerk, John C. Barnes, Sheriff, proclamation being made the court proceeded to business.

This day G. L. Rutherford, Clerk of the county court of said county of Lauderdale presented here in court a settlement made by him with Nancy Kidd, Administratrix on the estate of A. U. Kidd dec'd which is received by the court and ordered to be recorded.

This day Elnathan H. Condry presented in open court a commission from the Governor of the State of Tennessee authorizing him to discharge the duties of Justice of the peace in and for said county who took the several oaths of office and took his seat.

Ordered that Leroy Lockard be appointed Overseer of the road from Greens mill to the forks of the road near John Hogsett and that he have John Lockard,

Pg. 241 Thomas Lockard, William Boydstone, B. F. Boydstone, W. R. Ledbetter, C. T. Ledbetter, James J. Osteen and Drewry Massey and that he keep the same in repair as a second class road.

Ordered that Hiram Meadows be appointed Overseer of the road from John A. Hogset to stokes landing on Forkeddeer and that he have the following hands (to wit) Edmond Reynolds and Roberson Meadows, William Deason, John Wood, John Hogsette, G. Hogsette, Samuel Deason, Cain Acuff, E. Ballinger, John Langley, S. Johnson, Guy Stokces, Dicerson Jennings and sons and Jordan G. Stokes hands and that he keep the same in repair as a second class road.

Ordered that Henry R. Chambers, Esq. be paid five dollars out of any money in the hands of the hands of the Trustee not otherwise appropriated for holding an inquest over the dead body of Samuel Miskelly.

Ordered that court be adjourned until court in course.

J. H. Maxwell, J.P.
James Barfield, J.P.
Elnathan H. Condry, J.P.

Pg. 242 Be it remembered that at a county court began and held for the county of Lauderdale and State of Tennessee in the court house in the town of Ripley on the first Monday in October in the year of our Lord one thousand eight hundred and thirty nine it being the seventh day of said month present and presiding the worshipful Stith Richardson, Chairman and Esqs. Maxwell, Robertson, Crihfield, Gilliland, Barfield associate Justices sitting a county court for said county, G. L. Rutherford, Clerk and John C. Barnes, Sheriff, proclamation being made the court proceeded to business.

It is ordered that Champ C. Conner be permitted to list two tracts of land which was not listed for the tax for the year 1839 (to wit) a 200 acre tract and 226 acre tract both lying in the fifth district valued at one dollar per acre by the payment of the single tax.

Ordered that Daniel B. Turner be permitted to list a 1250acre tract of land valued at $1.00 per acre for the taxes for the year 1839 the same not having been listed.

This day Elijah Lake came into court and presented in open court a commission from the Governor of the State of Tennessee authorizing him to discharge the duties of a Justice of the peace in and for said countyand took
Pg. 243 the oaths of office agreeable to law.

This day William Strain proved by his own oath the killing of one wolf in the county of Lauderdale over the age of four months and is ordered to be certified to the Treasurer there being five Justices present.

This day Thomas Pewitte proved by his own oath the killing of one wolf in the county of Lauderdale over the age of four months which is ordered to be certified to the Treasurer there being five Justices present.

Ordered that Isaac Braden, Coroner of Lauderdale county be paid eight dollars out of any money in the hands of the Trustee not otherwise appropriated for holding an inquest over the dead body of a negro woman found dead on the Mississippi and for burying hhe same.

This day the jury of view that was appointed at the July session of the court to view the road leading from Ripley towards Dyersburg near H. A. G. Leas and report to this session the convenience or inconvenience that might
Pg. 244 result from changing said road reported to court which is received by the court and ordered to be established as marked by the jury.

It is ordered by the court there being a majority of all the Justices in said county present and voting in the affirmative that G. L. Rutherford, Clerk of the county court of said county of Lauderdale be paid fifty dollars for his ex-officio services for the year 1839 to be paid out of any money in the hands of the Trustee not otherwise appropriated.

Ordered by the court there being a majority of all the Justices in said

Pg. 244 cont. county present and voting in the affirmative that G. L. Rutherford, Clerk of the county court of said county be paid twenty five dollars and eighteen cents for making road orders, jury tickets, pauper orders, and the duplicate tax list for the year 1839 to be paid out of any money in the hands of the Trustee not otherwise appropriated.

Ordered that Archer Phillips be appointed Overseer of the Fulton road from Hurricane to Fulton from Hurricane Hill to where the Ripley road to Fulton intersects said road and that he have his own hands and Dr. Cousins and hands to work under him and that he keep the same in repair as a first class road.

Ordered that James E. Street be appointed Overseer of the road from Durhamville to Hurricane Hill and that he have the following hands to work
Pg. 245 under him (to wit) Milton G. Turner and hands, Robert West, Thomas Durham and hands, Rufus Inman, Christopher Watson, R. P. Russell, John Davis, Joseph Hays, Edwin Fitzpatrick and hands and all the hands belonging to James G. Anthony's plantation on the road from Durhamville to Fullens ferry.

Ordered that S. V. Gilliland, J. M. C. Robertson and John H. Maxwell, Esqs. be appointed commissioners to examine Charles Smoot and report to this court the propriety or impropriety of placing him on the pauper list.

This day the commissioners that was appointed at the August session to lay off to the widow of John Lockard dec'd a years provision report to court which is received by the court and ordered to be recorded.

Ordered by the court that Charles Smoot a pauper in said county be paid thirty dollars out of any money in the hands of the Trustee not otherwise appropriated to J. M. C. Robertson, Trustee for one year from this date.

It is ordered that John C. Barnes, Sheriff and Collector of the public taxes for the county of Lauderdale for the year 1839 be released from the payment of thirteen dollars and twenty four cents on account of insolvents
Pg. 246 for the year 1839 and that the same be certified to the Treasurer and County Trustee.

Ordered that the commissioners for the town of Ripley draft a plan for a court house to be built in the town of Ripley and report to the January session of this court.

It is ordered that court be adjourned until court in course.

Stith Richardson, Chairman
James Barfield, J.P.
J. H. Maxwell, J.P.

Pg. 247 Be it remembered that at a county court began and held for the county of Lauderdale and State of Tennessee in the court house in the town of Ripley on the first Monday in November in the year of our Lord one thousand eight hundred and thirty nine it being the fourth day of said month present and presiding the worshipful John H. Maxwell, Esq., Henry Crihfield, Elnathan H. Condry, Elijah Lake and James Barfield associate Justices sitting and holding a quorum court for said county, G. L. Rutherford, Clerk and John C. Barnes, Sheriff, proclamation being made the court proceeded to business.

John Nelson records his stock mark (to wit) a crop off of each ear and under bit in the left ear.

Ordered that Thomas Marchall be permitted to list a thousand acres tract of land lying in the fifth distrcit valued at $3000 for the year 1839.

Ordered that the following good and lawful men of the body of the county of Lauderdale be summoned as jurors for the next circuit court to be held for the county of Lauderdale on the third Monday in February next (to wit) John
Pg. 248 Darant, Samuel Owen, Shadrick Rice, John Watson, Jr., Lancy Graves, James A Morris, James S. Green, Joseph Wardlow, John H. Maxwell, Elijah Lake, James Barfield, Hiram C. Keller, James H. Johnson, James Hutcherson, Henry Willard, Robert C. Campbell, Elnathan H. Condry, Elijah B. Foster, John D. Nearn, Dickerson Jennings, Edmon Wright, Edwin Hinton, Caless Anderson, Mathew Porter,

Pg. 248 cont. and Edward Kennelly, A. G. W. Byron and Frederick Barfield, constables to wait on the court and jury.

Whereas it appearing to the satisfaction of the court that Mark Glidwell has departed this life and - Glidwell, widow of said Mark Glidwell dec'd relinquishing her right to the administration to Thomas L. Clark it is ordered that Thomas L. Clark have letters issued to him he having entered into bond with Thomas B. Cousins and Able H. Pope his securities in the sum of two hundred dollars conditioned and payable as the law directs and took the oath of administrator.

Ordered that court adjourn until court in course.

J. H. Maxwell, J.P.
James Barfield, J.P.
Henry Crihfield, J.P.

Pg. 249 Be it remembered that at a county court began and held for the county of Lauderdale and State of Tennessee in the court house in the town of Ripley on the first Monday in December in the year of our Lord one thousand eight hundred and thirty nine it being the second day of said month present the worshipful John H. Maxwell, Esqs. Barfield and Condry and Crihfield sitting and holding a county court for said county, G. L. Rutherford, Clerk and John C. Barnes Sheriff, proclamation being made the court proceeded to business.

It is ordered that the following men be appointed commissioners to lay off to the widow of Mark Glidwell dec'd a years provisions and report to the next term of this court (to wit) Robert West, Archer Phillips, and Caleb Arnold.

It is ordered that Samuel V. Gilliland, Joseph Currie and David C. Russell be appointed commissioners to lay off to the widow of William Fullen dec'd a years provision and report to the next term of this court.

Whereas it appearing to the satisfaction of the court that William Fullen has departed this life intestate and John Fullen applying for letters of administration on said estate and the court being satisfied with his claim to the right of administration he having entered into bond with Hiram C. Keller and William P. Gaines his security in the sum of five hundred dollars payable as the law directs and took the oath of administration it is there-

Pg. 250 fore ordered that he have letters accordingly.

It is ordered that court be adjourned until court in course.

J. H. Maxwell, J.P.
James Barfield, J.P.
Henry Crihfield, J.P.

Pg. 251 Be it remembered that at a county court began and held for the county of Lauderdale and State of Tennessee in the court house in the town of Ripley on the first Monday in January in the year of our Lord one thousand eight hundred and forty it being the sixth day of said month present the worshipful Stith Richardson, Esqs. S. V. Gilliland, E. Lake, James Barfield, H. Crihfield, Condry, Maxwell, Robertson and Foster Esqs. sitting and holding a county court for said county, G. L. Rutherford, Clerk and John C. Barnes, Sheriff.

Proclamation being made the court proceeded to business.

The court proceeded to elect a chairman for the year 1840 whereupon John H. Maxwell, Esq. was elected Chairman of said court for said year.

This day the courts proceeded to elect from their body a quorum to hold the monthly courts for said county for the 1840 whereupon Elnathan H. Condry, Elijah Lake and Henry R. Chambers, Esqs. was elected the quorum to hold said court.

The court proceeded to lay a county tax for county purposes for the year 1840. On motion of John H. Maxwell, Esq. to lay the following rates (to wit) Jury tax on each hundred dollars 2½ cents, contingent tax 2½ cents; road and bridge tax 2 cents; poor tax 3 cents; poor tax on each white poll 12½ cents;

Pg. jury tax on same $12\frac{1}{2}$ cents, the vote was taken, those that voted for said
252 rates were Esqs. Maxwell, Richardson, Gilliland, Lake, Barfield, Crihfield, Condry, and J. M. C. Robertson a majority of all the Justices in said county so said rates was laid Viz: total county tax on each hundred dollars ten cents; on each poll twenty five cents; county tax on privileges equal to that of the State.

It is ordered there being a majority of all the Justices present that Milton G. Turner, Esq. be appointed a revenue commissioner to take in a list of taxable property and polls for district no. 1, Lauderdale county for the year 1840;

It is ordered there being a majority of the Justices present that J. M. C. Robertson, Esq. be appointed a revenue commissioner to take in a list of taxable property and polls for the second district, Lauderdale county for the year 1840.

It is ordered there being a majority of the Justices present that Thomas J. Childress be appointed a revenue commissioner to take in a list of taxable property and polls for the third district, Lauderdale county for the year 1840.

It is ordered there being a majority of the Justices present that Henry Willard, Esq. be appointed a revenue commissioner to take in a list of taxable property and polls for the fourth district, Lauderdale county for the year 1840.

It is ordered there being a majority of the Justices present that Hennis Champ be appointed a revenue commissioner to take in a list of taxable proper-
Pg. ty and polls for the fifth district, Lauderdale county for the year 1840.
253 It is ordered there being a majority of the Justices present that Elnathan H. Condry, Esq. be appointed a revenue commissioner to take in a list of taxable property and polls for the sixth district, Lauderdale county for the year 1840.

It is ordered there being a majority of the Justices present that E. H. Hinton be appointed a revenue commissioner to take in a list of taxable property and polls for the seventh district, Lauderdale county for the year 1840.

It is ordered there being a majority of the Justices present that Henry R. Chambers, Esq. be appointed a revenue commissioner to take in a list of taxable property and polls for the eighth district, Lauderdale county for the year 1840.

This day G. L. Rutherford, Clerk of the county court of Lauderdale county present here in open court a settlement made by him with Dickerson Jennings, administrator of Richard Allison dec'd which was examined by the court and ordered to be recorded.

This day G. L. Rutherford presented in court a settlement made by him as Clerk with Samson Smith, guardian for the minor heirs of Arnold Burke dec'd which is received by the court and ordered to be recorded.

Pg. This day John Thompson, administrator of Samuel Rudder dec'd returned in
254 open court an inventory of the goods and chattels, rights and credits of S. Rudder dec'd which is received by the court and ordered to be recorded.

Ordered that Samuel V. Gilliland and R. L. Byron be appointed commissioners of the revenue to settle with the Trustee of Lauderdale county for the years 1838, 1839 & 1840.

This day G. L. Rutherford, Clerk of the county court of said county presents here in court a settlement made by him as clerk with John Thompson, administrator of Samuel Rudder dec'd which was examined by the court and ordered to be recorded.

This day G. L. Rutherford, Clerk of the county court of said county presented in court a settlement made by him with William T. Moorehead and Isaac Braden as administrator of Samuel G. Hogsette dec'd which is received by the court and ordered to be recorded.

This day Thomas L. Clark, administrator of Mark Glidwell dec'd presented in open court a sale bill which is received by the court and ordered to be recorded.

Pg. 254 cont. It is ordered that Sarah Coleman be allowed at the rates of one hundred dollars per annum for the support of John Williams a pauper in said county for the year 1840 to be paid out of any money in the hands of the Trustee not otherwise appropriated to be under the control of John Rudder.

Pg. 255 This day Jonathan Larry proved by his own oath the killing of one wolf in the county of Lauderdale over the age of four months which is ordered to be certified to the Treasurer there being five Justices present.

This day the commissioners that was appointed to lay off to the widow of Mark Glidwell a years provision reported to court which is received by the court and ordered to be recorded.

This day the commissioners for the town of Ripley in obedience to an order of the court made at the October session 1839 to draft a plan for a court house to be built in the town of Ripley presented to court a plan which was examinedby the court received and ordered to be filed in the Clerk's office.

It is ordered there being a majority of all the Justices in said county present and voting in the affirmative that the town commissioners proceed to collect the money due for lots to advertise and let out the building of said court house.

It is ordered that Charlotte Bibb bring his child, Moses, into the next county court to be held for the county of Lauderdale in the court house in the town of Ripley on the first Monday in February next that he may be provided for as the law in such cases directs.

Pg. 256 This day the commissioners that was appointed to lay to the widow of William Fullen dec'd a years provision report to court, was received by the court and ordered to be recorded.

This day John C. Barnes came into court and petitioned the court to have Thomas J. Childress qualified as deputy sheriff whereupon the said Thomas J. Childress came into court and took the several oaths of office agreeable to law.

It is ordered that court be adjourned until tomorrow morning 10 o'clock.

J. H. Maxwell, Chairman
J. M. C. Robertson, J.P.
Elnathan H. Condry, J.P.

Pg. 257 Tuesday morning court met pursuant to adjournment, present John H. Maxwell, Esq., Chairman and Esqs. Elijah Lake, Henry Crihfield, J. M. C. Robertson, Elnathan H. Condry, Henry Willard, James Barfield, and Sameel V. Gilliland associate Justices, G. L. Rutherford, Clerk and John C. Barnes, Sheriff.

It is ordered that James Barfield, Esq. be allowed the sum of five dollars for holding an inquest over the body of dead negro by the name of Warrar to be paid out of any money in the hands of the Trustee not otherwise appropriated.

It is ordered there being a majority of all the Justices present and voting in the affirmative that John C. Barnes, Sheriff be allowed the sum of fifty dollars for his ex-officio service for the year 1839 to be paid out of any money in the hands of the Trustee not otherwise appropriated.

It is ordered that John C. Barnes, Sheriff be paid out of any money in the hands of the Trustee not otherwise appropriated, twenty dollars for furnishing the court with wood and water for 1839.

It is ordered that the heirs of Charles I. Love be permitted to list a tract of land lying in the fifth district containing 1028 acres valued at $4.00 per acre.

It is ordered that John H. Maxwell, Esq. be allowed the sum of ten dollars and fifty cents out of any money in the hands of the Trustee not otherwise appropriated for holding the quorum courts for the year 1839.

Pg. 258 It is ordered that James Barfield, Esq. be allowed the sum of twelve dollars out of any money in the hands of the Trustee not otherwise appropriated

Pg. for holding the quorum courts for said county for the year 1839.
258 It is ordered that Henry Crihfield, Esq. be paid nine dollars for hold-
cont. ing the quorum courts for said county for the year 1839 to be paid out of
any money in the hands of the Trustee not otherwise appropriated.
Ordered that court adjourn for one Hour.
Court met pursuant to adjournment.
There being no further business before the court it is ordered that
court be adjourned until court in course.

J. H. Maxwell, Chairman
J. M. C. Robertson, J.P.
Elnathan H. Condry, J.P.

Pg. Be it remembered that at a county court began and held for the county of
259 Lauderdale and State of Tennessee in court house in the town of Ripley on the
first Monday in February in the year of our Lord, one thousand eight hundred
and forty it being the third day of said month, worshipful Elijah Lake,
Elnathan H. Condry and Henry R. Chambers, Esqs. commissioned and qualified as
the law directs and elected the quorum to hold the monthly court for said
county for the year 1840 and John H. Maxwell and Stith Richardson, Esqs.,
G. L. Rutherford, Clerk and John C. Barnes, Sheriff, proclamation being made
the court proceeded to business.
This day G. L. Rutherford, Clerk of the county court of said county
presented this court a settlement made by him with Gilly Hunter, guardian for
William Hunter, minor heir of Mabry Hunter dec'd which is received by the
court and ordered to be recorded.
It is ordered that Samuel V. Gilliland be paid out of any money in the
hands of the Trustee not otherwise appropriated for holding an inquest over
the dead body of William Fullen five dollars.
This day Johnathan Lancy proved by his own oath the killing of one wolf
in the county of Lauderdale over the age of four months which is ordered to
Pg. be certified to the Treasurer there being five Justices present.
260 This day Henry Sumrow proved by his own oath the killing of one wolf in
the county of Lauderdale over the age of four months which is ordered to be
certified to the Treasurer there being five Justices present.
It is ordered by the court that John C. Barnes, Sheriff and Tax Collector
for the year 1839 be released from the payment of four dollars and ninety six
cents it being the amount of the State and county tax on four tracts of land
improperly listed in the name of Mathew Picket and the same be certified to
the Treasurer.
It is ordered that Rezin L. Byron, David P. Posey and John Stone be
appointed commissioners to divide the estate of Samuel Rudder, dec'd and lay
off and divide said estate between John W. Rudder and Elizabeth Rudder and
report to the next term of the court.
This day Moses E. Stone came into court and was appointed guardian for
John W. Rudder, minor heir of Samuel Rudder dec'd and entered into bond in
the sum of two thousand dollars with John Thompson and John C. Barnes, his
securities and took the oath of guardian.
Pg. There being no other business before the court it is ordered that court
261 be adjourned until court in course.

Elijah Lake, J.P.
Elnathan H. Condry, J.P.
H. R. Chambers, J.P.

Pg. Be it remembered that at a county court began and held for the county of
262 Lauderdale and State of Tennessee in the court house in the town of Ripley on
the first Monday in March in the year of our Lord one thousand eight hundred
and forty it being the second day of said month present, Henry R. Chambers,

Pg. 262 cont. Elnathan H. Condry and J. M. C. Robertson, Esqs. holding the quorum court for said county, G. L. Rutherford, Clerk and John C. Barnes, Sheriff.

This day Henry Crihfield, Esq. presented to court his resignation as a Justice of the peace for said county which is received by the court.

This day G. L. Rutherford, Clerk of the county court presented a settlement made by him with David Nunn, administrator on the estate of Francis Nunn dec'd which is received by the court and ordered to be recorded.

It is ordered that Griffith W. Rutherford be released from the payment of the double tax on 552 acres of land by the payment of the single taxes for the year 1840.

Ordered that G. L. Rutherford be released from the payment of the double tax on 2290 acres of land in the seventh district for the year 1840 by the payment of the single tax.

Ordered that Jones and Henderson be released from the payment of the double tax on 480 acres of land in the seventh district for the year 1840 by the payment of the single tax.

Pg. 263 This day Edwin H. Hinton came into court and was appointed guardian for his daughter, Mary E. Hinton, a minor of the age of ten years and entered into bond and took the oath of guardian.

This day G. L. Rutherford, Clerk of the county court of said county presented to the court his resignation as Clerk of said court which is received by the court.

The court proceeded to appoint a Clerk protem to serve until the people elect a Clerk and he is qualified whereupon G. L. Rutherford was appointed and came into court and entered into bond conditioned and payable as the law directs and took the several oaths of office, which bond is in the words and figures following (to wit) We, G. L. Rutherford, Stith Richardson and Samuel Hooper, all of the county of Lauderdale and State of Tennessee are held and firmly cound unto his Excellency, James K. Polk, Esq., Governor of the State of Tennessee and his successors in the penal sum of five thousand dollars for the payment whereof we bind ourselves and each of our heirs, executors or administrators jointly, severally and firmly by these presents sealed with our seals and dated this second day of March 1840.

The condition of the above obligation is such that whereas the above bounden, G. L. Rutherford was this day elected by the county court, Clerk
Pg. 264 protem of the county court of Lauderdale county to serve until there can be one elected by the people and qualified, now if the above bounden G. L. Rutherford shall safely keep the records of said county court and pay over all the money by him collected by virtue of said office to those who are entitled by law and will and truly discharge the duties of Clerk of said court so long as he may continue in office then the above obligation to be void.

G. L. Rutherford (Seal)
Stith Richardson (Seal)
S. Hooper (Seal)

This day the last will and testament of Amos Rounsaville dec'd was produced in open court and proven by the oaths of Stith Richardson and William S. Walpole and is ordered to be recorded.

It is ordered that Hugh Smith be released from the payment of the double tax for the year 1840 by the payment of the single tax.

It is ordered that John Robbins and A. S. Martin be released from the payment of the double tax on 640 acres of land for the year 1840 by the payment of the single tax.

It is ordered that William G. Rounsaville be released from the payment of the double tax for the year 1840 by the payment of the single tax.

It is ordered that court be adjourned until court in course.

H. R. Chambers, J.P.
J. M. C. Robertson, J.P.

Elnathan H. Condry, J.P.

Pg. 265 Be it remembered at a Quarterly county court began and held for the county of Lauderdale and state of Tennessee in the court house in the town of Ripley on the first Monday in April in the year of our Lord, one thousand eight hundred and forty, it being the sixth day of said month present and presiding the worshipful Stith Richardson, Elnathan H. Condry, Elijah Lake, Henry Willard, John M. C. Robertson, James Barfield, Henry R. Chambers, Esqs. commissioned and qualified as the law directs, G. L. Rutherford, Clerk and John C. Barnes, Sheriff. Proclamation being made the court proceeded to business.

This day Isaac M. Steele presented in open court a certificate from John C. Barnes, Sheriff, of his having been elected by the qualified voters of Lauderdale county to the office of County Court Clerk for said county who took the several oaths of office agreeable to law and entered into bond which is the words and figures following (to wit)

State of Tennessee) We, Isaac M. Steele, Isaac D. Maxwell, Elnathan H.
Lauderdale County) Condry, John M. C. Robertson, Griffith L. Rutherford,
Pg. 266 and Samuel Lusk, jointly and severally acknowledge ourselves indebted to James K. Polk, Governor of the State of Tennessee for the time being and his successors in office in the penal sum of five thousand dollars for which payment well and truly to be made we bind ourselves, our heirs, executors and administrators jointly, severally and firmly by these presents sealed with our seals and dated the sixth day of April, 1840.

The condition of the above obligation is such that whereas the above bounden Isaac M. Steele was on the seventh day of March, 1840 duly and legally elected County Court Clerk of Lauderdale County as appears from the certificate of John C. Barnes, Sheriff of said county. Now if the above bounden Isaac M. Steele shall safaly keep the records of said county court and in all things well and truly discharge the duties of Clerk of said court so long as he may continue in office then the above obligation to be void otherwise to remain in full force and virtue.

Isaac M. Steele (Seal)
Isaac D. Maxwell (Seal)
Elnathan H. Condry (Seal)
J. M. C. Robertson (Seal)
G. L. Rutherford (Seal)
Sam Lusk (Seal)

Pg. 267 State of Tennessee) We, Isaac M. Steele, Isaac D. Maxwell, Elnathan H.
Lauderdale County) Condry, John M. C. Robertson, Griffith L. Rutherford and Samuel Lusk, jointly and severally acknowledge ourselves indebted to James K. Polk, Governor of the State of Tennessee for the time being and his successors in office in the penal sum of two thousand dollars for which payments well and truly to be made, we bind ourselves, our heirs, executors and administrators jointly and severally and firmly by these presents sealed with our seals and dated the sixth day of April, 1840.

The condition of the above obligation is such that whereas the above bounden Isaac M. Steele was on the seventh day of March, 1840, duly and legally elected Clerk of the county court of Lauderdale county. Now if the said Isaac M. Steele shall well and truly pay the Treasurer of the State all revenue by him collected or which ought to have been collected on or before the first day of October in each and every year during his continuance in the
Pg. 268 office of Clerk then the above obligation to be void otherwise to remain in full force and virtue.

Isaac M. Steele (Seal)
Isaac D. Maxwell (Seal)
Elnathan H. Condry (Seal)
J. M. C. Robertson (Seal)
G. L. Rutherford (Seal)
Sam Lusk (Seal)

Pg. 268 cont. State of Tennessee) We, Isaac M. Steele, Isaac D. Maxwell, Elnathan H.
Lauderdale County) Condry, John M. C. Robertson, Griffith L. Rutherford and Samuel Lusk jointly and severally acknowledge ourselves indebted to John H. Maxwell, Chairman of the county court of Lauderdale county for the time being and his successors in office in the penal sum of two thousand dollars for which payment well and truly to be made we bind ourselves, our heirs, executors and administrators jointly and severally and firmly by these presents sealed with our seals and dated this sixth day of April 1840.

The condition of the above obligation is such that whereas the above bounden Isaac M. Steele was on the seventh day of March, 1840 duly and legally elected Clerk of the county court of Lauderdale county. Now if the said

Pg. 269 Isaac M. Steele shall well and truly pay the Trustee of Lauderdale county, revenue by him collected or which ought to have been collected on or before the first day of October in each and every year during his continuance in the office of Clerk, then the above obligation to be void otherwise to remain in full force and virtue.

Isaac M. Steele (Seal)
Isaac D. Maxwell (Seal)
Elnathan H. Condry (Seal)
J. M. C. Robertson (Seal)
G. L. Rutherford (Seal)
Sam Lusk (Seal)

The said Isaac M. Steele and his securities acknowledging themselves indebted in open court in the sums mentioned in foregoing bonds.

This day G. L. Rutherford presented here in open court a certificate from John C. Barnes, sheriff of his having been elected sheriff of Lauderdale county for the ensuing two years from the first Saturday in March last and

Pg. 270 took the several oaths prescribed by law and entered into the several bonds required by law said bonds being in the following words and figures (to wit)

State of Tennessee) We, Griffith L. Rutherford, James L. Green, Henry F.
Lauderdale County) Rutherford, Stith Richardson, Henry R. Chambers and Samuel Hooper jointly and severally acknowledge ourselves indebted to James K. Polk, Governor of the State of Tennessee for the time being and successors in office in the penal sum of twelve thousand dollars for which payment well and truly to be made we bind ourselves, our heirs, executors and administrators jointly, severally and firmly by these presents sealed with our seals and dated the sixth day of April 1840.

The condition of the above obligation is such that whereas the bounden Griffith L. Rutherford was on the seventh day of March 1840 duly and legally elected Sheriff of Lauderdale county as appears from the certificate of John C. Barnes, sheriff of said county if therefore the said Griffith L. Rutherford shall well and truly execute and due return make of all process and precepts

Pg. 271 to him directed and pay and satisfy all fees and sums of money by him received or levied by virtue of any process in the proper office by which the same by the tenor thereof ought to be paid or to the person or persons to whom the same shall be due his, her or their executors, administrators, attorneys or agents and in all things well, truly and faithfully execute the said office of sheriff during his continuance therein then the above obligation to be void otherwise to remain in full force and virtue.

G. L. Rutherford (Seal)
James L. Green (Seal)
H. F. Rutherford (Seal)
S. Richardson (Seal)
H. R. Chambers (Seal)
Samuel Hooper (Seal)

Pg. 271 cont. State of Tennessee) Know all men by these presents that we, Griffith L. Lauderdale County) Rutherford, James L. Green, Henry F. Rutherford, Stith Richardson, Henry P. Chambers and Samuel Hooper all of the State and County aforesaid are held and firmly bound unto James K. Polk, Governor of the State of Tennessee for the time being and his successors in office for the use of

Pg. 272 said State in the sum of two thousand dollars to the payments of which well and truly to be made we bind ourselves, our heirs, executors and administrators jointly and severally, firmly by these presents sealed with our seals and dated the sixth day of April 1840.

The condition of the above obligation is such that whereas the bound Griffith L. Rutherford has been duly and constitutionally elected sheriff and collector of the public taxes of said county of Lauderdale for two years from the first Saturday in March 1840. Now if the said Griffith L. Rutherford shall well and truly collect all state taxes which by law he ought to collect and pay to the Treasurer of the state all taxes by him collected or which ought to have been collected on or before the first day of December in each and every year in which he shall collect the taxes then the above obligation to be void otherwise to remain in full force and virtue.

S. Richardson (Seal)
H. R. Chambers (Seal)
Samuel Hooper (Seal)
G. L. Rutherford (Seal)
James L. Green (Seal)
H. F. Rutherford (Seal)

Pg. 273 State of Tennessee) We, Griffith L. Rutherford, James L. Green, Henry F. Lauderdale County) Rutherford, Stith Richardson, Henry R. Chambers and Samuel Hooper, jointly and severally acknowledge ourselves indebted to John H. Maxwell, Esq., Chairman of the county court of Lauderdale county for the time being and his successors in office in the penal sum of four thousand dollars for which payment well and truly to be made, we bind ourselves, our heirs, executors and administrators jointly and severally, firmly by these presents sealed with our seals and dated the sixth day of April 1840. Whereas the said Griffith L. Rutherford was on the seventh day of March 1840 duly and legally elected sheriff and collector of the state and county taxes for Lauderdale county as appears from the certificate of John C. Barnes, sheriff of said county. Now if the said Griffith L. Rutherford shall well and truly collect and pay the Trustee of said county all county taxes by him collected or which ought to have been collected on or before the first Monday in October in each and every year which he shall collect the taxes then the above obligation to be void, otherwise to remain in full force and virtue.

G. L. Rutherford (Seal)
James L. Green (Seal)
H. F. Rutherford (Seal)
S. Richardson (Seal)
H. R. Chambers (Seal)
Samuel Hooper (Seal)

The said G. L. Rutherford and his securities acknowledge themselves indebted in open court in the sums mentioned in the foregoing bonds.

This day Edward H. Hinton and James L. Green produced here in open court commissions from James K. Polk, Governor of the State of Tennessee as Justices of the peace and took the several oaths prescribed by law and took their seat accordingly.

Green Baker proved by his own oath the killing of a wolf over the age of four months in Lauderdale county is ordered by the court that the same be certified to the Treasurer there being five Justices present.

Pg. Reuben Alphin proved by his own oath the killing of a wolf over four
275 months old in Lauderdale county it is ordered by the court that the same be
certified to the Trearurer there being five Justices present.

This day John M. C. Robertson produced in open court the cerfificate of
John C. Barnes certifying that he was duly and legally elected County Trustee
for two years from the first Saturday in March last whereupon said John M. C.
Robertson entered into bond conditioned and payable as the law directs and
took the several oaths prescribed by law he and his securities having first
acknowlegeed themselves indebted in open court in the sum mentioned in said
bond which bond is in the words and figures following (to wit)

State of Tennessee) We, J. M. C. Robertson, Stith Richardson, Robert West,
Lauderdale County) Elnathan H. Condry and Elijah Lake, jointly and severally acknowledge ourselves indebted to John H. Maxwell, Esq, Chairman of the
Pg. county court of Lauderdale county for the time being and his successors in
276 office in the penal sum of six thousand dollars for which payment well and
truly to be made we bind ourselves, our heirs, executors and administrators
jointly and severally, firmly by these presents sealed with our seals and
dated the sixth day of April 1840.

The condition of the above obligation is such that whereas the above
bounden J. M. C. Robertson was on the first Saturday in March, 1840 elected
county Trustee for the county of Lauderdale as appears from the certificate
of John C. Barnes, sheriff of said county. Now if the said J. M. C. Robertson
shall safely keep and pay over all county moneys which may be deposited in
his hands agreeable to the orders of the court and well and truly discharge
the duties of county trustee for said county in all things according to law
so long as he continues in office then this obligation to be void otherwise
to remain in full force and virtue.

J. M. C. Robertson (Seal)
S. Richardson (Seal)
R. C. West (Seal)
Elnathan H. Condry (Seal)
Elijah Lake (Seal)

Pg. The court proceeded to the election of a chairman protem, when J. M. C.
277 Robertson was elected Chairman.

This day A. G. W. Byrn, Samuel Thompson, Henry F. Rutherford and Joshua
Wright presented in open court certificate of their election to the office of
constables for said county from John C. Barnes, sheriff and entered into bond
conditioned and payable as the law directs and took the several oaths prescribed by law.

Whereas it appears to the satisfaction of the court that John Flippin
has departed this life intestate and John L. Flippin applying for letters of
administration and the court being satisfied as to his claim to the administration it is ordered that he have letters accordingly he having taken the oath
and entered into bond conditioned and payable as the law directs.

Whereas it appears to the satisfaction of the court that Philip Burrow
has departed this life intestate and the next of kin to the dec'd not making
claim to the administration and J. M. C. Robertson the largest creditor laying
Pg. claim to said administration proving his debt on oath it is ordered that he
278 have letters accordingly he having taken the oath and entered into bond conditioned and payable as the law directs.

Ordered by the court that Ezekial Farmer bring Moses, andillegitimate son
of Charlotte Bibb into court at the next term to be held in the court house in
the town of Ripley on the first Monday in May then and there to be dealt with
as the law directs.

It is ordered that William McFarlin be appointed Overseer of the road
from William P. Gaines old place to Silvertooth's landing on Hatchie river and

Pg. that he have the following hands (to wit) James Silvertooth, John D. Edney,
278 Mrs. Hunter's hands, William Hulm, R. Moore, F. Barfield, Henry Barfield,
cont. C. C. Dyer, J. C. Barnes, Mrs. Childress' hands, Thomas J. Gardner, Levi
Gardner, Elijah Lake's hands and Thomas L. Clark and that he keep the same
in repair as a second class road.

It is ordered by the court that Joseph Taylor be appointed overseer of
the road from Ripley towards Brownsville commencing in the town of Ripley and
to work to the cross road near Hennis Champ's old place and that he have the
Pg. following hands to work under him (to wit) William H. Stone, John Stone's
279 hands, Lee H. Burkes, R. C. Campbell's hands, Walter Glawson, Joseph Glawson,
William McClelland and hands, Samuel Dunlap, E. McLeod, N. McLeod, George
Milsaps, John Holliman and William Inman and McKennon and that he keep the
same in repair as a first class road.

It is ordered by the court that the following good and lawful men be appointed a jury of view (to wit) Joseph Taylor, R. L. Byrn, John Stone, Samuel Dunlap, P. C. Dyal, William H. Stone and Robert Walker to examine on the propriety or impropriety of altering the road leading from Ripley to Brownsville commencing on the forks of the old road where it formerly run so as to intersect said road between Labuns and Dyals and that they report to the July term of this court.

It is ordered by the court that Z. Mitchell be appointed Overseer of the road from Mill creek in the direction of Bucks ferry in the place of Lawson H. Dunaway and that he have the same hands Dunaway did and that he keep the same in repair as a second class road.

Pg. This day James Givins, administrator of the estate of Sarah Johnson
280 returned an additional inventory of the goods and chattels, rights and credits
that has come into his hands which is received by the court and ordered to be
recorded.

It is ordered by the court that B. F. Buck be appointed Overseer of the road from the bridge on Mill creek on the Dyersburg road to the key corner and that he have all the hands west of the Dyersburg road except Mathew Bradon and William O. Mohundra and that he keep the same in repair as a second class road.

It is ordered by the court that the following good and lawful men be appointed a jury of view to review and mark a road from the key corner to intersect the Dyersburg road near Henry Sumrow's the nearest and most practicable route, H. Rutherford, B. Porter, H. Crihfield, Robert Crihfield and Henry Summers and that they report to the July term of this court.

It is ordered by the court that the following good and lawful men be
appointed a jury of view or commissioners to inquire into and examine the
Pg. road leading from Durhamville to Williams Landing on Hatchie river and report
281 to the July term of this court whether said road ought to be changed or not
(to wit) George W. Young, Isaac D. Coachman, David M. Henning, Archer Phillips,
Edmund Fitzpatrick, Monroe P. Estes and William Crook.

It is ordered by the court that the following good and lawful men be appointed commissioners for the purpose of endeavoring to establishthe south-west corner of a tract of land granted by the state of North Carolina to Griffith Rutherford for 3000 acres by grant no. 37 which is the north-west corner of another tract of the same quantity of acres granted to the same man by grant no. 74 which likewise is the south-east corner of a tract granted to Benjamin Smith for 5000 acres by grant no. 165 and likewise the north-east corner of another tract granted to the same man for the same quantity of acres by grant no. 89 that is to say Stith Richardson, E. H. Hinton and M. B. Sawyers and report according to law.

Pg. It is ordered by the court that Samuel V. Gilliland, R. L. Byrn, J. R.
282 Stone, John Buchannon, C. Watson, S. W. Davenport and James G. Anthony, good
and lawful men be appointed a jury of view to review the Fulton road commencing at R. P. Russels apple orchard and running towards Durhamville and that they report to the July term of this court the utility or inutility of changing said road.

Pg. 282 cont. It is ordered by the court that the following tracts of land be released from double taxes by the payment of the single tax on the same

District No. 2	William Conner	1001 acres	Value	$2000.
" No. 3	John Donalson	2500 "	"	8000.
" " "	John C. McLemore	1500 "	"	3500.
" " "	William Cannon	320 "	"	640.
" " "	Heirs of Patience Wescott	2500 acres	value	$5000.
" " "	" " "	1421 "	"	2842.
" " "	" " "	1251 "	"	2500.
District No. 4	Mathew Barrow	84 "	"	240.
" " "	" "	100 "	"	300.
" " "	Heirs of James Trimble	64 & 232 "	"	600.
" " "	Malvina E. Trimble	109 & 500 "	"	1200.
District No. 5	Samuel Marshall	1100 "	"	2000.
District No. 6	Christopher Strong	428 "	"	1200.
Pg. " " "	" "	1000 "	"	2500.
283 District No. 7	Mathew Barrow	300 "	"	450.

It is ordered by the court that the clerk list for single taxes in district No. 1 the following property and polls (to wit) Joseph Currie 160 acres of land at four dollars per acre $640., one white poll, one slave value $500.; George Thumb one white poll.

Ordered by the court that Leonard Dunavant be released from paying double tax by the payment of the single tax.

Ordered by the court that the following good and lawful men be appointed commissioners to draft a plan and let out to the lowest bidder the building of a bridge across Bates creek on the Ashport road (Viz) H. C. Keller, G. L. Rutherford, Isaac Braden, E. P. Fuller, Abel H. Pope, J. L. Hearring.

It is ordered by the court there being a majority of all the Justices present and voting in the affirmative that G. L. Rutherford be allowed the
Pg. sum of ten dollars out of any money in the hands of the County Trustee not
284 otherwise appropriated for making duplicate tax list in 1838, issuing road orders in October 1839, issuing venire in November 1839, for 27 jury tickets October term 1839 and for issuing 21 jury tickets February term 1840.

This day G. L. Rutherford presented a settlement made by him as clerk of the county court with H. C. Keller as administrator on the estate of Imri Keller dec'd which is received by the court and ordered to be recorded.

Ordered by the court there being a majority of all the Justices present and voting in the affirmative that William T. Moorehead be paid three dollars out of any money in the hands of the Trustee not otherwise appropriated for two blank books furnished by him for the use of the county.

Ordered that the following good and lawful men of the body of the county of Lauderdale be summoned as jurors for the next circuit court to be held for the county of Lauderdale on the third Monday in June next (to wit) Milton G. Turner, Samuel V. Gilliland, William Turner, John Bradford, John Hearring,
Pg. Isaac D. Maxwell, Thomas W. Baker, F. W. Damon, John Stone, Abel H. Pope,
285 Thomas L. Clark, James Barfield, Isaac Braden, Samuel Givins, Josiah M. Alexander, Hennis Champ, John Fletcher, William Boydston, William R. Ledbetter, Armstead Wood, Leonard Dunavant, Henry Sumrow, H. Crihfield, James Salsberry and William B. Sawyers, and A. G. W. Byrn and Frederick Barfield constables to wait on the court and jury.

Ordered by the court that the following good and lawful men be appointed a jury of view to review and mark the nearest and best way for a road from Durhamville to the turnpike on the road from Brownsville to Covington (to wit) Isaac D. Coachman, David M. Henning, Archer Phillips, Edmond Fitzpatrick, Monroe P. Estes and William Crook and that they report to the July term of this court.

Ordered that the court adjourn until tomorrow morning nine o'clock.

Pg. 286 H. R. Chambers, J.P.
James Barfield, J.P.
Elnathan H. Condry, J.P.
James L. Green, J.P.

Tuesday morning the court met pursuant to adjournment present H. R. Chambers, James L. Green, Elnathan H. Condry and James Barfield, Esqs. Isaac M. Steele, Clerk and G. L. Rutherford, Sheriff. Proclamation being made the court proceeded to business.

Ordered that the court adjourn until court in course.

H. R. Chambers, J.P.
James Barfield, J.P.
Elnathan H. Condry, J.P.
James L. Green, J.P.

Pg. 289 Be it remembered that at a county court began and held for the county of Lauderdale and State of Tennessee in the court house in the town of Ripley on the first Monday in May in the year of our Lord one thousand eight hundred and forty it being the fourth day of said month present, Henry R. Chambers, Elnathan H. Condry and Elijah Lake, Esqs. commissioned and qualified as the law directs holding the quorum court for said county, Isaac M. Steele, Clerk and G. L. Rutherford, Sheriff. Proclamation being made the court proceeded to business.

Isaac M. Steele produced in open court a deputation from James Price, Register and took the several oaths prescribed by law.

This day William B. Sawyers produced in open court a commission from James K. Polk, Governor of the State of Tennessee as a Justice of the peace for Lauderdale county and took the several oaths prescribed by law and took his seat accordingly.

The court proceeded to elect a chairman of the quorum court whereupon H. R. Chambers was elected.

This day E. H. Hinton presented in open court an inventory of the goods and chattels, rights and credits of Mary E. Hinton that have come to his hands as guardian which is received by the court and ordered to be recorded.

Pg. 290 It is ordered by the court that the clerk list the following property belonging to Monroe P. Estes for single tax (to wit)

400 acres of land first district value $2000.
5 negroes " " " 2400.
1 white poll
1 pleasure carriage " 100.

Also Jonathan Jones taxable property in said district, two slaves value $900.

This day Isaac M. Steele, Clerk presented to the court a settlement made by him with James Givin, administrator of the estate of Sarah Johnson dec'd which is received by the court and ordered to be recorded.

This day Isaac M. Steele, Clerk pf the county court presented to the court a settlement made by him with Abel H. Pope as administrator of the estate of Lawson A. Henry dec'd which is received by the court and ordered to be recorded.

This day Ezekial Farmer in obedience to the order of this court at April term 1840 brought into court Moses Bibb an illegitimate child of Charlotte Bibb was bound an apprentice to Ezekial Farmer to learn the occupation of farming, Leroy F. Lockard becoming his security for the faithful performance of his duties to said apprentice and the payment of what the court directed
Pg. 291 him to be bound to pay said Moses Bibb at the age of twenty-one.

This day G. L. Rutherford petitioned to have Henry F. Rutherford sworn as deputy sheriff whereupon said H. F. Rutherford took the several oaths perscribed by law.

Pg. 291 cont. This day Joseph Wardlow informed the court that Thomas D. Fisher, guardian of Juretta Niswanger had gone to parts unknown, probably Texas, and that the estate of said Juretta G. Niswanger minor heir of Jacob Niswanger dec'd was suffering in consequence whereupon the court appointed William P. Gaines, guardian of said Juretta Niswanger who came into court with David P. Posey, R. C. Campbell and Hiram C. Keller his securities and entered into bond and took the oath of guardian according to law.

This day the court appointed Hiram C. Keller guardian of Hiram M. Keller minor heir of Imri Keller dec'd whereupon said Hiram C. Keller came into court with J. C. Barnes, Elijah Lake and G. L. Rutherford, his securities and entered into bond and took the oath of guardian according to law.

Pg. 292 There being no further business before the court it is ordered that the court be adjourned until court in course.

H. R. Chambers, Chairman
Elnathan H. Condry, J.P.
Elijah Lake, J.P.

Pg. 293 Be it remembered that at a county court began and held for the county of Lauderdale and state of Tennessee in the store house of William T. Moorehead in the town of Ripley on the first Monday in June in the year of our Lord one thousand eight hundred and forty, it being the first day of said month present and presiding H. R. Chambers, Esq. and Elijah Lake and Elnathan H. Condry, Esqs. holding the quorum court for said county, Isaac M. Steele, Clerk and G. L. Rutherford, Sheriff. Proclamation being made the court proceeded to business.

This day the resignation of Jessie R. Hutcherson, Constable for the fourth civil district of Lauderdale was presented in open court and received.

This day James Lewis produced in open court a commission from James K. Polk, Governor of the State of Tennessee as Justice of the peace for Lauderdale county whereupon he took the several oaths prescribed by law as a Justice of Peace.

It is ordered that Thomas Brim be appointed Overseer of the road leading from Mill creek to Bucks ferry from where Zachariah Mitchell stops to the county line and that he have all the hands between Mitchell and Hinton's
Pg. 294 boundaries and the county line that he keep the same in repair as a second class road.

This day the last will and testament of Susan C. Marley dec'd was presented and proved in open court by the subscribing witnesses, E. H. Hinton, Henry Sumrow and Guilford Jones and ordered to be recorded.

This day the court chose and appointed Reubin Alphine, guardian to John H. Johnson, Washington Johnston, Polly M. Johnson, Sally Johnson and Nancy Johnson, minor heirs of Sarah Johnson dec'd whereupon said Alphin came into court and entered into bond conditioned and payable as the law directs and took the oath of guardian.

It is ordered that the court adjourn until court in course.

H. R. Chambers, Chairman
Elijah Lake, J.P.
Elnathan H. Condry, J.P.

Pg. 295 Be it remembered that at a quarterly court began and held for the county of Lauderdale and State of Tennessee in the court house in the town of Ripley on the first Monday in July in the year of our Lord one thousand eight hundred and forty it being the sixth day of said month present and presiding the worshipful John H. Maxwell, Chairman and Esqs. Richardson, Hinton, Sawyers, Condry, Robertson, Lewis, Green, Vassor, Turner and Barfield, sitting and holding said court, Isaac M. Steele, Clerk and G. L. Rutherford, Sheriff. Proclamation being made the court proceeded to business.

Pg. 295 cont. This day A. H. Pope, J. L. Hearring and Elison P. Fuller appointed commissioners at the April term of this court reported that they have proceeded to draft a plan for a bridge across Bates creek on the Ashport road and offered the same to the lowest bidder, whereupon John Holliman bid seventy three dollars and fifty cents being the lowest bid the question being put, will the court accept of said report and order said commissioners to accept said bid; ayes, Condry, Green, Hinton, Lewis, Maxwell, Sawyers, Turner and Vassor; noes, Richardson.

Pg. 296 This day Joseph Taylor, R. L. Byrn, John Stone, Samuel Dunlap and P. C. Dyal who were appointed a jury of view at the April term of this court to examine on the propriety or impropriety of altering the road leading from Ripley to Brownsville reported which report is accepted and ordered to be recorded a majority of all the Justices present and voting.

This day Robert Crihfield, Benjamin Porter, Henry Rutherford and H. Crihfield who were appointed a jury of view at the April term of this court presented their report which report is accepted by the court there being a majority of all the justices present and voting in the affirmative.

This day Isaac Moore and John W. Nearn proved by their own oaths the killing of five wolves under four months old in the county of Lauderdale there being five Justices present and ordered that the same be certified to the Treasurer.

This day Onesimus Fudge proved by his own oath the killing of one wolf over four months old in the county of Lauderdale ordered that the same be certified to the Treasurer there being five Justices present.

Ordered that the county Trustee pay John L. Hearring nine dollars and fifty cents for 4 doors, for paper box, for 4 brass hinges, 4 dozen screws, hanging said door, for two locks, the vote on this appropriation were; ayes,
Pg. Condry, Barfield, Green, Hinton, Lewis, Maxwell, Richardson, Sawyers, Turner
297 and Vassor.

This day Elison P. Fuller praved by his own oath the killing of one wolf over four months old in the county of Lauderdale there being five Justices present ordered that the same be certified to the Treasurer.

This day Samuel V. Gilliland, Rezin L. Byrn, J. R. Stone, John Buchanon and C. Watson who were appointed a jury of view at the April term of this court reported which report was accepted and ordered to be recorded there being a majority of all the Justices present and voting in the affirmative.

This day John G. Flippin, administrator of the estate of John Flippin dec'd returned and sworn to in open court an inventory and sale bill of said estate which is received and ordered to be recorded.

This day H. A. G. Lee and Stith Richardson who were appointed executors of the last will and testament of Susan C. Marley dec'd which will was proven at the June term of this court came into court with H. C. Keller and E. H. Hinton their securities and entered into bond and took the oath of executors according to law whereupon it is ordered by the court that letters testamentary issue to them according to law.

Pg. 298 It is ordered that the county Trustee pay Isaac M. Steele, Clerk, twenty five dollars and 87½ cents for issuing four road orders April term, for issuing five orders for jurys of view from said term, for issuing venire facias, for circuit court, for the June term 1840, for one pauper order for John Williams, for issuing one road order from May term, for issuing twenty six jury tickets from June term of circuit court, for issuing three road orders from June term, for making the tax collectors book for 1840, for furnishing the county Trustee a statement of the amount of county revenue on the collectors book; ayes, Condry, Barfield, Green, Hinton, Maxwell and Lewis voting for said appropriation being one third of all the Justices in the county.

It is ordered that C. Watson be permitted to list 188 acres of land in the first district for single tax value $750.00 and that Calvin Jones be permitted to list 22 acres of land in the fifth district for single tax value $100.00.

Pg. It is ordered by the court that the following good and lawful men of the
298 body of the county of Lauderdale be summoned jurors for the next circuit to
cont. be held for the county of Lauderdale on the first Monday in October next (to wit) John M. Durant, Milton G. Turner, Samuel V. Gilliland, Samuel Gause, Joseph Taylor, R. L. Byrn, James A. Morris, James L. Green, John H. Maxwell,
Pg. John C. Barnes, Elijah Lake, Thomas J. Childress, John Vassor, John Brown,
299 John B. Fudge, Isaac Moore, E. B. Foster, R. Meadows, John Russell, H. Crihfield, Sr., E. H. Hinton, Edwin Fisher, William O. Mohundra, Sr., Laban Jones, and John Soward, and Joshua Wright and Samuel Thompson, constables to wait on said court and jury.

This day the court chose and appointed W. D. Lee, guardian of Malvina A. and Josiah C. Marley, minor heirs of Adum Marley dec'd in the place of Mrs. Susan C. Marley, former guardian dec'd, whereupon said William D. Lee with Stith Richardson and H. A. G. Lee, his securities came into court and entered into bond conditioned and payable as the law directs and took the oath prescribed by law for guardian.

It is ordered by the court that Milton G. Turner be paid by the county Trustee seven dollars and fifty cents for taking a list of taxable property and polls for the first civil district of Lauderdale county for the year 1840. The ayes and noes on this appropriation were; ayes, Condry, Barfield, Lewis, Maxwell, Sawyers and Turner; noes, Hinton and Richardson.

It is ordered by the court that John M. C. Robertson be paid by the
Pg. county Trustee seven dollars and fifty cents for taking a list of taxable
300 property and polls for the second civil district of Lauderdale county for the year 1840. The ayes and noes on this appropriation were; ayes, Condry, Barfield, Lewis, Maxwell, Sawyers, and Turner; noes, Hinton and Richardson.

It is ordered by the court that Thomas J. Childress be paid by the county Trustee seven dollars and fifty cents for taking a list of taxable property and polls for the third civil district of Lauderdale county for the year 1840. The ayes and noes on this appropriation were; ayes, Condry, Barfield, Lewis, Maxwell, Sawyers and Turner; noes, Hinton and Richardson.

It is ordered by the court that Henry Willard be paid by the county Trustee seven dollars and fifty cents for taking a list of taxable property and polls for the fourth civil district of Lauderdale county for the year 1840. The ayes and noes on this appropriation were; ayes, Condry, Barfield, Lewis, Maxwell, Sawyers and Turner; noes, Hinton and Richardson.

It is ordered by the court that Hennis Champ be paid by the county Trustee seven dollars and fifty cents for taking a list of taxable property and polls for the fifth civil district of Lauderdale county for the year 1840. The ayes and noes were; ayes, Condry, Barfield, Lewis, Maxwell, Sawyers and Turner; noes, Hinton and Richardson.

Pg. It is ordered by the court that Elnathan H. Condry be paid by the county
301 Trustee seven dollars and fifty cents for taking a list of taxable property and polls for the sixth civil district of Lauderdale county for the year 1840. The ayes and noes were; ayes, Condry, Barfield, Lewis, Maxwell, Sawyers and Turner; noes, Hinton and Richardson.

It is ordered by the court that Edwin H. Hinton be paid by the county Trustee seven dollars and fifty cents for taking a list of taxable property and polls for the seventh civil district of Lauderdale county for the year 1840. The ayes and noes on this appropriation were; ayes, Condry, Barfield, Lewis, Maxwell, Sawyers and Turner; noes, Hinton and Richardson.

It is ordered by the court that Henry R. Chambers be paid by the county Trustee seven dollars and fifty cents for taking a list of taxable property and polls for the eighth civil district of Lauderdale county for the year 1840. The ayes and noes on this appropriation were,ayes; Condry, Barfield, Lewis, Maxwell, Sawyers and Turner; noes, Hinton and Richardson.

It is ordered by the court that Hiram C. Keller, James L. Green and Elison P. Fuller be appointed commissioners for to let out to the lowest bidder to be done as soon as practicable the repairing the bridge over Cane creek

Pg. 302 on the road from Ripley to Ashport and that they report to the October term of this court.

Ordered that the court be adjourned until 8 o'clock tomorrow morning.

J. H. Maxwell, Chairman
James L. Green, J.P.
Elnathan H. Condry, J.P.

Teusday morning the court met pursuant to adjournment. Present the worshipful John H. Maxwell, Chairman and Esqs. Sawyers, Hinton, Green, Robertson, Chambers, Foster, Vassor, Barfield, Turner, Condray and Lewis, associate Justices, Isaac M. Steele, Clerk and G. L. Rutherford, Sheriff.

This day David P. Posey who was appointed at the June term 1839 of the court, guardian of Virginia Hill Keller, minor heir of Imry Keller dec'd returned in open court on oath an inventory of the property that has come to his hands of said estate which is received and ordered to be recorded.

This day Hiram C. Keller who was chosen and appointed at the May term 1840 of this court guardian of Hiram W. Keller, minor heir of Imry Keller dec'd returned in open court on oath an inventory of the property that has come to his hands of said estate which is received and ordered to be recorded.

Pg. 303 The court adjourned for half an hour.

The court met pursuant to adjournment.

This day the court proceeded to elect a Coroner for the county of Lauderdale for the next two years on counting out the votes it appeared that Isaac Braden was duly elected whereupon he came into court with Abel H. Pope and David P. Posey, his securities and entered into bond and the same was acknowledged in open court whereupon he took the several oaths prescribed by law.

This day the court proceeded to elect a Ranger for Lauderdale county for the ensuing two years whereupon John H. Maxwell was duly elected entered into bond with James L. Green and Isaac Braden for securities acknowledging themselves indebted in open court whereupon the several oaths prescribed by law was administered to him.

This day the court proceeded to elect an Entry Taker for Lauderdale county for the ensuing four years whereupon James Braden was duly elected entered into bond conditioned and payable as the law directs with Joseph Wardlow, William P. Gaines and Isaac Braden as securities acknowledging themselves indebted in open court whereupon the several oaths prescribed by law

Pg. 304 was administered to him.

This day the court proceeded to elect a County Surveyor for Lauderdale county for the ensuing four years whereupon Able H. Pope was duly elected entered into bond conditioned and payable as the law directs with William B. Sawyers, Hiram C. Keller, I. J. Penson and William P. Gaines as securities acknowledging themselves indebted in open court whereupon the several oaths prescribed by law was administered to him.

Ordered by the court that John L. Hearring be released from the payment of the tax on one slave valued at five hundred dollars and that the same be certified to the Treasurer and County Trustee.

Abel H. Pope came into court and requested to have William B. Sawyers qualified as Deputy Surveyor whereupon the several oaths prescribed by law for Surveyors was administered to him.

James L. Green records his stock mark (to wit) a slit in each ear.

Ordered that the court adjourn until court in course.

J. H. Maxwell, Chairman
James L. Green, J.P.
Elnathan H. Condry, J.P.

Pg. Be it remembered that at a county court began and held for the county of
305 Lauderdale and State of Tennessee in the court house in the town of Ripley on the first Monday in August in the year of our Lord one thousand eight hundred and forty and the sixty fifth year of American Independence it being the third day of said month. Present the worshipful H. R. Chambers, Chairman, Elnathan H. Condry, J. M. C. Robertson, Esqs. commissioned and qualified as the law directs holding the quroum court for said county, Isaac M. Steele, Clerk and G. L. Rutherford, Sheriff, proclamation having been made the court proceeded to business.

It is ordered that John H. Maxwell agent of the heirs of John Pope be released from the double tax on 500 acres of land listed in seventh district belonging to said heirs by paying the single tax thereon and the commissioners fee for listing and that the sheriff be allowed a credit for the same tract erroneously listed in the sixth district and the same be certified to the county Trustee.

It is ordered that William Campbell be released from the double tax on 1050 acres of land in the seventh civil district by the payment of the single tax and the commissioners fee for listing the same.

The court adjourned until 2 o'clock.

Pg. The court met pursuant to adjournment.

306 This day Isaac M. Steele, Clerk of the county court presented a settlement made by him with A. R. Carrigan, Administrator of William Carrigan dec'd which is received by the court and ordered to be recorded.

John H. Maxwell, Esq. appeared and took his seat as one of the court.

This day H. A. G. Lee and Stith Richardson, Executor of the last will and testament of Susan C. Marley dec'd returned on oath into court an inventory of said estate which is received and ordered to be recorded.

This day John M. C. Robertson, Trustee of Lauderdale county came into court with Pleasant G. Davenport and Carter Whitson, his securities and entered into bond conditioned and payable as the law directs for the safe keeping and paying over of the common school fund.

This day Pleasant G. Davenport produced in open court the last will and testament of George Moore dec'd wherein he is appointed Executor and offered the same for probate. The valedity of said will was contested by William A. Cleaves who entered into bond as the Executor mentioned in said will for the
Pg. sum of five hundred dollars to be void on condition he prosecutes said suit
307 to effect or in case of failure to pay all cost.

Ordered that the court adjourn until court in course.

H. R. Chambers, Chairman Quorum Court
Elnathan H. Condray, J.P.
J. H. Maxwell, J.P.

Pg. Be it remembered that at a county court began and held for the county of
308 Lauderdale and State of Tennessee in the court house in the town of Ripley on the first Monday in September in the year of our Lord, one thousand eight hundred and forty and the sixty fifty year of American Independence, it being the seventh day of said month. Present the worshipful Henry R. Chambers, Chairman and Elijah Lake and Elnathan H. Condray, Esqs. commissioned and qualified as the law directs holding the quorum court for said county, Isaac M. Steele, Clerk and Griffith L. Rutherford, Sheriff. Proclamation having been made the churt proceeded to business.

It appearing to the satisfaction of the court that I. D. Coachman has died leaving no will and Mrs. C. A. R. Coachman having relinquished her right to the administration in favor of Benjamin S. Tyus and Thomas W. Tyus and they having entered into bond conditioned and payable as the law directs and took the oath of administrators it is ordered that letters of administration issue to them.

It is ordered that William Turner be released from the payment of the state and county tax on lot No. 33 in the town of Ripley valued at $120. erroneously listed and that the same be certified to Comptroller of the Treasury and County Trustee.

Pg. 311 It is ordered that John M. Durant be released from the payment of the tax on 80 acres of land vlaued at $1000. and one slave valued at $500. erroneously listed and that the same be certified to the Comptroller of the Treasurer and County Trustee.

It is ordered that William Turner, David M. Henning, Thomas Rice and John Rice be appointed commissioners to lay off to C. A. R. Coachman, widow of I. D. Coachman dec'd her years provision and that they report to the November term of this court.

Henry Sumrow records his stock mark (to wit) a smooth crop of off the right ear and a split in the left.

It is ordered that Charles Jones be released from the payment of double tax on 1930 acres of land by the payment of the single tax and that the same be certified to the Comptroller and County Trustee.

This day Reubin Alphin who was appointed guardian of John H. Johnson, Washington Johnson, Polly M. Johnson, Sally Johnson and Nancy Johnson, minor heirs of Sally Johnson dec'd came into court and resigned said appointment
Pg. whereupon the court chose and appointed James H. Givin guardian in his place
312 whereupon said Givin came into court and took the oath of guardian accordingly, having entered into bond conditioned and payable as the law directs.

Ordered that court adjourn until court in course.

H. R. Chambers, Chairman Quorum Court
Elijah Lake, J.P.
Elnathan H. Condray, J.P.

Pg. 313 Be it remembered at a county court began and held for the county of Lauderdale and State of Tennessee in the house of Ezekial Farmer, the circuit court being in session in the court house in the town of Ripley on the first Monday in October in the year of our Lord one thousand eight hundred and forty and the sixty fifth year of American Independence it being the fifth day of said month, present and presiding the worshipful John H. Maxwell, Esq., Chairman and Esqs. E. H. Condray, J. L. Green, James Lewis, H. R. Chambers, Sawyers, Barfield, Richardson, Willard commissioned and qualified as the law directs holding the court for said county, Isaac M. Steele, Clerk and Griffith L. Rutherford, Sheriff. Proclamation having been made the court proceeded to business.

Fernifer McCoy records his stock mark (to wit) a swallow fork in the right ear and an under half crop in the left ear.

This day John H. Maxwell, Esq., Chairman of the county court called on Isaac M. Steele, Clerk of the county court for his receipts which he produced are in the words and figures following (to wit)

Comptrollers Office
Nashville, Tennessee
Sept. 7, 1840

Pg. 314 Received from I. M. Steele his Statement of Revenue collected as Clerk of Lauderdale County Court from April 6, 1840 to Sept. 1, 1840.

Amount collected	$84.96
Commissions	2.12
Warrant No. 1062 this day for	$82.84

Daniel Graham, Comptroller

$82.84 No. 1062
Jackson, October 2, 1840

Received from Isaac M. Steele eighty two dollars and eighty four cents audity to him by No. 1062 and due on account of Revenue collected as Clerk

Pg. 314 cont. of Lauderdale County Court from April 6, 1840 to Sept. 1, 1840.
Signed duplicates John M. Campbell, Cas. for
Treasurer of Tennessee

Trustees Office
Ripley, Tennessee
Sept. 16, 1840

Received from I. M. Steele his Statement of Revenue collected as Clerk of Lauderdale County Court from April 6, 1840 to Sept. 1, 1840.

Amount collected	$72.00
Commissions	1.80

J. M. C. Robertson
Trustee of Lauderdale County

Received from Isaac M. Steele seventy dollars and twenty cents the
Pg. amount due and oweing from him on account of revenue collected as clerk of
315 Lauderdale County Court from the sixth of April, 1840 to first of Sept., 1840.
Givin under my hand at office this 25th day of Sept., 1840.

J. M. C. Robertson
Trustee of Lauderdale County

Ordered that the County Trustee pay Isaac M. Steele Clerk of the county court sixty six dollars sixty two and a half cents for issuing six road orders at July term for issuing seven orders for juries of view at said term, issuing venire facias for circuit court at July term, for issuing three road orders September term, for recording settlement with William T. Moorehead, former County Trustee, for recording settlement with himself as County Court Clerk, for all services in regard to common schools for the year 1840, for ex-officio services for the year 1840 and for one blank book bought for the use of the county. Present and voting for said appropriation, Maxwell, Richardson, Lewis, Condray, Chambers, Green, Turner, Barfield, Sawyers and Willard a majority of all the Justices of said county.

Ordered that the county Trustee pay Isaac Braden seventy four dollars for building a bridge over Bates fork of Cane creek on the Ashport road, Present and voting for said appropriation Esqs., Maxwell, Richardson, Lewis,
Pg. Condray, Chambers, Green, Turner, Barfield, Sawyers and Willard a majority of
316 all the Justices of said county.

Ordered that the County Trustee pay Isaac Braden, Coroner of Lauderdale County five dollars for holding and inquest on the body of John Cochrane. Present and voting for said appropriation, Esqs. Maxwell, Richardson, Lewis, Condray, Chambers, Green, Turner, Barfield, Sawyers and Willard.

This day James Barfield presented to the court his resignation as a Justice of the Peace for the third civil district of Lauderdale county which was accepted by the court.

The court adjourned until four o'clock.

The court met pursuant to adjournment.

Ordered that the county trustee pay Elijah B. Foster, Esq. five dollars for holding an inquest on the body of Joseph Rodgers. Present and voting for said appropriation, Maxwell, Lewis, Richardson, Chambers, Condray, Sawyers.

Ordered that William W. Lea be released from the payment of double tax on all his property in Lauderdale county by the payment of the single tax and that the same be certified to the Comptroller and County Trustee.

This day E. P. Fuller proved by his own oath the killing of one wolf in the county of Lauderdale over four months old there being five Justices present ordered that same be certified to the Comptroller.

Pg. This day John H. Maxwell, Esq., Chairman of the county court called on
317 G. L. Rutherford late Clerk of the county court for his receipts which he

Pg. 317 cont. produced which are in the words and figures follwing (to wit)

Comptrollers Office
Nashville, Tennessee
Sept. 7. 1840

Received from G. L. Rutherford his statement of revenue collection as late Clerk of Lauderdale county court.
From Sept. 1, 1839 to April 6, 1840

Amount collected	$218.62
Commissions off	5.45
Warrant No. 1061 this day for	$213.17

Daniel Graham, Comptroller

$213.17 No. 1061

Jackson, October 2, 1840.

Received from G. L. Rutherford two hundred and thirteen dollars and seventeen cents audited to him by No. 1061 and due on account of revenue collected as former Clerk of Lauderdale County Court from Sept. 1, 1839 to April 1, 1840. Signed duplicates.

John M. Campbell, cas for
Treasurer of Tennessee

Pg. 318 Received of G. L. Rutherford late Clerk of Lauderdale County Court seventy two dollars and twenty five cents in full of the revenue collected by him by virtue of said office from merchants, peddlers and privileges from the first of Sept., 1839 to the sixth of April, 1840.
Sept. 25, 1840

J. M. C. Robertson
Trustee of Lauderdale County

Received of G. L. Rutherford, Sheriff of Lauderdale County one hundred and twenty eight dollars and eighty cents in county claims and cash in part of the county tax for which he is bound for the year 1840.
Sept. 25, 1840

J. M. C. Robertson
Trustee of Lauderdale County

Ordered that the court adjourn until ten o'clock tomorrow morning.

J. H. Maxwell, Chairman
James L. Green, J.P.
Elnathan H. Condry, J.P.

Tuesday morning court met pursuant to adjournment.

It appearing to the satisfaction of the court that Jeremiah Cotter has died leaving no will and Absolum G. W. Byrn having applied for letters of administration on said estate and the court being satisfied as to his claim to the said administration and he having entered into bond conditioned and payable as the law directs and took the oath of Administrator, it is there-
Pg. fore ordered that he have letters of administration accordingly.
319 It appearing to the satisfaction of the court that John Cochrane has died leaving no will and the court being satisfied to John Fletchers claim to letters of administration and he having entered into bond conditioned and payable as the law requires and took the oath of administrator, it is therefore ordered that he have letters of administration accordingly.

Pg. 319 cont. This day James Hodges proved by his own oath the killing of one wolf over four months old in Lauderdale county there being five Justices present ordered that the same be certified to the Comptroller.

Ordered that the County Trustee pay William Williams thirty dollars for repairing the bridge on Cane creek on Ashport road. Ayes on this appropriation were Chambers, Lewis, Condray, Richardson, Turner and Maxwell.

Ordered that G. L. Rutherford, Sheriff of Lauderdale County be allowed a credit of fourteen dollars and seventy cents for insolvents, persons removed from the county and errors in tax list and that the same be certified to the Comptroller and County Trustee.

Pg. 320 Ordered that the court adjourn for one hour.

The court met pursuant to adjournment.

This day the last will and testament of George Moore dec'd was produced in open court and the execution thereof proved by the subscribing witnesses, Carter Whitson and James M. Barber the same is ordered to be recorded and that Pleasant G. Davenport the executor named in said will have letters testamentary he having entered into bond conditioned and payable as the law directs and took the oath of Executor.

This day the court proceeded to appoint judges and clerks for the several precincts of Lauderdale county to hold the election for President and vice President of the United States (to wit)

For first district D. M. Herring, John M. Durant and John Bradford for Judges, James G. Anthony, John N. Golding and Samuel L. Gause, Clerks.

For second district R. L. Byrn, John H. Maxwell and Robert C. Campbell, Judges, William T. Moorehead, R. H. McGaughey and I. R. Pinson, Clerks.

For the third district A. H. Pope, H. C. Keller and John C. Barnes, Judges, C. C. Dyer, T. J. Childress and James Barfield, Clerks.

For the fourth district John Vassor, Samuel Givins and J. M. Alexander, Judges, Henry Willard, James Givin and William M. Lea, Clerks.

Pg. 321 Fifth district W. H. Haralson, R. G. Henley, and John Brown, Clerks, G. Temple, John Fletcher and B. Dunn, Judges.

Sixth district A. Wood, Isaac Moore and E. B. Foster, Judges, W. Boydston, W. R. Ledbetter and John W. Nearn, Clerks.

Seventh district E. Wright, E. H. Hinton and H. Crihfield, Jr., Judges, W. D. Lee, W. Wright and J. W. Richardson, Clerks.

Eighth district Benjamin Porter, John Soward and L. H. Duanway, Judges, William B. Sawyers, C. Rounsaville and O. R. Willis, Clerks.

Ordered that Hiram C. Keller, John M. C. Robertson and Milton G. Turner be appointed a committee to examine all applicants for the benefit of the Pauper Laws in Lauderdale County for the next twelve months whereupon said committee came into court and took the oath prescribed by law.

Ordered that the following good and lawful men of the county of Lauderdale be summoned as jurors for the next circuit court to be held for the county of Lauderdale on the first Monday in February next (to wit) Cyrus Webb, William Turner, Pleasant C. Dyal, Christopher Watson, Lancy Graves, Isaac D. Maxwell, John B. Byrn, A. Phillips, John J. Nelson, Hiram C. Keller, Benjamin Whitson, Thomas L. Clark, James Givin, John Acre, Leroy F. Lockard,

Pg. 322 Armstead Wood, Dickerson Jennings, Hiram Meadows, Leonard Dunavant, H. Crihfield, Esq., Henry Sumrow, William Misskelly, James Soward and Richard Parr and Fred Barfield and Absolam G. W. Byrn, Constables to wait on the court and jury.

It is ordered that the court adjourn until 8 o'clock tomorrow morning.

S. Richardson, Chairman Protem
J. M. Lewis, J.P.
Elnathan H. Condry, J.P.

Wednesday morning court met pursuant to adjournment.

This day the court chose and appointed David A. Bradford guardian of

Pg. William T.,Mary Jane, Eleanor Ann, Robert A. and Caledonia T. Burk, minor
322 heirs of Arnold Burk dec'd in the place of Sampson Smith former guardian
cont. dec'd whereupon said Bradford came into court, entered into bond conditioned and payable as the law directs and took the oath of guardian.

It appearing to the satisfaction of the court that Michael Cleaves has died leaving no will and William A. Cleaves having applied for letters of
Pg. administration and the court being satisfied as to his claimto the adminis-
323 tration and he having entered bond conditioned and payable as the law directs. It is therefore ordered that he have letters of administration.

Ordered that the court adjourn until court in course.

Stith Richardson, Chairman Protem
E. H. Hinton, J.P.
Elnathan H. Condry, J.P.

Pg. Be it remembered that at a county court began and held for the county of
324 Lauderdale and state of Tennessee in the court house in the town of Ripley on the first Monday in November in the year of our Lord one thousand eight hundred and forty and the sixty fifth year of American Independence it being the second day of said month. Present and presiding the worshipful J. M. C. Robertson, Chairman Protem, Esqs. Lake and Condry commissioned and qualified as the law directs holding the quorum court for said county, Isaac M. Steele, Clerk and Griffith L. Ruthesford, Sheriff. Proclamation having been duly made the court proceeded to business.

It is ordered that John Smith be permitted to list 100 acres of land in the seventh civil district of Lauderdale county for the single tax for the year 1840.

This day the last will and testament of Jonathan Jones dec'd was produced in open court and the execution thereof proved by Lovick Lanier and Pleasant Gardner subscribing witnesses thereto and ordered to be recorded that John H. Lanier one of the executors named in said will have letters testamentary he having entered into bond conditioned and payable as the law directs and took the oath of executor.

Pg. This day A. G. W. Byrn, administrator of the estate of Jeremiah Cotter
325 dec'd returned his inventory of said estate upon oath which is received and ordered to be recorded.

This day John Fullen, administrator of the estate of William Fullen dec'd returned on oath an additional sale bill of said estate which is ordered to be recorded.

It is ordered that court adjourn until court in course.

J. M. C. Robertson, J.P.
Elijah Lake, J.P.
Elnathan H. Condry, J.P.

Pg. Be it remembered that a county court began and held for the county of
326 Lauderdale and state of Tennessee in the court house in the town of Ripley on the first Monday in December in the year of our Lord one thousand eight hundred and forty and the sixty fifth year of American Independence it being the seventh day of said month. Present and presiding the worshipful E. Lake, Chairman Protem and E. H. Condry and John Maxwell, Esqs. holding the quorum court for said county, Isaac M. Steele, Clerk and G. L. Rutherford, Sheriff. Proclamation having been duly made the court proceeded to business.

This day D. M. Herring, William Turner, Thomas G. Rice and John P. Rice commissioners appointed at the September term of this court to lay off to C. A. R. Coachman, widow of I. D. Coachman dec'd her years provision reported to court which report is received and ordered to be recorded.

Ordered that Sarah Coleman be paid by the county Trustee fifteen dollars and fifty cents for the funeral expenses of John Williams a pauper.

This day P. G. Davenport, administrator of the estate of James W. Cheek dec'd returned in open court on oath an inventory of said estate which is received and ordered to be recorded.

Pg. 327 Ordered that James A. Morris bring Sarah Jackson an orphan into court at the next term to be dealt with according to law.

Ordered that the court adjourn until court in course.

Elijah Lake, Chairman Protem
of the quorum court
Elnathan H. Condray, J.P.
J. H. Maxwell, J.P.

Be it remembered that at a county court began and held for the County of Lauderdale and State of Tennessee in the court house in the town of Ripley on the first Monday in January in the year of our Lord one thousand eight hundrec and forty one it being the fourth day of said month and the sixty fifty year of American Independence, Present the worshipful J. H. Maxwell, E. Lake, Samuel V. Gilliland, James L. Green, J. M. C. Robertson, E. H. Hinton, E. H. Condray and Turner and W.B. Sawyers, Esqs. sitting and holding a County Court for said county, Isaac M. Steele, Clerk and G. L. Rutherford, Sheriff. Proclamation being made the court proceeded to business.

The court proceeded to elect a Chairman for the year 1841, whereupon James L. Green was duly elected.

Pg. 328 This day Moses E. Stone, guardian of John W. Rudder one of the heirs of Samuel Rudder dec'd made a report on oath in open court of the property belonging to said heirs which was received and ordered to be recorded.

Ordered that the County Trustee pay Abel H. Pope twenty five dollars, thirty three and one third cents for running and marking the boundary line between Lauderdale and Dyer Counties.

This day A. H. Pope, County Surveyor returned to court the survey of the line between Lauderdale and Dyer Counties which is ordered to be recorded.

This day Hiram C. Keller, guardian of Hiram W. Keller one of the heirs of Imri Keller dec'd returned on oath in open court a report of the property belonging to said heir which was received and ordered to be recorded.

This day John Fletcher, administrator of the estate of John Cochrane dec'd returned on oath in open court a sale bill of said estate which is received and ordered to be recorded.

It appearing to the satisfaction of the court that Charlotte Andrews has died leaving no will and Samuel P. Andrews having applied for letters of
Pg. administration and the court being satisfied with his claim to the administra-
329 tion and he having entered into bond with approved security and took the oath of Administrator it is therefore ordered that he have letters of administration.

Ordered by the court that Abel H. Pope be appointed to make a general plan or map of the County of Lauderdale and that he have the same done by the October term of this court.

This court proceeded to lay a county tax for the year 1841 whereupon the following rates were laid to wit, Jury tax 21½ cents on each hundred dollars worth of property, contingent tax on the same 2½ cents, road and bridge tax on the same 2½ cents, poor tax on the same 2½ cents, jury tax on polls 12½ cents, poor tax on same 12 cents, tax on privileges the same as state tax. Those who voted for said rates were Turner, Gilliland, Robertson, Green, Maxwell, Lake, Condray, Hinton and Sawyers, a majority of all the Justices for said county.

The court proceeded to elect a commissioner to take the census of Lauderdale County whereupon E. H. Hinton was duly elected.

Pg. 330 It appearing to the court that Mathew Turner has died leaving no will and Jonathan Larry having applied for letters of administration and the Court being satisfied with his claim to the administration and he having given bond with approved security and took the oath of Administrator, it is therefore

Pg. 330 cont. ordered that he have letters of administration accordingly, ten voting in the affirmative a majority of all the Justices being present.

Ordered that the County Trustee pay G. L. Rutherford, Sheriff seventy dollars for his ex-officio services and for furnishing wood and water for the court for the year 1840.

This day Blair H. Lee proved by his own oath the killing of one wolf over the age of four months in the county of Lauderdale therebeing five Justices present. Ordered that the same be certified to the treasurer.

This day the court proceeded to elect a quorum to hold the monthly courts for the year 1841 whereon James L. Green, E. H. Hinton and John H. Maxwell, Esqs. were duly elected.

Ordered that the county Trustee pay H. R. Chambers nine dollars for holding the quorum courts for the year 1840.

Ordered that the County Trustee pay E. H. Condray thirteen dollars and fifty cents for holding the quorum courts for the year 1840.

Pg. 331 Ordered that the county Trustee pay Elijah Lake nine dollars for holding the quorum courts for the year 1840.

Ordered that the County Trustee pay Samuel V. Gilliland five dollars for settling with G. L. Rutherford, Clerk and William T. Moorehead, County Trustee as commissioner of Revenue for the year 1840.

Ordered that the County Trustee pay Rezin L. Byrn five dollars for settling with G. L. Rutherford, Clerk and William T. Moorehead, County Trustee as commissioner of Revenue for the year 1840.

Ordered there being a majority of all the Justices present that Milton G. Turner be appointed a revenue commissioner to take a list of taxable property and polls for the first district of Lauderdale County for the year 1841.

Ordered there being a majority of all the Justices present that John H. Maxwell be appointed a revenue commissioner to take a list of taxable property and polls for the second district of Lauderdale County for year 1841.

Pg. 332 Ordered there being a majority of all the Justices present that Elijah Lake be appointed a revenue commissioner to take a list of the taxable property and polls for the third district of Lauderdale County for the year 1841.

Ordered there being a majority of all the Justices present that Henry Willard be appointed a revenue commissioner to take a list of the taxable property and polls for the fourth district of Lauderdale County for the year 1841.

Ordered there being a majority of all the Justices present that Rezin G. Henly be appointed a revenue commissioner to take a list of the taxable property and polls for the fifth district of Lauderdale County for the year 1841.

Ordered there being a majority of all the Justices present that E. H. Condray be appointed a revenue commissioner to take a list of the taxable property and polls for the sixth district of Lauderdale County for the year 1841.

Ordered there being a majority of all the Justices present that E. H. Hinton be appointed a revenue commissioner to take a list of the taxable property and polls for the seventh district of Lauderdale County for the year 1841.

Ordered there being a majority of all the Justices present that William

Pg. 333 B. Sawyers be appointed a revenue commissioner to take in a list of taxable property and polls for the eighth district of Lauderdale County for the year 1841.

Ordered there being a majority of all the Justices present that Samuel V. Gilliland and Rezin L. Byrn be appointed commissioners of Revenue to settle with the county officers for the year 1841.

This day H. A. G. Lee one of the Executors of the last will and testament of Susan C. Marley dec'd returned in open court on oath a sale bill of said estate which is received and ordered to be recorded.

This day John H. Lanier, Executor of the last will and testament of Jonathan Jones dec'd returned in open court on oath a sale bill of said estate

Pg. which is received and ordered to be recorded.
333 Ordered that the court adjourn until nine o'clock tomorrow morning.
cont.

James L. Green, Chairman
J. H. Maxwell, J.P.
Elnathan H. Condray, J.P.

Tuesday morning the court met pursuant to adjournment.

Pg. This day Isaac M. Steele presented to court a settlement made by him as
334 Clerk with P. G. Davenport, Administrator of James W. Cheek dec'd which was received and ordered to be recorded.

Ordered that the County Trustee pay Isaac M. Steele four dollars and 43$\frac{3}{4}$ cents for issuing jury tickets, road orders, etc.

This day David A. Bradford, guardien of the minor heirs of Arnold Burke, dec'd returned on oath in open court a report of the property which has come to his hands by virtue of his appointment to said guardianship which is received and ordered to be recorded.

Ordered by the court that Elijah Lake, James B. Crook, Henry Willard, George R. Williams and William Williams be appointed commissioners to view and examine the bridge across cane creek on the Fulton road and report to the April term of this Court the propriety or impropriety of building another bridge across the same or of receiving the one already built.

The court adjourned until court in course.

James L. Green, Chairman
J. H. Maxwell, J.P.
E. H. Condray, J.P.

Pg. Be it remembered that at a County Court began and held for the County of
335 Lauderdale and State of Tennessee in the court house in the town of Ripley on the first Monday in February in the year of our Lord one thousand eight hundred and forty one it being the first day of said month, present the worshipful James L. Green, Chairman, John H. Maxwell and Elnathan H. Condray, Esqs. sitting and holding a quorum court for said county, Isaac M. Steele, Clerk and G. L. Rutherford, Esq., Sheriff. Proclamation being made the court proceeded to business.

This day Isaac M. Steele presented a settlement made by him as clerk with William G. Rounsaville, Administrator of Amos Rounsaville dec'd which was received and ordered to be recorded.

E. H. Hinton, Esq. appeared and took his seat.

Ordered that the commissioners for the town of Ripley shall cause the stumps and other obstructions to be removed off of the site for the court house.

Pg. This day James B. Hutcherson produced to court the certificate of G. L.
336 Rutherford, Sheriff of his election as constable for the fourth civil district of Lauderdale County and entered into bond with approved security and took the several oaths prescribed by law for constable.

This day the court proceeded to bind Mary Jane Dyal and orphan to Mary Elkins and ordered that P. C. Dyal have his apprentice bond given up to him and be released from any further liability on said orphans account.

Ordered that the court adjourn for one hour.

The court met pursuant to adjournment.

This day John L. Flippin, Administrator of John Flippin dec'd returned an additional inventory of said estate on oath which is received and ordered to be recorded.

This day Ezekial Farmer who was charged with having begotten an illegitimate child on the body of Charlotte Bibb came into court and entered into bond with approved security to the Chairman of the county courts, he and his securities acknowledging themselves indebted, conditioned for the faithful

Pg. payment to said Charlotte Bibb of the money allowed her by law.
336 This day Isaac J. Pinson who was charged with having begotten an illegit-
cont. imate child on the body of Delphia Byler came into court and entered into
Pg. bond with approved security he and his securities acknowledging themselves
337 indebted in open court for the faithful payment to said Delphia of the penalty
mentioned in said bond.

It is ordered that the court adjourn until court in course.

James L. Green, Chairman
J. H. Maxwell, J.P.
E. Hinton, J.P.

Pg. State of Tennessee, Lauderdale County Court, March Term
338 Be it remembered that at a County Court began and held for the County of
Lauderdale and State of Tennessee in the Court House in the Town of Ripley on the first Monday in March in the year of our Lord one thousand eight hundred and forty one it being the first day of said month and the Sixty fifty year of American Independence, present the worshipful James L. Green, Esq., Chairman, John H. Maxwell and E. H. Hinton, Esqs., duly commissioned and qualified as the law directs holding a quorum court for said county, Isaac M. Steele, Clerk and Griffith L. Rutherford, Sheriff. Proclamation being made the court proceeded to business.

This day Isaac M. Steele presented to court a settlement made by him as clerk of the county court with Gilly Hunter, guardian of William Hunter, minor heir of Mabry Hunter dec'd which was received and ordered to be recorded.

This day Abel H. Pope produced to court a commission from his Excellency, James K. Polk, Governor of the State of Tennessee as a Justice of the Peace for Lauderdale County whereupon by order of the court the several oaths prescribed by law was administered to him.

This day Henry Crihfield, Sr., Administrator of Joseph H. Adams dec'd returned on oath in open court an additional inventory of said estate which is received and ordered to be recorded by the court.

Pg. March Term 1841
339 This day Jonathan Laney, Administrator of the estate of Mathew Turner
dec'd returned on oath in open court an inventory and also a sale bill of said estate which is received and ordered to be recorded by the court.

Ordered that court adjourn until court in course.

James L. Green, Chairman
J. H. Maxwell, J.P.
E. H. Hinton, J.P.

Be it remembered that at a county court began and held for the County of Lauderdale and State of Tennessee in the court house in the town of Ripley on the first Monday in April in the year of our Lord one thousand eight hundred and forty one it being the fifth day of said month and the sixty fifty year of American Independence. Present and presiding the worshipful James L. Green, Esq., Chairman and Sawyers, Chambers, Hinton, Richardson, Condray, Maxwell, Robertson, Turner, Gilliland and Lake, Esqs., duly commissioned and qualified according to law sitting and holding a county court for said county, Isaac M. Steele, Clerk and Griffith L. Rutherford, Esq., Sheriff. Proclamation being first made the court proceeded to business.

Pg. This day Isaac M. Steele, Clerk of this court agreeable to law called
340 upon Griffith L. Rutherford, Esq., Sheriff and collector of the public taxes
for the County of Lauderdale to renew his revenue bonds whereupon he entered into the following bonds with his securities he and they acknowledging ~~thems elves~~ said bonds in open court (Viz)

State of Tennessee) Know all men by these presents that we, Griffith
Lauderdale County) L. Rutherford, Robert C. Campbell, Stith Richardson

Pg. 340 cont. and James L. Green, all of the State and County aforesaid are held and firmly bound unto James K. Polk, Governor of the State of Tennessee for the time being and his successors im office for the use of said state in the sum of two thousand dollars to the payment of which well and truly to be made we bind ourselves, our heirs, executors and Administrators jointly and severally firmly by these presents sealed with our seals and dated the fifth day of April 1841.

The condition of the above obligation is such that whereas the above bound Griffith L. Rutherford has been duly and constitutionally elected Sheriff and Collector of the public taxes of said County of Lauderdale for two years from the first Saturday in March 1840. Now if the said Griffith L.
Pg. 341 Rutherford shall well and truly collect all state taxes which by law he ought to collect and pay to the treasurer of the state all taxes by him collected or which ought to be collected or which ought to have been collected on or before the last day of December in each and every year in which he shall collect the taxes then the above obligation to be void, otherwise to remain in full force and virtue.

Acknowledged in open Court
Isaac M. Steele, Clerk

G. L. Rutherford, (Seal)
R. C. Campbell (Seal)
S. Richardson (Seal)
James L. Green (Seal)

State of Tennessee) We, Griffith L. Rutherford, Robert C. Campbell and
Lauderdale County) Stith Richardson jointly and severally acknowledge ourselves indebted to James L. Green, Esq., Chairman of the county court of Lauderdale County for the time being and his successors in office in the penal sum of four thousand dollars for which payment well and truly to be made we bind ourselves, our heirs, executors and administrators jointly, severally, firmly by these presents sealed with ourseals and dated the fifth day of April 1841.

Pg. 342 Whereas the said Griffith L. Rutherford on the seventh day of March 1840 duly and legally elected sheriff and collector of the State and County taxes for Lauderdale County for two years from the first Saturday in March 1840. Now if the said Griffith L. Rutherford shall well and truly collect and pay the Trustee of said County all county taxes by him collected or which he ought to have collected on or before the first Monday in October in each and every year in which he shall collect the taxes then this obligation to be void, otherwise to remain in full force and virtue.

Acknowledged in open court
James L. Green, Chairman

G. L. Rutherford (Seal)
R. C. Campbell (Seal)
S. Richardson (Seal)

Ordered that the County Trustee pay Isaac Braden, Coroner of Lauderdale five dollars out of any money in the County Treasury not otherwise appropriated for holding an inquest on the body of a negro belonging to Edmond Fitzpatrick; ayes, Esqs. Green, Richardson, Condray, Hinton, Sawyers and Turner.

Pg. 343 L. M. Sweet records his stock mark (to wit) a poplar leaf in the left ear and a hook in the right.

Ordered that Charles Smoot a pauper be allowed thirty dollars for the year 1841 under the superintendence of Milton G. Turner, Esq. and that the County Trustee pay the same quarterly out of any money in the county treasury not otherwise appropriated; ayes, Green, Richardson, Turner, Condray, Hinton, Gilliland, Sawyers and Chambers, Esqs.

Ordered that Rebecca Boswell a pauper be allowed forty dollars for the year 1841 under the superintendence of Green Baker as trustee and that the County Trustee pay the same quarterly out of any money in the county treasury not otherwise appropriated; ayes, Green, Richardson, Turner, Condray, Hinton, Gilliland, Sawyers and Chambers, Esqs.

Pg. 343 cont. This day Samuel P. Andrews, Administrator of the estate of Charlotte Andrews, dec'd returned on oath in open court an inventory of said estate which is received and ordered to be recorded.

Pg. 344 This day William P. Gaines, guardian of Juretta Niswanger returned on oath in open court an inventory of the goods and chattels, rights and credits of said ward which has come to his hands by virtue of his appointment which is receivable and ordered to be recorded.

Ordered that James McElyea be paid seven dollars sixty and a half cents by the County Trustee out of any money in the County Treasury not otherwise appropriated for funeral expenses incurred by him in the burial of James Neary a stranger; ayes, Lake, Sawyers, Condray, Chambers, Hinton, and Maxwell, Esqs.

This day Robert H. Hamil produced in court the certificate of G. L. Rutherford, Esq., Sheriff of Lauderdale of his election to the office of Constable for the second civil district of Lauderdale County, whereupon said Hamil entered into bond with approved security and took the several oaths prescribed by law.

This day Frederick Barfield produced to court the certificate of G. L. Rutherford, Esq., Sheriff of Lauderdale of his election to the office of Constable for the third civil district of Lauderdale County, whereupon said Barfield entered into bond with approved security and took the several oaths prescribed by law.

Pg. 345 Ordered by the court that the Clerk be authorized to release all persons from double taxes that may make application for the same during one month from this time and also that all persons may list their property on application to the Clerk by paying his fees for doing the same.

Ordered that the County Surveyor run off and sufficiently mark the prison bounds of Lauderdale County according to the Statute in that case made provided making said bounds one mile square taking the court house for the center and that he make a plot of said survey and state in his report explicitly the mark by which he has designated said bounds and that he make said report to the July term of this court.

Ordered by the court Elijah Lake, James B. Crook, Henry Willard, George R. Williams and William Williams be appointed commissioners to examine and
Pg. report to the July term of this court on the propriety or impropriety of re-
346 ceiving the bridge across Cane creek on the Fulton road and the value of said bridge, its condition, durability or the propriety or impropriety of building another bridge on said creek where the Fulton road crosses. That they also report what they believe to be the value of the present bridge if taken by the county without obligation to be kept up five years from the time of building the same and also what amount would be reasonable whould Dr. Lee give security to keep the same up five years from the time of building the same.

Pg. 347 Ordered that the following good and lawful men of the body of the County of Lauderdale be summoned as jurors for the next term of the circuit court to be held for the County of Lauderdale on the first Monday in June (to wit) David A. Bradford, Edmond Fitzpatrick, John P. Rice, Richard W. Green, John F. Jett, Robert C. Campbell, James Whitson, William Lunsford, Thomas J. Childress, Elijah Lake, Ellison P. Fuller, David C. Russell, John Vassor, Henry Willard, John Fletcher, James H. Hogsette, Eli Coble, Benjamin Nearn, James Long, Elnathan H. Condray, Henry Crihfield, Jr., John W. Nearn, Samuel Strickland, James A. Freeman and Henry Pitts, Sr., and Samuel Thompson and Robert H. Hamil, Constables to wait on the court and jury.

This day the court proceeded to appoint five Trustees of the Ripley Academy according to the Statute in such case made and provided whereupon the following men were appointed that is to say James L. Green, Stith Richardson, Griffith L. Rutherford, Rezin L. Byrn and Isaac M. Steele.

Ordered that Milton G. Turner be allowed the sum of seven dollars and
Pg. fifty cents for taking in a list of taxable property and polls for the first
348 civil district of Lauderdale County for the year 1841 to be paid by the County Trustee out of any money in the County Treasury not otherwise appropriated;

Pg. 318 cont. ayes, Esqs. Sawyers, Condray, Gilliland, Chambers, Hinton, Maxwell, Richardson and Green.

Ordered that John H. Maxwell be allowed the sum of seven dollars and fifty cents for taking in a list of taxable property and polls for the second civil district of Lauderdale County for the year 1841 to be paid by the County Trustee out of any money in the County Treasury not otherwise appropriated; ayes, Esqs. Sawyers, Condray, Gilliland, Chambers, Hinton, Maxwell, Richardson and Green.

Ordered that Elijah Lake be allowed the sum of seven dollars and fifty cents for taking in a list of taxable property and polls for the third civil district of Lauderdale County for the year 1841 to be paid by the County Trustee out of any money in the County Treasury not otherwise appropriated; ayes, Esqs. Sawyers, Condray, Gilliland, Chambers, Hinton, Maxwell, Richardson and Green.

Pg. 349 Ordered that Henry Willard be allowed the sum of seven dollars and fifty cents for taking a list of taxable property and polls for the fourth civil district of Lauderdale County for the year 1841 to be paid by the County Trustee out of any money in the County Treasury not otherwise appropriated; ayes, Esqs. Sawyers, Condray, Gilliland, Chambers, Hinton, Maxwell, Richardson and Green.

Ordered that Rezin G. Henley be allowed the sum of seven dollars and fifty cents for taking a list of taxable property and polls for the fifth civil district of Lauderdale County for the year 1841 to be paid by the County Trustee out of any money in the County Treasury not otherwise appropriated; ayes, Esqs. Sawyers, Condray, Gilliland, Chambers, Hinton, Maxwell, Richardson and Green.

Ordered that Elnathan H. Condray be allowed the sum of seven dollars and fifty cents for taking a list of taxable property and polls for the sixth civil district of Lauderdale County for the year 1841 to be paid by the County Trustee out of any money in the County Treasury not otherwise appropriated;
Pg. 350 ayes, Esqs. Sawyers, Condray, Gilliland, Chambers, Hinton, Maxwell, Richardson and Green.

Ordered that E. H. Hinton be allowed the sum of seven dollars and fifty cents for taking a list of taxable property and polls for the seventh civil district of Lauderdale County for the year 1841 to be paid by the County Trustee out of any money in the County Treasury not otherwise appropriated; ayes, Esqs. Sawyers, Condray, Gilliland, Chambers, Hinton, Maxwell, Richardson and Green.

Ordered that William B. Sawyers be allowed the sum of seven dollars and fifty cents for taking a list of taxable property and polls for the eighth civil district of Lauderdale County for the year 1841 to be paid by the County Trustee out of any money in the County Treasury not otherwise appropriated; ayes, Esqs. Sawyers, Condray, Gilliland, Chambers, Hinton, Maxwell, Richardson and Green.

Pg. 351 Ordered that the court adjourn until eight o'clock tomorrow morning.

James L. Green, Chairman
Samuel V. Gilliland, J.P.
H. R. Chambers, J.P.

Tuesday morning April the sixth.

Court met pursuant to adjournment.

It appearing to the satisfaction of the court that Alexander Strickland has died leaving no will and Griffith L. Rutherford having applied for letters of administration and the court being satisfied with his claim to the administration and he having entered into bond with approved security and took the oath prescribed by law for administrator it is therefore ordered that he have letters of administration accordingly.

Griffith L. Rutherford, Esq., Sheriff and Collector of the public taxes for the County of Lauderdale took the oath of revenue collector as provided by the Statute in such cases.

Pg. 352 Ordered that court adjourn until court in course.

James L. Green, Chairman
Sam V. Gilliland, J.P.
Elnathan H. Condray, J.P.

May Term 1841

Be it remembered that at a county court began and held for the County of Lauderdale and State of Tennessee in the court house in the town of Ripley on the first Monday in May it being the third day of said month in the year of our Lord one thousand eight hundred and forty one and the sixty fifty year of the Independence of the United States of America. Present and presiding the worshipful James L. Green assisted by E. H. Hinton and John H. Maxwell, Esqs. all duly commissioned and qualified as the law directs sitting and holding a quorum court for said county, Isaac M. Steele, Clerk and Griffith L. Rutherford Esq., Sheriff. Proclamation being duly made the following proceedings were had and done in said court (to wit)

Pg. 353 This day Griffith L. Rutherford, Administrator of the estate of Alexander Strickland dec'd returned on oath in open court an inventory of said estate which is received and ordered to be recorded.

This day Isaac M. Steele, Clerk of the county court presented to the court a settlement made by him with Hiram C. Keller, Administrator of Joel J. Reynolds dec'd which was received and ordered to be recorded.

This day Isaac M. Steele, Clerk of the County Court presented to the court a settlement made by him with Hiram C. Keller, Administrator of James Curtis dec'd which was received and ordered to be recorded.

This day Isaac M. Steele, Clerk of the County Court presented to the court a settlement made by him with David A. Bradford, guardian of William T. Burke, Mary J. Burke, Eleanor A. Burke, Robert A. Burke and Caledonia T. Burke,

Pg. 354 minor heirs of Arnold Burke, dec'd which was received and ordered to be recorded.

Ordered that the court adjourn for one hour.

The court met pursuant to adjournment.

This day Stith Richardson, E. H. Hinton and William B. Sawyers, Commissioners appointed at the April term of this court for the purpose of endeavoring to establish the south-west corner of a tract of land granted by the State of North Carolina to Griffith Rutherford for 3000 acres reported to court which report was received and ordered to be recorded.

Ordered that the court adjourn until court in course.

James L. Green, Chairman
J. H. Maxwell, J.P.
E. H. Hinton, J.P.

Pg. 355 Be it remembered that at a quorum court began and held for the county of Lauderdale and State of Tennessee in the house of Isaac J. Pinson, Esq. (the circuit court being in session in the court house) on the first Monday in June it being the seventh day of said month in the year of our Lord one thousand eight hundred and forty one and the sixty fifth year of American Independence. Present and presiding the worshipful James L. Green, Esq. assisted by E. H. Hinton and H. R. Chambers, Esq., Isaac M. Steele, Clerk and G. L. Rutherford, Esq., Sheriff by his lawful deputy H. F. Rutherford, Esq. Proclamation being duly made the following proceedings were had on said court.

The settlement of the clerk with David P. Posey as guardian of Virginia H. Keller was examined, received and ordered by the court to be recorded.

This day Samuel P. Andrews, Administrator of Charlotte Andrews dec'd returned on oath in open court an account of the sale of said estate which is received and ordered to be recorded.

Pg. Ordered that the court adjourn for two hours.
356 The court met pursuant to adjournment.
Stith Richardson, Esq. appeared and took his seat.
Ordered that the court adjourn until court in course.

James L. Green, Chairman
S. Richardson, J.P.
E. H. Hinton, J.P.

Pg. Be it remembered that a county court begun and held for the county of
357 Lauderdale and state of Tennessee in the court house in the town of Ripley on the first Monday in July it being the fifth day of said month in the year of our Lord one thousand eight hundred and forty one and the sixty sixth year of the Independence of the United States of America, present J. H. Maxwell, Esq., Henry Willard, Elijah Lake, E. H. Condray, M. G. Turner, A. H. Pope, J. M. C. Robertson, Stith Richardson, S. V. Gilliland and E. H. Hinton, Esqs. commissioned and qualified as the law directs holding a court for said county, Isaac M. Steele, Clerk and Griffith L. Rutherford, Esq., Sheriff.

This day Isaac Moore proved by his own oath the killing of six wolves in the county of Lauderdale two of which were over the age of four months and four under the age of four months which is ordered to be certified to the Treasurer there being eight Justices present.

Pg. Ordered by the court those voting in the affirmative were Esqs. Willard,
358 Lake, Condry, Turner, Pope, Richardson and Maxwell, that the County Trustee pay to Isaac M. Steele, Clerk of the county court out of any money in his hands not otherwise appropriated, thirty one dollars, eighteen and $\frac{3}{4}$ cents for furnishing tax book to Sheriff, issuing road orders, etc.

Ordered that the settlement of the commissioners with the County Trustee be received and recorded.

This day the court chose and appointed Joshua Wright, guardian of Damorias Reynolds, one of the minor heirs of Joel Reynolds, whereupon said J. Wright, John H. Maxwell and Samuel Lusk, his securities entered into bond conditioned and payable as the law directs whereupon said Wright took the oath prescribed by law for guardian.

Ordered that the County Trustee pay Griffith L. Rutherford twelve dollars and 73 cents for releases not admitted by the Comptroller out of any money in the County Treasury not otherwise appropriated, ayes, Esqs. Willard, Lake, Condray, Turner, Pope, Richardson, Maxwell.

Pg. Ordered that the Trustee pay G. L. Rutherford out of any monies in his
359 hands not otherwise appropriated five dollars for keeping G. R. Williams and James Hinson, those voting in the affirmative were Esqs. Willard, Lake, Condray, Pope, Richardson, Maxwell and Hinton.

It appearing to the satisfaction of the court that Mary Graves, alias Mary Young has died leaving no will and Lance Graves having applied for letters of administration and the court being satisfied with his claim to the administration and he and his securities, Rezin L. Byrn and Absolam G. W. Byrn having entered into bond conditioned and payable as the law directs and he having took the oath of administration according to law. It is therefore ordered that he have letters of administration accordingly.

Ordered by the court that C. G. Fisher, Entry Taker of Tipton County be authorized and employed to furnish to the Entry Taker of Lauderdale County a true transcript of all surveys of that part of the 11 surveyors district
Pg. located in Lauderdale County in a well bound book with an index to the same
360 and that he be allowed twenty five cents for each copy of survey when completed and received by the court, the transcript to be finished and submitted at the October term of this court.

Ordered by the court that the Trustee pay to A. H. Pope, County Surveyor twelve dollars out of any money in his hands not otherwise appropriated for laying off the prison bounds of Lauderdale County and that he pay A. H. Pope

Pg. 360 cont. the chain carriers and markers one dollar each. The Justices present and voting in the affirmative were Esqs. Willard, Gilliland, Condray, Lake, Hinton, Maxwell and Richardson.

Ordered by the court there being a majority of all the Justices of said county present and voting in the affirmative that William W. Lea be paid out of any money in the hands of the Trustee not otherwise appropriated two hundred dollars for the building of a bridge across Cane Creek on the road leading from Ripley to Fulton and keeping the same in repairs for five years.

Ordered by the court that Richard H. McGaughey be appointed Trustee for the benefit of William T. Moorehead and Marena O. Moorehead in a marriage contract in place of H. A. G. Lea, dec'd.

This day Isaac M. Steele, Clerk of the County Court of Lauderdale County presented a settlement by him with Edwin H. Hinton, guardian of Mary E. Hinton which is ordered to be received and recorded.

Pg. 361 This day Abel H. Pope, County Surveyor of Lauderdale County returned into court a plan of the prison bounds of said county which is ordered to be received and recorded.

This day Robert McMordie recorded his stock mark (to wit) a smooth crop off of the right ear.

This day Edwin H. Hinton legally elected by the county court a commissioner to take and make out in writing an accurate and complete list of the numbers of free white male inhabitants of Lauderdale County who are twenty one years of age and upwards and who are resident citizens of said county on the first day of January 1841 made return of such list so taken and certified according to law to the Clerk of the county court. Whereupon it appears that the aggregate number of free white male inhabitants is five hundred and thirty eight.

Ordered by the court that court adjourn until tomorrow morning 9 o'clock.

J. H. Maxwell, Chairman Protem
Elijah Lake, J.P.
Elnathan H. Condray, J.P.

Pg. 362 July 6, 1841, Tuesday Morning.

Court met pursuant to adjournment, J. H. Maxwell, Esq., Chairman Protem, E. Lake, S. Richardson, A. H. Pope, J. M. C. Robertson, E. H. Condray, H. Hillard, Esqs., I. M. Steele, Clerk and G. L. Rutherford, Esq., Sheriff.

This day William W. Lea came into court and entered into bond with Joseph Wardlow and J. M. C. Robertson his securities in the penal sum of four hundred dollars, conditioned for extending a certain bridge built by him across Cane Creek about twenty feet and to guarantee the permanence of the same and to keep it in good repair for the term of five years from the first of September 1840. Which was acknowledged in open court and ordered to be received and recorded.

Ordered one third of all the Justices of said county present and voting in the affirmative that E. H. Condray, Jonathan L. Hearing and A. H. Pope be appointed commissioners to draft a plan for a bridge on Cane Creek on the road leading from Ripley to Isaac Moores and let out the building of the same to the lowest bidder taking bond with approved security for the completion of the same against the October term of this court according to contract and for the keeping the same in good repair for the term of five years from the time the same is completed.

Pg. 363 Ordered that the following good and lawful men of the body of the County of Lauderdale be summoned as jurors for the next term of the circuit court to be held for the county of Lauderdale on the first Monday in October next (to wit) Pleasant C. Dial, Smith Kent, Jeremiah Penick, Joseph Currie, Rezin L. Byrn, John B. Byrn, Isaac D. Maxwell, Jonathan L. Hearing, John Watson, Jr., Archer Phillips, David P. Posey, William Strain, Nathaniel W. Barnes, Sugar T. Evans, James H. Givins, James Hubbard, Armstead Wood, Roberson Meadows, Henry Shearer, Willie Dodd, Zachariah Mitchell, Henry Sumrow, Edmund Wright, Richard

Pg. 363 cont. Parr and John Soward, and Samuel Thompson and Frederick Barfield constables to wait on the court and jury.

Ordered that court be adjourned until court in course.

J. H. Maxwell, Chairman Protem
S. Richardson, J.P.
A. H. Pope, J.P.

Pg. 364 Be it remembered that at a quorum court began and held for the county of Lauderdale and state of Tennessee in the court house in the town of Ripley on the first Monday in August it being the second day of said month in the year of our Lord one thousand eight hundred and forty one and the sixty sixth year of the Independence of the United States of America present E. H. Hinton, John H. Maxwell, E. H. Condray, Esqs., Isaac M. Steele, Clerk and Griffith L. Rutherford, Sheriff. Proclamation being duly made the court proceeded to business.

The court choose E. H. Hinton, Chairman Protem.

It appearing to the satisfaction of the court that George Williams has died leaving no will and David Williams having applied to court for letters of Administration and the court being satisfied with his claim to the administration and he and his securities having entered into bond conditioned and payable as the law directs and acknowledged the same in open court, it is ordered that he have letters of administration accordingly.

Pg. 365 Ordered that the court adjourn for two hours.

The court met pursuant to adjournment.

Ordered that the court adjourn until court in course.

E. H. Hinton, Chairman Protem
Elnathan H. Condray, J.P.
J. H. Maxwell, J.P.

Pg. 366 September Term 1841.

Be it remembered that at a quorum court began and held in the court house in the town of Ripley in the county of Lauderdale and State of Tennessee on the sixth day of September it being the first Monday in said month in the year of our Lord one thousand eight hundred and forty one, present the worshipful James L. Green, Stith Richardson and John H. Maxwell, Esqs., Isaac M. Steele, Clerk with G. L. Rutherford, Sheriff by his legally authorized deputy, H. F. Rutherford.

Ordered by the court that Rezin L. Byrn, William Conner and Robert C. Campbell, Esqs. be appointed commissioners to make division of five slaves belonging to the estate of Mary A. Graves, Alias Mary A. Young between Lancy Graves and the heirs of William P. Young and that they report to the October term of this court.

This day Isaac M. Steele presented to court a settlement made by him as Clerk of this court with Leroy F. Lockard, Administrator of the estate of John Lockard which is approved and ordered to be recorded.

Pg. 367 September sixth, 1841.

Ordered that the court adjourn until one o'clock P. M.

The court met pursuant to adjournment.

This day John M. C. Robertson, Trustee of Lauderdale County entered bond with Archer Phillips and Isaac M. Steele, his securities conditioned and payable as the law directs for the safe keeping of Common School money he and them acknowledging the same in open court which is ordered to be recorded.

John M. C. Robertson, Esq. appeared and took his seat.

This day Stith Richardson, Esq. tendered his resignation as a Justice of the peace for Lauderdale County which was accepted by the court.

Ordered that the court adjourn until court in course.

Pg. 367 cont.
James L. Green, Chairman
J. H. Maxwell, J.P.
J. M. C. Robertson, J.P.

Pg. 368
October Term 1841

Be it remembered that a county court began and held for the County of Lauderdale and State of Tennessee in the court house in the town of Ripley on the first Monday in October, it being the fourth day of said month in the year of our Lord one thousand eight hundred and forty one and the sixty sixth year of American Independence. Present James M. Lewis, John M. C. Robertson, Abel H. Pope, Elnathan H. Condray, John H. Maxwell, Henry R. Chambers, William B. Sawyers and Elijah B. Foster, Esqs. commissioned and qualified as the law directs holding a court for said county, Isaac M. Steele, Clerk by his deputy William T. Morehead and Griffith L. Rutherford, Esq., Sheriff. Proclamation being made the following proceedings were had and done in said court.

The court chose James M. Lewis, Esq., Chairman Protem.

This day William T. Moorehead came into open court and took the oath of office of Deputy Clerk of this court.

This day Henry Willard proved by his own oath the killing of one wolf in Lauderdale County over the age of six months there being five Justices of said county present and voting in the affirmative.

Pg. 369
Ordered by the court there being a majority of all the Justices of said county present and voting in the affirmative that Isaac M. Steele be allowed sixty four dollars and 87½ cents for his ex-officio services and for all services in relation to common schools, etc.for the year 1841 out of any money in the hands of the Trustee not otherwise appropriated.

Ordered by the court there being a majority of all the Justices of said county present and voting in the affirmative that the Trustee pay to Isaac M. Steele fifteen dollars for furnishing a Registers Book out of any monies in his hands not otherwise appropriated.

This day Benjamin L. and T. W. Tyus, administrators of the estate of Isaac D. Coachman dec'd returned on oath in open court an inventory of said estate which is received and ordered to be recorded.

Court adjourned for one hour.

Court met pursuant to adjournment.

This day James M. Lewis, Chairman Protem of the county court called on Isaac M. Steele, Clerk of the county court for his receipts which he produced which are in the words and figures following (to wit)

Pg. 370

Comptrollers Office
Nashville, Tennessee
September 9, 1841

Received from Isaac M. Steele his statement of revenue collected as Clerk of Lauderdale County Court from Sept. 1, 1840, to Sept. 1, 1841.

Amount Collected		$84.68
Commissions	$2.11	
Paid Byrn & Gilliland	5.00	
		7.11
Warrant No. 1367 this day for		$77.57

Daniel Graham
Comptroller

No. 1367 $77.57

Branch Union Bank Tennessee
Jackson, September 21, 1841

Received from Isaac M. Steele seventy seven dollars and fifty seven cents audited to him by Warrant No. 1367 and due on account of revenue

Pg. 370 cont. collected as Clerk of Lauderdale County Court from first September 1840 to first September 1841, for which I have signed duplicate receipts.

John M. Campbell, Cash.
B. C. Keatts, C. M.

$113.07½

Ripley Tennessee
September 30, 1841

Received from Isaac M. Steele one hundred and thirteen dollars, seven and a half cents the amount due on account of revenue collected as Clerk of Lauderdale County Court from first September 1840 to first September 1841.

J. M. C. Robertson
Trustee of Lauderdale County

Pg. 371 This day David Williams, Administrator of the estate of George Williams dec'd returned on oath in open court an inventory of said estate which is received and ordered to be recorded.

This day James Hutchison proved by his own oath the killing of one wolf in said county over the age of four months which is ordered to be certified to the Comptroller there being five Justices present.

Ordered by the court there being one third of all the Justices of said county present and voting in the affirmative that Charles G. Fisher be paid forty dollars by the Trustee for furnishing the transcript of the plots and certificates of that part of the eleventh surveyors district situated in Lauderdale County.

Ordered by the court there being one third of all the Justices of said county present and voting in the affirmative that A. H. Pope be paid two dollars and ninety cents for plots and certificates for land lying in said county by the Trustee out of any money in the hands not otherwise appropriated obtained by mail from Trenton.

Pg. 372 This day William D. Lee returned an inventory in open court upon oath of the effects which has come into his hands as guardian for Josiah and Malvina Marley, minor heirs of Adam Marley dec'd which was received and ordered to be recorded.

This day G. L. Rutherford, sheriff and collector of the public taxes for Lauderdale County presented in open court upon oath the following statement of removals from the county off of whom he could not collect the tax (to wit)

Wilson C. Baker	1 poll	left Cty	25¢
D. Millsap	1 "	" "	25¢
Neill McLeod	1 "	" "	25¢
Wiley Voss	1 "	" "	25¢
Henry Edney	1 dead		25¢
R. F. Moore	1 poll	left Cty	25¢
Elisha Roberson	1 "	" "	25¢
James Bowk	1 "	" "	25¢
Michael Bricoe	1 "	" "	25¢
H. W. Caulkins	1 "	" "	25¢
James Conway	1 "	" "	25¢
William Carrol	1 "	" "	25¢
John Conley 1st	1 "	" "	25¢
John Conley 2nd	1 "	" "	25¢
William Conley	1 "	" "	25¢
William Coyle	1 "	" "	25¢
William Carson	1 "	" "	25¢
James Donaldson	1 "	" "	25¢

Pg. 373

Gabriel Frasier	1	"	"	"	25¢
Michael Holham	1	"	"	"	25¢
James Lancy	1	"	"	"	25¢
James Murphy	1	"	"	"	25¢
John Martin	1	"	"	"	25¢
Thomas Shanly	1	"	"	"	25¢
John Garvin, Jr.	1	Double	"	"	50¢
Abram Moss	1	"	"	"	50¢
William McAllister	1	"	"	"	50¢
W. B. Ramsey	1	Poll	"	"	25¢
Simpson	1	"	"	"	25¢
J. C. Newly	1	"	"	"	25¢
John B. Acree	1	"	"	"	25¢
William Saunders	1	"	"	"	25¢
Mary Ramsey 3 slaves left the County					$1.80
					$11.55

I, G. L. Rutherford, Sheriff and Collector of the public taxes for the County of Lauderdale for the year 1841 do solemnly swear that the foregoing list insolvents by me exhibited is just and true to the best of my knowledge, etc., and that said list fully sets forth the name of each delinquent, the amount of tax they owe and the nature and kind of taxable subjects from which derived and the year for which it accrued and that I have used all legal ways and means in my power to collect the taxes contained in the said list from the time that I received the tax list of my county from the Clerk thereof this fourth day of October 1841.

Sworn to in open court.

G. L. Rutherford, Sheriff & Collector
for Lauderdale County

Pg. 374 It is ordered that G. L. Rutherford, Sheriff and Collector be allowed a credit for eleven dollars and fifty five cents the amount of the foregoing statement for the county revenue for the year 1841.

Ordered by the court that Abel H. Pope be allowed the further time of three months for making a general plan of Lauderdale County.

Ordered that the court be adjourned until tomorrow morning 9 o'clock.

J. M. Lewis, Chairman Protem
Elnathan H. Condray, J.P.
A. H. Pope, J.P.

Tuesday Morning, October 5, 1841

Court met pursuant to adjournment.

This day Pleasant G. Davenport, Executor of the estate of George Moore dec'd returned in open court on oath an inventory of said estate which was received and ordered to be recorded.

Ordered by the court there being a majority of all the Justices present and voting in the affirmative that the Trustee pay to David Gilliland seven dollars and fifty cents for one record book bought and paid for by him out of any monies in his hands not otherwise appropriated.

Pg. 375 This day J. M. C. Robertson, Esq. tendered his resignation as Trustee of Lauderdale County which was received by the court and ordered to be recorded.

This day John H. Maxwell, Esq. tendered his resignation as Ranger of Lauderdale County which was received by the court and ordered to be recorded.

Ordered by the court there being a majority of all the Justices of said county present and voting in the affirmative that Jessie Ledbetter be paid eighty four dollars by the Trustee out of any monies in his hands not otherwise appropriated for building a bridge across Cane Creek on the road from Ripley to Isaac Moore.

This day Jessie Ledbetter came into court and entered into bond with

Pg. 375 cont. William R. Ledbetter, Drewry Massy and Calvin F. Ledbetter, his securities in the penal sum of one hundred and sixty eight dollars conditioned for the keeping in good repair a bridge built by him across Cane Creek on the road from Ripley to Isaac Moore for the space of five years from the fifth day of October 1841, which was acknowledged in open court and ordered to be received and recorded.

Pg. 376 Whereas it appearing to the satisfaction of this court that Henry A. G. Lee has departed this life and Margaret Lee widow of the said H. A. G. Lee dec'd, relinquishing her right to the administration to William D. Lee. It is ordered that William D. Lee have letters issued to him he having entered into bond with Guilford Jones and Benjamin T. Porter his securities in the sum of thirty hundred dollars conditioned and payable as the law directs and took the oath of Administrator.

This day the court proceeded to elect a Master for the County of Lauderdale in the place of J. M. C. Robertson resigned. Whereupon John H. Maxwell was duly elected, who took the oath of office and entered into bonds with security which are in the following words and figures (to wit)

State of Tennessee)
Lauderdale County) Know all men by these presents that We, John H. Maxwell, John C. Barnes and Elnathan H. Condray are held and firmly bound unto Robert P. Currin, Superintendent of Common Schools and his successors in office in the penal sum of one thousand and four hundred dollars for the payment of which well and truly to be made we bind ourselves, our heirs, executors and administrators jointly and severally, firmly by these presents sealed with our seals and dated the fifth day of October 1841.

Pg. 377 The condition of the above obligation is such that whereas John H. Maxwell was this day elected by the County Court, County Trustee in the place of John M. C. Robertson resigned. Now should the above bounden John H. Maxwell safely keep and pay over according to law all monies which may come into his hands an account of common schools then the above obligation to be void else to remain in full force and virtue.

J. H. Maxwell (Seal)
J. C. Barnes (Seal)
Elnathan H. Condray (Seal)

State of Tennessee)
Lauderdale County) Know all men by these presents that we, John H. Maxwell, John C. Barnes and Elnathan H. Condray, jointly and severally acknowledge ourselves indebted to James L. Green, Chairman of the County Court of Lauderdale County for the time being and his successors in office in the penal sum of two thousand dollars for which payment well and truly to be made we bind ourselves, our heirs, executors and administrators jointly and severally, firmly by these presents sealed with our seals and dated the fifth day of October 1841.

Pg. 378 The condition of the above obligation is such that whereas the above bounden John H. Maxwell has been this day elected by the County Court of said County, County Trustee in the place of John M. C. Robertson resigned as appears of record in said court. Now if the said John H. Maxwell shall safely keep and pay over all county monies which shall come into his hands by virtue of said office agreeable to the orders of the court made pursuant to the laws of this state and at the expiration of the term of his office for which he was elected shall pay over to his successor all the county money which is in his hands or which ought to be in his hands and well and truly discharge the duties of County Trustee for said County in all things according to law so long as he continues in office then this obligation to be void otherwise to remain in full force and virtue.

J. H. Maxwell (Seal)
J. C. Barnes (Seal)
Elnathan H. Condray (Seal)

Pg. 379 cont. This day the last will and testament of John Warpool, dec'd was produced in open court and proven by Edmund Wright, Zachariah Mitchell and John Russell the subscribing witness which was ordered to be recorded whereupon William Warpool and Benjamin Warpool who being appointed Administrator in said will, it is ordered that William Warpool and Benjamin Warpool have letters issued to them, they having entered into bond with Robert Crihfield, Benjamin T. Porter, Thomas D. Warpool and John Russell, their securities in the sum of six thousand dollars conditioned and payable as the law directs and took the oath of Administrators.

This day the court proceeded to elect a Ranger for the County of Lauderdale in place of John H. Maxwell resigned, whereupon Elnathan H. Condray was duly elected who entered into bond conditioned and payable as the law directs and took the oath of office.

Wednesday morning sixth of October.

Court met pursuant to adjournment.

Ordered that court be adjourned until court in course.

J. M. Lewis, Chairman Protem
Elnathan H. Condray, J.P.
William B. Sawyer, J.P.

Pg. 380 Be it remembered that at a County Court began and held in the Court House in the town of Ripley for the County of Lauderdale and state of Tennessee on the first Monday in November it being the first day of said month in the year of our Lord one thousand eight hundred and forty one and the sixty sixth year of American Independence. Present James M. Lewis, E. H. Hinton and John H. Maxwell, Esqs. elected to hold the quorum court for said County, Isaac M. Steele, Clerk with Griffith L. Rutherford, Esq., Sheriff.

James M. Lewis, Esq. was appointed Chairman Protem in the absence from the court of James L. Green, Esq. the regular Chairman.

Ordered that the following good and lawful men be appointed commissioners to value and divide the slaves hereinafter named between the heirs of John Walpole dec'd according to the provisions of his will (to wit) John Russell, Samuel C. Robertson and William B. Sawyer, the slaves to be divided are Martha, Holly, James, Ebberlina, Rose, Eunice, June and Minerva.

Pg. 381 It appearing to the satisfaction of the court here that Robert Ford has died intestate and Henry F. Rutherford having applied for letters of Administrator on said estate and the court being satisfied with his claim to the administration and he having given bond with Stith Richardson and John L. Flippin as securities and he and they having acknowledged the same in open court, therefore it is ordered that letters of administration issue on said estate to the said Henry F. Rutherford.

This day William D. Lee, Administrator of the estate of Henry A. G. Lee dec'd returned on oath in open court an inventory of said estate which is received and ordered to be recorded.

This day William L. Walpole and Benjamin F. Walpole, Executors of the last will and testament of John Walpole dec'd returned on oath in open court an inventory of said estate which is received and ordered to be recorded.

Pg. 382 This day John L. Flippin, administrator of all and singular the goods and chattels, rights and credits of John Flippin dec'd returned on oath in open court an additional inventory of said estate which is received and ordered to be recorded.

It appearing to the satisfaction of the court that Green B. Temple is dead leaving no written will and Nancy Temple having applied for letters of administration and the court being satisfied with her claim and she having entered into bond with Robert C. Campbell and William D. Lee, her securities she and they acknowledging said bond in open court, it is therefore ordered that letters of administration be issued to her accordingly.

Ordered that Stith Richardson, Henry F. Rutherford and Samuel Hooper be

Pg. 382 cont. appointed commissioners to lay off and set apart to Margaret E. Lee, widow relic of Henry A. G. Lee dec'd her years provision and that they report to the January term of this court.

Pg. 383 The court here chose and appointed R. B. Blackwell guardian of Hariet E. Blackwell, Thomas J. J. Blackwell, Henry F. Blackwell and June I. V. Blackwell, minor heirs of Robert Blackwell whereupon said R. B. Blackwell came into court with Archer Phillips and James A. Lackey, his securities and entered into bond conditioned and payable as the law directs, whereupon the oath of guardian was administered to said Robert B. Blackwell.

Ordered that the court adjourn until court in course.

J. M. Lewis, Chairman Protem
J. H. Maxwell, J.P.
E. H. Hinton, J.P.

Pg. 384 State of Tennessee, Lauderdale County
December Term 1841

Be it remembered that at a County Court began and holden in the town of Ripley for the County of Lauderdale on the sixth day of December in the year of our Lord one thousand eight hundred and forty one, it being the first Monday in said month of December present the worshipful James M. Lewis, Elnathan H. Condray and E. H. Hinton, Esqs., Isaac M. Steele, Clerk with Griffith L. Rutherford, Sheriff.

Whereas heretofore (to wit) on the first day of March being also the first Monday of said month in the year of our Lord one thousand eight hundred and forty one, this court appointed A. H. Pope, County Surveyor of Lauderdale County to survey and mark the prison bounds of the aforesaid County of Lauderdale directing him to report to the July term of this court and whereas said A. H. Pope made said report to the July term of this court agreeable to the order of this court and the act of the General Assembly in that case made and

Pg. 385 provided and whereas the Clerk of this court by mistake recorded said report in the Deed Book and whereas the said Act of the General Assembly requires said report to be entered upon the Minutes. Therefore it is ordered that said report be received now as before and spread on the minutes which said report is in the words and figures following (to wit)

State of Tennessee) In pursuance to an order to me directed from the wor-
Lauderdale County) shipful County Court of the County of Lauderdale, I have surveyed and caused to be marked and measured the prison bounds around the town of Ripley agreeable to an act of the General Assembly of the aforesaid state passed for that purpose. Beginning at a dogwood and black gum marked P B and with a blaze and three chops above and below and a beach pointer marked with a blaze two chops above and two below standing 160 poles north, 160 poles west from the center of the court house and runs thence south at 95 poles cross the road leading from Ripley to Ashport at a white oak and poplar marked P B at 266 poles cross the road leading from Ripley to H. C. Kellers at a black gum marked P B and with a blaze and three chops above and below and two dogwoods and an ash marked with a blaze and two chops above and below thence east at 78 poles cross the road leading from Ripley to Fulton at a oak marked P B at 226 poles cross the road leading from Ripley to Brownsville at a small Spanish oak marked P B in all 320 poles to a small persimmon marked P B with a blaze and three chops above and below and a red bud and dogwood pointers marked with a blaze with two chops above and below thence north at 134 poles cross the road leading from Ripley to R. L. Byrns at an ash and poplar marked P B in all 320 poles to an elm and horn beam marked P B and a blaze with three chops above and below with a dogwood and an elm pointers marked with a blaze with two chops above and below thence west at 44 poles cross the road leading from Ripley to Dyersburg at a white oak and black gum marked P B in all 320 poles to the beginning the lines marked with a blaze and

Pg. 385 cont. a chop above. Surveyed the thirtyth of June 1841.

R. L. Byrn)
&) C. C.
R. H. Hammill)

A. H. Pope, C. S.

James Braden, Marker

Griffith L. Rutherford, Sheriff of Lauderdale County and Collector of the public taxes for the said County made the following report which is received by the court and ordered to be spread on the minutes which is the words and figures following.

I, G. L. Rutherford, Sheriff and Collector of the public tax for the County of Lauderdale for the year 1841 hereby report to court the following list of insolvents.

To Wit		Polls	Tax
Neil McLeod	Left the County	1	12½
William D. Cooper	Insolvent	1	12½
Michael Horner	Left the County	1	12½
F. McCoy	Left the County	1	12½
Daman Millsaps	Left the County	1	12½
Henry Edney	Left the County	1	12½
Lazarus Inman	Left the County	1	12½
Richard F. Moore	Left the County	1	12½
Elisha Roberson	Left the County	1	12½
James Bourk	Left the County	1	12½
Pg. 388 Michael Briscoes	Left the County	1	12½
Hiram W. Calking	Left the County	1	12½
James Conway	Left the County	1	12½
Michael Conway	Left the County	1	12½
William Carrol	Left the County	1	12½
John Connelly, 1st	Left the County	1	12½
John Connelly, 2nd	Left the County	1	12½
William Connelly	Left the County	1	12½
William Coil	Left the County	1	12½
William Carson	Left the County	1	12½
James Donalson	Left the County	1	12½
Gabriel Frazier	Left the County	1	12½
Michael Hoolham	Left the County	1	12½
James Lancy	Left the County	1	12½
James Murphy	Left the County	1	12½
John Martin	Left the County	1	12½
Thomas Shanley	Left the County	1	12½
John Brown	Left the County	1	12½
William B. Raney	Left the County	1	12½
Simpson	Left the County	1	12½
J. C. Newley	Left the County	1	12½
John B. Acre	Left the County	1	12½
John B. Fudge	Left the County	1	12½
William Sanders	Left the County	1	12½
Samuel P. Anders	Left the County	1	12½
		25	4.37½

I, G. L. Rutherford, Sheriff and Collector of the public taxes for the
Pg. 389 County of Lauderdale for the year 1841 do solemnly swear that the foregoing list of insolvents by me exhibited is just and true to the best of my knowledge and that said list fully sets forth the name of each delinquent in my county the amount of tax they owe for the year 1841 and that I have used all legal ways and means in my power to collect the taxes contained in the said list from the time that I recoveredthe tax list of my County from the Clerk thereof

Pg. 389 cont. and I could find no property to enable me to collect the said taxes this sixth day of December 1841.

G. L. Rutherford, Sheriff

Sworn to in open court
This 6th day of December 1841
Test. Isaac M. Steele, Clerk

Whereupon it is ordered by the court that G. L. Rutherford, Sheriff as aforesaid be allowed a credit from the state tax on said insolvents amounting in all to the sum of four dollars and thirty seven and a half cents and that the same be certified to the Comptroller of the Treasury.

Pg. 390 This day Willie Dodd presented the following petition
State of Tennessee
Lauderdale County Court December Term 1841

Your petitioner respectfully represents to your worships that whereas heretofore (to wit) at the January term 1841 of this court your petitioner became security of Samuel P. Anders as administrator of Charlotte Anders dec'd and whereas your petitioner conceives himself in danger of becoming liable by reason of the conduct of said administrator and he believes he has good reason for such fear therefore your petitioner prays your worships to order a summons to issue forth with for said Samuel P. Anders made returnable to the next term of this court requiring him to give new and counter security or in case he fails to appoint another administrator in his place, this 6th day of December 1841.

Sworn to in open court
This 6th day of December 1841
Test. Isaac M. Steele, Clerk

Willie Dodd

Pg. 391 Whereupon it is ordered by the court that a summons issue in accordance with said petition.

This day the following report was received and ordered to be spread on the minutes (to wit)

We, the commissioners appointed by the county court of Lauderdale County at November term 1841 to divide and appropriate the negroes mentioned in the order or decree by which we were appointed have met together on the premises and after being duly sworn have performed the duties assigned to us as follows (Viz) Lot No. 1 we have alloted to Caroline a negroe girl Martha valued $450 and pay No. 8 $150, No. 2 Thomas a negroe girl named Hally at $450 pay No. 9 $150, No. 3 Francis a negroe James at $400 pay No. 9 $100, No. 4 John negroe girl Eveline at $325 pay No. 9 $25, No. 5 William a negroe Rose at $ 375 pay to No. 7 $50 and to No. 9 $25, No. 6 Catherine a negroe girl Eunice at $300, No. 7
Pg. 392 Benjamin a negroe girl Jane at $250 to receive of No. 5 $50, No. 8 Mary a negroe girl Minerva at $150 to receive of No. 1 $150, No. 9 Rebecca to receive $300 as follows of No. 2 $150 of No. 3 $100 of No. 4 $25 of No. 5 $25. Witness our hands and seals this 20th day of November 1841.

Samuel C. Robinson (Seal)
John Russell (Seal)
William B. Sawyer (Seal)

This day the court chose and appointed Isaac Braden, guardian of Mahala Braden, John Braden, Martha Braden, Elizabeth Braden, Wiley Braden, Hariet Braden, Robert Braden and Sarah Jane Braden, minor heirs of Martha Yergen, whereupon the said Isaac Braden and Robert C. Campbell and A. H. Pope, his securities came into court here and entered into bond in the sum of $400 conditioned and payable as the law directs acknowledging the same in open court whereupon the oath of guardian was administered to said Isaac Braden.

This day William D. Lee, Administrator of H. A. G. Lee dec'd returned into court here on oath an account of the sales of the dec'd estate which is received and ordered to be recorded.

Pg. 393 It appearing to the satisfaction of the court that Eleanor Wood has died leaving no will and William Wood having applied for letters of administration on said estate and the court being satisfied with his claim to the administration and he having entered into bond conditioned and payable as the law directs with Joseph Taylor and Jonathan L. Hearring as securities he and they acknowledging the same in open court and the said Wood having taken the oath of administration it is therefore ordered by the court letters of administration issue accordingly to him.

Ordered that the following good and lawful men of the body of the County of Lauderdale be appointed Jurors for the February term of the circuit court of this county (to wit) Peter T. A. Walker, E. S. Campbell, Samuel A. Givin,
Pg. 394 A. H. Pope, James B. Crook, George R, Williams, William Williams, Robert C. Campbell, John F. Jett, Joseph Taylor, Lancy Graves, David Walker, John Buchanon, Thomas G. Rice, P. G. Davenport, David C. Russell, Robert P. Russell, Dickerson Jennings, Jesse Ledbetter, Moses B. Chisom, Henry Crihfield, Jr., Edward Fisher, William B. Sawyer, Henry R. Chambers and S. Hooper, and Samuel Thompson and Fred K. Barfield, Constables to wait on the court and Jury.

Ordered that the Clerk issue notices to Gilly Hunter, guardian of William Hunter, Robert West, guardian of Francis,Marion, Rachael, Caroline and Virginia Millen and Moses E. Stone, guardian of John Rudder requiring them and each of them to appear at the next term of this court and give new and counter security.

The court this day chose James M. Lewis, Chairman Protem.

Ordered that the court adjourn until court in course.

James M. Lewis, Chairman Protem
Elnathan H. Condray, J.P.
E. H. Hinton, J.P.

Pg. 395 State of Tennessee) January Term 1842
Lauderdale County)

Be it remembered that at a County Court began and holden at the court house in the town of Ripley for Lauderdale County on third day of January in the year of our Lord one thousand eight hundred and forty two it being the first Monday in said month of January. Present H. R. Chambers, S. V. Gilliland, J. M. Maxwell, E. H. Condray, M. G. Turner, A. H. Pope, William B. Sawyer and Elijah Lake, Esqs., Isaac M. Steele, Clerk with Griffith L. Rutherford, Sheriff.

This day the court chose and appointed John H., Chairman of this court.

This day Green Baker proved by his own oath the killing of one wolf in the County of Lauderdale over the age of four months there being five Justices present ordered that the same be certified to the Comptroller of the Treasury.

Pg. 396 This day James H. Givin proved by his own oath the killing of one wolf over the age of four months in the County of Lauderdale their being five Justices present ordered that the same be certified to the Comptroller of the Treasury.

This day Robert C. West, guardian of Francis, Marian, Rachael, Caroline, and Virginia Millen, minor heirs of Robert K. Millen came into court here with Lance Graves, Milton G. Turner, his securities and entered into bond in the sum of three thousand dollars conditioned and payable as the law directs he and they acknowledging the same in open court as the law directs.

This day Gilly Hunter, guardian of William Hunter, Minor heir of Mabry Hunter came into court here with William P. Gaines and Hiram C. Keller, her securities and entered into bond in the sum of eight hundred dollars conditioned and payable as the law directs, her and her securities acknowledging the same in open court as the law directs.

This day Moses E. Stone, guardian of John M. Rudder, minor heir of Samuel Rudder came into court here with Griffith L. Rutherford and John Thompson his securities and entered into bond in the sum of three thousand

Pg. 397 dollars conditioned and payable as the law directs him and his securities acknowledging the same in open court according to law.

Whereas it appears to the court that Henderson Jones is dead and having made no will or testament and application being made by Joseph Currie to have letters of administration granted to him on the estate of the said Henderson Jones dec'd he having given bond and security as by law in such case is required and taken oath as is required by law he and his securities having acknowledged said bond in open court the court therefore orders that he have letters accordingly.

It is ordered by the court that Griffith L. Rutherford, Sheriff of this County be allowed the sum of fifty dollars for his ex-officio service for the year 1841 to be paid by the County Trustee out of any money in his hands not otherwise appropriated, Ayes on said appropriation were Elnathan H. Condray, Henry R. Chambers, Samuel V. Gilliland, Elijah Lake, Able H. Pope and William B. Sawyer, Esqs. one third of all the Justices of said county, Noes none.

Pg. 398 It is ordered by the court that Griffith L. Rutherford, Sheriff of this county be allowed the sum of twenty dollars for furnishing wood and water for the courts of this county for the year 1841 to be paid by the county Trustee out of any money in his hands not otherwise appropriated, Ayes on said appropriated were Elnathan H. Condray, Henry R. Chambers, Elijah Lake, Abel H. Pope and William B. Sawyers, Esqs. one third of all the Justices in said county, Noes, none.

Ordered by the court that James M. Lewis, Esq. (elected one of the quorum in the place of James L. Green absent at the General Assembly) be paid by the county Trustee three dollars for holding the quorum court at November and December terms, Ayes on said appropriation were Elnathan H. Condray, Henry R. Chambers, Samuel V. Gilliland, Abel H. Pope, and William B. Sawyer, Esqs., one third of all the Justices of said county, Noes, none.

Pg. 399 Ordered by the court that James L. Green, Esq. be paid by the County Trustee out of any money in his hands not otherwise appropriated the sum of seven dollars and fifty cents for holding the quorum courts five days in the year 1841, Ayes on said appropriation were Elnathan H. Condray, Henry R. Chambers, Samuel V. Gilliland, Abel H. Pope and William B. Sawyers, Esqs., one third of all the Justices in said County, Noes, none.

Ordered by the court that John H. Maxwell, Esq., be paid by the county Trustee out of any money in his hands not otherwise appropriated the sum of seven dollars and fifty cents for holding the quorum court five days in the year 1841, Ayes on said appropriation were Elnathan H. Condray, Henry R. Chambers, Samuel V. Gilliland, Abel H. Pope and William B. Sawyer, Esqs., one third of all the Justices in said County, Noes, none.

Pg. 400 Ordered by the court that E. H. Hinton, Esq. be paid by the county Trustee out of any money in his hands not otherwise appropriated the sum of nine dollars for holding the quorum courts six days in the year 1841, Ayes on said appropriation were Elnathan H. Condray, Henry R. Chambers, Samuel V. Gilliland, Elijah Lake, Abel H. Pope and William B. Sawyer, Esqs., one third of all the Justices in said County, Noes, none.

It is ordered by the court present and voting for the same Elnathan H. Condray, Henry R. Chambers, Samuel V. Gilliland and Elijah Lake, John H. Maxwell, Abel H. Pope, William B. Sawyer and Milton G. Turner, Esqs., a majority of all the Justices of said county that David C. Russell, Joseph Currie, Samuel A. Thompson, Thomas Fitzpatrick, Edmund Fitzpatrick, David P. Posey and Joseph Hays, good and lawful men of the body of the County of Lauderdale be appointed a jury of view to review the road leading from Fullen's Ferry to Durhamville and report on the propriety or impropriety of changing the same taking into consideration the public good as well as private convenience so
Pg. 401 as to straighten said road by commencing at the corner of Joseph Currie's fence and running a straight direction through the planation of Samuel V. Gilliland, Esq. and that they report to April term of this court.

Whereas at the December term of this court, Willie Dodd, one of the securities of Samuel P. Anders, Administrator of all and singular the goods

Pg. and chattels, rights and credits of Charlotte Anders, dec'd made oath in open
401 court that he concieved himself in danger of becoming liable by reason of the
cont. conduct of the said Samuel P. Anders, Administrator as aforesaid and whereas
said court ordered the Clerk to issue a notice against Samuel P. Anders commanding him to appear at the present term of this court to give new and counter security as administrator as aforesaid or to surrender said estate to such person as the court might appoint and the said notice did issue accordingly on the seventh day of December last passed and was placed in the hands of
Pg. Griffith L. Rutherford, Sheriff of Lauderdale County and the said Griffith L.
402 Rutherford, Sheriff as aforesaid made this day return of said notice into
open court with the following return endorsed thereon "Came to hand the day issued, G. L. Rutherford, Sheriff, S. P. Anders not to be found in my County, G. L. Rutherford, Sheriff" On motion of the said Willie Dodd security as aforesaid founded on his affidavit at the December term of this court. It is ordered by this court that an alias order be issued by the Clerk of this court directing the Sheriff to summon the said Samuel P. Anders to be and appear at the February term of this court on the first Monday thereof in the court house in the town of Ripley then and there to give new and counter security in the place of said Willie Dodd or said administration will be taken from him.

It is ordered by the court present and voting for the same Elnathan H. Condray, Henry R. Chambers, Samuel V. Gilliland, Elijah Lake, John H. Maxwell, Abel H. Pope, William B. Sawyer and Milton G. Turner, Esqs. a majority of all the Justices of said County that Stith Richardson, B. Foster, Henry Sumrow,
Pg. Benjamin Nearn, Jesse Ledbetter and Ancel Reynolds, good and lawful men of
403 the body of the County of Lauderdale be appointed a jury of view to view and
mark a road from Boling Fishers on the Dyersburg road to the Ashport turnpike road near Samuel Deasons the nearest and best route taking into consideration as well the public good as private convenience should said jury think said road would be of public advantage if laid out and that they report to the April term of this court.

This day Jesse P. Fullen came into court here and brought with him Pleasant G. Davenport and William P. Gaines for securities and be they entered into bond in the sum one hundred and thirty six dollars payable to John H. Maxwell, Chairman of the County Court of said county conditioned for the said Jesse P. Fullens keeping in good repair a bridge by him built on Bates Fork of Cole Creek for the County for the term of five years from the date and leaving the same in good repair at the end of said term said Jesse P. Fullen
Pg. and Pleasant G. Davenport and William P. Gaines acknowledging said bond in
404 open court.

This day Henry F. Rutherford, Administrator of all and singular the goods and chattels, rights and credits of Robert Ford dec'd returned on oath here in open court and inventory of said estate which is received and ordered to be recorded.

It is ordered by the court that James Hubbard, Dr. E. S. Campbell and Rezin G. Henley (freeholders unconnected either by affinity or consanguinity with Nancy Temple widow of Green B. Temple dec'd) be appointed commissioners to set apart so much of the crop, stock, provision and monies on hand or due or other assets of the estate of the said Green B. Temple dec'd as may be necessary for the support of the said Nancy Temple widow as aforesaid and her
Pg. family until the expiration of one year from the decease of her husband the
405 said Green B. Temple and that they report to the April term of this court.

This day Stith Richardson, H. F. Rutherford and Samuel Hooper commissioners appointed at the November term of this court to set apart to Margaret Lee widow of H. A. G. Lee her years provision reported to court which report is received and ordered to be recorded.

This day Nancy Temple, Administratrix of all and singular the goods and Chattels, rights and credits of Green B. Temple dec'd returned on oath here in open court and inventory and account of sales of said estate which received and ordered to be recorded.

Pg. 405 cont. This day William Wood, Administrator of all and singular the goods and chattels, rights and credits of Eleanor Wood dec'd returned here in open court on oath an inventory of said estate which is received and ordered to be recorded.

Pg. 406 This day J. C. Barnes, H. C. Keller, John Fletcher, John C. Nevils and Begnal Crook a jury of view appointed at the October term of this court to view and mark out a road from Ashport to the mouth of Cole Creek reported to court which report is in the words and figures following (to wit)

We, the undersigned Jurors having been sworn according to law have proceeded to view and mark the road from the mouth of Cole Creek to Ashport commencing at the creek thence up the Missippi on the highest ground to J. C. Nevils, thence to J. C. Barnes, thence to John Fletchers, thence to Booths, thence to the place known as the Hale place, thence to John Nixons, thence to Ashport which we submit to the worshipful County Court. This 19th day of November 1841.

H. C. Keller
John Fletcher
John C. Nevils
Begnal Crook

Whereon said report was accepted and ordered to be recorded present and voting for the same Elnathan H. Condray, Henry R. Chambers, Samuel V. Gilliland, Elijah Lake, John H. Maxwell, Abel H. Pope and William B. Sawyer, Esqs.

Pg. 407 It is ordered by the court present and voting for the same Elnathan H. Condray, Henry R. Chambers, Samuel V. Gilliland, Elijah Lake, John H. Maxwell, Abel H. Pope and William B. Sawyer, Esqs., that John Nixon be appointed Overseer to cut out the road from Ashport to the mouth of Cole Creek as viewed out by the jury of view from Ashport to John Booths and that he have the hands in Ashport and in the vicinity and that he report to the April term of this court.

It is ordered by the court present and voting for the same Elnathan H. Condray, Henry R. Chambers, Samuel V. Gilliland, Elijah Lake, John H. Maxwell, Abel H. Pope and William B. Sawyer, Esqs., that J. C. Nevils be appointed Overseer to cut out the road from Ashport to the mouth of Cole Creek as viewed out by the jury of view commencing at the mouth of Cole Creek cutting to John Booths and that he have all the hands in the point and that he report to the April term of this court.

Pg. 408 Ordered by the court that Blair H. Lee be appointed Overseer of the road leading from Ripley to Dyersburg working from the old Dyer County line to the north boundary line of Boling Fishers tract of land and that he have the following hands (to wit) all his own hands, Henry Sumrow, James Sumrow and Onesemus Fudge and that he keep the same in repair as first class road.

Ordered by the court that George Chapman be appointed Overseer of the road leading from Ripley to Dyersburg working from the north boundary line of L. Dunavants tract of land to the forks of the road near H. Sumrows and that he have the hands in the following bounds (to wit) Commencing at Dunavants north boundary line thence west with the same line to the Byler road thence with the said road to the forks of the same near H. Crihfields thence west to the old district line thence east with said line far enough to include the hands on R. P. Currin's plantation thence west toa point east of Dunavants north east corner and that he have the hands of E. Wright and William Wright and that he keep the same in repair as a first class road.

Pg. 409 Ordered by the court that Samuel A. Thompson be appointed a Revenue Commissioner to take a list of taxable property and polls for the first civil district of Lauderdale County for the year 1842.

Ordered by the court that John H. Maxwell be appointed a Revenue Commissioner to take a list of taxable property and polls for the second civil district of Lauderdale County for the year 1842.

Ordered by the court that Elijah Lake be appointed a Revenue Commissioner to take a list of taxable property and polls for the third civil district of

Pg. Lauderdale County for the year 1842.
409 Ordered by the court that Henry Willard be appointed a Revenue Commis-
cont. sioner to take a list of taxable property and polls for the fourth civil district of Lauderdale County for the year 1842.

Ordered by the court that Rezin G. Henley be appointed a Revenue Commissioner to take in a list of taxable property and polls for the fifth civil district of Lauderdale County for the year 1842.

Ordered by the court that Elnathan H. Condray be appointed a Revenue Commissioner to tkae a list of taxable property and polls for the sixth civil district of Lauderdale County for the year 1842.

Ordered by the court that E. H. Hinton be appointed a Revenue Commissioner to take a list of taxable property and polls for the seventh civil district of Lauderdale County for the year 1842.

Ordered by the court that William B. Sawyer be appointed a Revenue Commissioner to take a list of taxable property and polls for the eighth civil district of Lauderdale County for the year 1842.

This day the court here chose and appointed Isaac D. Maxwell, guardian of Dulcinia Maxwell, Mary Maxwell, Soloman Maxwell, Isaac Maxwell, James Maxwell and Elvira Maxwell his own children and heirs at law of Nancy Maxwell his dec'd wife formerly Nancy Byler. Whereupon said Isaac D. Maxwell came into court and entered bond in the sum of $400 with John H. Maxwell and Isaac M. Steele, his securities conditioned and payable as the law directs the said Isaac D. Maxwell, John H. Maxwell and Isaac M. Steele acknowledging said bond in open court which was ordered to be entered of record, whereupon the oath of guardian was administered to the said Isaac D. Maxwell.

This day the court here chose and appointed John H. Maxwell, guardian of Abraham B. Maxwell, Bedford C. Maxwell, Elizabeth Maxwell and John Maxwell, his own children and minor heirs at law of Elvira Maxwell, his dec'd wife formerly Elvira Byler. Whereupon the said John H. Maxwell came into court with Isaac D. Maxwell, Isaac M. Steele and Abel H. Pope, his securities and entered into bond in the sum of four hundred dollars conditioned and payable as the law directs he and his securities acknowledging the same in open court which was ordered to be recorded, whereupon the oath of guardian was administered accordingly.

Pg. Ordered by the court that the court adjourn until tomorrow at 9 o'clock.
412

J. H. Maxwell, Chairman
Elnathan H. Condray, J.P.
A. H. Pope, J.P.

Tuesday Morning

Court met pursuant to adjournment.

It is ordered by the court that Samuel V. Gilliland, Esq., Commissioner of Revenue be paid two dollars and fifty cents by the County Trustee out of any money in the County Treasury not otherwise appropriated for settling with John M. C. Robinson, County Trustee for the year 1840, Ayes on said appropriation were Elnathan H. Condray, Elijah Lake, Samuel V. Gilliland, Abel H. Pope and Henry Willard, Esqs., Noes, none.

It is ordered by the court that Rezin L. Byrn, Esq., Revenue Commissioner be paid two dollars and fifty cents by the County Trustee out of any money in County Treasury not otherwise appropriated for settling with John M. C. Robertson, County Trustee for the year 1840, Ayes, on said appropriation were Elnathan H. Condray, Elijah Lake, Abel H. Pope, Samuel V. Gilliland and Henry Willard Esqs.

Ordered by the court that Benjamin T. Porter be appointed Overseer of New Road from Henry Sumrows to the key corner working from the Center of the
Pg. bridge to the key corner and that he have the following hands to work under
413 him (to wit) Benjamin Porter's hands, O. R. Willis, A. H. Thurman, Rezin Porter, Haukin's hands, William Spence and William Adams and that he keep the same in repair as a second class road.

Pg. 413 cont. Ordered by the court that Saml V. Gilliland and Rezin L. Byrn, Esquires be appointed commissioners of Revenue to settle with the County Officers for the year 1842.

This day Isaac M. Steele produced here in open court a settlementmade by him as clerk of this court with Moses E. Stone, Guardian of John W. Rudder, minor heir of Samuel Rudder which settlement was received by the court.

This day Isaac M. Steele, Clerk of this court produced here in open court a settlement made by him with John Fullen, Administrator of William Fullen, deceased which was received by the court.

Pg. 414 This day Isaac M. Steele, clerk of this court produced here in open court a settlement made by him with James H. Given, Guardian of William W. Johnson, Polly W. Johnson, Sarah A. Johnson and Nancy T. Johnson, minor heirs of Sarah Johnson, which said settlement was received and approved by the court.

This day Isaac M. Steele, clerk of this Court produced here in open court a settlement made by him with Robert C. West, Guardian of Francis Marion Millen and Rachel Caroline Virginia Millen minor heirs of Robert K. Millen which settlement was approved and received by the court.

This day, Isaac M. Steele, clerk of this court produced here in open court a settlement made by him with Robert Jordan, Administrator of William Jordan deceased wihich was received and approved by the court.

This day the court proceeded to elect three Justices of their own body to hold the quorum courts for the year 1842, whereupon John H. Maxwell, Elnathan H. Condray and Henry Willard, Esquires were duly elected.

It was proposed to lay a county Tax at the following rates (To Wit) a Jury Tax on each hundred dollars worth of property on which a state Tax is laid two and a half cents Poor Tax on the same Two and half cents Road and Bridge Tax on the same Two and half cents contingent Tax on the same $2\frac{1}{2}$ cts Jury Tax on each White Poll $12\frac{1}{2}$ cts Contingent Tax on White polls twelve and a half cents County Tax on all License Privileges the same as the State Tax, ayes for said rates were Elnathan H. Condray, Samuel V. Gilliland, Elijah Lake, John H. Maxwell, Abel H. Pope, Wm. B. Sawyer, Milton G. Turner and Henry Willard, Esquires a majority of the Justices in said County so said Tax was laid accordingly.

It is ordered by the court that the County Trustee pay C. G. Fisher Five dollars for selecting paper for McEntry taker of this county and C. out
Pg. of any money in the county Treasury not otherwise appropriated, ayes, Con-
416 dray, Gilliland Lake, Turner and Willard, Esqr. one third of all the Justices in said County, Noes, None.

It is ordered by the court that James Braden, Entry Taker of said county be paid by the County Trustee out of any money in the county Treasury not otherwise appropriated the sum of Ten Dollars for producing papers for said office from 11th and 13th District, ayes, Condray, Gilliland, Lake, Turner, and Willard, Esquires one third of all the Justices of said County Noes, None.

Whereas the clerk has reported to this court that H. A. G. Lee one of the security of William D. Lee, Guardian of Malvina A. Marley andJosiah C. Marley orphan and minor heirs of Adam Marley and Susan C. Marley has died. It is therefore ordered by the court the clerk issue a notice directed to the sheriff of this County commanding him to notify the said William D. Lee ten days before the next term of this court to be and appear in this court on the first Monday in February next than and there to give new and counter security in
Pg. place of the said H. A. G. Lee, deceased or deliver up the said estate.
417 Ordered that court adjourn until Court in course.

J. H. Maxwell, Chairman
Elnathan H. Condray, J. P.
Elijah Lake, J. P.

Pg. 418 Be it remembered that at a county court began and held in the Court House in the town of Ripley for the county of Lauderdale and State of Tennessee on the first Monday in February. It being the Seventh day of said month in the year of our Lord one thousand Eight Hundred and Forty two and the 66th year of American Independence. Present John H. Maxwell, Elnathan H. Condray, and Henry Willard, Esquires, elected to hold the quorum Court for said County, Isaac M. Steele, clerk by his deputy Wm. T. Moorehead with Griffith L. Rutherford Esqr., Sheriff.

John H. Maxwell, Esqr. was elected, chairman of said court.

Whereas notice having been served on William D. Lee, Guardian for Josiah and Malvina Marley, Minor Heirs of Adam Marley Decd to come before this court and give Counter security. And Guilford Jones came before the court and offered himself as security which was received and ordered to be recorded.

This day Isaac M. Steele, Clerk by his Deputy Wm. T. Moorehead presented to court the settlement made with him and John L. Flippin, Administrator of John Flippin Decd which was received and ordered to be recorded.

Ordered by the court that James Sherman be appointed overseer of the Ashport Rod from the forks East of Stephen Guardner and working to the bridge on Cane Creek in the place of James Gillespie and that he have the same hands to work said Road that Gillispie had.

This day Isaac M. Steele, Clerk by his Deputy Wm. T. Moorehead presented to Court the settlement made by him with William P. Gains Guardian for Juretta Nesivanger, Minor Heir of Jacob Nesivanger Decd. which was received and ordered to be recorded.

This day Joseph Currie administrator of all and singular the goods and chattels, rights and credits of Henderson Jones Dec'd. returned on oath here in open Court an inventory and account of sales of said Estate which was received and ordered to be recorded.

This day William A. Wood, Administrator of all and singular the goods and chattels, rights, and credits of Eleanor Wood, Deceased returned on oath here in open Court an inventory and account of sales of said Estate which was received and ordered to be recorded.

Pg. 420 This day the Jury of view appointed at the last term of this court to view and determine the propriety of turning that part of the road leading from Fullens Ferry to Durhamville over which James H. Cleaves is overseer, returned the following report which was received and ordered to be recorded (To Wit) State of Tennessee) We the undersigned be appointed and sworn to Lauderdale County) view and determine on the propriety of turning that part of the public road leading from Fullen's Ferry to Durhamville over which Jas. H. Cleaves is overseer do report that in our opinion the said road ought to be changed as follows (To Wit) beginning one hundred yards West of the corner of Joseph Curries fence thence through the plantation of S. V. Gilliland so as to intersect the old road below the Negro Cabins all of which is respectfully submitted to the consideration of the Court this 4th day of Febry 1842.

S. A. Thompson
David P. Posey
Thos. Fitzpatrick
Joseph Currie
David C. Russell

This day A. G. W. Byrn administrator of all and singular the goods and chattels, rights and credits of Jeremiah Cotter Deceased returned on oath here in open court an inventory and account of sales of said Estate which was received and ordered to be recorded.

Pg. 421 Ordered by the Court that Samuel P. Anders Administrator of Charlotte Anders, Deceased be notified by the Sheriff of Dyer County to appear before this Court at the next term thereof to give counter security otherwise the effects of said Estate will be required to be given up to Willie Dodd who has made oath according to law in such cases made and provided.

Ordered by the Court that Arthur Williams be appointed overseer of the

Pg. 421 cont. Fulton Road commencing at the Lauderdale and Haywood Counties line to Durhamville and that he have the hands of Mary I. Lea to work the same.

It appearing to the satisfaction of the court here that Williamson price has died intestate and James Price having applied for letters of Administration on said Estate and the court being satisfied with his claims to the administration and he having given bond with Archer Phillips and Edmund Fitzpatrick his securities and he and they having acknowledged the same in open court, therefore, it is ordered by the Court that letters of Administration Jessie on the said Estate to the said James Price.

Pg. 422 This day the court chose and appointed Ransome Hawkins, Guardian of Catherine Hawkins, minor Heir of Martha Hawkins, Dec'd, formerly Martha Williams, whereupon the said Ransome Hawkins with Henry Willard and Abel H. Pope his securities came into Court and entered into bond conditioned and payable as the law directs and took the oath prescribed by law for Guardians.

Ordered by the court that court be adjourned until Court in Course.

J. H. Maxwell, Chairman
Elnathan H. Condray, J. P.
Henry Willard, J. P.

Pg. 423 Be it remembered that at a quorum Court began and holden for the County of Lauderdale and State of Tennessee in the Court House in the Town of Ripley on the First Monday in March it being the seventh day of said Month In the year of our Lord, one thousand Eight hundred and forty Two and the Sixty Sixth year of American Independence. Present, John H. Maxwell, Esq. Chairman of said court together, E. H. Condray and Henry Willard, Esq. with Isaac M. Steele clerk andGriffith L. Rutherford, Esq. Sheriff.

This day came into open court, Griffith L. Rutherford and produced before the court his certificate of his election as Sheriff of Lauderdale County and Executed the following bonds for the faithful performance of his duties as such Sheriff and Collector of the public Tax for the County of Lauderdale which said Bonds are in the following words and figures viz)

Pg. 424 State of Tennessee) We, Griffith L. Rutherford, James L. Green, Henry Lauderdale County) F. Rutherford and Edwin H. Hinton jointly and severally acknowledge ourselves indebted to James C. Jones, Governor of the State of Tennessee for the time being and his successors in office, in the penal sum of Twenty thousand dollars; for which payment will and turly to made, we bind ourselves, our heirs, executors, and administrators, jointly and severally, formly by these presents; sealed with our seals and dated the 7th day of March 1842.

The condition of the above obligation is such, that whereas, the above bounden Griffith L. Rutherford, has been duly and constitutionally elected Sheriff and collector of the Public taxes of the county of Lauderdale aforesaid, for two years from the first Saturday in March 1842, as appears from the certificate of Isaac Braden Coroner of said county, if therefore the said Griffith L. Rutherford shall will and truly execute, and due return make af all process and precepts to him directed, and pay satisfy all fees and sums of money by him received or levied by virtue of any process in the

Pg. 425 proper office, by which the same by the tenor thereof ought to be paid, or to the person or persons to whom the same shall be due, his, her or their executor, administrator, attorney or agents, and in all things will, truly and faithfully execute the said office of Sheriff during his continuance therein, then the above obligation to be void; otherwise to remain in full force and effect.

Acknowledged in open Court. J. H. Maxwell Chairman County Court

Griffith L. Rutherford (Seal)
Jas. L. Green (Seal)
Henry F. Rutherford (Seal)
E. H. Hinton (Seal)

Know all men by these presents, that we Griffith L. Rutherford, James L. Green, Henry F. Rutherford and Edwin H. Hinton all of Lauderdale County and State of Tennessee, are held and formly bound until James C. Jones, Governor of State of Tennessee, for time being and his successors in office,

Pg. 425 cont. for the use of Said State, in the penal sum of Two thousand dollars for which payment well and truly to be made, we bind ourselves, our heirs, executors and administrators, jointly and severally, firmly by these presents, sealed with our seals and dated the 7th day of Mardh 1842.

Pg. 426 The condition of the above obligation is such, that whereas, the above bounden Griffith L. Rutherford has been duly and constitutionally elected Sheriff and collector of the public Taxes of said Lauderdale county, for two years from the first Saturday in March last passed 1842. Now if the said Griffith L. Rutherford shall well and truly collect all State Taxes which by law he ought to collect, and pay to the Treasurer of the State all State Taxes by him collected, or which ought to have been collected; on or before the last day of December in each and every year in which he shall collect the Taxes; then the above obligation to be void, otherwise to remain in full force and virtue.

Acknowledge in	Griffith L. Rutherford	(Seal)
Open Court	Jas. L. Green	(Seal)
J. H. Maxwell	H. F. Rutherford	(Seal)
Chairman County Court -	E. H. Hinton	(Seal)

State of Tennessee) We, Griffith L. Rutherford, James L. Green, Henry
Lauderdale County) F. Rutherford and Edwin H. Hinton jointly and

Pg. 427 severally adknowledge our selves indebted to John H. Maxwell, Chairman of the County Court of Lauderdale County for time being and his successors in office, in the penal sum of two thousand dollars; for which payment well and truly to be made, we bind ourselves, our heirs, executors and administrators, jointly and, severally firmly by these presents; sealed with our seals and dated the 7th day of March 1842. Whereas the said Griffith L. Rutherford was on 5th day of March 1842 duly and legally elected, Sheriff and collector of the Public Taxes for the County of Lauderdale. Now if the said Griffith L. Rutherford shall, well and truly collect and pay to the Trustee of said county of Lauderdale, all county Taxes by him collected, on or before the last day of December in each and every year in which he shall collect the Taxes, Then the above obligation to be void, otherwise to remain in full force and virtue.

Acknowledged in	Griffith L. Rutherford	(Seal)
Open Court	Jas. L. Green	(Seal)
J. H. Maxwell,	H. F. Rutherford	(Seal)
Chairman County Court -	E. H. Hinton	(Seal)

Whereupon the several oath prescribed by law was administered to the

Pg. 428 said Griffith L. Rutherford all of which said bonds, and various signature of the parties were duly acknowledged in open court, in pursuance to the Statute in such case made and provided and ordered to be recorded.

This day came into open court Gilford Jones and produced the Certificate of Isaac Braden, Coroner of Lauderdale County of his Election as Trustee of said County of Lauderdale for two years from the first Saturday in March 1842 and Executed the following Bond for the safe keeping of County Revenue and the faithfully, performance of his duties which said bond is in the words and figures following - (To Wit) -

State of Tennessee) We, Gilford Jones, William D. Lee, and E. H. Hinton
Lauderdale County) all of the County of Lauderdale are held and firmly bound unto John H. Maxwell chairman of the County Court of said County and his successors in office in the penal sum of Two thousand dollars, for which payment will and truly to be made we bind ourselves our heirs executors and ad-

Pg. 429 ministrators jointly and severally firmly by these presents, sealed with our seals and dated the 7th day of March 1842.

Whereas the above bound Guilford Jones was on the 5 day of March 1842 duly and legally elected Trustee of Lauderdale County, as appears from the certificate of Isaac Braden, coroner of said County; now the condition of this obligation is such that if the said Guilford Jones shall safely Keep and faithfully pay out all county monies which shall be deposited in his hands agreeable to the orders of the County Court of said County of Lauder-

Pg. dale and otherwise faithfully discharge the duties of his office accord-
429 ing to law in all things then this obligation to be void, otherwise to
cont. remain in full force and virtue. -

Acknowledge in Open Court Isaac M. Steele, Clerk -

Guilford Jones, J. P.
William D. Lee (Seal)
E. Hinton (Seal)

Pg. and the said Guilford Jones entered into the following bond for the safe
430 keeping of common School monies (To Wit).

State of Tennessee) We, Guilford Jones, William D. Lee and E. H. Hin-
Lauderdale County) ton all of the State of Tennessee and county of Lauderdale are held and firmly bound unto Scott Terry, Superintendent of public instruction and his successors in office in the penal sum of Fifteen hundred dollars for which payment well and truly to be made, we bind ourselves, our heirs, executors and administrators jointly and severally, firmly by these presents sealed with our seals and dated the 7th day March 1842.

Whereas the above bound Guilford Johns was on the 5th day of March 1842 duly and legally elected Trustee of Lauderdale County as appears from the certificate of Isaac Braden Coroner of said County - Now the condition of this obligation is such that if the said Guilford Jones shall faithfully pay according to law all monies which may come in into his hands on account of common Schools then this obligation to be void, otherwise to remain in
Pg. full force and virtue.
431 Acknowledged in) Open Court) Isaac M. Steele) Clerk)

Guilford Jones (Seal)
William D. Lee (Seal)
E. H. Hinton (Seal) -

Whereupon the said Guilford Jones took the several oaths prescribed by law.

This day James Price came into Court and produced the Certificate of Isaac Braden Coroner of Lauderdale County certifying that he was duly elected Register of said County and Executed the following bonds - (To Wit) -

State of Tennessee) We, James Price, David Gilliland, William P. Gaines
Lauderdale County) and H. C. Keller, all of the County of Lauderdale are held and firmly bound unto James C. Jones, Governor of the State of Tennessee for the time being and his successors in office in the penal sum of Twelve Thousand, Five hundred Dollars for which payment well and truly
Pg. to be made, we bind ourselves, our heirs, executors and administrators,
432 jointly and severally, firmly by these presents; sealed with our seals and dated the 7th day of March 1842. Whereas, the above bound James Price was on the 5th day of March 1842 duly and legally elected Register of Lauderdale County by the qualified voters thereof as appears from the certificate of Isaac Braden, Coroner of said County. Now the condition of this obligation is such that if the said James Price Shall, truly, and faithfully discharge the duties of his office according to law in all things, then this obligation to be void, otherwise to remain in full force and virtue.

Acknowledged in) Open Court) Isaac M. Steele)

David Gilliland (Seal)
Wm. P. Gaines (Seal)
H. C. Keller (Seal)

Whereupon the oaths prescribed by law were taken by the said Price.

This day Samuel A. Thompson came into Court and produced a certificate of Isaac Braden, Coroner of Lauderdale County Certifying that he was duly elected by the qualified voters of the first civil district a Constable of
Pg. said County, whereupon he entered into bond in the sum of eight thousand dol-
433 lars with Hiram C. Keller, Jonathan L. Hearring and Guilford Jones, securities condition or payable as the law directs; he and they acknowledging the same in open court according to the form of statute in such case made and provided which said bond was ordered to be recorded whereupon the several oaths prescribed by law for a constable was administered to the sd. Samuel A. Thompson.

This day Thomas J. Keeton and William A. Wood came into court and pro-

Pg. 433 cont. duced the certificate of Isaac Braden, Coroner of said County of Lauderdale of their election as Constables of the second civil district of said County and entered into bond with securities condition payable as the law directs which was ordered to be recorded and the several oaths of law for constablex administered to the Said William A. Wood and Thomas J. Keeton.

This day Marshall A. Posey came into court and produced the certificate of Isaac Braden, Coroner of Lauderdale County of his Election as a Constable for the Third Civil District of Said County and entered into bond wibhssecurity conditioned and payable as the law directs which was
Pg. 434 ordered to be recorded and the several oaths prescribed by law for a constable was administered to the said Marshall A. Posey.

This day Samuel Deason came into Court and produced the certificate of Isaac Braden coroner of Lauderdale County of his Election as a constable for the 6th Civil District of Said County and entered into bond conditioned and payable as the law directs and took the several oaths prescribed by law for a constable.

This day Robert Crihfield came into court and produced the certificate of Isaac Braden Coroner of Lauderdale County of his Election as a Constable for the Seventh Civil District of said County and enéered into bond with securities conditioned and payable as the law directs and took the several oaths prescribed law for a constable.

Pg. 435 It appearing to the satisfaction of the court that Gilbert Elam has died leaving no will and Ezekiel Farmer having applied for letters of Administration on said estate in consequence of being a credition and having proved his debt on Oath and the Court being satisfied as to his claims to the Administration and he having given bond and security as required by law and took the oath prescribed by law for Administrator it is therefore ordered that he have letters accordingly.

James Price who was appointed at the last term of Court, Administrator of the estate Williamson Price dec'd. came into court this day and took the oath prescribed by law for Administration.

This day Benj. H. Walpole one of the Executors of John Walpole deceased returned into Court on oath an account of the Sales of said Estate which was received and ordered to be recorded.

Pg. 436 This day Ezekiel Farmer Administration of the estate of Gilbert Elam, deceased, returned an oath in open court an Inventory of said Estate which was received and ordered to be recorded.

Ordered by the Court that Rewben Kennedy be appointed overseer of the Buck's Ferry and Stokes landing Road in the place of Joshua Wright, deceased and that he have the following hands to work under him (To Wit) - John Langley, A. J. Langley, Hezekial Henderson, D. Jennings, W. Jennings, Thomas Jennings, Samuel Lusk, John Lockard and George W. Lumpkin and that he keep the same in repair as a second Class road.

The Court adjourned until Court in Course.

J. H. Maxwell, Chairman,
Elnathan H. Condray, J. P.
Henry Willard, J. P.

Pg. 437 Be it remembered that at a County Court began and holden for the county of Lauderdale and State of Tennessee in the Court House in the Town of Ripley on the first Monday in April it being the forrth day of said month in the year of our Lord one-thousand eight-hundred and forty-two and the sixty-sixth year of the Independence of the United States of America present the worshipful, John H. Maxwell, A. H. Pope and E. H. Condray, Esquires, with Isaac M. Steele, clerk and Griffith L. Rutherford, Esquire Sheriff.

A Commission from James C. Jones Governor of the State of Tennessee was produced here in open court at it appearing from the inspection of the same that H. S. Payton, T. G. Rice, J. H. Maxwell, A. H. Pope, J. R. Hutcheson, E. S. Campbell, E. H. Condray, Wm. R. Ledbetter, E. Fishher are commissioned Justices of the peace for the county of Lauderdale County whereupon

Pg. the several oaths prescribed by law were administered to the according to
437 the form of Statutes in such case made and provided said Justices so sworn
cont./ then proceeded to organize by the Election of J. H. Maxwell, Chairman of
Pg./ said Court.
438 This day Griffith L. Rutherford came into court and produced the certificate of Isaac Braden, Coroner of Lauderdale County of his election to the office of shff of sd county and entered into the following bonds.

To Wit:-

State of Tennessee) We, Griffith L. Rutherford, H. F. Rutherford, J. L.
Lauderdale County) Hearring and Robert C. Campbell jointly and severally acknowledge ourselves indebited to James C. Jones, Governor of the State of Tennessee for the time being and his successors in office in the penal sum of Twenty thousand dollars for which payment well and truly to be made we bind ourselves, our heirs, executors and administrator, Jointly and severally firmly by these presents sealed with our seals and dated the 4th day of April 1842. The condition of the above obligation is such that whereas the above bounden, Griffith L. Rutherford was on the first saturday in March 1842 duly and legally elected by the qualified voters of Lauderdale County Sheriff of said
Pg. County if therefore the said Griffith L. Rutherford shall well and truly exe-
439 cute and return make of all process and precepts to him directed and satisfy all fees and sums of money by him received or Levied by virtue of any process in the precepts office by which the same by the tenor thereof ought to be paid or to the person or persons to whom the same shall be due his, her or their executors administrators attorneys or agents and in all things well and truly and faithfully execute the said office of sheriff during his continuance therein then the above obligation to be void otherwise to remain in full force and virtue.

Acknowledged in) G. L. Rutherford (Seal)
Open Court) H. F. Rutherford (Seal)
Test - J. H. Maxwell) J. L. Hearring (Seal)
Chairman-Lauderdale Cty) R. C. Campbell (Seal)

State of Tennessee) We, Griffith L. Rutherford, H. F. Rutherford, J. L.
Lauderdale County) Hearring and Robert C. Campbell jointly and severally acknowledge ourselves indebted to James C. Jones, Governor of the State of Tennessee for the time being and his successors in office in the penal
Pg. sum of two thousand dollars for which payment, well and truly to be made we
440 bind ourselves, our heirs, executors, and administrators jointly and severally firmly by these presents sealed with our seals and dated the 4th day of April 1842.

Whereas the said Griffith L. Rutherford was on the 5th day of March 1842 duly and legally elected to serve as sheriff and collector of the State and County Taxes for Lauderdale County as appears from the certificate of Isaac Braden Coroner of said County. Now if the said Griffith L. Rutherford shall well and truly collect and pay to the Treasurer of the State all Taxes by him collected or which ought to have been collected on or before the last day of December in each and every year in which he shall collect the Taxes then the above obligation to be void otherwise to remain in full force and virtue.

Acknowledged in) G. L. Rutherford (Seal)
Open Court on the) H. F. Rutherford (Seal)
4th day of April 1842) J. L. Hearing (Seal)
Test. J. H. Maxwell) R. C. Campbell (Seal)
Chairman Lauderdale Cty)

Pg.
441 State of Tennessee) We, Griffith L. Rutherford, H. F. Rutherford, J. S.
Lauderdale County) Herring and Robert C. Campbell jointly and severally acknowledge ourselves indebted to J. H. Maxwell, chairman of the County Court for the time being and his successors in office in the penal sum of Two thousand dollars for which payment well and truly to be made we bind ourselves, our heirs, executors and administrators jointly and severally firmly by these pre-

Pg. sents, sealed with our seals and dated the 4th day of April 1842. Whereas
441 the said Griffith L. Rutherford was on the 5th day of March 1842 duly and leg-
cont. ally elected Sheriff and collector of the State and County Taxes for Lauderdale County as appears from the certificate of Isaac Braden Coroner of said county. Now if the said Griffith L. Rutherford shall well and truly collect and pay to the County Trustee of said county all Taxes by him collected or which ought to have been collected on or before the last day of December in
Pg. each and every year in whtth he shall collect the Taxes then the above obliga-
442 tion to be/void otherwise to remain in full force and virtue.

Acknowledged in)	G. L. Rutherford (Seal)
Open Court)	H. F. Rutherford (Seal)
Test. J. H. Maxwell)	J. L. Hearring (Seal)
Chairman, Lauderdale County)	R. C. Campbell (Seal)

All of which said bonds and various signatures of the parties were duly acknowledged in open court in pursuance to the Statute in such case made and provided and ordered to spread on the minutes. Whereupon the several oaths prescribed by law for to be taken by the Sheriff were administered to the said Griffith L. Rutherford according to the form of the Statutes in such made and provided.

This day James Price came into Court and produced the certificate of Isaac Braden, coroner of Lauderdale County of his Election as Register of said County and entered into the following bond(To Wit):-

State of Tennessee) We, James Price, J. H. Maxwell, William P. Gaines,
Pg. Lauderdale County) James A. Lackey and John C. Barnes all of the county
443 of Lauderdale and State aforesaid were held and firmly bound unto James C. Jones, Governor of the State of Tennessee for the term being and his successors in office in the penal sum of Twelve Thousand; five hundred Dollars for which payment well and truly to be made we bind ourselves our heirs, Executors and Administrators jointly and severally, firmly by these presents, sealed with our seals and dated the 4th day of April 1842.

Whereas, the above bound James Price was on the 5th day of March 1842 duly and legally elected Register of Lauderdale County by the qualified voters thereof as appears from the certificate of Isaac Braden Coroner of said County. Now the condition of this obligation is such that if the said James Price shall, truly and faithfully discharge the duties of his office according to law in all things then this obligation to be void otherwise to remain in full force and firtue.

Acknowledge in)	James Price (Seal)
Open Court)	J. H. Maxwell (Seal)
Test. Isaac M. Steele-Clk.)	Wm. P. Gaines (Seal)
	James A. Lacky(Seal)
	J. C. Barnes (Seal)

Pg. Which bond with the several signatures of the parties thereto was duly
444 acknowledged in open court in pursuance to the statute in such case made and provided and ordered to be recorded on the minutes, whereupon the several oaths presctibed by law for Register were duly administered to said James Price.

This day Guilford Jones came into Court and produced the certificate of Isaac Braden, Coroner of Lauderdale County of his election to the office of Trustee of Ladderdale County and entered into the following bond-(To Wit):0

State of Tennessee) We, Guilford Jones, S. Richardson and Edward Fisher Lauderdale County) all of the county of Lauderdale are held and firmly bound unto John H. Maxwell, Chairman of the County Court of said County and his successors in office in the penal sum of Two thousand dollars for which payment well and truly to be made we bind ourselves our heirs executors and administrators jointly and severally firmly by these presents, sealed with
Pg. our seals and dated the 4th day of April 1842.
445 Whereas the above bound Guilford Jones was on the 5th day of March 1842 duly and legally elected Trustee of Lauderdale County as appears from the Certificate of Isaac Braden, Coroner of said County: Now the condition of this

Pg. 445 cont. obligation is such that if the said Guilford Jones shall safely keep and faithfully pay out all county monies which shall be deposited in his hands agreeably to the orders of the county court of said county of Lauderdale and otherwise faithfully discharge the duties of his office according to law in all things then this obligation to be void otherwise to remain in full force and virtue.

Acknowledged in) Guilford Jones (Seal)
Open Court) S. Richardson (Seal)
Test. Isaac M. Steele-Clk.) Edwd. Fisher (Seal)

State of Tennessee) We, Guilford Jones, S. Richardson and Edward Fisher Lauderdale County) all of the County of Lauderdale are held and firmly bound unto Scott Terry, Superintendant of Public Instruction and his successors in office in the penal sum of fifteen hundred dollars for which payment well and truly to be made we bind ourselves, our heirs, executors and administrators, jointly and severally firmly by these presents sealed with our seals and dated the 4th day of April 1842. Whereas the above bound Guilford Jones was on the 5th day of March 1842 duly and legally elected Trustee of Lauderdale County as appears from the Certificate, Isaac Braden, Coroner of said County:- Now the condition of this obligation is such that if the above bound Guilford Jones shall faithfully pay according law all monies which may come into his hands on account of common Schools then this obligation to be void, otherwise to remain in full force and virtue.

Acknowledged in) Guilford Jones (Seal)
Open Court) S. Richardson (Seal)
Test. Isaac M. Steele-Ck.) Edwd. Fisher (Seal)

Which said Bonds with the signatures thereto were acknowledged in open court in pursuance to the statute in such case made and provided and ordered to be recorded in the minutes.

Whereupon the several oaths prescribed by law for Trustee were duly Administered to said G. Jones.

Pg. 447 It appearing to the satisfaction of the Court here from the inspection of the Certificate of Isaac Braden, Coroner of Lauderdale County that Samuel A. Thompson was on the 5th day of March 1842 duly elected to serve as constable for the first district of Lauderdale County, William A. Wood and Tho. J. Keeton for the 2nd district of said County Marshall A. Posey for the 3rd district of Said County James H. Given for the 4th district of said County, James Johnson for the 5th district of said County, Samuel Deason for the 6th district of said County and Robert Crihfield for the 7th district of said County. Whereupon the Constables Elect before named severally came into Court and Entered into bond conditioned and payable as the law directs with Securities approved by the Court and took the oaths prescribed by law for constables.

Pg. 448 Ordered by the Court that the County Trustee pay Isaac M. Steele assignee of Jesse P. Fullen for the building of the bridge on Bates Forke of Cane Creek by said Fullen the sum of Sixty-Eight Dollars and Twenty-five cents, Ayes, Condray, Campbell, Fisher, Hutcheson, Ledbetter, Maxwell, Peyton, Pope, and Rice, Esqrs. a majority of all the Justices of said County.

Ordered by the Court that the county Trustee pay Isaac M. Steele for three Record Books paid for by him for the use of the office of Circuit Court Clerk and Register of this County the sum of Twenty-four Dollars and Seventy-five cents, ayes, Esquires, Condray, Campbell, Fisher, Hutcheson, Ledbetter, Maxwell, Peyton, Pope, and Rice, a majority of all the acting Justices of the peace of said County.

Ordered by the Court that the County Trustee pay Samuel V. Gilliland, Esq. Commissioner of Revenue, Two Dollars and fifty cts. for one day Settling

Pg. 449 with John H. Maxwell, late Trustee of this County, Ayes, Esqs. Condray, Campbell, Fisher, Ledbetter, Maxwell, Peyton, Pope and Rice, Noes, None.

Ordered by the Court that the County Trustee pay Rezin L. Byrn, Esq. Commissioner of Revenue, Two-Dollars and fifty cents for settling with John H. Maxwell, late Trustee of this county, ayes, Esquires, Condray, Campbell, Fisher, Ledbetter, Maxwell, Peyton, Pope and Rice.

Pg. 449 cont. Ordered by the Court that the County Trustee pay Samuel A. Thompson, Ten-Dollars for taking in a list of Taxable property and polls in the first Civil District of this County for the year 1842 ayes, Esquires, Condray, Campbell, Maxwell, Peyton, Pope, Rice and Fisher, Noes, Esquires Ledbetter and Hutcheson.

Ordered by the Court that the County Trustee pay John H. Maxwell, Ten-Dollars for taking in a list of Taxable property and polls in the second civil district of Lauderdale County for the year 1842 ayes, Esquires, Condray, Campbell, Fisher, Maxwell, Peyton, Pope and Rice, Noes Esquires, Ledbetter and Hutcheson.

Pg. 450 Ordered by the Court that the County Trustee pay Elijah Lake, Ten-Dollars for taking in a list of Taxable property and polls for the 3rd civil district of Lauderdale County for the year 1842 ayes, Esquires Condray, Campbell, Fisher, Maxwell, Peyton, Pope, and Rice, Noes, Esquires, Ledbetter and Hutcheson.

Ordered by the court that the County Trustee pay Henry Willard Ten-Dollars for taking in a list of Taxable property and polls for the 4 civil district of Lauderdale County for the year 1842 ayes, Esquires, Condray, Campbell, Fisher, Maxwell, Peyton, Pope and Rice. Noes, Esquires Ledbetter and Hutcheson.

Ordered by the court that the County Trustee pay Rezin G. Henley, Ten-Dollars for taking in a list of Taxable property and polls for the 5 civil district of Lauderdale County for the year 1842, ayes, Esquires, Condray, Campbell, Fisher, Maxwell, Peyton, Pope, and Rice, Noes, Esquires, Ledbetter and Hutcheson.

Pg. 451 Ordered by the court that the County Trustee pay E. H. Condray, Ten-Dollars for taking a list of Taxable property and polls for the 6th civil district of Lauderdale county for 1842, ayes, Esquires, Condray, Campbell, Fisher, Maxwell, Peyton, Pope, andRice, Noes, Esquires, Ledbetter and Hutcheson.

Ordered by the court that the County Trustee pay E. H. Hinton, Ten-Dollars for taking a list of Taxable property and polls in the 7th civil district of Lauderdale County for the year 1842, ayes, Esquires, Condray, Campbell, Fisher, Maxwell, Peyton, Pope and Rice, Noes, Esquires, Ledbetter and Hutcheson.

Ordered by the Court that the County Trustee pay Wm. B. Sawyer Ten-Dollars for taking a list of Taxable property and polls in the 8th civil district of Lauderdale County for the year 1842, ayes, Esquires, Condray, Campbell, Fisher, Maxwell, Pope and Rice, Noes, Esquires, Ledbetter and Hutcheson.

Pg. 452 On motion, G. L. Rutherford ordered by the Court that Daniel Cherry be released from payment of double taxes on 2560 acres of land in the 4th civil district of Lauderdale County valued at $8960 by the payment of the single Tax for the year 1842.

On motion of G. L. Rutherford, ordered by the court that William Bradshaw be released from the payment of double Taxes on 200 acres of land in the 4 civil district of Lauderdale County valued at $600 by the payment of the single Taxes on the same.

Ordered by the Court on motion of G. L. Rutherford that James Trimble heirs be released from the payment of double Taxes on 70 acres of land lying in the 4th civil district of Lauderdale County valued at $250 by the payment of Single Tax on the same.

On motion of G. L. Rutherford ordered by the Court that the heirs of James Trimble be released from the paymentof double Tax on 1360 acres of land lying in the 4th civil district of Lauderdale County valued at $2720 by

Pg. 453 the payment of Single Taxes on the same.

On motion of G. L. Rutherford, ordered by the Court that Marget and Trimble be released from the payment of Double Taxes on 64 acres of land lying in the 4th civil district of Lauderdale County valued at $232 by the payment of the single Taxes on the same.

On motion of G. L. Rutherford, ordered by the Court that Malvina E. Trimble

Pg. 453 cont. be released from the payment of Double Taxes on 109 acres of land lying in the 4th civil district of Lauderdale County valued at $500 by the payment of Single Taxes on the same.

On motion of G. L. Rutherford, ordered by the Court that Lynn Rhodes be released from the payment of double Taxes on 497 acres of land lying in the 1st civil district of Lauderdale County valued at $1500 by the payment of single Taxes on the same.

Pg. 454 On motion of G. L. Rutherford ordered by the court that James Caldwell be released from the payment of double Taxes on 800 acres of land lying in the 8th civil district of Lauderdale County valued at $2000 by the payment of single Taxes on the same.

On motion of G. L. Rutherford ordered that the heirs of John Kennelly be released from the payment of double Taxes on 263 acres of land lying in the 8th Civil District of Lauderdale County valued at $500 by the payment of Single Taxes on the same.

On motion of G. L. Rutherford ordered that the heirs of John Kennelly be released from the payment of double Taxes on two lots in Canton Lying in Civil District No. 8 of Lauderdale County valued at $300 by the payment of single Taxes on the same.

Ordered by the court that G. L. Rutherford be released from the payment of double Taxes on 128 acres of land lying in the 8th civil district of Lauderdale County valued at $256 by the payment of single Taxes on the same.

Pg. 455 On motion of G. L. Rutherford ordered by the Court that Paschal W. Sanders be released from the payment of double Taxes on one Lot in Canton lying in Civil District No. 8. Valued at $50.00 by the payment of Single Taxes on the same.

On motion ordered by the Court that Wm. D. Lee be released from the payment of double Taxes on 337 acres of land lying in civil No. 8 valued at $1350 by the payment of the single Taxes on the same.

On motion ordered that Daniel B. Turner be released from the payment of Double Taxes on 1250 acres of land lying in Civil District No. 4 valued at $2500 by the payment of the single Taxes on the same.

On motion of Abel H. Pope ordered by the court that Wm. W. Woodfolk be released from the payment of double Taxes on 20 acres of land valued at $100 lying in Civil District No. 4.

Pg. 456 Ordered that the following report be received and recorded and the road established accordingly:- A majority of all the Justices present and voting for the same - (To Wit). To the worshipful County Court of Lauderdale County.

The undersigned free holders having been summoned by the Sheriff of Lauderdale County and duly sworn as a jury of view and to lay off the road described in the annexed order have proceeded to perform the duty assigned them and do agree upon and make the following report-(To Wit)-The said road shall begin at Ashport, Tennessee, near Samuel Deasons and running on the ridge with the old road and near it until it intersects the Dyersburg road at B. Fishers.

They have thus laid out said road to the greatest advantage to the inhabitants and as little as may be to the prejudice of enclosures to best of their knowledge and skill all of which they respectfully submit to the consideration of the worshipful Court. This 1st day of April, 1842.

S. Richardson (Seal)
Jesse Ledbetter (Seal)
Benjamin Nearn (Seal)
Ancel Reynolds (Seal)
Henry Sumrow (Seal

Pg. 457 A. G. W. Byrn and E. H. Hinton appearing and the Court being Satisfied from an inspection of the same that they are Regularly Commissioned by James C. Jones, Governor of the State of Tennessee as Justices of the peace for the County of Lauderdale. Whereupon the several oaths prescribed by law was administered to them and they took their seats as members of this court.

This day James Braden came into open court here and in pursuance to the Act of the General assembly of the State of Tennessee passed at their Session

Pg. 457 cont. in the winter of 1841 and 1842 entered into the following bond - (To Wit)-
State of Tennessee) We, James Braden, A. G. W. Byrn, J. L. Hearring,
Lauderdale County) R. C. Campbell, J. C. Barnes, R. S. Byrn, J. H. Maxwell and G. L. Rutherford jointly and severally, acknowledge ourselves indebted to the State of Tennessee in the penal sum of Seventy Thousand dollars for which payment well and truly to be made we bind ourselves, our heirs,
Pg. 458 executors and administrators jointly and severally, firmly by these presents sealed with our seals and dated the 4th day of April 1842. The condition of the above obligation is such that if the above bound James Braden Entry Taker of the county of Lauderdale shall faithfully perform the several duties of his office as required by law and shall faithfully account for and pay over according to law all moneys by him received in payment for land entered in his office then the above obligation to be void otherwise to remain in full force and virtue.

Acknowledged in)
Open Court)
Test. I. M. Steele-Clk.)

A. G. W. Byrn (Seal)
R. C. Campbell(Seal)
J. L. Hearring(Seal)
Rezin L. Byrn (Seal)
G. L. Rutherford(Seal)
I. H. Maxwell (Seal) -

I, James Braden do solemnly swear that I will faithfully and honestly discharge all the duties appertaining to my office as Entry taker for Lauderdale County as directed by law to the best of my ability and that I will faithfully and honestly account for and pay over all monies by me received
Pg. 459 in payment for any land entered in my office as required by law. So help me God.

James Braden-

The foregoing oath was duly administered to and Subscribedly said James Braden Entry Taker of said County of Lauderdale on this 4th day of April A.D. 1842 and ordered by the Court to be recorded on the minutes of said court.

This day Samuel V. Gilliland and Rezin L. Byrn, Esqr. Commissioners of Revenue appointed by this court to Settle with the County Officers made report of their settlement with John H. Maxwell, late Trustee of Lauderdale which is received and ordered to be recorded as the Statute requires.

Ordered by the court that David P. Posey be permitted to list 80 acres of land lying in the 2nd civil district for Single Taxes said Land valued at $4.00

Ordered that court adjourn for one hour.

Court met pursuant to adjournment.

Ordered that the Commissioners of the Town of Ripley lay off and sell a lot of the commons of said Town to include the old Court House on one and two years credit. Taking bond with good security and report to the July Term of this court.

Ordered that James Price overseer of the Fulton road have in addition to the hands allowed him by his present order Joseph Wardlow and hand and that he keep the same in repair as a secon Class road.

This day James Price administrator of all and singular the goods and chattels, rights and credits of Williamson Price, deceased, returned in open court on oath an inventory of said estate which is received and ordered to be recorded.

Ordered that John Thompson, A. G. W. Byrn and James Price be appointed commissioners to draft a plan for a bridge and let out to the lowest bidder the building of the same taking bond with sufficient security for the comple-
Pg. 461 tion of the same. The said bridge to be built on Matthews Fork of Cane Creek on Brownsville road leading by Byrns and to be completed by and the commissioners to report to the October Term of this Court.

Ordered by the Court that John W. Hammil be paid by the County Trustee Five-dollars for making a Coffin for Isaac Peterson, Ayes, Esquires, Byrn, Campbell, Fisher, Ledbetter, Maxwell, Peyton, Pope, Rice and Hinton, None, None.

Pg. 461 cont. Ordered that Nancy Grant a pauper be allowed the sum of Forty-Dollars for the year 1842 to be paid by the County Trustee quarterly to be paid to and under the management of John H. Maxwell as Trustee, Ayes, Esquires, Byrn, Condray, Campbell, Fisher, Ledbetter, Maxwell, Peyton, Pope, and Rice, Noes, None.

Ordered that Abel H. Pope be paid by the County Trustee quarterly Two Dollars during the year 1842 to be applied to the support of Rebecca Boswell a pauper, ayes, Esquires, Byrn, Condray, Campbell, Fisher, Ledbetter, Maxwell, Peyton, Pope, Rice and Hinton.

Pg. 462 Ordered that H. S. Peyton, Esq. be paid by the County Trustee, Thirty-Dollars for the year 1842 in quarterly installments to be applied to the support of Charley Smoot a pauper, ayes, Esquires, Condray, Campbell, Fisher, Ledbetter, Maxwell, Peyton, Pope, Rice, and Hinton, Noes, None.

Ordered by the court that John Nixon who was appointed at the January Term of This court to cut out that part of this road leading from Ashport to the mouth of Cole Creek lying between Ashport and John Booths be allowed until the October Term of this court to complete the same.

Ordered by the court that J. C. Nevils who was appointed at the January term of this court to cut out that part of the road leading from Ashport to the mouth of Cole Creek lying between Booths and the mouth of said creek be allowed until the October Term of this Court to complete the same.

Pg. 463 Ordered that the Sheriff of Lauderdale County Summon the following good and lawful men of the body of County of Lauderdale as a Venire for the June Term of the Circuit Court of said County, (To Wit) - George W. Young, Samuel Owen, S. Rice, Edmund Fitzpatrick, William Hafford, A. G. W. Byrn, Walter Glawson, Archer Phillips, Thomas J. Childress, N. W. Barnes, Daniel Williams, Tho. L. Clark, James B. Hutcheson, E. Wakefield, E. S. Campbell, John H. Nixon, Drury Massey, Robertson Meadows, Benjamin Nearn, James H. Hagsette, E. H. Hinton, Caleb W. Anderson, Edmund Wright, James Soward, and Henry Pitts, together with William A. Wood and Thomas J. Keeton, Constables to wait on the Court and Jury.

This day the court proceeded according to the form of the Statute to elect five Trustees for the Ripley Academy - Whereupon Stith Richardson, G.L. Rutherford, J. L. Green, J. W. Durant and Isaac M. Steele were duly elected. The vote being for S. Richardson 9, for G. L. Rutherford, nine, J. L. Green, Eight, for John W. Durant Five, for Rezin L. Byrn four, and for Isaac M. Steele, Nine.

Pg. 464 This day at the request of G. L. Rutherford, Shff. and etc.- H. F. Rutherford, Esq. was sworn according to law as Deputy Sheriff of Lauderdale County.

Ordered that Court adjourn until tomorrow Morning at 9'O'clock, A. M. - J. H. Maxwell, Chairman, A. G. W. Byrn, J. P., H. L. Peyton, J. P.

Tuesday Morning, April 5th 1842, Court met pursuant to adjournment. Present; John H. Maxwell, Chairman together, with, Esquires, H. S. Peyton, Thomas G. Rice, A. G. W. Byrn, E. H. Condray, Edward Fisher and Wm. R. Ledbetter, Isaac M. Steele, clerk and Griffith L. Rutherford, Sheriff.

At the request of James Price, Isaac M. Steele was qualified according to law as deputy Register.

This day the Court proceeded to appoint Three Justices of their own body to hold the quorum Courts for the year 1842. Whereupon, John H. Maxwell, H. S. Peyton and E. H. Condray were appointed.

It appearing to the satisfaction of the court here that Joshaa Wright has departed this life intestate and the widow having relinquished her Right
Pg. 465 to the administration in favor of G. L. Rutherford and the next of kin not applying for letters of Administration and the said G. L. Rutherford having entered into bond with approved security according to law and took the oath of Administrator therefore it is ordered by the Court that he have Letters accordingly.

It appearing to the satisfaction of the Court that Robert Maxwell has departed this life intestate and Joel Kirby having applied for Letters of Administration and the court being satisfied with his caaim to the administration and he having entered into bond with security and took the oath prescribed by

Pg. 465 cont. law. Therefore it is ordered by the Court that he have letters accordingly.
This day Ellison P. Fuller proved by his own oath the killing of one wolf in the County of Lauderdale over the age of four months there being five Justices present. Ordered that the same be certified to the Comptroller of the Treasury.

Pg. 466 Ordered that Jordan W. Richardson be appointed overseer of that part of the public road leading from Ripley to Dyersburg situated between the West End of B. Fishers plantation and the Bridge on Carruths fork of Cane Creek and that he have the following hands to work under him - (To Wit) - B. Fishers hands S. Richardson hands, E. Fisher's hands and John Pewitt and that he keep the same in repair as a first class road.

H. R. Chambers, Esq. appearing and it appearing from the commission filed that he is regularly commissioned a Justice of the peace for Lauderdale County. Therefore the several oaths prescribed by law were administered to him and he therefore took his seat as member of this court.

Ordered by the court present and voting for the same a majority of all the Justices of the county that E. Fisher be appointed overseer to open a road from B. Fishers to the western end of Ancel Reynolds Field with the hands of Jordan W. Richardson and Blair H. Lee and that he cut out said road as a second class road and that he report to the October Term of this Court.

Pg. 467 Ordered by the court present and voting for the same a majority of all the Justices of said County that John Wood be appointed overseer to open a road from Ancel Reynolds to the Ashport Turnpike near Samuel Deasons and that he have the following hands - (To Wit)- Eli Goble hands and Drewry Massey hands, Reuben Cannaday hands and John A. Hogsette and hands and that he cut out the same as a second class road and that he report to the October Term of this court.

Ordered by the Court present and voting for the same Esquires, Condray, Fisher, Peyton, Pope, Ledbetter, Rice, Chambers, and Maxwell a majority of all the Justices of the county that Daniel Williams, James B. Crook, Isaac Braden, E. P. Fuller, David Williams, Green Baker, James Sherman, good and lawful men of the body of the County Lauderdale be appointed a jury of view to view and lay out (if in their opinion the public interest would be promoted thereby) a road to leave the Fulton Road Two miles east of Mrs. Bakers
Pg. 468 running by the peace known as the Hodge place and intersecting the Ashport road at or near Wm. Nashes, 4 miles from Ripley the nearest and best route taking into consideration as well public good as private convenience and that they report to the July Term of this Court.

On motion it is ordered by the court the following Tracts of land be released from the payment of Double Taxes by the payment of single Tax - (To Wit) - Samuel V. Gilliland one tract of Land 4th District 320 acres value $1000, James Taylor heirs 4th Dst. 640 valued at $2000, Same 640 acres 4th Dist. same value $2000. Isaac Taylor 155 - 4 district valued at $500.

Ordered by the Court that Abel H. Pope be paid by the County Trustee, one-hundred and Sixty-dollars for making a plan of Lauderdale County, ayes, Esquires, Condray, Peyton, Pope, Fisher, Ledbetter, Rice, Chambers and Maxwell, a majority of all the Justices of said County, Noes, Byrn.

Ordered that the court adjourn for one hour -

Court met pursuant to adjournment.

Pg. 469 Ordered by the Court that Isaac Braden, Coroner of Lauderdale County be paid by the County Trustee, Ten-Dollars for holding the popular election in March 1842, ayes, Chambers, Condray, Fisher, Ledbetter, Maxwell, Pope, Peyton and Rice, Noes, None.

Ordered by the Court that the Clerk be authorized to procure a Seal for this Court on as good terms as possible and that the Court will reimburse him for the same, ayes, Condray, Peyton, Pope, Fisher, Ledbetter, Rice, Byrn, Chambers and Maxwell, Noes, None.

Ordered by the Court that the court adjourn until court in Course.

J. H. Maxwell, Chairman
A. H. Pope, J. P.
Wm. R. Ledbetter, J. P.

Pg. May Term - 1842 -
470 Be it remembered that at a quorum court began and held for the county of Lauderdale and State of Tennessee in the Court house in the Town of Ripley on the first Monday in May it being the second day of said month in the year of our Lord - One-thousand, Eight-Hundred and forty-Two and the Sixty-Sixth year of the Independence of the United States of America. Present the Worshipful J. H. Maxwell, H. S. Peyton and E. H. Condray, Esquires, appointed to hold the quorum courts of said County of Lauderdale with I. M. Steele, Clerk and Griffith L. Rutherford, Esquire Sheriff.

This day Griffith L. Rutherford, Sheriff and Collector of the Public Taxes for the County of Lauderdale came into open court here and took and subscribed the following oath -, (To Wit) - You, Griffith L. Rutherford do solemnly swear that you will faithfully collect and account for all Taxes for your County or cause the same to be done according to law and to the best of your
Pg. Judgement and that you will use all lawful means in your power to find out
471 such property as may not have been listed for taxation in your county and that you will return a list of property to the clerk of the County Court. So help you God.

Sworn to and subscribed) G. L. Rutherford
in Open Court May 2nd, 1842)
Test. -Isaac M. Steele, Clk.)

It appearing from inspection that J. M. Alexander and O. R. Willis are regularly commissioned Justices of the Peace for the County of Lauderdale by James C. Jones, Governor of the State of Tennessee for the time being whereupon the several oaths prescribed by law was administered to them accordingly.

This day, Joel W. Kirby, Administrator of all and singular the goods and chattels, Rights and credits of Robert Maxwell, deceased, returned on oath in open court an inventory of said estate which is received and ordered to be recorded.

Pg. This day, Isaac Braden, Coroner of Lauderdale County presented to Court
472 Two Inquisitions held by him on the bodies of Henry Kimmons and a person unknown, which is received and ordered to be certified to the County Trustee.

This day, Griffith L. Rutherford, Administrator of all and singular, the good and chattels, rights and Credits of Joshua Wright deceased returned on oath in open court an inventory of said estate which is received and ordered to be recorded.

This day, Thomas J. Childress produced here in open a Commission from James C. Jones, Governor of the State of Tennessee as a Justice of the Peace for the County of Lauderdale - Whereupon the several Oaths prescribed by law was administered to him.

Ordered that adjourn to Court in Course.

J. H. Maxwell, Chairman,
Elnathan H. Condray, J. P.
Henry L. Peyton, J. P.

Pg. June Term - 1842 - Monday, June 6, 1842.
473 Be it remembered that a County Court began and held for the County of Lauderdale and State of Tennessee in the Court House in the Town of Ripley-On the first Monday in June it being the Sixth day of said month in the year of our Lord one-thousand, Eight-hundred and forty-two and Sixty-seventh year of American Independence. Present, John H. Maxwell, Henry L. Peyton, Elnathan H. Condray, Esquires Commissioned and qualified as the law directs appointed to hold the quorum courts for said County with Isaac M. Steele by his Deputy William T. Moorehead, Clerk and Griffith L. Rutherford, Esq. Sheriff. Proclamation being made the following proceedings were had and done in said Court.

Ordered by the Court that John Nixon, Rezin G. Henly and E. S. Campbell free holders unconnected by affinity or consanguinity with --- Temples be appointed Commissioners to Set apart so much of the Crop, Stock provisions and monies on hand of the Estate of Green B. Temple as may be necessary

Pg. for the support of --- Temples widow of G. B. Temples Dec'd until the ex-
473 piration of one year after the decease of said entestate.
cont. Ordered by the court that George W. Gause be appointed overseer of
the road from Durhamville to Williams Ferry on Hatchie River in stead of
Pg. Shadrach Ric e and have the same hands that Rice had and that he keep the
474 same in repair as a second Class road.

This day, Samuel Hooper returned his order as overseer of the Dyersburg road from the north Boundary of Leonard.Dunavants land to Mill Creek. and it is ordered by the Court that Jack Fowler be appointed Overseer of said Road in the place of Saml Hooper and that he have the same hands that Hooper had and that he be required to keep the same in repair as a first Class road.

This day Isaac M. Steele, Clerk by his deputy, William T. Morehead, presented to court the Settlement made with him and David A. Bradford, Guardian of William T. Burke, Mary J. Burke, Eleanor A. Burke, Robert A. Burke, and Caledonia T. Burke, minor Heirs of Arnold Burke Dec'd which was received and ordered to be recorded.

Ordered by the Court that Armslead Wood, Samuel Lukk, and William Deason, free holders unconnected by affinity or consanguinity to Mary Wright be appointed commissioners to set apart so much of the crop stock, provisions and monies, on hand of the Estate of Joshua Wright Dec'd as may be necessary for the support of the said Mary Wright - Widow of Joshua Wright Dec'd until the expiration of one year after the Decease of said intestate.

Pg. Monday June 6th, 1842.
475 Ordered by the Court that Benjamin Nearn, Jesse Ledbetter and William
R. Ledbetter, free holders unconnected by affinity or consanguinity with Nancy Maxwell a child under fifteen years of age, minor Heir of Robert Maxwell, Dec'd. be appointed commissioners to set apart so much of the Crop, Stock, provisions and monies on hand, or due, or other assets of the Estate of Robt. Maxwell, Dec'd as may be necessary for the support of the said Nancy Maxwell, minor Heir of Robt. Maxwell, Dec'd. until the expiration of one year after the decease of the said intestate.

This day James Price Administrator of Williamson Price Deced. returned an additional inventory of said Estate upon Oath which is received and ordered to be recorded.

Ordered by the Court that the Clerk issue a summons directed to the Sheriff of Lauderdale County to notify Joel W. Kearly,Administrator of the Estate of Robert Maxwell, Dec'd. to be and appear before this Court at the next Term thereof to give additional security.

This day, Joel W. Kearly, Administrator of the Estate of Robert Maxwell Dec'd. returned hereupon oath an additional inventory of Property of said Estate which is received and ordered to be recorded.

Pg. Monday June 6th, 1842.
476 This day Joel W. Kearly, Administrator of the Estate of Robert Maxwell
Dec'd. returned on oath his sale Bill of said Estate which is received and ordered to be recorded.

This day Jesse R. Hutcheson overseer of the Fulton Road from Cane Creek Bridge to Fulton Turn-Pike returned his road order and it is ordered by this court that Miles D. Wakefield be appointed overseer of said Road in the place of J. R. Hutcheson and that he have the same hands that Hutcheson had and that he keep the same in repair as a first Class road.

Ordered by the Court that Court be adjourned until Court in Course.

J. H. Maxwell, Chairman,
Hennis L. Peyton, J. P.
Elnathan H. Condray, J. P.

July Term 1842.

Be it remembered that at a County Court began and held for the County of Lauderdale and State of Tennessee at the Court House in the Town of Ripley on the first Monday in July being the fourth day of said month in the year of our Lord one-thousand, Eight-hundred and Forty-Two and the 66th year

Pg. of American Independence. Present the worshipful, John H. Maxwell, Chair-
476 man together with Esquires, Childress, Condray, Peyton, Rice, Alexander,
cont. Hutcheson, Pope, Ledbetter, Isaac M. Steele, Clerk and Griffith L. Rutherford, Esquire, sheriff, the following proceedings were had in said court.

This day Jas. L. Green duly commissioned a Justice of the peace for
the County of Lauderdale aforesaid appeared and took the several oaths prescribed by law for Justices and took his seat as a member of this court.

This day David Walker returned his order as overseer of the road leading from Ripley to the County-Line near Champ C. Conner which is received.

Pg. Ordered that John Laird be appointed overseer of the road leading from
478 Ripley to the County-Line near Champ C. Conners and that he have the following hands to work under him (To Wit) David Walker, Jas. A. Morris, A. G. W.
Byrn hands, A. Vickery, M. Hamer, Wm. Hafford, Jerry Riddle, Lance Greaves,
John B. Byrn and Joseph Glawson and hands and that he keep the same in repair
as a second class road.

This day Griffith L. Rutherford, Administrator and etc. of the estate of
Joshua Wright returned on oath in open Court an account of the sales of said
Estate which is received and ordered to be recorded.

This day James Price returned his order as overseer of the Public Road
from Ripley to Fulton road as far as the old Fulton road which is received.

Ordered that Isaac Thompson be appointed overseer of Fulton road from
Ripley to the old Fulton Road near Gaines Old place and that he have the fol-
Pg. lowing hands - (To Wit) - John McCall, Joseph Wardlaw and hands and James
479 Price and that he keep the same in repair as a second class Road.

This day, Andrew Caplerger proved by his own oath the killing in the
County of Lauderdale of one wolf over the age of four months there being five
Justices present. Ordered that the same be certified to the Comptroller of
the Treasury.

This day the Court proceeded to establish a Ferry on Hatchie River on
the road from Durhamville to Covington at the place called and known as Williams Old Ferry.

Whereupon the Court orders adjudges and decrees that said ferry be established enjoying all the rights profits and privileges of a public ferry
and that George W. Gause and Richard W. Green be appointed keepers of said ferry
and that they be liable according to the farm of the Statute as such keepers
of a public ferry and they entered into bond and security as required by law
whereupon George W. Gause came into court and entered into bond, conditioned
Pg. and payable as the directs with John W. Durant and Thomas G. Rice for his
480 securities. It is further ordered and Decreed that the said Gause and Green
may take demand and receive the following rates and no higher.

For wagon drawn by four horses, mules, or oxen or mare	-	.37 cts.
For every Two horse carriage	-	.25
For every two wheele carriage	-	.25
For man and horse	-	.12½
For each horse in a drove or led	-	.06¼
For each head of cattle	-	.03
For each head of hogs or sheep	-	.01
For each footman	-	.06¼

And then terms the above rates for long Ferriage.

Ordered that the County Trustee pay Isaac M. Steele, Clerk of this
Court one-dollars for a blank book purchased of James A. Lackey in the year
1840 to make the sheriff Tax list in one-dollars for ditto purchased of
James J. Robinson for fifty-cents for ditto purchased of Durant and Hearring
for the same for the year 1842. One-dollar for furnishing the sheriff bond
to the Comptroller for the year 1842. As per receipt one-dollar for recording
Pg. settlement with the County Trustee in the year 1842. One-dollars and Seventy-
481 five cents for Issuing Twenty-eight Jury Tickets from the October Term of the
Circuit Court of Lauderdale County 1841. One-dollar fifty-six and one-fourth
cents for issuing Twenty-five Jury Tickets from the Febry. Term 1842 of the
Circuit Court for said county one-dollar Sixty-two and one-half cents for issuing

Pg. Twenty-Six Jury Tickets from the June Term 1842 of the Circuit Court for
481 said County, one-dollar and fifty-cents for all services in relation to
cont. three paupers-(To Wit)-Rebecca Boswell, Charles Smoot and Nancy Grant for
the year 1842. One-dollar and fifty-cents for Issuing eight Road and two
orders for Juries of view from October Term 1841, twelve and one-half Cents
for issuing one road order from December Term 1841, one-dollar twelve and
one-half cents for issuing five road orders and two orders for Juries of
view from the January Term 1842. Twenty-five cents for issuing two road
orders from the Febry. Term 1842. One-dollar for issuing six road orders
Pg. and one order for a Jury of view at April Term 1842. Thirty-Seven and a
482 half cents for issuing Three Road orders at June Term 1842. $20.00 furn-
ishing Sheriff with Tax list for 1842. One-dollar for Issuing Venire facias
for Febry. and June Terms 1842. of the Circuit Court for said County in all
the sum of Thirty-six Dollars and $37\frac{1}{2}$ cents the, ayes, for said Appropriation
was Alexander, Childress, Condray, Green, Hutcheson, Ledbetter, Maxwell, Pope,
Peyton and Rice, Noes, None.

Ordered that Rezin L. Byrn, Treasurer of the Commissioners of the Town
of Ripley be allowed to return as a compensation for his services Three per
centum on all monies received and three per centum on all monies paid out
the, ayes, for said Allowance were Alexander, Childress, Condray, Green, Ledbetter, Maxwell, Pope, Peyton, and Rice, Noes, None.

Ordered by the Court that I. M. Steele, G. L. Rutherford and Jonathan
L. Hearring be appointed Commissioners to divide the negroes devised by the
Pg. last will of Amy Richardson deceased to Rebecca A. Lackey formerly Rebecca
483 A. Richardson, Mary A. Richardson and Virginia A. Richardson, Children of
S. Richardson and report to the October Term of this Court.

This day Joel W. Kirby, Administrator of the estate of Robert Maxwell,
deceased, returned on oath into open court an additional inventory and additional Sale Bill of said Estate which received and ordered to be recorded.

Ordered that the County Trustee pay Isaac Braden, Coroner of Lauderdale
County, Six Dollars and fifty-cents, funeral charges incurred by him in burying Henry Kimmons and a person whose name is unknown, ayes, on said Appropriation were Alexander, Condray, Childress, Green, Hutcheson, Maxwell, Peyton, Pope, Rice and Ledbetter.

Pg. Ordered that the following good and lawful men of the body of the
484 County of Lauderdale be appointed a jury of view to view out and mark a public road (if in their opinion the public interest will be promoted thereby)
into consideration the public good as well as private convenience from the
most convenient point near Joseph Curries in the direction of Fulton to intersect the Fulton Road near James B. Crooks that is to say David Fitzpatrick, Elijah Lake, John McWhite, James B. Crook, A. H. Pope, Thomas J.
Childress, and George Thum and that they report to the October Term of This
Court present and voting for said order, Esquires Alexander, Childress, Condray, Green, Hutcheson, Ledbetter, Maxwell, Pope, Peyton, a majority of all
the Justices of said County.

Pg. This day Isaac Moore proved by his own oath the killing of Four Wolves
485 in the County of Lauderdale one over and three under the age of four months.
There being five Justices present it is ordered that the same be certified
to Comptroller of the Treasury.

Ordered that the County Trustee pay Abel H. Pope, Surveyor of Lauderdale County, Three-Dollars for surveying and making a plot and certificate
of said survey of the Lot in the Town of Ripley on which the Old Court House
is situated the ayes, on said appropriation were, Alexander, Childress, Don-
dray, Green, Hutcheson, Ledbetter, Maxwell, Peyton, and Rice, Noes, None.

Pg. Ordered that Archer Phillips, Overseer of the public road from Hurricane
486 Hill to the forks of the same near James Whitson's have the following hands
in addition to those allowed him by his former order - (To Wit) - John Price,
W. Boyd and John Boyd and that he keep the same in repair as a second Class
road.

Pg. 486 cont. This day the court chose and appointed John Thompson Guardian of John W. Rudder an orphan and minor heir of Same Rudder in the room and stead of Moses E. Stone former Guardian whereupon the said John Thompson came into Court and entered into bond conditioned and payable as the law directs with A. P. Thompson and William A. Wood as his securitys.

Ordered that James W. Reynolds be appointed overseer of the road from Ripley towards Dyersburg in the place of William Lunsford and that he have the following hands to work under him - (To Wit) - Guilford Jones and hands, William Inman, Damon Thomas Milsapp, George Millsapp, John H. Maxwell, and
Pg. 487 hands, J. D. Maxwell and hands, John J. Nelson and hands, William Lunsford and hands, Alfred Denny, Nicholas Reynolds, Walter Caruth, William Caruth and Armstead B. Nealy and that he work from Ripley to the North Bank of Caruths Creek and that he keep the same in repair as a first class road.

This day, Ezekiel Farmer admr. and etc. of the estate of Gilbert Elam, deceased returned on oath in open court an account of Sales of said Estate which is received and ordered to be recorded.

This day Gilly Hunter, Guardian of William Hunter a minor orphan came into court and renewed her bond as required by law and gave Abel H. Pope and Wm. P. Gaines as her securities.

This day Robt B. Blackwell, Guardian of Harriet E. Blackwell, Thomas J. J. Blackwell and June A. V. Blackwell, minor orphan s came into court with Archer Phillips and R. H. McGaughy as his securities he and they en-
Pg. 488 tered bond conditiones and payable as the law directs.

This day the Court Chose and appointed Elizabeth Reaves, Guardian of William Inman, a minor orphan, whereupon the said Elizabeth Reaves came into Court and entered into bond conditioned and payable as the law directs with G. L. Rutherford and Nicholas Reynolds as securities and took the oath prescribed law.

This day Joel W. Kerby, Admr. and etc. of Robert Maxwell, decd. being solemnly called to come into court and give additional security in accordance with the order of this Court at the last Term thereof which had been made known to him as appears by the return of the Sheriff of this County came and refused to give additional security. It is therefore ordered that he be dismissed from any further administering on said estate and it is further ordered that Samuel Hawkins be appointed Administrator of said es-
Pg. 489 tate in the room and stead of the said Joel W. Kerby - Whereupon the said Samuel Hawkins came into court and entered into bond with S. Richardson, Joseph Taylor, William P. Lee and R. C. Campbell for securities conditioned and payable as the law directs.

The oath prescribed by law for Administrator having been administered to the said Saml Hawkins, the court therefore order that he have letters accordingly.

This day, William D. Lee, Guardian of Malvina A. Marley and Josiah C. Marley minor orphans came into court and renewed his bond as Guardian as aforesaid giving Stith Richardson, Guilford Jones and R. Campbell as securities.

This day the court proceeded to elect a coroner for said County-Whereupon Isaac Braden was unanimously elected and came into court and entered into bond, conditioned and payable as the law directs with Archer Phillips, R. P. Russell and Jno. W. Durant for his securities and took the several oaths prescribed by law for said office.

Pg. 490 State of Tennessee) To the Sheriff of said County Greeting you are
Lauderdale County) hereby commanded to summon the following good and lawful men of the body of Lauderdale County to attend at the next Term of the Circuit Court to be held for the County of Lauderdale aforesaid on the first Monday in October Next at the Court House in Town of Ripley then and there to serve as Grand or petit Jurors as the case may be - (To Wit)- S. S. Gause, William Turner, Joseph Currie, Monroe P. Estes, John J. Nelson, Rezin L. Byrn, Isaac D. Maxwell, William McClelland, Joseph Churchwell,

Pg. 490 cont. James Sherman, James Gillespie, Leevy F. Lockard, Henry Willard, Sugar T. Evans, Jas. Hubbard, Lee H. Rucker, Henry Shearer, Calvin F. Ledbetter, William Jennings, Jesse Ledbetter, John W. Nearn, Benjamin Brown, George Chipman, Wm. B. Sawyer and James Salisberry and Samuel Deason and Robert Crihfield constable to attend said Court and Jury.

Pg. 491 The following report was received and ordered to be recorded and the road established accordingly - (To Wit) - We the undersigned jurors having been sworn have proceeded to discharge the duties assigned as commencing on the Ashport Road near William Nash, Thence with road as cut by the citizens and to intersect the road Turner Williams all of which is respectfully submitted to the worshipful Court t his 30 daynof June 1842.

Ellison P. Fuller,
David Williams,
Daniel Williams,
Green Baker,
Jas. B. Crook-

Present and voting for said reception and order a majority of all the Justices of said County.

Ordered that the Court adjourn until tomorrow morning at 9 o'clock.

J. H. Maxwell, Chairman-
Henry S. Peyton, J. P. -
Elnathan H. Condray, J. P. -

Pg. 492 Court met pursuant to adjournment. Present the worshipful J. H. Maxwell, E. H. Condray, T. J. Childress, A. G. W. Byrn, Jas. L. Green, Wm. R. Ledbetter, H. S. Peyton, A. H. Pope, Thos. G. Rice, Esqrs. a majority of all the Justices of said Court Isaac M. Steele, Clerk with G. L. Rutherford, Esquire, Sheriff.

This day, A. G. W. Byrn, Esquire returned aa Inquisition by him held on the body of William Y. Dreskell, which is received and ordered to be certified to the County Trustee.

Ordered that R. L. Byrn, Archer Phillips and Elijah Lake be appointed Commissioners to receive proposals for the purchasing a site and Erecting the necessary buildings for a poor house for Lauderdale County and that they report to the October Term of this court present and voting for said Order, Esquires, Condray, Childress, Byrn, Green, Ledbetter, Maxwell, Peyton, Pope, and Rice a majority of all the Justices of said County.

Pg. 493 This day David P. Posey, Guardian of Virginia H. Keller a minor orphan and one of the heirs of Imri Keller and Wesley Keller came into open court and renewed his bond according law giving for security, Archer Phillip and Wm. P. Gaines.

Ordered that Benjamin Whitson be appointed overseer to but out a road from the Ashport Road near William Nash's and intersecting the Fulton Road East of Turner Williams as viewed by the Jury of view and that he have the following hands to cut said road H. C. Keller and hands, Jno. Chapman, Walace Rooks, Isham Robinson, Jas. H. Johnson, Jas. Sherman, E. P. Fuller and hands, Jonathan Gardner, Jas Hodges and James Gillespie and that he cut out the same as second class road and that he report to the October Term of this court.

This day Jas. H. Given proved by his own oath the killing of Six Wolves, one over and five under the age of four months in the County of Lauderdale there being five Justices present ordered that the same be certified to the Comptroller of the Treasury.

Pg. 494 Ordered that William McFarlan overseer of the road from Hatchie to Fulton road at Stephen Guardners and have the following hands to work under him-(To Wit) - John McWhite, J. Churchwell, J. P. Silvertooth, J. D. Edney, J. G. Childress, William T. Hulm, John C. Barnes and hands, Nancy Childress hands, Elijah Lake hands, Milton F. Lake, B. Gilstrap, E. Gilstrap, Lacey and sons and that he keep said road in repair as a second class road.

Ordered that James B. Crook, overseer on the Fulton Road from Cane Creek

Pg. 494 cont. to the Lake road about one mile East of Turner Williams have the following hands, Merril Churchwell, David Williams, William Williams, George R. Williams, Wm. Cauley, Ransom Hawkins, Green Baker, Noah Baker, Robert Baker, E. Smith, Daniel Williams, James B. Crooks hands, Benj. Hammil, T. Williams, and S. Laney and that he keep the same in repair as Second Class road.

Pg. 495 Ordered that Abner Pitts be appointed overseer of the Fulton road from the Lake road about one mile East of Turner Williams to the Ripley Road east of S. Gardner old place and that he have the following hands to work under him - (To Wit) - his own hands Josiah Blankenship, Wesley Blankenship, F. Barfield, Henry Barfield, W. D. Barfield, Jno. Floyd and hands, Tho. L. Clark, Stephen Gardner, Wm. Prescott, L. F. Lockard, Thos. Lockard, Moses Lockard and that he keep the same in repair as a Second Class road.

This day William P. Gaines, Guardian of Juretta G. Neiswanger a minor orphan came into court and renewed his bond as said Guardian giving for security, David P. Posey, and Griffith L. Rutherford as required by law.

This day David A. Bradford, Guardian of the minor heirs of Arnold Burke came into Court and renewed his bond as required by law giving John Bradford, Joseph Wardlaw, L. A. Thompson, J. L. Hearring as securities.

Pg. 496 Ordered that the Clerk of this Court notify all Guardians appointed by this court heretofore and who have failed to come into court at this court and renew their bonds as by law they were bound to do to come forward at the August Term of this court and renew their bond ayes, Byrn, Green, Maxwell, Peyton, and Rice, Noes, Condray, Ledbetter and Pope.

Ordered that the Court be adjourned until Court in Course.

J. H. Maxwell, Chairman,
A. H. Pope, J. P.
Elnathan H. Condray, J. P.

Pg. 497 August Term 1842.

Be it remembered that on this the first Monday in August one-thousand, Eight-hundred and forty-two, it being the first day of said month, a quorum Court was began and holden at the Court House in the town of Ripley for the County of Lauderdale Present and holding said Court the Worshipful John H. Maxwell, Chairman presiding and A. G. W. Byrn and Elnathan H. Condray, Esquires, Isaac M. Steele, Clerk with Griffith L. Rutherford, Esq. Sheriff of Lauderdale County. When the following proceedings were had.

This day Isaac M. Steele, clerk of this court presented to court a settlement made by him with Hiram C. Keller, Guardian of H. M. Keller which is received and ordered to be recorded.

This day, Isaac M. Steele, clerk of this Court presented to Court a Settlement made by him with David P. Posey, Guardian of Virginia H. Keller, which is received and ordered to be recorded.

Pg. 498 This day James H. Given, Guardian of John H. Johnson, Washington Johnson, Polly W. Johnson and Nancy Johnson, minor orphans and heirs of Sally Johnson came into court and renewed his bond in the sum eighteen-hundred Dollars giving H. C. Keller and J. R. Hutcheson for security.

This day, H. C. Keller, Guardian of H. C. Keller came into court and renewed his bond as required by law giving G. L. Rutherford and James H. Given for security.

This day, James Johnson came into court and resigned the office of Constable of the 5th Civil District of Lauderdale County.

Ordered that Court adjourn until Court in Course.

J. H. Maxwell, Chairman,-
Elnathan H. Condray, J. P.-
A. G. W. Byrn, J. P. -

Pg. 499 State of Tennessee-

Be it remembered that on this the first Monday in September, one-thousand, Eight-hundred and forty-two, it being the fifth day of said month, a quorum Court was began and holden at the Court House in the Town of Ripley for the County of Lauderdale in the State aforesaid. Present and holding said

Pg. 499 cont. court the Worshipful John H. Maxwell, Chairman presiding and H. S. Peyton and Elnathan H. Condray, Esquires, Isaac M. Steele, Clerk with Griffith L. Rutherford, Esquire Sheriff of Lauderdale County, when the following proceedings were had.

Erasmus D. Thurmond Records his stock mark - (To Wit) - a smooth crop and under bit in each ear.

This day Isaac M. Steele, Clerk of the County Court presented to court a settlement made by him with Stith Richardson President and Griffith L. Rutherford, Treasurer of the board of Trustee of Ripley Academy which is received and ordered to be recorded according to Law.

Pg. 500 Ordered that Pendleton G. Gaines be appointed overseer of the Public Road leading from Covington to Ripley working from Fullen's Ferry to Curries and that he have the hands in following bounds to work under him--- (To Wit) - Commencing at E. Nevils runninghthence a direct line to Joseph Curries from thence due North to Barnes Creek thence down said Creek to Hatchie River thence to the beginning and that he keep the same in repair as a second Class road.

Ordered that John Laird overseer of the Brownsville road from Ripley to the County-line near C. C. Conner have the following hands in addition to those allowed him by his former order - (To Wit) - Amos C. Lathum, Jeremiah Cheek and Wm. Reed and that he keep said road in order as a Second Class road.

Ordered that Isaac Thompson overseer of Fulton Road near Gaines old place have the following hands to work under him to Wit John McCall, Joseph Wardlaw and hands, James Price and John Whitson and all hands that are

Pg. 501 or may come into the bonds of the before mentioned hands and that he keep the same in repair as a Second Class road.

Ordered that Bruce McCray be appointed Overseer of the Old Dyersburg-Covington road from the south bank of Cane Creek to where the said road intersects the Road from Ripley to Dyersburg intersects the same and that he have the following hands to work under him - (To Wit) - David Harris, Curtis Ellis and the hands on Loves Tract of Land and that he keep the same in repair as second class road.

This day Ranzom Hawkins, Guardian of Catherine Hawkins came into Court and renewed his bond giving for security H. C. Keller and A. H. Pope he and they acknowledging said bond in open Court.

Ordered that John D. Edney be appointed overseer of that part of the

Pg. 502 public road between Wm. P. Gaines old place and Silvertooths Landing and that he have the following hands to work under him - (To Wit* - James Silvertooth, Mrs. Hunters hands, William T. Halem, F. Barfield, J. C. Barnes, Mrs. Childress hand, Henry Barfield, Elijah Lakes, hands and Thomas L. Clark, John McWhite, J. Churchwell, J. G. Childress, Milton F. Lake, B. Gilstrap and Lacy and sons and William McFarland and that he keep the same in repair as a second class road.

State of Tennessee) Personally appeared in Open Court Samuel Hooper,
Lauderdale County) one of the Subscribing Witnesses to the last will and testament of Henry Chambers deceased, who being first sworn deposes and says that he saw him sign, seal, and publish the same as his last will and testament and that he subscribed the same as a witness in the testators presence and William Pillow being first sworn in open court deposes and says that he saw the said Henry R. Chambers, sign, seal and Execute the same for his last will and Testament ordered that the same be admitted of

Pg. 503 record and that Henry F. Rutherford and Martha H. Chambers the Executor and Executrix therein named have Letters testamentary on entering into bond with sufficient security and qualifying according law to witness Isaac M. Steele, Clerk of said Court this 5th day of Septem1842.

Isaac M. Steele, Clk.-

And thereupon came here into Courte the Henry F. Rutherford and Martha H. Chambers and there came along with them G. L. Rutherford and William P.Gaines

Pg. and entered into bond jointly in the sum of four-thousand Dollars and the
503 oath prescribed by law was duly administered to the said H. F. Rutherford
cont. and Martha H. Chambers and etc.

Ordered that Court adjourn until Court in Course.

J. H. Maxwell, Chairman-
Elnathan H. Condray, J. P. -
Henry S. Peyton, J. P. -

Pg. Monday, October 3rd, 1842.
504 Be it remembered that a County Court began and held for the County of Lauderdale and State of Tennessee. At the Court House in the Town of Ripley on the First Monday in October being the third day of said month in the year of our Lord, one-thousand, Eight-Hundred and Forty-Two and the 66th year of American Independence. Present the Worshipful John H. Maxwell, Chairman together with Esqrs. Condray, Peyton, Rice, Byrn, Pope, Fisher, Campbell, Childress and Ledbetter.

Isaac M. Steele, Clerk by His Deputy Wm. T. Morehead, Samuel A. Thompson, Deputy Sheriff, the following proceeding were had in said Court.

m This day, Christopher Watson returned his road order and it is ordered by the Court that John Watson be appointed overseer of his stead of the Road leading from Durhamville in a Northern direction by Joseph Murphys have the hands in the following bounds - (To Wit) - : Commencing at the forks of the roads leading from Brownsville to Ripley and Brownsville to Fulton running west by Northwest with the Ripley Road until it intersects the Road from Hurricane Hill to Joseph Taylors thence with the Hurricane Hill road to Walsons Creek or branch thence down said Branch to the Fulton Road thence East with said road to the beginning. Including James E. Street and the hands of Mary J. Lee, and he have in addition to the hands in said bounds. James C. Lovelace and hands, George W. Tatum and hands and Jeremiah Penick and hands.

Pg. Ordered that the County Trustee pay Isaac M. Steele, Clerk of the County
505 Court 50 cents for Issuing Venire Facias for the October Term of the Circuit Court of Lauderdale County $1.00 for issuing 8 road orders from July Term of the County Court 25 cents for issuing one order for Jury of view from July Term of the County Court $1.00 for notifying two Guardians to renew their bonds by order of the County Court $2.00 for settling with the Trustees of Ripley Academy $1.00 for recording settlement with himself as clerk of the County Court $1.00 for recording settlement with David Gilliland, Clerk of the Circuit Court of Lauderdale County 62½ cents for issuing 5 Road orders from September Term of the County Court $1.00 being the amount paid by him for writing chair for the Clerks office $15.00 for all services in relation to Common schools for the year 1842 and $50.00 for Ex officio services for the year 1842 making in all the sum of $73.37½, ayes, Esqrs. Maxwell, Condray, Peyton, Rice, Byrn, Pope, Fisher, Ledbetter and Childress, Noes, None.

Ordered that the County Trustee pay Jonathan L. Hearring five-Dollars for making writing Desk for Clerk of the County Court and 75 cents for furnishing and putting on Lock on same. Six-Dollars for making writing Desk for sheriff 75 cents for furnishing and putting on Lock on same, ayes, Esqrs. Maxwell, Condray, Peyton, Rice, Burn, Pope, Fisher, Ledbetter and Childress, Noyes, None.

Pg. Monday Oct. 3, 1842.
508 This day, Wm. B. Chambers returned his road orderas overseer of Road. And it is ordered that William Curtis be appointed overseer in his stead of the following Road From the Bridge on Mill Creek on the Dyersburg road to the Key Corner and that he have all the hands west of the Dyersburg road except Matthew Brandon and that he keep the same in repair as a second Class road.

This day Drury Massey returned his road order as overseer of Road and it is ordered that Benjamin F. Boydson be appointed in his stead, overseer of the road leading from Ripley to intersect the Bucks ferry road at Isaac

Pg. Moores and that he have the following hands to work under him - (To Wit)-
508 Thomas Lockard, Moses Lockard, Drury Massey, Moses B. Chism, George W. Chism,
cont. Elijah Chism, Roland Ledbetter, J. I. Osteen, Hiram Meadows, William Sayyer and Calvin F. Ledbetter and that he keep the same in repair as a second class road.

This day Cyrus Webb proved by his own Oath the killing of one Wolf over four months of age in the County of Lauderdale there being five Justices present. Ordered that the same be certified to the Comptroller of the Treasury.

This, Ellison P. Fuller proved by his own oath the killing of one Wolf over four months of age in the County of Lauderdale there being five Justices present. Ordered that the same be certified to the Comptroller of the Treasury.

Pg. Monday, Oct. 3rd. 1842.
509 At their valuation - (To Wit) - Four Hundred and fifty-dollars and is also to receive from Mary A. Richardson Eight 33/100 Dollars and to Mary A. Richardson, we assign Berry at Mima at their Valuation - (To Wit) - Four hundred and Seventy-five Dollars paying R. A. Lackey and Virginia Al Richardson, Eight 33/100 Dollars each, all which respectfully submitted to Court September 23rd. 1842.

Isaac M. Steele-
G. L. Rutherford-
J. L. Hearring*

It is ordered by the Court that the above report be confirmed in all things and that the property be vested as set forth in said report.

It is ordered that William Turner, James C. Lovelace, Smith Kent, Thomas Blackwell, Asa Pate, John P. Rice and David A. Bradford be appointed a jury of review to review a road to leave the road leading from Durhamville to Brownsville at or near Mr. Thomas Blackwells and intersect the road leading from Durhamsville to William's old Ferry at the new Methodist Church on said road near Mr. James C. Lovelace's and that they report to the next January Term of this Court.

Ordered that the Trustee pay to G. L. Rutherford, Sheriff four-dollars for work done on Jail and 12½ cents for one pound of nails, as per receipt, out of any money in his hands not otherwise appropriated.

Pg. Monday, Oct. 3, 1842.
510 This day William A. Wood, Constable tendered his resignation as Constable which was received and ordered to be recorded.

This day, Samuel L. Gaase returned his road order and it is ordered that Monroe P. Estes be appointed overseer in his stead of the road from Thomas G. Rices Gin to the Haywood County line, and that he have Saml L. Guase hand, the hands of Shadrach Rice and his own hands and that he keep the same in repair as a second class road.

This day, James H. Cleaves returned his road order and it is ordered by the Court that David Fitzpatrick be appointed overseer in his stead of the Road from Durhamville towards Covington as far as Joseph Curries and that he have the hands in the following bounds - (To Wit) - West of Williams Ferry Road to the spring branch of Mrs. Thompson thence with said Creek to Hatchie River and south of said Road to the River. Except the hands on Wardlaws plantation, P. G. Davenport, Carter Whitson and Nevils and that he keep the same in repair as a first Class Road.

This day, Benjamin Whitson who was appointed at the last July Term of this Court overseer to cut out a road fromthe Ashport Road near Wm. Nash's and intersecting the Fulton Road East of Turner William's returned his road order, Endorsed. "The within or executed by cuttin out the within named road and etc. September the 15th, 1842"- Benj. Whitson.

Pg. Monday Oct. 3rd. 1842.
511 This day John Wood who was appointed at the April Term of this Court, overseer to open a road from Ancel Reynolds to the Ashport Turnpike near Sam'l Deasons, returned his order, Endorsed, "I, return my order executed according to law."- J. Wood.

Pg. 511 cont. This day, Matthew Brandon returned his road order, and it is ordered that James Soward be appointed, in his stead, overseer of the Dyersburg Road from Mill Creek to the Dyer County-line, and that he have all hands East of said road and north of Mill Creek and all hands on Matthew Brandon's Place and Orvel Thirmond place and that he keep the same in repair as a first Class road.

This day, Gordon W. Stone returned his road order, and it is ordered by the Court that Marshall A. Posey be appointed in his stead overseer of the Road leading from Ripley towards Covington Commencing at Bates Fork of Cane Creek and working to John Fullens field and that he have the same hands that Stone did to work under him, and that he keep the same in repair as a first Class road.

Ordered that Court be adjourned until tomorrow morning 10 o'clock.

J. H. Maxwell, Chairman-
A. H. Pope, J. P.-
Thos. J. Childress, J. P.-

Pg. 512 Tuesday Morning , Oct. 4th, 1842.

Court met pursuant to adjournment.

Ordered that the Trustee pay Hermis Champ, seven Dollars, Eighty-seven and a half-cents for boarding a run away negro twenty-one days. Out of any monies in his hands not otherwise appropriated.

This day, William Walpole returned his road order, and it is ordered that Caleb W. Anderson be appointed in his stead, overseer of the road from Mill Creek in the direction of Buck's Ferry and that he have the same hands that Walpole had. And that he keep the same in repair as a second Class road.

This day, John H. Maxwell, Chairman of the County Court called on Isaac M. Steele, Clerk of the County Court for his receipts for County Revenue which he produced which are in the following words and figures following - (To Wit) -

Received of Isaac M. Steele, Clerk of the County Court of Lauderdale County his Statement of Revenue collected from 1st. Sept. 1841 to 1 Sept. 1842. Amount collected $179.50.

Cr. by rendering statement -	$1.00		$179.50
" by Commissions at 2½ pr.ct.	4.48 3/4	-	- 5.48 3/4
	$5.48 3/4	/--	$174.01 1/4

Balance due/

Guilford Jones, Trustee
of Lauderdale County --

Received of Isaac M. Steele, one-hundred and Seventy-four Dollars - 1¼ cents in full of Revenue collected as Clerk of the

Pg. 513 Oct. 4, 1842 -

County Court of Lauderdale County from 1st Sept. 1841 to 1st. September, 1842.

Oct. 1st. 1842- Guilford Jones, Trustee -
of Lauderdale County.

This day, William D. Lee, returned his road order and it is ordered that William T. Morehead be appointed in his stead overseer of the Road leading from Ripley to Brownsville commencing at the town of Ripley and working to the cross road near Hermis Champ's old place, and that he have the following hands to work said Road. Robt. C. Campbells hands, Benjamin Watkins and hands --- Dunlap, John F. Fossett, Joseph Taylor, William D. Lee and hands, Alexander McKinnon, William McClelland, Thomas Hazlewood and hands --- Dunahow's and hands, Walter Glosson and that he keep the same in repair as a first class road.

This day, James Gillespie proved by his own oath the killing of one wolf over the age of four months in Lauderdale County there being five Justices present. Ordered that the same be certified to the Comptroller of the Treasury.

Ordered by the Court that Rezin L. Byrn, Elijah Lake and John H. Maxwell be appointed Commissioner to procure a site and have the necessary buildings erected for a poor house for Lauderdale County to be completed by the next January Term of this Court and that they report to the next term of this Court.

Pg. 514 October 4th, 1842.-

Ordered by the Court that Nicholas Reynolds, Jr. be appointed overseer of

Pg. the Road leading from Boling Fisher's to Ashport. Commencing at Boling
514 Fisher's lane and work to where it intersects the Bucks Ferry Road and
cont. that he have the following hands to work said Road. The hands of Edward
Fisher, William Nearn, and Ancel Reynolds, and That he keep the same in
repair as a second Class Road.

Ordered by the Court that Elijah Lake be appointed Overseer to cut
out the West end of the new road, marked out from Joseph Currie's to intersect the Fulton Road West of Green Baker's Commencing where said road
crosses the Silvertooth Road, and that he have the hands in the following
bounds, beginning at the Fulton Road where the Silvertooth Road intersects
it and running with Silvertooth road to Edneys, thence with the road to
Childress Old Ferry on Hatchie River, thence down the River to the mouth
of Cane Creek, thence up said Creek opposite Benjamin Hamil's thence south
including Hamil to the Fulton Road East of Turner Williams and with the
Fulton Road to the beginning and that he report to the next January term
of this Court.

Ordered by the Court that George Thumb be appointed overseer to cut
out the East end of the new Road marked out from Joseph Currie's to inter-
Pg. sect the Fulton Road west of Green Bakers commencing at Curries and opening
515 it to where it crosses the Silvertooth Road, and that he have the hands in
the following Bounds:- Beginning at the Covington Road at Hurricane Hill,
thence with that Road to Fullen's Old Ferry on Hatchie River, thence down
said River to Childress' Old Ferry, thence with that road to Edney's thence
with the Silvertooth Road to the Fulton Road near Gardner's Old place,
thence with said road to Hurricane Hill, the beginning. And that he report
to the next January term of this court.

Ordered by the Court that, that part of the old Bucks Ferry and Stokes
Landing Road over which Joshua Wright was overseer be discontinued.

Ordered that George W. Lumpkins be appointed overseer of the new Road
from the North West Corner of Ancel Reynolds field to intersect the turnpike Road near Samuel Deasons and that he have the following hands to work
said road, John L. Ledbetter, Samuel Lusk, William Jennings, Thomas Jennings,
Green B. Jennings, Samuel Jennings, Reuben P. Kennedy, John Langley, Andrew
Langley, Hesekiah Henderson and James J. Osteen and that he keep the same
in repair as a second class road.

Pg. October 4, 1842.-
516 Ordered that Court be adjourned until Court in Course.

J. H. Maxwell, Chairman-
Elnathan H. Condray, J. P.-
E. H. Hinton, J. P.-

Pg. November Term, 1842-
517 State of Tennessee-

Be it remembered that on this the 7th day of November, one-thousand,
Eight-hundred and forty-two, it being the first Monday in said Month of
November, a quorum Court was begun and holden at the Court House in the
town of Ripley for the County of Lauderdale, present and hold said Court
the Worshipful Hohn H. Maxwell, Chairman and Henry S. Peyton and E. H. Condray, Esquires duly commissioned and qualified and assigned to hold the
quorum Courts for the County aforesaid when the following proceedings were
had.

Whereas at the October session 1842 of this Court Thomas M. Blackwell
proved by his own oath the killing of one wolf in the County of Lauderdale
over the age of four months and whereas the Clerk failed to enter the same
on the minutes. Therefore ordered that the following entry be made nunc
pro tunc.

This day Thomas M. Blackwell proved by his own oath the killing of one
wolf in the County of Lauderdale over four months old there being five Jus-
Pg. tices present, ordered that the same be certified to the Comptroller of the
518 Treasury.

Pg. 518 cont. This day, Isaac M. Steele presented to court a distribution pro rata made by him as Clerk of this Court of the estate of Jeremiah Cotter deceased. Whereupon it ordered adjudged and decreed by the Court that said report and distribution be in all things confirmed and that said settlement be recorded and that Absolum G. W. Byrn administered make payment to the creditors in accordance with said report and settlement.

This day, William R. Chisholm, administrator of all and singular the goods and chattels Rights and credits of Jemimah F. Chism, deceased returned on oath here in open court an inventory of said estate which is received and ordered to be recorded.

This day, Isaac Braden, Coroner of Lauderdale County returned into Court an inquisition held by him over the body of Eward Harris which is ordered to be certified to the County Trustee to be paid for according to law.

Pg. 519 This day, John H. Maxwell, chairman of this Court bound by the direction of the Court W. Robison, an orphan to Hiram Meadows which Indenture is in the words and figures following - (To Wit) -

State of Tennessee-

I, John H. Maxwell, Chairman of the County Court of Lauderdale County in the State aforesaid by the direction of the Court and in their behalf do hereby bind Elijah W. Robison an orphan of the age of eleven years, the 12th of March 1842 to Hiram Meadows with to live and work as an apprentice until he attains tb the age of twenty-one years during which time the said Elijah W. Robison shall obey the lawful commands and faithfully serve the said Hiram Meadows and be in all respects subject to his authority and control according to law and his duty as an apprentice. And the said Hiram Meadows on his part covenants that he will teach and instruct the said Elijah M. Robison in the trade and occupation of a Farmer and to read and write and some good

Pg. 520 Arithmetic or cause the same to be done if he have sufficient capacity. And he will also constantly find for the said Elijah W. Robison sufficient diet, lodging, washing, and apparel and other necessaries suited to an apprentice both in sickness and health and also take care of his morals and treat him with humanity and at the end of the time will give him one horse, saddle and bridle worth seventy-five dollars, one good feather bed and two good suits of clothes. This 7th day of November, 1842.

J. H. Maxwell, Chairman- (Seal)-
H. Meadows - (Seal) -

Secutity for the performance of the above indenture -

Wm. R. Chisholm - (Seal) -

Which said indenture was acknowledged in open court according to law.

Ordered that Wm. J. Connelly be appointed overseer of the Ashport Road from Cane Creek to the bluff of Cale Creek and that he have the following hands to work under - (To Wit) - E. Balinger, John Rockly, --- Rockly, John

Pg. 521 Arnold and hands, Thomas Turner, John King, Charles Black, John Geness, and that he keep the same in repair as a first class road.

Wm. R. Ledbetter, Esq. appeared and took his seat as a member of this court.

Rezin L. Byrn, John H. Maxwell, and Elijah Lake, who were appointed commissioners of a poor house at the October Session of this court came into open court here and was duly sworn according to law.

This day, James J. Robinson produced in open the Certificate of Griffith L. Rutherford, Sheriff of Lauderdale County of his election in the second District of said County to serve as a constable in s'd. county whereupon said James J. Robinson entered into bond, conditioned and payable as the law directs with Robert C. Campbell, James Whitson and William P. Gaines as his securities, he and they acknowledging the due execution of the same in open court, whereupon said Robinson was duly qualified according to law.

Pg. 522 Ordered that Court adjourn until Court in Course.

J. H. Maxwell, Chairman-
Elnathan H. Condray, J. P. -
Henry L. Peyton, J. P.-

Pg. 523 December Term, 1842-

State of Tennessee-

Be it Remembered that at a quorum court began and held for the county of Lauderdale in the state aforesaid in the Court House in the Town of Ripley on the first Monday in December it being the fifth day of said month in the year of our Lord one-thousand, eight-hundred and forty-two, present and holding said court, J. H. Maxwell, E. H. Condray and A. G. W. Byrn, Esquires commissioned and qualified according to law the following proceedings was had in said Court.

This day, Isaac M. Steele, Clerk of this court proceeded to the Court here a settlement by him made with P. G. Davenport, Executor of the last will and Testament of George Moore, Dec'd which being examined by the Court and fully understood. It is ordered that the same be in all things confirmed and that the same be recorded.

This day Isaac M. Steele, Clerk of this court produced to the court here a settlement by him made with John Fletcher, Administrator of all and singular the goods and chattels rights and credits which were of John Cochrane deceased which being examined and fully understood by the Court here it

Pg. 524 is ordered that the same be recorded and in all things be confirmed.

It appearing to the satisfaction of the court here that Rezin G. Henry, Revenue Commissioner of the 5th Civil District committed a clerical mistake in putting down the valuation of 435 acres of Land in said district belonging to the Union Bank of Tennessee puting it down at $21750 when in fact he ought and intended to put it at $2175. It is therefore ordered that said Union Bank be released from the payment of $982 State Tax and$19.64 County Tax erroneously Taxed as above and that the same be certified to the Comptroller of the Treasury and County Trustee.

This day, Wm. R. Chisholm administrator of all and singular the goods and chattels, rights and credits which were of Jeremiah F. Chisholm deceased returned into open Court here on oath an account of sales of said Estate which were received and ordered to be recorded.

Pg. 525 This day, William A. Cleaves, administrator of all and singular the goods and chattels, rights and credits which were of Michael Cleaves returned into open court here an Inventory and account of Sales of said estate on oath which was received and ordered to be recorded.

State of Tennessee) Personally appeared in open court here William
Lauderdale County) Elmore and William Ball subscribing witnesses to the last Will and testament of Ann Lytte who being first sworn depose and say that they saw her Execute the same and subscribed the same as witness in her presence. Ordered that the same be admitted of record.

G. L. Rutherford, Sheriff and collector of the Public Taxes for the County of Lauderdale make the following report which is ordered to be recorded.

A. List of Insolvents on the Tax book for the year 1842.

John W. Bishop	1 poll left the county	37½
George Bradford	1 poll left the county	37½
Elisha Donnahoe	1 poll Insolvent	37½
William Donnahoe	1 poll left the cty	37½
Pg. John J. Davis	1 poll left the county	37½
526 A. J. Fullen	1 poll Insolvent	37½
Jonathan Ozement	1 poll Insolvent	37½
William Sanders	1 poll Insolvent	37½
William Allen	1 poll Insolvent	75
Stephen Austin	1 poll Insolvent	37½
Thomas J. Keetpn	1 poll left the county	37½
Angus McCleod	1 poll left the county	37½
Isham Robeson	1 insolvent	37½
Stephen Gardner	1 insolvent	37½
Griffy George	1 poll insolvent	37½

Pg.	W. T. Hulme	1 poll insolvent	37½
526	Jacob Linville	1 poll insolvent	37½
cont.	Wiley Voss	1 poll left the county	37½
	Andrew Finn	1 poll left the county	37½
	John King	1 poll left the county	37½
	John Vossor	1 slave left before Tax book was made	75
	William Carol	1 poll left the county	75
	John Moss	1 poll died insolvent	75
	Josiah Kettle	1 poll left the county	37½
	Corneleus Durden	1 poll insolvent	75
	William Watkins	1 poll Insolvent	75
	Joseph Barber	1 left the county	37½
	Isaac Edmonson	1 poll insolvent	37½
	John King	1 poll insolvent	37½
	A. J. Langley	1 poll left	37½
	Elihue Randolph	1 poll left	37½
	Hiram Slater	1 poll insolvent	37½
	Abraham Humble	1 poll insolvent	37½
Pg. 527	Thomas D. Walpole	1 pole and 1 slave value at $300 left the County	77½
	A. Humble	1 poll insolvent	75

State of Tennessee) Personally appeared in open court, G. L. Ruther-
Lauderdale County } ford, Sheriff and so forth and made oath in due form of law that the foregoing list of insolvents and etc. by him exibited is just and true to the list of his knowledge and that said list fully sets forth the name of each delinquent in his county the amount of Tax he owes and the nature and kind of Taxable property subjects from which derived and the year from which it accrued and that he has used all legal ways and means in his power to collect the Taxes continued in said list from the time he received the Tax list of his county from the clerk thereof and that he could not find any property to enable him to collect the said taxes sworn to and subscribed in open court Dec. 5th, 1842.

Test. - Isaac M. Steele - G. L. Rutherford.

Whereupon it is ordered by the Court that G. L. Rutherford, sheriff as
Pg. aforesaid be allowed a credit for the State and County Tax on said Insolvent's
528 and that the same be certiffed to the Comptroller of the Treasury and County Trustee.

Ordered that the following good and lawful men of the body of the County of Lauderdale be summoned to appear before the Judge of the tenth Judicial Circuit at a Circuit Court to be held for the county of Lauderdale at the Court House in the Town of Ripley on the first Monday in February then and there to serve as grand or petit Jurors as the case may be - (To Wit) - S.V. Gilliland, Cyrus Webb, Asa Pata, R. P. Russell, Wm. Lunsford, A. S. Tucker, James Whitson, J. L. Hearring, Abner Pitts, Wm. Steven, E. P. Fuller, D. C. Russell, A. Caplinger, H. Super, John C. Barnes, Wm. L. Mitchell, John Arnold, Sam'l. Lusk, John A. Hogsett, Hiram Meadows, J. J. Smith, C. G. Manning, B. M. Flippin, Edward Kennelly, and Claiborne, Rounsaville with Samuel A. Thompson and Jas. J. Robinson, as constables to attend the Court and Jury.

Pg. Ordered that William Bibb be appointed overseer of that part of the Pub-
529 lic Road leading from Ripley to Brownsville by the way of C. C. Conners lying between the forks of the road near James Price's and Haywood County-line and that he have the following hands to work under - (To Wit) - James A. Morris, Wm. Hafford, David Walker, J. Cheek, Amos C. Latham, Wm. Reed, James Bragden, Absolam Vickory, John B. Byrn, J. W. Holliman, Joseph Clawson and Joseph Lowry and that he keep the same in repair as a second class road.

Ordered that Court adjourn until Court in Course.

J. H. Maxwell, Chairman-
Elnathan H. Condray, (J. P.)-
Absolam G. W. Byrn, (J. P.)-

Pg. January Term - 1842-

530 Be it remembered that at a County Court began and held for the County of Lauderdale in the State of Tennessee in the Court House in the Town of Ripley on the first Monday in January it being the sedond day of said Month in the year of our Lord one-thousand, eight-hundred and forty-three and of the United States of America the Sixty-Seventh. Present and holding said Court, A. G. W. Byrn, Elnathan H. Condray, William R. Ledbetter, A. H. Pope, Jas. L. Green, Henry S. Peyton, T. G. Rice, Esquires, commissioned and qualified according to law when the following proceedings were had.

John L. Robbins produced a commission from James C. Jones, Governor of the State of Tennessee as a Justice of the Peace for Lauderdale County, whereupon the several oaths prescribed by law were duly administered to him and he took his seat as a member of this court.

The Court proceeded to elect a chairman whereupon James L. Green, Esqr. was duly Elected.

Pg. Ordered by the Court that Tho. G. Rice, Esquire be appointed a Revenue

531 Commissioner to take a list of Taxable property and polls for the first Civil District of said County of Lauderdale for the year 1843.

Ordered by the Court that A. G. W. Byrn, Esquire be appointed a Revenue Commissioner to take a list of Taxable property and polls for the Second Civil District of said County of Lauderdale for the year 1843.

Ordered by the Court that A. H. Pope, Esquire be appointed a Revenue Commissioner to take a list of Taxable property and polls for the Third Civil District of said County of Lauderdale for the year 1843.

Ordered by the Court that J. M. Alexander, Esq. be appointed a Revenue Commissioner to take a list of Taxable property and polls for the Fourth Civil District of said County of Lauderdale for the year 1843.

Ordered by the Court that E. S. Campbell, Esq. be appointed a Revenue

Pg. Commissioner to take a list of Taxable property and polls for the Fifth Civ-

532 il District of said County of Lauderdale for the year 1843.

Ordered by the Court that E. H. Condray, Esq. be appointed a Revenue Commissioner to take a list of Taxable property and polls for the Sixth Civil District of said County of Lauderdale for the year 1843.

Ordered by the Court that Edward Fisher, Esq. be appointed a Revenue Commissioner to take a list of Taxable property and polls for the Seventh Civil District of said County of Lauderdale for the year 1843.

Ordered by the Court that John S. Robbins, Esq. be appointed Revenue Commissioner to take a list of Taxable property and polls for the Eight Civil District of said County of Lauderdale for the year 1843.

The Court proceeded to elect three members of their own body to hold the quorum Court for the year 1843, whereupon Jas. L. Green, A. G. W. Byrn and Abel H. Pope, Esqs. were duly elected.

Pg. This day the Court here chose and appointed Joseph Hays, Guardian to

533 Jesse J. Moore, Betsy A. Moore and George W. Moore, whereupon said Joseph Hays, Joseph Wardlaw and Samuel A. Thompson his securities came into Court and entered into bond in the sum of three-hundred Dollars conditioned and payable as the law directs he and they acknowledging the same in open court, whereupon the said Hays took the oath of Guardian according to law.

This day, the Court proceeded to elect a Treasurer of the poor house, whereupon Rezin L. Byrn was unamimously elected and entered into bond according to law with Samuel V. Gilliland and David Gilliland for securities he and they acknowledge the same in open court.

This day, Elnathan H. Condray, Esq. tendered his resignation as Ranger of Lauderdale County which is accepted by the Court.

This day, Elijah Lake and Rezin L. Byrn, two of the Commissioners of the poor house make a report in the words and figures following - (To Wit)-

State of Tennessee) In pursuance of the order of your worships we the un-
Lauderdale County) dersigned Commissioners of the poor house have proceeded to examine the various sites offered to us for the erection of the poor

Pg. house and after carefully examining the same both with reference to helth
533 and cheapness have contracted for the occupant claim on which Joseph Glaw-
cont. son resides consisting of Seventy-seven acres between Twelve and fifteen
acres of which are in cultivation we have agreed to pay for said occupant
claim the sum of one-hundred and fifty-dollars, Seventy-three dollars of
which is to be paid but of the Tax of the year 1842. And the remainder out
of the Tax of the year 1843 - We have not caused a house to be built accord-
Pg. ing to the order of your worships because we had not sufficient time but
535 there is a cabin on said place which will (in our opinion) answer the purposes contemplated by your worships for one year all of which is respectfully submitted to your consideration. This 31st day of December 1842.

Elijah Lake) Coms-
Rezin L. Byrn)

Which said report is accepted by the Court.

Ordered by the Court that the County Trustee pay John W. Hamil Five-dollars for making a coffin to bury Rebecca Boswell a pauper out of any money in his hands not otherwise appropriated, ayes, Esquires, Byrn, Condray, Green, Ledbetter, Robbins, Rice, Peyton, and Pope, Noes, None.

Ordered by the Court that the County Trustee pay Griffith L. Rutherford,
Sheriff of Lauderdale County, fifty-dollars for his Ex-officio services for
the year 1842 out of any money in his hands not otherwise appropriated, ayes,
Pg. Esquires Byrn, Condray, Green, Ledbetter, Robbins, Rice, Peyton, and Pope, a
536 majority of all the Justices in the County, Noes, None.

Ordered by the Court that the County Trustee pay Griffith L. Rutherford, sheriff of Lauderdale County, Twenty-dollars for furnishing wood and water four the Courts and taking care of the Court House and one-dollar twelve and one-half cents for postage by him paid on commissions of Justices of the peace for his said County, Ayes, Esqrs, Byrn, Condray, Green, Ledbetter, Robbins, Rice, Peyton and Pope, Noes, None.

Ordered by the Court that the County Trustee pay James Hodges one-dollar and fifty-cents out of any money in his hands not otherwise appropriated for Hawling coffin for Rebecca Boswell from Ripley to the Burying ground, Ayes, Esqrs. Byrn, Condray, Green, Ledbetter, Robbins, Rice, Peyton and Pope, Noes, None.

Ordered by the Court that the County Trustee pay John H. Maxwell, Twelve-dollars out of any money in his hands not otherwise appropriated for hold-
Pg. ing the quorum Courts of Lauderdale County eight days for the year 1842, ayes,
537 Esqrs. Byrn, Condray, Green, Ledbetter, Robbins, Rice, Peyton and Pope, Noes,
None.

Ordered by the Court that the County Trustee pay Elnathan H. Condray twelve-dollars for holding the quorum Court for Lauderdale County eight days for the year 1843, ayes, Esqr. Byrn, Condray, Green, Ledbetter, Robbins, Rice, Peyton and Pope, Noes, None.

Ordered by the court that the County Trustee pay Henry S. Peyton six-dollars for holding the quorum Court four days for Lauderdale County for the year 1842, ayes, Esqrs, Byrn, Condray, Green, Ledbetter, Robbins, Rice, Peyton and Pope, Noes, None.

Ordered by the Court that the County Trustee pay Henry Willard, three-dollars for holding the quorum court two days for Lauderdale County for the year 1842, ayes, Byrn, Condray, Green, Ledbetter, Robbins, Rice, Peyton, and Pope, Noes, None.

Pg. Ordered that the County Trustee pay Absolum G. W. Byrn three-dollars out of
538 any money in his hands not otherwise appropiated for holding the quorum Court
two days for Lauderdale County for the year 1842, ayes, Esqrs. Byrn, Condray,
Green, Ledbetter, Robbins, Rice, Peyton and Pope, Noes, None.

Ordered by the Court that all of that portion of Lauderdale County lying North of Forked Deer River be erected into a Civil District to be called and known as Civil District No. 9 and that the election ground be at house of Wm. L. Mitchell, present and voting for said order, Esquires, Condray, Byrn,

Pg. 538 cont. Green, Ledbetter, Robins, Rice, Peyton and Pope a majority of all the Justices in said County.

This day the Court proceeded to elect Commissioners of Revenue to settle with the County Officers whereupon, Rezin L. Byrn and Samuel V. Gilliland were unanimously elected.

Pg. 539 This day the Court proceeded to lay a County Tax for the year 1843 when the following rates were laid - (To Wit) - Contingent Tax on each hundred dollars worth of Taxable property three cents; Jury Tax on the same three cents; poor Tax on the same three cents; Road and Bridge Tax on the same three cents; Jury Tax on each white poll Twelve and one-half cents; Contingent Tax on the same Twelve and one-half cents; poor tax on the same twelve and one-half cents; County Tax on all License privileges the same as the State Tax present and voting for the rates aforesaid, Esquires, Byrn, Condray, Green, Ledbetter, Robbins, Rice, Peyton and Pope a majority of all the Justices of said County of Lauderdale.

This day Isaac M. Steele presented to court a settlement by him made as Clerk of this Court with John H. Lanier, Executor of the last will and testament of Jonathan Jones which was approved by the Court. Ordered to be recorded and that the same be in all things confirmed.

Pg. 540 Ordered by the Court that Saban Jones be appointed overseer of that part of the public road leading from Ripley to Dyersburg lying between Mill Creek and the Dyer County-line and that he have all the hands east of said road and north of Mill Creek in our said County of Lauderdale and the hands on Matthew Brandons and Orville Thurmonds plantations and that he keep the same in repair as a first class road.

This day the Court proceeded to elect a Ranger of Lauderdale County in the place of Elnathan H. Condray resigned, whereupon Isaac D. Maxwell was unanimously elected came into court and entered bond conditioned and payable as the law directs with Hiram C. Keller and William Lunsford for securities he and they acknowledging said bond in open court and took the several oaths prescribed by law.

Ordered by the Court that Peter R. Winningham be appointed overseer of that part of the public road leading from Brownsville to Fulton lying between Haywood County-line and Durhamville and that he have the hands of Mary J. Lee to work the same and that he keep the same in repair as a first class.

Pg. 541 The following report was received and ordered to be recorde - (To Wit)- We the Jury of view have this day reviewed and marked a road according to the above - commencing on the Brownsville Road near Camp Creek Bridge and from thence west to William Turner West boundary line and from thence South-west near Daniel Cherrys and David A. Bradford corner. From thence alond Bradford's and Rhodes line to the Durhamville road given under our hands this 29th Decr. 1842.Thomas Blackwell, Smith Kent, John P. Rice, James C. Lovelace, William Turner, A. Pate. Whereupon it is ordered that said report be confirmed and the road established in accordance therewith present and voting for the same a majority of all the Justices of said county.

Ordered by the Court that William Turner be appointed overseer to cut out and open a public road from the Brownsville and Fulton road commencing near Camp Creek bridge and intersecting the road from Durhamville Green and Gause ferry at St. Paul's Chapel as viewed and marked out by the Jury of view and that he have J. P. Rice and hands, Thomas Blackwells hands, John
Pg. 542 Bradford's hands, Smith Kent's hands, James C. Lovelace and hands to cut out said road and that he report to the April session of this court.

Ordered by the Court that J. F. Jett, Jas. Taylor, J. Faucett, Tarlton Durham, Alex L. Tucker, Robert Walker and Samuel Dunlap good and lawful men be appointed a jury of view to view and mark out public road(if in their opinion a public good require it) commencing on the Ashport Turnpike a few rods west of Mr. Hazlewoods house and running south by Robert Walker's and from thence westwardly to Hurricane Hill and that they report to the April session

Pg. 542 cont. of this Court present and voting for the same, Esquires, Byrn, Condray, Green, Ledbetter, Robbins, Rice, Peyton, and Pope a majority of all the Justices in the County.

Ordered by the Court that the Coroner of Lauderdale County take possession of and sell the property of Edward Harris and appropriate the same to the payment of his burial expences and report his proceeding to this Court.

Pg. 543 Ordered by the Court that Lee H. Rucker be appointed a Revenue Commissioner to take a list of Taxable property and polls for the 9th Civil District of Lauderdale County for the year 1843.

Ordered that the Court adjourn until 9 o'clock tomorrow morning.

Jas. L. Green, Chmn.-
A. H. Pope, J. P. -
Abs. G. W. Byrn, J. P. -

Tuesday Morning, Janurry 3rd. 1843-

Court met according to adjournment, Present the owrshipful Jas. L. Green, Esquire, Chairman and Esquires, William R. Ledbetter, Absolam G. W. Byrn, Abel H. Pope, and E. H. Condray, and E. H. Hinton.

Ordered by the Court that Elijah Lake be appointed overseer of that part of the public road leading from Joseph Curries to the Fulton road lying between the Fulton road and the east end of the first bridge, East of said Lake's and that he have the hands of his own plantation and that he keep the same in repair as a second class road.

Pg. 544 Ordered by the Court that Marshal A. Posey, overseer of part of the Ripley and Covington road work from Bates fork of Cane Creek to Fullen's field and that he have J. Currie and hands, D. C. Russell and hands, the hands on Gilliland plantation, the hands on D. P. Poseys plantation, Joshua R. Stone, G. W. Stone, Wm. Spence and the hands on J. Buchannon's plantation and that he keep the same in repair as a first class road.

Elijah Lake who was appointed overseer to open a road from Joseph Curries to the Fulton road reported, that he had opened said road in good order.

Ordered that Pendleton G. Gaines, overseer of part of the Ripley and Covington road, work from Fullen's ferry to Fullen's field and that he have the hands in the following bounds to work under him - (To Wit) commencing at E. Nevils running thence due North to Barnes Creek, thence down said creek to Hatchie River, thence to the beginning and that he keep the same in repair as a first class road.

Pg. 545 Ordered by the Court that Benjamin T. Porter be appointed overseer of the New Road from near Henry Sumrows to the Key Corner working from the center of the Bridge to the Key Corner and that he have the following hands to work under him - (To Wit) - Benjamin Porter's hands, Rezin Porter, Hawkins hands and William Spence and John Thurmond and that he keep the same in repair as a second Class road.

Ordered that Alfred Kennedy be appointed overseer to cut and open, a public road from the termination of Eaton and Fulton road at Haywood County-line to the termination of Eaton and Fulton Turnpike and that he keep said road when opened in order as a first class road and that he have the following hands to work under him - (To Wit) - Dabney P. Phillips, Wm. H. Howard, John B. Dodd, Wm. Dodd, Jas. Ingraham.

Ordered by the Court that the County Trustee pay James A. Lackey, five-dollars for medical services rendered, Rebecca Boswell, a pauper, Ayes, Esquires, Byrn, Condray, Green, Hinton, Ledbetter and Pope.

Pg. 546 At the request of Isaac D. Maxwell, Ranger of Lauderdale County, Isaac M. Steele took the several oath prescribed by law for Deputy Ranger.

Ordered that court adjourn until court in course.

Jas. L. Green, Chmn.-
A. H. Pope, J. P. -
E. H. Hinton, J. P. -

Pg. February Term, 1843-
547 State of Tennessee-
cont. Be it remembered that at a quorum court began and held for the County of Lauderdale in the State aforesaid in the Court House in the Town of Ripley on the first Monday in February it being the Sixth day of said month in the year of our Lord, one-thousand, eight-hundred and forty-three. Present and holding said Court, James L. Green, Abel H. Pope and A. G. W. Byrn, Esquires, Commissioned and qualified according to law the following proceedings were had and done in said Court.

This day Caleb W. Anderson appeared in open Court and made Oath in due form of law that the testatrix signed and published the writing annexed to this Commission and certificate as her last will and testament that she was of disposing mind and memory and that he subscribed his name thereto in the presence of the testatrix at her request.

Ordered that the same be certified to the County Court of Caroline County in the State of Virginia to be there recorded.

This day, Isaac M. Steele, Clerk of this Court produced to the Court here a settlement by him made with James H. Given, Guardian of John H. Johnson, Wm. H. Johnson, P. W. Johnson, Nancy Johnson, and Sally Johnson, which being ex-
Pg. amined by the Court and fully understood it is ordered that the same be con-
548 firmed in all things and that the same be recorded.

This day, Isaac M. Steele, Clerk of this Court produced to the Court here a settlement by him made with John Thompson, Guardian of John W. Rudder which being examined by the Court and fully understood.

It is ordered that the same be confirmed in all things and that the same be recorded.

This day Isaac M. Steele, Clerk of this Court produced to the Court here a settlement made by him with William G. Rounsaville, Administrator of all and singular the goods and Chattels, rights and Credits of Amos Rounsaville, Decd which being examined by the Court and fully understood. It is ordered that the same be confirmed in all things and that the same be recorded.

This day, Isaac M. Steele, Clerk of this Court produced to the Court here a settlement by him made with Robert B. Blackwell, Guardian of Harriet E. Blackwell, Thomas J. J. Blackwell, Henry F. Blackwell, and Jane A. V. Blackwell, which being examined by the Court and fully understood.

It is ordered that the same be confirmed in all things and that the same be recorded.

Ordered by the Court that John Boyd be appointed overseer of the public road from Hurricane Hill to the forks of the same near James Whitsons and
Pg. that he have the following hands - (Viz) - William Boyd, Griffin George, John
549 Alverson, and sons and Samuel W. Davenport and sons and John Fullen and that he keep the same in repairs as a second class road.

This day, the Court here chose and appointed James H. Cleaves, Guardian to Alfred D. Conner commonly called Alfred D. Moore. Whereupon said James H. Cleaves, A. S. Durham and Joseph Hayes his securities came into court and entered into Bond in the sum of five-hundred Dollars conditioned and payable as the law directs, he and they acknowledging the same in open court. Whereupon the said Cleaves took the oath of Guardian according to law.

This day, Isaac M. Steele, Clerk of this Court produced to the Court here a settlement by him made with William A. Cleaves, Administrator of Michael Cleaves, Decd. which being examined by the Court and fully understood.

It is ordered that the same be confirmed in all things and that the same be recorded.

Pg. This day Guilford Jones, Trustee for the County of Lauderdale produced
550 here in open Court upon oath a statement of County money which came into his hands for the year 1842 and the disbursements of the same which report is in the words and figures following - (To Wit) -

State of Tennessee) I, Guilford Jones, Trustee of Sd. County certify
Lauderdale County) that the following is a true statement of all the

Pg. 550 cont. County money that came into my hands for the year 1842 and the disbursement of the same. April 5th Amt. received from Jno. H. Maxwell, former Trustee. Good money - $416.83

Mississippi money - $2511-

	May 7th	- from Edward Kennelly on Stray	10.00
	Oct. 1st-	" I. M. Steele of Cty Ct on privileges	174.01¼
	Oct. 1st-	" S. V. Gilliland, clk of Ct. Cty revenue	14.00
	Nov. 3rd-	" Samuel Hawkins on Stray	25.00
	Dec.14th-	" Cain Acuff on Stray	7.50
		Amount of good money received ----	$647.94¼
		Disbursements	
	April 5th	- Pd I. M. Steele, order for bridge	68.25
	" "	- DoDo for Ct. Clk and Registers Books -	24.75
	" "	- " " Green Baker for Rebecca Boswell, pauper, 4th installment for 1841 ----	10.00
	" "	- " " H. S. Peyton for C. Smoot - (Pauper) -	10.00
	" "	- " " E. H. Condray Revenue Commissioner -	10.00
	" "	- " " A. H. Pope for County Plan	160.00
	" "	- " " A. Phillips Jury Ticket	4.00
	" "	- " " " " " "	3.00
	" "	- " " Henry Sumroe " "	3.00
	" "	- " " D. P. Posey " "	3.00
Pg.	" "	- " " E. H. Hinton-Revenue Commissioner -	10.00
551	" "	- " " Jno. H. Maxwell -" " " -	10.00
	April 8th	- " " Elijah Lake - " " "	10.00
	" "	- " " S. V. Gilliland, Commissioner of Revenue-	2.50
	" "	- " " R. L. Byrn - " " " " -	2.50
	" 9th	- " " J. H. Maxwell for pauper -	10.00
	" 13th	- " " Levi Gardner - Jury Ticket -	2.00
	" 13th	- Pd.- David Fitzpatrick" " -	2.00
	" "	- " " G. W. Tatum - " " -	2.00
	" "	- " "Roberson Meadows-" " -	3.00
	" "	- " " John L. Flippin -" " -	2.00
	April/16th	- " " Joseph Taylor -" " -	2.00
	" "	- " " Samuel Thompson-Revenue Commissioner -	10.00
	" 18th	- " " Jno. W. Hamils for coffin for Isaac Peterson- (order)	5.00
	May 2nd	- " " R. G. Henley, Revenue Commissioner -	10.00
	" "	- " " Isaac Braden, order for holding Election -	10.00
	" "	- " " " " " " 2 inquests -	10.00
	June 7th	- " " R. C. Campbell, Jury Ticket -	2.00
	" "	- " " Henry Willard, Revenue Commissioner -	10.00
	June 4th	- " " Thos. J. Keyton, Const. waiting on Court -	3.00
	" "	- " " Thos. L. Clark, Jury Ticket -	2.00
	" 6th	- " " Fred Barfield, Const. Waiting on Court -	3.00
	" "	- " " I. M. Steele, C. Court - Allowance -	36.37½
	Aug. 26th	- " " Fred Barfield, Const. Waiting on Court -	2.00
	" "	- " " James Crook, Jury Ticket -	2.00
	" "	- " " Caleb W. Anderson, Jury Ticket -	2.00
	" 27th	- " " N. W. Barnes, " " -	3.00
	Sept. 5th	- " " Wm. A. Wood, Const. Waiting on Court -	3.00
	" 20th	- " " Fred Barfield,-" " " " -	4.00
	Oct. 1st	- " " D. Gilliland, bill of Cost State vs F. McCoy-	8.62½
Pg.	" 3rd	- " " A. G. W. Byrn for holding inquest -	5.00
552	" "	- " " I. M. Steele, C. Court order -	73.37½
	" "	- " " A. H. Pope for Rebecca Boswell-pauper -	10.00
	" "	- " " Jno. H. Maxwell, Nancy Grant-pauper, 2 and 3 installment -	20.00
	" "	- " " H. L. Peyton for C. Smoot-pauper -	7.00

Pg. Nov. 2nd - Pd Leroy F. Lockhart, Jury Ticket - $ 4.00
552 " 19th - " D. Gilliland bill of Cost State vs. Wm Hulm 12.18 3/4
cont. Dec. 24th - " Do. Do. - State vs R. Hamile 13.00
Trustee's Commissions on $416 received from Maxwell 2½ percent $10.42 - 5 per ct Do on $231.11¼ - $11.50½ -) $624.56 ¼
21.92½
$646.48 3/4

Balance in the hands of Trustee - 1.45½

State of Tennessee) I, Guilford Jones, Trustee of Lauderdale County in
Lauderdale County) said State do certify that the foregoing is a true Statement of all the County money that came into my hands for the year 1842 and the disbursements of the same given under my hand this 6th day of February 1843.

Guilford Jones, Trustee,
of Lauderdale County -

Test.)
Sworn to in open Court)
this 6th day of February 1843)
Isaac M. Steele, Clerk)
By Wm. P. Morehead, D. Clk.)

Pg.
553 It appearing to the satisfaction of this court that Eleanor Wood has heretofore obtained letters of administration upon the Estate of Sabret Wood, Decd from the County Court of Tipton County and that the said Administratrix before the expiration of her administration departed this life, and William A. Wood having applied for letters of administration De bonus non and he having entered into bond with security and took the oath prescribed by law.

It is therefore ordered by the Court that he have letters accordingly.

Ordered by the Court that court be adjourned until tomorrow morning 10 o'clock.

Jas. L. Green, Chairman-
A. H. Pope, J. P. -
Absolum G. W. Byrn, J. P.-

Tuesday Morning - 10 o'clock-

Court met pursuant to adjournment, Present James L. Green, Esqr. Chairman, Abel H. Pope and Absolum G. W. Byrn.

This day, George Thum who was appointed overseer to cut out the east end of the new Road marked out from Joseph Curries to intersect the Fulton Road west of Green Bakers handed in his report, which report is in the words and figures following - (To Wit) - To the Worshipful Court of Lauderdale County, I hereby return my order the road cut agreeable to order and recommend W. H. Fisher as overseer which report was received and ordered to be recorded.

Pg.
554 This day, Joseph Hayes, Guardian for the minor Heirs of Jesse Moore, appeared in open Court and made oath that Fifty-four-dollars and 93 cents is the amount which has come in to his hands as Guardian which Statement was received and ordered to be recorded.

Ordered that Alfred Kenedy, overseer to cut out the road from Haywood County-line to the termination of the Fulton and Eaton Turnpike have the following hands to help cut said road in addition to the hands allowed him by his farmer order - (To Wit) - The hands living between Tisdal Creek and R. P. Currins West boundary line and Rutherfords Creek.

Ordered that the Court be adjourned until Court in Course.

Jas. L. Green, Chairman-
A. H. Pope, J. P. -
Absolum G. W. Byrn, J. P. -

State of Tennessee) Be it remembered that at a quorum Court began and
Lauderdale County) held for the County of Lauderdale in the State aforesaid at the Court House in the Town of Ripley on the first Monday in March it being the sixth day of saad month in the year of our Lord one-thousand, eight-hundred and forty-Three. Present and holding said court James L. Green, Esquire, Chairman and Esquires, Absolum G. W. Byrn and Abel H. Pope, Commissioned, qualified and appointed to hold the quorum court for said County in said State.

Pg. Ordered that Absolum Bostick be released from the payment of Double Tax on
554 Lots No. 4, 5, 11, 45, 47, 81 and 87 in the Town of Ripley.
cont. Ordered that Nicholas T. Perkins be released from the payment of Double Tax on 274 acres of land in the 6th Civil District.

Ordered that Isaac Taylor be released from the payment of Double Tax on 155 acres of land in the 6th Civil District.

Ore'd that James P. Taylors heirs be released from the payment of double
Pg. Tax on Two tracts of land lying in the 4th Civil District containing 640 acres
556 each.

Ordered that Isabella Wilson be released from the payment of Double Tax on Slave valued at $500.

Ordered that Cark Cample & Co. be permitted to list 200 acres of land in the 6th Cilil for single Tax valued at $300.

Ordered that Alden Gifford be released from the payment of Double Tax on the following tracts of land - (To Wit) - 640 acres in the Sixth District -274 acres in the same 3000 acres in said District and 4000 acres in the 7 Civil District.

Ordered that Absolam Vickory be appointed overseer of that part of the public road leading from Ripley to Brownsville by the way of Champ C. Conner's lying between the forks of the road near James Prices and Haywood County-line and that he have the following hands to work under him - (To Wit) - William Bibb, James A. Morris, Wm. Hafford, David Walker, J. Cheek, Amos Latham, Wil-
Pg. liam Reed, James Bragden, Jr., Wi Holliman, Joseph Glawson and Joseph Lowry
557 and that he keep the same in repair as a second class road.

Ordered that Robert Black be released from the payment of double Tax on 400 acres of land lying in the 3 Civil District.

This day the Clerk of this Court presented to Court a settlement made by him with Gilly Braden alias Gilly Hunter, Guardian of William Hunter which was examined and approved by the court and ordered to be recorded.

The Clerks presented to court a settlement made by him with Isaac Braden, Guardian of Mahala Braden & others which was approved and ordered to be recorded.

This day the Clerk presented to court a settlement made by him with Jonathan Lancy, Administrator of Matthew Turner dec'd which was approved and ordered to be recorded.

Pg. Ordered that Samuel V. Gilliland be released from the payment of double
558 Tax on 320 acres of Land lying in the 4th Civil District.

Ordered that Calvin Jones be released from the payment of Double Tax on the following tracts of land lying in the 5th Civil District - (To Wit) - One tract of 750 acres, one tract of 127 acres, one tract of 50 acres and one tract of 22 acres.

Ordered that Court adjourn until Court in Course.

Jas. L. Green, Chairman-
Absolum G. W. Byrn, J. P. - A.H. Pope, J.P.-

State of Tennessee) Be it remembered that at a County Court began and held
Laurderdale County) for the County of Lauderdale in the State aforesaid in the Court House in the Town of Ripley on the first Monday in April in the year of our Lord one-thousand, eight-hundred and forty-three, it being the third day of said Month and the Sixty-Seventy year of the Independence of the United States present A. G. W. Byrn, A. H. Pope, E. H. Condray, W. R. Ledbetter, J. M. Alexander, J. H. Maxwell, E. Fisher, and T. J. Childress, Esquires, Commissioned and sworn according to law holding said Court.

The court appointed Edward Fisher, Esquire Chairman-protempore.

This day, Isaac M. Steele, Clerk of this Court called upon Griffith L. Rutherford, Sheriff and Collector of the State and County Taxes for the County of Lauderdale to renew his Revenue bonds according to Law, Whereupon the said, G.L. Rutherford and his securities entered into the following bonds he and they acknowledging the same in open court - (To Wit):-

Pg. State of Tennessee) Know all men by these presents, that we, Griffith L.
560 Lauderdale County) Rutherford, Henry F. Rutherford and William P. Gaines, all of the State and County aforesaid are held and firmly bound unto James C.

Pg. 560 cont. Jones, Governor of the State of Tennessee for the lime and his successors in office for the use of said State, in the sum of one-thousand dollars; for the payment of which well and truly to be made-we bind ourselves, our heirs, executors and administrators, jointly and severally, firmly by these presents, sealed with our seals and dated the 3rd day of April A. D. 1843.

The condition of the above obligation is such that whereas, the above bound Griffith L. Rutherford, was duly and legally elected Sheriff and collector of the State and County Taxes for the County of Lauderdale, for two years from the first Saturday in March A. D. 1842. Now if the said Griffith L. Rutherford, shall, well and truly collect all State Taxes which by law he ought to collect, and pay to the Treasurer of the State all Taxes by him collected, or which ought to have been collected on or before the last day of December in

Pg. 561 each and every year in which he shall collect the Taxes, then the above obligation to be void, otherwise to remain in full force and virtue.

Acknowledged in open) G. L. Rutherford - (Seal)
Court, April 3rd.1843) H. F. Rutherford - (Seal)
Test.) Wm. P. Gaines - (Seal)
Isaac M. Steele, Clerk)

State of Tennessee) Know all men by these presents, that we, Griffity L. Ru-
Lauderdale County) therford, Henry F. Rutherford, William P. Gaines, all of the State and County aforesaid, are held and firmly bound unto James L. Green, Chairman of the County Court for the County of Lauderdale for the time being and his successors in office for the use of said County,in the sum of Two-Thousand dollars; for the paymentof which well and truly to be made, we bind ourselves, our heirs, executors, and administrators, Jointly, and severally, firmly by these presents; sealed with our seals and dated the 3rd day of April A.D.-1843.

The condition of the above obligation is such that whereas the above bound, G. L. Rutherford, was duly and constitutionaly elected Sheriff and Collector of

Pg. 562 the State and County Taxes for the County of Lauderdale for two years from the first Saturday in March A. D.-1842: Now if the said Griffith L. Rutherford, shall, well and truly collect all County Taxes which by law he ought to collect, and pay to the County Trustee of the County aforesaid, all Taxes by him collected, or which ought to have been collected, on or before the last day of December in each and every year in which he shall collect the Taxes, then the above obligation to be void, otherwise to remain in full force and virtue.

Acknowledged in open) G. L. Rutherford - (Seal)
Court April 3rd.-1843) H. F. Rutherford - (Seal)
Test.-) Wm. P. Gaines - (Seal)
Isaac M. Steele, Clerk)

Ordered by the Court that the County Trustee pay Isaac M. Steele one-dollar and fifty-six ¼ cents for Issuing Twenty-five Jury Tickets from the October Term of the Ciruuit Court, one-dollar and sixty-two and one-half cents for issuing thirteen Road orders from the October session of this court Twenty-five cents for Issuing order for Jury of view from said Session. Twelve and one-half cents for issuing one road order from the November session of this court, Twel-

Pg. 563 ve and one-half cents for issuing one road order from the December session of this Court-Fifty cents for issuing the Writ of Venire Facias from the December Session of this Court, Eighteen and three-fourth cents Postage paid on a letter from the Secretary of State, Eighty-seven and one-half cents for Issuing Seven Road orders from the January Session of this court, Twenty-five cents for one Jury of view at the January Session of this Court, one-dallar and forty-three and three-fourth cents for issuing Twenty-three Jury Tickets from the Bebruary Term of the Circuit Court, Twenty-five cents for Two Road orders at February Session of this court-Twelve and one-half cents for one road order at March Session, one-Dollar for chah paid for the delivery of Two Copies of Caruthers & Nicholsons completion of the Statutes of the State of Tennessee for the 9th Civil District and Sixteen-Dollars and forty-Seven and one-half cents for cash paid in part pay for a Minute book for the Circuit Court making in the whole the sum of

Pg. Twenty-four dollars and Seventy-Eight and 1 fourth cents, ayes for said ap-
563 propriation were Esquires, Alexander, Byrn, Condray, Fisher, Ledbetter, Max-
cont. well and Pope, Noes, None.

Pg. Ordered that the County Trestee pay Abel H. Pope Seven Dollars, Seventy-
564 six cents, it being the amount paid by him for burial clothes for Rebedca Boswell, a pauper, Ayes, Alexander, Byrn, Condray, Childress, Fisher, Pope, Ledbetter and Maxwell, one-third of all the Justices in said County.

Ordered by the Court that Rezin L. Byrn, be allowed on settlement of his account as Treasurer of the Commissioners of Ripley Twenty-three Dollars for thirty-six chairs furnished for the use of the Court House and Five-dollars and Twenty-six cents for four pair Andirons for the Court House, Ayes, Alexander, Byrn, Condray, Childress, Fisher, Ledbetter, Maxwell and Pope a majority of all the Justices in said County.

Ordered that William W. Lea be released from the payment of double Taxes on all property listed in his name in the County of Lauderdale.

Ordered that the heirs of John Pope be permitted to list 500 acres of land in the 7th Civil District valued at $1500 for the single Tax.

Pg. Ordered that if the Poor Tax for the year 1842 has been paid by the Sher-
565 iff and Collector to the County Trustee that the said Trustee pay over the part of the same which is unexpended to Rezin L. Byrn, Treasurer of the Commissioners of the Poor House and that if the same remains in the hands of the Sheriff and Collector that he pay the same to the said Byrn Treasurer as aforesaid and that the Sheriff and Collector when the Poor Tax for the year 1843 is collected pay the same to the said Byrn Treasurer as aforesaid or his successor in office, ayes, Esquires, Alexander, Byrn, Condray, Childress, Fisher, Ledbetter, Maxwell and Pope a majority of all the Justices of said County.

This day Rezin L. Byrn, one of the Commissioners for the Town of Ripley presented to Court here a plan for Railing in the Court House which said plan being examined and fully understood by the Court, it is ordered that the same be let out according to said plan by the Commissioners of said Town, Ayes, Al-
Pg. exander, Byrn, Condray, Childress, Fisher, Ledbetter, Maxwell, and Pope, a ma-
566 jority of all the Justices in the County.

Ordered that the heirs of Joshua Wright be released from the payment of Double on one Slave valued at $400.

Ordered that Patience Wescott be released from the payment of Double Tax on 1603 acres of Land lying in the 3 Civil District valued at $3206 and that John Donalson be released from the payment of Double Tax on 2500 acres valued at $5000 in same District.

Ordered that the following good and lawful men of the body of the County of Lauderdale be summoned by the Sheriff to attend the next term of the Circuit Court to be held in the Court House in the Town of Ripley on the first Monday in June next then and there to serve as Grand or Petit Jurors as the case may be - (To Wit) - William J. Crocker, Pleasant C. Dial, John Watson, Thomas Fitspatrick, Isaac D. Maxwell, John Thompson, William A. Wood, William Hafford,
Pg. Green Baker, George R. Williams, Josiah Blankenship, George Thurmon, Henry Wil-
567 lard, Samuel A. Given, John A. Clark, Isaac Moore, D. Jinnings, John Wood, William Boydstun, Henry Somero, E. Fisher, C. Rounsaville, John Oliver, William B. Sawyer and Lee H. Rucker and Marshall A. Posey and James H. Given, constables to attend the Court and Jury.

Ordered that John Fletcher be released from the payment of Double Tax.

The following report was presented to court by Rezin L. Byrn.

To Wit:-

State of Tennessee) To the Worshipful County Court April Session 1843. I, Re-
Lauderdale County) zin L. Byrn, Treasurer of the Commissioners of Ripley Respectfully beg leave to report to your worships the following amounts as collected from the Sales of Ripley Town lots and the amounts yet due and the manner in which the same has been expended - (To Wit):-

	Purchaser's Names	No. of Lots	Amt.Sold for	Amt.Paid	Balance due
Pg. 567 cont.	Hiram C. Keller	1	$466.00	$561.61	$ 49.00
	Thomas J. Dobyns	4 & 5	260.00	289.18	00.00
	Mark Watson	13	136.25	136.25	161.91
Pg.	William T. Morehead	15-54-97	234.00	279.79	00.00
568	J. L. Green	18-19-66-69	745.00	1093.24	----
	Christopher Watson	21	125.00	114.95	26.62
	James A. Morris	24-46-47	362.00	25.01	432.41
	William H. Walkers	25& 85	290.00	52.25	218.32
	Armour & Lake	29	200.00	224.98	----
	Henry R. Crawford	30 & 81	361.00	84.43	356.74
	Josiah K. Goodwin	32	103.00	114.80	----
	William Turner	33 & 35	295.00	287.81	44.25
	William Conner	36 & 45	270.00	277.37	----
	James Hubbard	38-39-44	426.00	505.50	----
	H. B.SWilliams	48	50.00	52.53	----
	Hermis Champ	53	65.00	68.16	----
	William D. Cooper	55	78.00	12.50	66.60
	Samuel Oldham	40	190.00	190.00	----
	Wm. H. Fisher	41	290.00	344.31	----
	Levi Gardner	45	40.00	44.50	----
	D. & D. Williams	51 & 73	42.25	43.80	----
	James Price	50	16.00	18.74	----
	Lee H. Burks	49	40.00	42.00	----
	P. G. Davenport	7 & 9	363.00	139.30	307.69
	T. G. Brooks	8 & 11	115.00	76.81	57.83
	A. B. Gaines	69 & 71	151.00	178.65	----
	A. H. Howard	56	90.00	91.35	----
	A. H. Pope	59	32.00	35.09	----
	Joseph Wardlow	57-58-60	240.00	282.72	----
	S. V. Gilliland	77	90.00	90.00	----
	P. W. Sanders	76	80.00	86.00	----
	R. C. Campbell	76	58.00	75.29	----
Pg.	Stephen M. Sullivan	80	16.50	18.47	----
569	Peyton Hickson	79	67.00	33.50	45.24
	Rezin S. Byrn	78	90.00	90.00	----
	John Goodwin	63 & 90	102.00	67.85	67.00-lost
	J. M. C. Robertson	61-95-98	91.00	215.20	----
	William Laird	62	80.00	46.00	53.60
	(I. J. Pinson	34	285.00	364.91	----) All
	(T. Caruth	71 & 72	148.00	55.48	14.08)per-
	(William S. Reed	93	150.00	192.20	----)sons
	William S. Reed	42	175.00	100.00	210.00
	G. L. Rutherford	82-85-84	282.00	00.00	379.04
	John W. Holliman	87	131.00	134.95	----
	Solomon D. Spain	88-89-94	212.00	212.00	----
	Isaac D. Maxwell	91-96	115.00	25.00	118.42
	Ivey Chandler	37	187.00	-----	239.00
	John Stone	101	43.00	43.50	----
	William Braden	100	26.00	----	34.19
				7414.86	3059.38

Total 3

In the following cases the purchasers and all their securities have proved insolvent and the Commissioners will be compeled to take the lots back. To Wit:

James N. Smith -	26-65-64-86-92-99-102	$ 695.50
Isaac Vann	3	190.00
Dan Vaught	12	335.00

Pg.	David S. Hill	14	$ 170.00
569	S. D. Holmes	10-16-17-22-27-28-31	982.00
cont.	Armstead Morehead	23-20-68	361.00
	Alexander McKorkle	26	300.00
	William D. Cooper	52	32.00
		Total ---	$3085.50
	To which add J. Goodwin		67.00
		Total amt. ---	$3152.50

Pg. Expenditures-

570	1 - To postage on letter	$ 0.10
	2 - For Printing done	5.00
	3 - For " "	1.50
	4 - To this amt. padd Hearing first installment on for building Court House	1110.00
	5 - Paid for Building Jail	1935.00
	6 - Attorney fees	10.00
	7 - For digging up stupps on C 76 site	6.00
	8 - Costs at Covington	51.37½
	9 - This amt. lost by depreciating of money	5.00
	10- Postage on 2 notices of Bankruptcy	0.20
	11- Paid J. S. Hearring & Green for Build C. H. last payment	3300.00
	12- This amt. paid for painting C. H.	140.00
	13- This amt. paid for 36 chairs delivered	23.00
	14- This amt. padd for 4 pr. andirons, C. H.	5.26
		$ 6582.43
	Amount received -	7414.86
	Deduct amount paid out -	6582.43
		$ 832.43
	Deduct my Commissioners -	222.44 for receiving
		$ 609.99
	Deduct my Commissioners for paying out -	197.47
	Balance in my hands) -	$ 412.52

Amount of debits yet due believed to be from solvent persons or such at least as can be collected $2992.38.

All which is respectfully submitted to your worships and request your
Pg. worships to appoint a committee of your body to examine the vouchers and com-
571 pare them with the foregoing statement and if the same be found correct in all things that it may be taken and accepted as a settlement and ordered to be recorded as such. I would just State to your worships that I charged and received from J. L. Hearring $18. Interest on advances I made him which we were not to do by contract and which was done at my own risk.

Rezin L. Byrn.

Whereupon the Court appointed A. H. Pope, J. H. Maxwell and Thos. J. Childress, Esquires, a Committee to examine said report who make the following report - (To Wit) -

We, the Committee appointed to examine the within report submitted to the Court by R. L. Byrn after examining the same, Say, we believe the same to be correct in all things as set forth in said report and that we believe said Byrn ought not to be charged with $18. Interest received from Hearring. Given under our hands, This 3rd April, 1843.

Al H. Pope-
J. H. Maxwell-
Thos. J. Childress-

Whereupon, it is ordered by the Court that said report be in all things be confirmed and that the same be recorded.

Pg. Ordered that James Soward be permitted to list one-hundred acres of land
572 in the 8th Civil District, valued at $400, for single Tax and 200 acres of land in said District valued at $300 for single Tax.

Pg. Ordered that the County Trustee pay Thomas G. Rice, Esq. Ten Dollars for
572 his services as Revenue Commissioner in the first Civil District for the year
cont.1843, ayes, Alexander, Byrn, Condray, Childress, Fisher, Maxwell, and Pope,
Noe-Ledbetter.

Ordered that the County Trustee pay A. G. W. Byrn, Esq. Ten Dollars for his services as Revenue Commissioner in the Second Civil District for the year 1843, ayes, Alexander, Byrn, Condray, Childress, Fisher, Maxwell, and Pope. Noe, Ledbetter.

Ordered that the County Trustee pay A. H. Pope, Esq. Ten Dollars for his services as Revenue Commissioner in the third Civil District for the year 1843, ayes, Alexander, Byrn, Condray, Childress, Fisher, Maxwell and Pope. Noe, Ledbetter.

Pg. Ordered that the County Trustee pay J. M. Alexander Ten Dollars for his
573 services as Revenue Commissioner in the 4 Civil District for the year 1843.
Ayes, Alexander, Byrn, Condray, Childress, Fisher, Maxwell and Pope. Noes,
Ledbetter.

Ordered that the County Trustee pay E. S. Campbell Ten Dollars for his services as Revenue Commissioner for the 5th Civil District for the year 1843. Ayes, Alexander, Byrn, Condray, Childress, Fisher, Maxwell and Pope. Noe Ledbetter.

Ordered that the County Trustee pay Elnathan H. Condray Esq. Ten Dollars for his services as Revenue Commissioner for the 6th Civil District for the year 1843. Ayes, Alexander, Byrn, Condray, Childress, Fisher, Maxwell, and Pope, Noe Ledbetter.

Ordered that the County Trustee pay Edward Fisher Ten Dollars for his services as Revenue Commissioner for the 7th Civil District for the year 1843. Ayes, Alexander, Byrn, Condray, Childress, Fisher, Maxwell and Pope. Noe, Ledbetter.

Pg. Ordered that the County Trustee pay John L. Robins Ten dollars for his
574 services as Revenue Commissioner for the 8th Civil District for the year 1843.
Ayes, Alexander, Byrn, Condray, Childress, Fisher, Maxwell and Pope, Noes-Ledbetter.

Ordered that John A. Pewitt be appointed overseer of that part of the public road leading from Ripley to Dyersburg lying between the North Bank of Caruths Creek and the North end of Bolling Fisher's field and that he have the following hands to work under him:- Bolling Fisher's hands, H. T. Blythe, W. H. Richardson, Jas. L. Fort and Jordan W. Richardson, Onesemus Fudge, Thomas Hutcheson and S. Richardson and that he keep the same in repair as a first class road.

Ordered that Henry Shearer be appointed overseer of that part of the pub-
lic road of the Bucks Ferry Road lying between the North West Corner of Ancel
Reynolds' field and Haywood County-Line and that he have the following hands
Pg. to work under him - (To Wit)-:- Richard Hill, E. G. Chism, Tho. Wilcox, Henry
575 Reynolds, Henry Shearer's hands, Isaac Reynolds, Daniel and Datid Reynolds and
Benjamin Brown and that he keep the same in repair as a second Class road.

Ordered by the court that Nicholas Reynolds, overseer of that part of the public road leading from Bolling Fishers to Ancel Reynolds have John Hodge in to the hands heretofore allowed him.

Ordered that Bell be appointed overseer to cut out that part of the public road reviewed out from Ashport to the mouth of Cole Creek lying between Ashport and Booths and that he have all hands from Booths to Ashport inclusive and that he report to July session of this Court.

Ordered that John C. Nevils be appointed overseer to cut out the road from
Pg. Booths to the Mouth of Cole Creek and that he have all hands from Booths to the
576 Mouth of Creek and that he report to the July Session of this court.

Ordered that B. F. Jordan be released from the payment of Double Tax on Lot No. 61 and 63 in the town of Ripley valued No. 61 at $150. No. 63 at $10.50.

Ordered that Frances Shoemake be released from the payment of Double Tax on Lot No. 7 in the Town of Ripley valued at $200.00.

Pg. 576 cont. Ordered that the Court adjourn until Court in Course.

Edward Fisher, Chm. Protem-
J. H. Maxwell, J. P. -
Elnathan H. Condray, J. P. -

Pg. 578 May Term 1843-

State of Tennessee) Be it remembered that at a quorum Court began and Lauderdale County) held for the County of Lauderdale aforesaid, in the State aforesaid, at the Court House in the Town of Ripley on the first Monday in May it being the first day of said Month in the year of our Lord, one-thousand, eight-hundred and forty-three, and the Sixty-Seventy year of the Independence of the United States of America, Present, and holding said court the Worshipful, James L. Green, Esq. C. Thurmond and Esqrs. A. G. W. Byrn, and A. H. Pope, duly commissioned and qualified and appointed to hold the quorum Court of said County.

This day Isaac M. Steele, Clerk of this court, presented to Court a settlement made by him with Wm. P. Gaines, Guardian of Janalta G. Neiswanger, which being examined by the Court and fully understood. It is ordered that the same be in all things confirmed and that the same be recorded.

Pg. 579 This day, Griffith L. Rutherford, Administrator of all and singular the goods and chattels, rights, and Credits which were of Alexander Stricklen, deceased, returned on oath here in open court an account of sales of said Estate which is received and ordered to be recorded.

It appearing to the satisfaction of the Court that Samuel W. Hawkins has departed this life without making any last will and testament and application being made to the Court by Caroline Hawkins to have letters of administration granted to her on the estate of the said deceased and the Court being satisfied as to her claim to the administration, and she having entered into bond and giving security according to Law and took the oath prescribed by law. It is therefore ordered by the Court that letters of Administration issue to her accordingly.

Ordered that Court adjourn until Court in Course.

Jas. L. Green, Chairman-
A. H. Pope, J. P. -
Abs. G. W. Byrn, J. P.-

Pg. 580 State of Tennessee) Be it remembered that at a quorum Court began and held Lauderdale County) for the County of Lauderdale aforesaid at the Court House in the Town of Ripley on the first Monday in June it being the fifth day of Said Month in the year of our Lord, one-Thousand, Eight-Hundred and forty-three and the sixty-seventy year of American Independence. Present and holding said Court the Worshipful James L. Green, Esqr., Chairman and Abel H. Pope and A. G. W. Byrn, Esqrs. duly Commissioned and qualified and appointed to hold the quorum Courts of said County.

Ordered that George W. Young be appointed overseer of the Road from Durhamville to Williams Ferry on Hatchie River instead of George W. Gause and that he have the same hands that Gause had and that he keep the same in repair as a second Class Road.

William Salisbury records his Stock mark - (To Wit) - a crop off of the right ear and an under bit in the left ear.

Zachariah Mitchell records his stock Mark - (To Wit) - a crop and a split in the right ear, and a split in the left ear.

Pg. 581 This day, the clerk presented to Court a settlement made by him with Stith Richardson, Executor of Susan C. Marley, Deceased which was approved and ordered to be recorded.

This day, Rezin L. Byrn and Samuel V. Gilliland Commissioners of Revenue for Lauderdale County presented to Court a settlement made by them with Guilford Jones, Trustee of said County which was approved and ordered to be recorded.

This day, A. G. W. Byrn produced in open Court a paper writing purporting to be the last will and Testament of James E. Street and thereupon personally appeared in open Court, Rezin L. Byrn and John Watson subscribing witness thereto

Pg. who being first solemnly sworn depose and say that they saw James E. Street
581 sign, seal and publish the same as his last will and Testament and that they
cont. subscribed the same as Witnesses in his presence and at his request and that the said James E. Street was of sound and deposing mind and memory at the time of making and publishing said last will and testament. Whereupon it is ordered that the same be admitted of record.

Court adjourned until 4 o'clock.

Pg. 4 o'clock --- Court met pursuant to adjournment.

582 Ordered that P. F. Critchfield be appointed Overseer of the Dyersburg Road from Leonard Dunavants land to Mill Creek instead of Jack Fowler and that he have the same hands that Fowler hadd and that he keep the same in Repair as a first Class Road.

A Commission from James C. Jones, Governor of the State of Tennessee was produced here in open Court and it appearing from the inspection of the same that James Soward was commissioned Justice of the Pease for the County of Lauderdale, whereupon the several oaths prescribed by law was administered to him according to the form of Statutes in such case made and provided.

Ordered by the Court that William D. Lee, Guardian for Malvina A. Marley and Josiah C. Marley be required to come forward at the next July Term of this Court and give additional security on his Guardian Bond.

State of Tennessee) We, Rezin L. Byrn, and Samuel V. Gilliland, Commiss-
Lauderdale County) ioners of Revenue for the County aforesaid have pro-
Pg. ceeded to settle with Guilford Jones, Trustee and find the affairs of his of-
583 fice as follows-Viz:-

Guilford Jones, Trustee Dr to Lauderdale County.

To Amount received from former Trustee	$ 416.83
" " " " E. Kennelly on Stray	10.00
" " Revenue from County Clerk	174.01¼
" " " " Circuit Clerk	14.00
" " " Samuel Hawkins on Stray	25.00
" " Cain Acuff on Stray	7.50
" " James B. Hutcheson on Stray	6.00
" " Saml Hoope " "	2.25
" " John Fletcher " "	10.00
" " Dickerson Jennings " "	2.25
" " Isaac D. Maxwell " "	6.25
" " Reuben Alfin " "	4.00
Amount due on rangers book not Collected - viz:	
" " from Jas. H. Hogsette on 3 Strays	13.00
" " Saml Lusk on 1 Stray	2.50
" " P. C. Dial - Stray Hog -	.75
Said for Leonard Dunavant on Stray	18.00
" " Mary J. Lee " "	12.00
" " John Barnes " "	13.00
Amt. due on Tax list after deducting $126.42½) for the Poor House paid to Commiss.)	709.82 3/4
Cr.-----	$1447.77
By amt. paid I. M. Steele, order for bridge -	$ 68.25
" " " " " " , order for Books & etc.	27.75
" " Balance of allowance to R. Boswell for 1841-	10.00
" " E. H. Condray Ct. order	10.00
" " A. H. Pope order for County plan	160.00
	$ 273.00

Pg.

584

Cr. by Amt. Brot over	$273.00
Cr. by Amt. paid A. Phillips - Jury Ticket -	4.00
" " " " A. Phillips - Jury Ticket -	3.00
" " " " Henry Sumeroe- " " -	3.00
" " " " D. P. Posey - " " -	3.00
" " " " E. H. Hinton - Revenue Commiss.-	10.00

Pg.	Cr. by amt. paid Jno. H. Maxwell - Revenue Commiss.-	$ 10.00
584	" " " " E. Lake - " " -	10.00
cont.	" " " " S. V. Gilliland - Commiss. of Rev.-	2.50
	" " " " R. L. Byrn - " " " -	2.50
	" " " " John H. Maxwell for Nancy Grant, pauper-	40.00
	" " " " Levi Gardner, Jury Ticket -	2.00
	" " " " David Fitzpatrick - Jury Ticket -	2.00
	" " " " Geo. W. Tatum - " " -	2.00
	" " " " Roberson Meadows - " " -	3.00
	" " " " Jno. L. Flippin - " " -	2.00
	" " " " Joseph Taylor - " " -	2.00
	" " " " Samuel Thompson, Rev. Commis.-	10.00
	" " " " John W. Hamil - Ct. Order -	5.00
	" " " " R. G. Henly - Rev. Commiss.-	10.00
	" " " " Isaac Bradin - Ct. Order -	10.00
	" " " " " " - 2 inquests -	10.00
	" " " " R. C. Campbell - Jury Ticket -	2.00
	" " " " Henry Willard, Rev. Commiss.-	10.00
	" " " " Thos. J. Keeton, Const. Court -	3.00
	" " " " Thos. L. Clark, Jury Ticket -	2.00
	" " " " Fred Barfield, Const. on Court	3.00
	" " " " Isaac M. Steele - Ct. Order	36.37½
	" " " " F. Barfield - Const. Court	2.00
	" " " " J. B. Crook - Jury Ticket	2.00
	" " " " Caleb W. Anderson-Jury Ticket	2.00
	" " " " N. W. Barnes - " "	3.00
Pg.	" " " " W. A. Wood, Const.-1 court	3.00
585	" " " " F. Barfield- " 1 "	4.00
	" " " " Bill Cost-State vs F. McCoy	8.62½
	" " " " A. G. W. Byrn, inquest	5.00
	" " " " Isaac M. Steele-Ct. order	73.37½
	" " " " A. H. Pope for R. Boswell, pauper-	30.00
	" " " " L. F. Lockard-Jury Ticket-	4.00
	" " " " Bill Cost State vs. Wm. Hulm	12.18 3/4
	" " " " " " State vs. R. H. Hamil	13.00
	" " " " Jas. Currie - Jury Ticket	3.00
	" " " " Ezk. Wakefield -" "	3.00
	" " " " G. W. Young - " "	3.00
	" " " " Sugar T. Evans- " "	3.00
	" " " " J. H. Hogsette- " "	3.00
	" " " " J. H. Nixon - " "	3.00
	" " " " E. S. Campbell- " "	3.00
	" " " " R. Meadows - " "	3.00
	" " " " Richard Parr - " "	3.00
	" " " " Drury Massy - " "	3.00
	" " " " E. H. Hinton- " "	3.00
	" " " " E. Wright - " "	3.00
	" " " " E. Wright - " "	3.00
	" " " " James Sales berry- Jury Ticket-	4.00
	" " " " Henry Willard - " " -	4.00
	" " " " Benjamin Brown - " " -	4.00
	" " " " James Shearman - " " -	4.00
	" " " " Wm. Turner - " " -	4.00
	" " " " Sam'l. S. Gause- " " -	4.00
	" " " " C. F. Ledbetter - " " -	4.00
	" " " " W. P. Estes - " " -	4.00
	" " " " Wm. McClelland - " " -	4.00
Pg.	" " " " J. D. Maxwell - " " -	4.00
586	" " " " M. B. Chism- " " -	4.00

Pg.	Cr. by	Amt.	paid	H. Crichfield, Jr. -	Jury	Ticket	$ 2.00
586	"	"	"	H. Pitts -	"	"	2.00
cont.	"	"	"	Saml. A. Givens -	"	"	2.00
	"	"	"	Jno. F. Jett -	"	"	2.00
	"	"	"	A. G. W. Byrn -	"	"	2.00
	"	"	"	Dickerson Jennings -	"	"	2.00
	"	"	"	Wm. Hafford -	"	"	2.00
	"	"	"	David Walker -	"	"	2.00
	"	"	"	G. R. Williams -	"	"	2.00
	"	"	"	Wm. B. Sawyer -	"	"	2.00
	"	"	"	Lance Graves -	"	"	2.00
	"	"	"	E. Lake -	"	"	2.00
	"	"	"	G. L. Rutherford, Cty. allowance for Wood-			21.12½
	"	"	"	" " " , Ex officio services -			50.00
	"	"	"	Isaac Braden for inquest-			5.00
	"	"	"	J. H. Maxwell for holding quorum courts-			12.00
	"	"	"	L. Deason Const. one Court-			4.00
	"	"	"	George Chitman Jury Ticket-			4.00
	"	"	"	Jesse Ledbetter-	"	" -	4.00
	"	"	"	J. W. Nearn -	"	" -	4.00
	"	"	"	Jas. Hubbard -	"	" -	4.00
	"	"	"	J. Churchwell-	"	" -	4.00
	"	"	"	Smith Kent-	"	" -	3.00
	"	"	"	T. J. Childress-	"	" -	3.00
	"	"	"	Z. Mitchell-	"	" -	3.00
	"	"	"	P. S. Davenport-	"	" -	2.00
	"	"	"	R. C. Campbell-	"	" -	2.00
	"	"	"	B. Nearn,-	"	" -	2.00
	"	"	"	Wm. Williams-	"	" -	2.00
Pg.	"	"	"	Jno. W. Hamil, Ct. Order -			5.00
587	"	"	"	J. Gillespie- Jury Ticket -			4.00
	Trustee's Commission-						65.15½
							$945.84¼

Amt. of Debt - $1447.77
Amt. of Debt - --945.84½
Balance in the hands of Trustee ---------------------- 501.92 3/4
Also $250.00 in Mississippi Money not
included in the above-

May 26th, 1843- Rezin L. Byrn-) Commissioners
Saml. V. Gilliland-)

It appearing to the satisfaction of the Court that Isaac Reynolds has departed this life intestate and David Reynolds having applied for letters of administration and the Court being satisfied with his claim to the administration and he having entered into bond with security and took the oath prescribed by law. Therefore it is ordered by the Court that he have letters accordingly.

Ordered that Court be adjourned until Court in Course.

Jas. L. Green, Chairman-
Abs. G. W. Byrn, J. P. -
A. H. Pope, J. P. -

Pg. 588 July Term- 1843-
State of Tennessee-

Be it remembered, that a County Court began and held for the County of Lauderdale in the State aforesaid, at the Court House in the town of Ripley, on the first Monday in July, it being the third day of said Month, in the year of our Lord, one-thousand, eight-hundred and forty-three, and the Sixty-Sixth year of American Independence. Present and holding said court the worshipful James L. Green, Chairman, together with Absolam G. W. Byrn, Elnathan H. Condray, William R. Ledbetter, Edward Fisher, John H. Maxwell, Henry S. Peyton,

Pg. Abel H. Pope, John L. Robbins, Thomas G. Rice, E. H. Hinton, T. J. Childress
588 and James Soward, Esquires, Commissioned and qualified according to law, hold-
cont. ing said Court.

Ordered by the Court that the County Trustee pay Isaac M. Steele, sixty-two and a half cents for Road orders at the last April session of this Court fifty cents for issuing the Venire facias at said session $1 for furnishing Revenue bond of the Sheriff for the year 1843; $2.56¼ for issuing forty-one Jury tickets from the June Term of the Circuit Court, twenty-five cents for
Pg. two road orders at June session of this Court, twenty Dollars for furnishing
589 the Sheriff the tax list for the year 1843, and two Dollars for revenue heretofore erroneously collected and paid into the treasury. Being in all the sum of Twenty-six Dollars, ninety-three and three-fourth cents, ayes, Esquires, Condray, Fisher, Green, Ledbetter, Maxwell, Peyton, Pope, Robbins, Rice and Soward, one-third of all the Justices of said County.

This day Caroline Hawkins, Admrx. of Samuel W. Hawkins returned in open Court on oath an account of sales of said Estate which is received and ordered to be recorded.

Ordered that Rezin L. Byrn, James Price and John Thompson be appointed Commissioners to view the bridge built on Matthews fork of Cane Creek on the Byrn Road, and they report to this term of this Court the value of the same and what in their opinion the County ought to pay for the same-(if anything)-

Pg. Ordered that Peter R. Winningham overseer of the Durhamville road have in
590 addition to Mrs. Lee's hands, his own and Thos. Tuggle's hands.

Ordered that George W. Young, Sam'l. Owen, Sam'l. S. Gause, J. P. Rice, D. A. Bradford, William Turner and S. M. Sweat all good and lawful men of the County of Lauderdale be appointed a Jury of View to view and lay off-(if in their opinion the public good demand the same)- A rout for a road from a point on the road leading from Durhamville Via Green and Gause's, ferry to Covington commencing at the mouth of the lane between S. S. Gause and G. W. Young and intersecting, the Brownsville road and that they report to the October session of this Court, those who voted for said order were Esquires, Byrn, Condray, Childress, Fisher, Green, Hinton, Ledbetter, Maxwell, Peyton, Pope, Robbins, Rice and Soward a majority of all the Justices in said County.

Pg. This day Bridget Street and A. G. W. Byrn, Executrix and Execution of
591 the last will and testament of James B. Street, Deceased, came into Court and entered into bond and gave James C. Lovelace and J. H. Maxwell as their securities, they and their securities acknowledging said bond in open Court according to law which said bond is ordered to be recorded and the said Bridget Street and A. G. W. Byrn having been qualified according to law, it is ordered that they have Letters testamentary accordingly.

This day Charles Black proved by his own oath the killing of one wolf in the County of Lauderdale over four Months old; their being five Justices present, ordered that the same be certified to the Comptroller of the Treasury.

This day Benjamin Whitson proved by his own oath the killing of six wolves in the County of Lauderdale under the age of four months; there being five Justices present. Ordered that the same be certified to the Comptroller
Pg. of the Treasury.

592 Ordered that the County Trustee pay Rezin L. Byrn, Two dollars and fifty-cts for settling with the County Trustee for the year 1843, ayes, Esquires, Condray, Fisher, Green, Hinton, Ledbetter and Maxwell, one-third of all the Justices, in said County.

Ordered that the County Trustee pay Sam'l. V. Gilliland, Two-dollars and fifty-cents for settling with the County Trustee for the year 1843, Ayes, Esquires, Condray, Fisher, Green, Hinton, Ledbetter, and Maxwell, one-third of all the Justices in said County.

Ordered that Wm. Turner be appointed overseer of the public road leading from the Brownsville road near Thomas Blackwell's and intersecting the road from Durhamville to Green and Gause ferry at the Methodist Churdh and that he have the following hands to work under him - (To Wit) - J. W. Winfred, J. P. Rice,

Pg. and hands, Thomas Blackwell's hands, Robert Hurt, James C. Lovelace and Jere-
592 miah Penick's hands and that he keep the same in repair as a second Class road.
cont/ Ordered that the County Trustee pay Isaac M. Steele two-dollars thirty-
Pg./ seven and one-half cents for a Docket purchase d for the office of the Clerk
593/ of the Circuit Court, Ayes, Esquires, Byrn, Condray, Childress, Fisher, and
Green, one-third of all the Justices of said County.

Ordered that the County Trustee pay H. S. Peyton, Seven-dollars and fifty cents for a Revenue book furnished by him for the Clerk of the County court's
office, ayes, Esquires, Byrn, Condray, Childress, Green, Ledbetter, Maxwell,
Robbins, Rice and Soward.

Ordered that the following good and lawful men of the body of the County
of Lauderdale be summoned by the Sheriff as the law directs to attind at Oct-
ober Term of the Circuit Court for Lauderdale County to serve as grand or pet-
Pg. it Jurors as the case may be- (To Wit) - Archer Phillips, Saml. L. Gause, Jo-
594 seph Currie, Monroe P. Estes, John J. Nelson, B. Griffith, Wm. P. Gaines, Wm.
McClelland, Milton F. Lake, J. D. Edney, L. F. Lockard, Fred Barfield, Sugar
T. Evans, Jas. Hutcheson, Jas. Hubbard, R. E. Campbell, William G. Hogsette,
Cain Acuff, R. Meadows, Wm. R. Chism, L. Dunavant, Edward Wright, Wm. Curtes,
John Soward and Wm. L. Mitchell with Robert Crichfield and James J. Robinson
to attend the Court and Jury, as Comstables.

Ordered that the County Trustee pay Absolum Vickery forty-five Dollars
for building a bridge on Matthews fork of Cane Creek and it is further ordered
that the Clerk shall not issue a copy of this order until the said Vickery
shall produce satisfactory evidence of his having completed said bridge by putting three pancheons at each end of said bridge and completing the butments at
both ends and that he be required to keep said bridge in repair five years,
Pg. ayes, Byrn, Condray, Childress, Fisher, Green, Ledbetter, Maxwell, Peyton, Rob-
595 bins, Rice and Soward.

This day, David Reynolds who was at the last term of this Court appointed
Administrator of the estate of Isaac Reynolds came into Court and resigned said
appointment and surrendered his Letters of Administration which said resignation was accepted by the Court.

This day, Ellison P. Fuller proved by his own oath the killing of one
wolf in the County of Lauderdale under the age of four months-there being five
Justices present. Ordered that the same be certified to the Comptroller of the
Treasury.

Ordered that the following good and lawful men be appointed Judges for the
popular election to be held on the first Thursday in August next - (To Wit) -
1st District, Joseph Currie, A. Phillips and S. Rice.
2nd- J. D. Maxwell, R. S. Byrn and L. Gaines.
3rd- E. Lake, Abel H. Pope and David C. Russell.
4th- Saml. A. Given, Henry Willard and James B. Hutcheson,
5th- James Hubbard, E. S. Campbell and John Nixon.
6th- Armstead Wood, Jesse Ledbetter and Samuel Lusk.
7th- Edmund Wright, Jno H. Somero and H. Crihfield, Junr.
8th- Richard Parr, Wm. B. Sawyer and John Soward.
9th- Wm. L. Mithhell, James Lewis and Lee H. Rucker.

Ordered that the County Trustee pay Lee H. Rucker, Ten-Dollars for taking
in a list of taxable property and polls for the 9th Civil District of Lauderdale
County for the year 1843, ayes, Esquires, Byrn, Condray, Childress, Fisher, Green,
Hinton, Ledbetter, Maxwell, Peyton, Robbins, Rice,and Soward one-third of all the
Justices in said County.

Pg. Ordered that John W. Durant, Thos. G. Rice and Samuel Owen be appointed com-
597 missioners to draught a plan and let out to the lowest bidder the building of a
bridge on the Slough on the road leading to Green and Gause ferry on Hatchie River and that they report to the October Term of this Court.

Ordered that Thomas Hutcheson be appointed overseer of the Key corner road
from the forks of the same, at the Corner of the Benjamin Fisher field, to Haywood
County-line and that he have the hand of Mrs. Isabella Wilson and that he keep the

Pg. same in repair as a second Class road.

597 This day Guilford Jones, Trustee of Lauderdale County came into Court and
cont. entered into bond with Wm. D. Lee and Hiram C. Keller for securities, conditioned for the safe keeping and paying over the Com mon School Moneys of said County he and they acknowledging the same in open Court according to law.

Pg. Ordered that the Commissioner of Ripley proceed to have the inside paint-
598 ing of the Court House executed immediately, Ayes, Esquires, Byrn, Condray, Childress, Fisher, Green, Hinton, Ledbetter, Maxwell, Pope, Peyton, Robbins, Rice and Soward, a majority of all the Justices of said County.

This day William D. Lee, Guardian of Malvina A. Marley and Josiah C. Marley came into Court and gave Martha A. Shephard and Chloe Lee as additional security as such Guardian he and they acknowledging said bond in open court according to law which is accepted by said Court as, additional security and said bond is ordered to be recorded.

Ordered thatCourt adjourn until 8 o'clock - tomorrow morning, Jas. L. Green, Chairman, Abs. G. W. Byrn, J. P., A. H. Pope, J. P.

Pg. Tuesday Morning, July 8th, 1843-
599 Court met according to adjournment, present the Worshipful James L. Green, Chairman and Esquires, Abel H. Pope and Absalam G. W. Byrn.

Ordered that Court adjourn until Court in course.

Jas. L. Green, Chairman-
Abs. G. W. Byrn, J. P. -
A. H. Pope, J. P. -

Pg. State of Tennessee) Be it Remembered that at a quorum Court, began and held for
600 Lauderdale County) the County aforesaid in the State aforesaid, in the Court House in the town of Ripley, on the first Monday, Agust, it being the sixth day of said month, in the year of our Lord one-thousand eight-hundred and forty-three, and the Sixth-eighth-year of the Independence of the United States. Present and holding said court the Worshipful James L. Green, Absolam G. W. Byrn and A. H. Pope, Esquires, Commissioned qualified according to law.

James Salisbury records his Stock mark to wit:- A swallow fork in the right ear, a crop and an under nick in the left ear.

Robertson Meadows records his stock mark to wit:- A swallow fork in the right ear, and an under half Crop off the left Ear.

Pg. This day, Isaac M. Steele, Clerk of this Court presented to Court a set-
601 tlement made by him with Hiram C. Keller Guardian of Hiram C. Keller which is approved by the Court and ordered to be recorded.

This day, Isaac M. Steele, Clerk of this Court presented to Court a settlement made him with Wm. A. Wood, Administrator of all and singular the goods and chattels which were of Eleanor Wood, Deceased which said settlement is approved by the Court and ordered to be recorded.

This day, Bridget Street and A. G. W. Byrn the Executor and Executrix of the last Will and testament of James E. Street, returned into open Court on oath an inventory and Sale Bill of the property of said Estate not specifically devised which is received and ordered to be recorded.

Whereas it appears to the Court now in session that Samuel Deason has
Pg. died leaving no will and William Deason having applied for letters of adminis-
602 tration and the Court being satisfied with his claim to the administration, the widow and relect having waived her right in his favor as appears by his own oath, and the said William Deason having given bond and qualified according to law. The Court therefore order that he have letters accordingly.

Ordered that Armstead Wood, John A. Hogsette and Joel Sawyer freeholders unconnected either by affinity or Consanguinity with the widow of the late Samuel Deason be appointed Commissioners, to set apart to said Widow (on oath to act impartially) so much of the Crop, stock, provisions and monies on hand, or due, or other assets as may be necessary for the support of said widow and her family, until one year from the decease of her husband the said Samuel Deason.

Ordered that Court adjourned until Court in Course.

Pg. 602 cont.

Jas. L. Green, Chairman-
A. H. Pope, J. P.-
A. G. W. Byrn, J. P.-

Pg. 604 Be it remembered that at a quorum Court began and held in the Court House in the town of Ripley for the County of Lauderdale in the State of Tennessee on the first Monday in September in the year of our Lord one-thousand, eight-hundred and forty-three, it being the 4th day of said month before the Worshipful Abel H. Pope, Henry S. Peyton and A. G. W. Byrn, Esqrs. the following proceeding were had to wit:-

This day, Isaac Moore produced in open Court here the Certificate of G.L. Rutherford Sheriff and etc. of his having been elected in the 6th District to serve as a constable in said County and entered into bond and security and was qualified according to law.

Ordered that David Harris be appointed overseer of the old Dyersburg road from the South bank of Cane Creek to where said road intersects the road from Ripley to Dyersburgh and that he have the following hands to work under him to wit:- Brice McElroy, Curtis Ellis and the hands on Loves tract of land and that he keep the same in repair as a second Class road.

Pg. 605 Ordered that Charles G. Manning be appointed overseer of the road from Ripley towards Dyersburg and that he have the following hands to work under him -(To Wit)- Guilford Jones and hands, William Inman, James Reynolds, Damon Millsap,Thomas Millsap, John H. Maxwell's hands, Isaac D. Maxwell and hands, John J. Nelson and hands, Alfred Denney, Nicholas Reynolds, Walter Caruth, William Caruth, Armstead B. Neely and Wm. Lunsford and hands and that he work from Ripley to the North Bank of Caruths Creek and that he keep the same in repair as a first Class road.

The day R. C. Campbell produced in open Court here a Commission from the Governor of the State of Tennessee as a Justice of the Pease for Lauderdale County whereupon the several oaths prescribed by law was administered to him.

Pg. 606 Cyrus Webb records his stock mark to wit:- A crop and Split in the left ear, and a Crop and under bit in the right ear.

This day, Isaac M. Steele, Clerk of the County Court presented to Court a settlement made by him with David P. Posey, Guardian of Virginia H. Keller which is approved by the Court and ordered to be recorded.

This day, William Deason, Administrator of the Estate of Samuel Deason Deceased returned into open court on oath an inventory and account of sales of said estate which ordered to be recorded.

This day, Wm. A. Summers produced in open Court here the Certificate of G. L. Rutherford, Shff and etc of his having been elected in the 5th District of Lauderdale County to serve as a constable in said county, whereupon he entered into bond gave security and qualified according to law.

Pg. 607 Ordered that court adjourn until Court in course.

A. H. Pope, Chairman, P.T.-
Henry L. Peyton, J. P.-
A. G. W. Byrn, J. P.-

Pg. 608 October 1843 -

State of Tennessee-

Be it remembered that a County Court began and held for the County of Lauderdale and State aforesaid at the Court House in the Town of Ripley on the first Monday in October it being the second day of said Month in the year of our Lord, one-thousand, Eight hundred and forty-three and the sixty-seventh year of American Independence. Present and holding said Court the Worshipful James L. Green, Chairman, John H. Maxwell, Thomas J. Childress, Martin R. Alexander, Henry S. Peyton, Elnathan H. Condray, Thos. G. Rice, William R. Ledbetter, A. G. W. Byrn and Abel H. Pope, Esquires. Commissioned and qualified according to law holding said Court. The following proceedings were had and done-(To Wit)-

Ordered that James P. Ledbetter be appointed in the stead of Benjamin F. Boydston. Overseer of the Road leading from Ripley to intersect the Bucks Ferry

Pg. 608 cont. Road at Isaac Moores and that he have the following hands to work under him- (To Wit) - John B. Moore, Drewry Massey, Mosey B. Chism, Benj'm. F. Boydson, John Meadows, Roland Ledbetter, Hiram Meadow, William R. Chism and William Boydson and that he keep the same in repair as a second Class Road.

Pg. 609/ Ordered that Henry Crihfield be appointed overseer of the Dyersburg road from Leonard Dunavant's land to Mill Creek, Instead of P. F. Crihfield and that he have the same hands that P. F. Crihfield had, and that he keep the same in repair as first Class Road.

Ordered by the Court that the County Trustee pay Robert H. Hamil five-Dollars for making coffin for John Blackwell out of any monies in his hands

Pg. 610 not otherwise appropriated. Justices present and voting in the affirmative, were, John H. Maxwell, Thomas J. Childress, Martin R. Alexander, Henry S. Peyton, A. G. W. Byrn and Abel H. Pope, those voting in the negative were, James L. Green, E. H. Condray, Thomas G. Rice and Wm. R. Ledbetter.

It appearing to the satisfaction of the Court that Sarah Cook has departed this life intestate and William Turner having applied for letters of administration and the Court being satisfied with his claim to the administration and he having entered into bond with security and took the oath prescribed by law, therefore it is ordered by the Court that he have letter accordingly.

This day the Jury of View appointed at the last Term of this Court to view and lay off - (if in their opinions the public good demanded the same)- a route for a road, from a point on the Road leading from Durhamville Via Green and Gause's Ferry to Covington Commencing at the mouth of the lane between S. S. Gause and G. W. Young and intersecting the Brownsville Road; and were required to report to the October session of this Court, returned the following report to wit:-

Pg. 611 State of Tennessee) The undersigned having been summoned by the Sheriff
Lauderdale County) of Lauderdale County as a Jury of view and duly sworn, proceeded to lay out a road in pursuance of the within order, commencing at the mouth of the lane between G. W. Young and S. S. Gause on the Durhamville Road, thence, east keeping the Road already opened as near as practicable and intersecting the Brownsville road near the Corner of J. C. Coggshell's field, distance about $1\frac{1}{4}$ miles, having viewed the same, do not think the public good demands the same as the order directs, but that the public good would be promoted and the Convenience of the neighborhood all of which is respectfully submitted.

Geo. W. Young-
Samuel Owen-
Sam'l. S. Gause-
D. A. Bradford-
William Turner-

It is therefore ordered that the said road be established as a second Class road and that George W. Young be appointed overseer of the same, and that he have his own hands to cut out and keep the same in repair as a second Class Road. It is further ordered that Geo. W. Young have S. S. Gause's hands, S. Rice's hands, J. L. Gause's hands and M. P. Estes' hands to cut out said

Pg. 612 Road and build a bridge across the Creek on said Road.

Ordered that John J. Nelson be appointed overseer of the Road leading from Ripley to Dyersburg to commence at the East mouth of the lane between Said Nelson and Isaac D. Maxwell and to work to the Carruth Branch of Cane Creek on said Road, and to have his own hands, Walter and William Corruth to work said road, and that he keep the same in repair as a first Class Road.

Ordered that Joseph Currie be appointed overseer of the Road leading from Covington to Ripley, from Fullen's field to the South East corner of Joshua Stones' field and that he have Sam'l. V. Gillilands hands, Gordon Stone, and his own hands to work said Road, and that he keep the same in repair as a first Class Road.

Ordered that William P. Posey be appointed overseer of the Covington and Rip-

Pg. 612 cont. ley Road from the South east Corner of Joshua Stones field to Beaties fork of Cane Creek and that he have David P. Posey's hands, John Buchanan and hands and Joshua R. Stone and that he keep the same in repair as a first Class Road.

Pg. 613 Nicholas Reynolds, Senior records his Stock mark, (To Wit)- a swallow fork in the right ear.

John C. Barnes records in addition to his stock mark already recorded, two splits in the dewlap of the Cattle Stock.

This day, Samuel V. Gilliland, Guardian for the heirs of Sabret Wood, Deceased, returned on oath in open Court an inventory of the effects of said Words which is received and ordered to be recorded.

Ordered that the County Trustee pay Isaac M. Steele, the sum of Fifty Dollars for his ex-officio services as Clerk of the County Court of this County for the year 1843. Ayes, Esquires, Green, Childress, Alexander, Peyton, Condray, Rice, Ledbetter, and Pope.

Ordered that the County Trustee pay Isaac M. Steele, $112½ for one blank Book for the office, 50 cents for issuing the Veniri Facias, 25 cents for issuing order for jury of view, 62½ cents for issuing 5 road orders, $1.00 for recording settlement with self, $1.00 for recording settlement with the Clerk of the Circuit Court, $2.00 for settling with Treasurer of Ripley Academy, $15.00

Pg. 614 for all services in relation to common schools in 1843. Making in all the sum of twenty-one dollars and fifty-cents, ayes, Esquires, Green, Childress, Alexander, Peyton, Condray, Rice, Ledbetter and Pope.

Ordered that the County Trustee pay Thomas D. Hart the sum of four Dollars and Sixty-three cents for goods furnished by him for the Burial of John Blackwell, out of any monies in his hands not otherwise appropriated, ayes, Esquires, Childress, Alexander, Peyton, Pope and R. C. Campbell.

Ordered that Edmund Fitzpatrick be appointed overseer of the road from Durhamville to Hurricane Hill and that he have the following hands to work under him-(To Wit)-his own hands, Jas. Anthony's hands, Cyrus Webb, S. Durham, ----- Durham, M. Starnes, J. Price, R. P. Russell and David Fitzpatrick's hands and that he keep the same in repair as a first Class Road.

Ordered that Right Koonce be appointed overseer of the Road from Durhamville to the West end of James Anthony's land and that he have the following hands to work said road -(To Wit) - Caleb Arnold, John Arnold, M. Arnold, James Brown, James Cleaves, William Cleaves, ----- Pitman, Joseph Hayes, John Holmes,

Pg. 615 Wm. Matthews, Sam'l. Thompson hands and William Thompson and Wm. Holmes and that he keep the same in repair as a first Class road.

Benjamin F. Jordan, this day proved by his own oath the killing of one wolf in Lauderdale County over the age of four months, there being five Justices present. Ordered that it be certified to the Comptroller of the Treasury.

Ordered that Thomas Fitzpatrick be appointed overseer of the Road from the West end of James Anthony's land to the road near Joseph Currie's and that he have his own hands to work said Road, and that he keep the same in repair as a first Class road.

Ordered that Hiram Meadows, Isaac Moore, H. Shearer, T. Wilcox and Wm. R. Ledbetter be appointed a jury of view to examine into the propriety or impropriety of turning the road leading from Ripley to Isaac Moore's at the Corner of Benj'm. F. Boydson's field and report to the next January Term of this Court.

Pg. 616 Ordered that Abraham L. McMordie be released from the payment of seven dollars and 72 cents, County Tax and the sum of three dollars and 22 cents, state Tax, incorrectly charged to him on 4827½ acres of Land. It appearing to the satisfaction of the Court that the Revenue Commissioner Committed on error in putting down the value of said land at $9655,. When he ought and indended to put down the same at $3218. Ordered that the same be certified to the Comptroller of the Treasury and the County Trustee.

Ordered that Rezin L. Byrn, Asa Pate, Archer Phillips, Thomas Durham and John Price, Good and lawful men of the County of Lauderdale be appointed a jury of view to view out a road leaving the Road leading from Durhamville and run with the line of C. Watson and Marshall Starne's land so as to intersect the Road

Pg. leading from Durhamville to Hurricane Hill at or near the corner of Milton G.
616 Turner's field and report to the next January Term of this Court.
cont.-----Ordered by the Court that, that portion of the Fulton Road from Cane Creek
Pg. /Bridge to Vasser's old place be divided and that James B. Hutcheson be appoint-
617/ ed overseer of the lower part, to work from the ten mile post from Fulton to Vasser's old place and that all persons living in the 4th district West of the West Boundary line of the Hatchie Connection lands be assigned and bound to work under him.

Ordered by the Court that David Williams be appointed overseer of that portion of the Fulton Road from Cane Creek Bridge to the Ten mile post from Fulton, and that all persons liable to work on roads living between Cane Creek and Cole Creek, South of the old Ashport Road except John King and Thomas Turner and east of the west boundary of the Hatchie Connection hands, be assigned and bound as hands to work under him.

Ordered by the Court that Benjamin Whitson be appointed overseer of the Road from the Ashport Road west of William Nash's old place to the Fulton Road, and that he have the following hands to work said Road. To Wit:- Ellison P. Fuller and hand, John Wardlow, Benjamin Hamil and Turner Williams and that he keep the same in repair as a second Class Road.

Pg. Ordered by the Court that John Boyd be appointed overseer of the road from
618 Hurricane Hill to the Ripley Road east of Wm. P. Gaines old place on the same road, and that he have the following hands to work said Road- (To Wit)- William Boyd, William Spence, Samuel Davenport, Thomas Davenport, John Fullen, John Alverson, Bluford Alverson, Wade Alverson, Josiah Blankenship and James Blankenship and that he keep the same in repair as a second Class Road.

Ordered by the Court that George Thumb be appointed overseer of the Fulton Road from Josiah Curries to the east end of the first bridge east of Elijah Lake's and that he have the following hands to work said road -(To Wit)- William Fisher, Nancy Fisher's hands, Adolphus Carrigan, Albert Durham, David C. Russell and Hand, Leroy F. Lockard, Thomas Lockard, Moses Lockard, William McPharlin, Zachariah Norman, Stephen Gardner and William T. Hulme, and that he keep the same in repair as a second Class road.

Pg. Ordered by the court that James Shearman be appointed Overseer of the Ash-
619 port Road commencing at the fork west of Gaine's old place working to Cane Creek Bridge, and that he have the following hands to work under him-(To Wit)- John Floyd and hand, William Strain, Jr., John S. Pope, John Chapman, Hiram C. Keller and hands, Wallis Rooks and James Gillespie and that he keep the same in repair as a second Class road.

Ordered that Abner Pitts be appointed Overseer of the Fulton Road from the forks of the Road east of Wm. P. Gaines old place to the fork that leaves the Same for Elijah Lakes, east of Turner William's and the he have the following hands to work said road - (To Wit) - Isaac Braden, John Braden, Elihu Nelson, John Prescott, James Prescott, Thomas S. Clark, Nathaniel W. Barnes, Henry P. Barfield, William D. Barfield, Frederick Barfield, and his own hands, and that he keep the same in repair as a second Class Road.

This day, James L. Green, Chairman of the County Court of Lauderdale County called on Isaac M. Steele, Clerk of the County Court of said County for his receipts for County Revenue, which he produced which are in the following words and figures following -(To Wit)-

Pg. Trustee's office, Ripley, Tenn. 8 Sept.-1843.
620 $69.68 3/4 - Received from Isaac M. Steele, Clerk of Lauderdale County Court sixty-nine Dollars sixty-eight and three-fourth cents in full of Revenue collected from 1st. Sept. 1842 to 1st. Sept. 1843.

Guilford Jones, Trustee, and etc.

Trustee's office, Ripley, Tenn. 8 Sept.-1843.

Received of I. M. Steele, his statement of Revenue collected as clerk of Lauderdale County Court from 1st. Sept. 1843 to 1st. Sept. 1843. Amount Collected-
$72.50. $72.50

Commissions - $1.81¼)
Cr. by rendering Settlement $1.00)

2.81¼

Balance Due $61.68 3/4 -

Pg. Guilford Jones, Trustee and etc.
620 It appearing to the Satisfaction of this Court that James Barfield has
cont. departed this life intestate. And Frederick R. Barfield having applied for letters of Administration and the Court being satisfied with his claim to the administration and he having entered into Bond with security and took the oath prescribed by Law. Therefore it is ordered by the Court that he have letters accordingly.

This day, Jesse R. Hutcheson, resigned his Commission as a Justice of the peace for this Cty.

Pg. This day, Pendleton G. Gaines proved by his own oath the killing of four
621 wolves in this County under the age of four months there being five Justices present. Ordered that it be certified to the Comptroller of the Treasury.

It is ordered by the Court that the Commissioners for the Town of Ripley have a well dug on the public square in said Town. And it is further ordered that said Commissioners have the necessary repairs done to the cupolo on the Court House.

Ordered by the Court that the hands of Samuel Owen and R. W. Green be added to the list of George W. Young's order on the William's Ferry Road subject to work said road.

Ordered by the Court that John Edmoson be appointed overseer of the Road leading from the North West Corner of Ancel Reynold's field and intersects the Ashport Turnpike road near Samuel Deason's and that he have the following hands in the following bounds to work under him - (To Wit) - commencing at the North West Corner of Ancel Reynold's field running with said Road to the
Pg. North East Corner of Hiram Slater's field and thence North so as to include
622 Mashack Price to Dickison Jennings including William Jennings, thence from the said Jenning's with the Road to Coal Creek, thence up Coal Creek to where the path crosses the Creek, running from the Northwest Corner of Ancel Reynold's field and that he keep the same in repair as a second Class Road.

Ordered by the Court that Noah Sawyers be appointed overseer of the Road from the North east corner of Hiram Slater's field to the Turn Pike road near Samuel Deason's place, and that he have the following hands to work said Road- (To Wit)- Cain Acuff, B. C. Acuff, John Langley, Benjamin Deason, William Deason, John A. Hogsette, William G. Hogsette, John Wood, William Wood and Hezekiah Henderson, and that he keep the same in repair as a second Class Road.

This day, Isaac M. Steele, Clerk of the County Court of Lauderdale County presented to Court a settlement made by him with the Treasurer of the Board of Trustee's of Ripley Academy, which was examined by the Court, received, and ordered to be recorded.

Pg. This day, Isaac M. Steele, Clerk of the County Court of Lauderdale County
623 presented to Court a settlement made by him with William S. Walpole and Benjamin H. Walpole, Executors of the last will and testament of John Walpole, Deceased, which was examined by the Court, received, and ordered to be recorded.

Ordered by the Court that Milton Lake be appointed overseer of the Road commencing at the Cross Road between Edney's and Barfields and work to the Fulton Road near Stephen Gardners old place, and that he have the following hands to work said Road - (To Wit)- John McWhite, Samuel White, James P. Silvertooth, John C. Barnes, Joel G. Childress, John D. Edney, and Benjamin F. Childress and hands and that he keep the same in repair as a second class Road.

Ordered that Court be adjourned until Tomorrow morning 9 O'clock.

Jas L. Green, Chairman,
A. H. Pope, J. P.,
Thos. J. Childress, J. P.

Pg. October 3rd, 1843-
624 Court met pursuant to adjournment.

This day, Henry F. Rutherford, Executor of Henry R. Chambers, deceased, returned here in open court on oath an inventory of the notes, accounts, Judgements and Executors that have come into his hands as Executor of said estate, which was received and ordered to be recorded.

It appearing to the satisfaction of the Court that Benjamin Walker,

Pg. 624 cont. Guardian of Benjamin R. Walker, Minor orphan, has departed this life. The Court therefore, this day proceeded to choose and appoint James P. Walker, Guardian for Benjamin R. Walker, Minor orphan, in the room and stead of Benjamin Walker, Dec'd. Whereupon the said James P. Walker, David M. Henning and James J. Alison, his securities came into Court and entered into Bond in the sum of Five-Thousand Dollars, conditioned and payable as the law directs, he and they acknowledging the same in open Court, whereupon the said Walker took the oath of Guardian according to law.

Ordered by the Court that Elijah Lake, Thomas Golding and Abel H. Pope be appointed Commissioners to lay off one year's allowance for Francil Barfield, widow of James Barfield, Deceased.

Pg. 625 This day, the following report of the Commissioner's of the Town of Ripley was presented and ordered to be recorded. (To Wit).

We, the undersigned Commissioners of the Town of Ripley having been directed by the County Court at the April session 1843 to let out the enclosing of the Court House agreeable to the plan exhibited to sd court proceeded to let out sd work to the lowest bidder. When Joseph Wardlow became the undertaker agreeing to complete the same by the first day of Oct. 1843. Which has not been done. All of which is respectfully submitted. G. L. Rutherford-
H. C. Keller-
Rezin L. Byrn-
R. C. Campbell-

Ordered by the Court that Joseph Wardlow be allowed the further time, until the first Monday in December next to complete the Court House enclosure. It is further ordered that the Commissioners for said Town be authorized to have the trees on the public square topped and remove such as they may think proper to have removed and the Stumps removed from within the Court House enclosure.

Pg. 626 Ordered by the Court that Joseph Currie, David Gilliland and William P. Posey be appointed Commissioners to examine into the propriety of building a bridge across the middle slough in Hatchie bottom on the Ripley and Covington Road and ascertain the probable amount of the cost of such bridge; and that they report to the next January term of this Court.

Ordered that Thomas G. Rice, Shadrach Rice and Samuel Gause be appointed Commissioners to lay off one years allowance for Sarah Crook, Widow of William D. Crook, Deceased.

Ordered by the Court that James H. Bates be appointed overseer of the Ripley and Covington Road from Fullen's Ferry to Fullens Field and that he have the following hands to work said Road -(To Wit) - his own hand, P. G. Gaines and hand , A. J. Fellens, J. B. Mosely, James Wardlow, Joseph Crocker, Geo. L. Johnson's hands, Gerome Roy, David L. Bishop, John Bishop, Perry Nevils, Edmund Nevils, the hands on Jas. Wardlows Hatchie plantation, Carter Whitson, Wm. P. Johnson, Daniel Borum and Elup Wardlow and that he keep the same in repair as a first Class Road.

Pg. 627 Ordered by the Court that David Williams overseer of the Fulton Road in addition to the hands already assigned him have the hands of W. W. Lea of Fulton to work under him.

It appearing to the satisfaction of the Court that William D. Crook has departed this life intestate, and James B. Crook having applied for letters of administration and the court being satisfied with his claim to the administration. And he having entered into Bond and security and taken the oath prescribed by law. It is therefore ordered by the Court that he have letter accordingly.

Ordered that Court be adjourned until Court in Course.

Jas. L. Green, Chairman-
Thomas J. Childress, J. P.-
Thos. G. Rice, J. P.

Pg. 629 November Term-1843-
State of Tennessee.

Pg. 629 cont. Be it Remembered, that at a quorum court began and held for the County of Lauderdale in the State aforesaid in the Court House in the town of Ripley on the first Monday in November it being the sixth day of said month, in the year of our Lord one-thousand, eight-hundred and forty-three, and the Sixty-eight year of American Independence present and holding said court the worshipful James L. Green, Esquire, Chairman and Abel H. Pope and Absolam G. W. Byrn, Esquires, Justices of the peace for the County aforesaid, duly Commissioned and qualified and appointed to hold the quorum courts for said county in said State.

Whereas it appears to the satisfaction of the Court that Nancy Childress has died leaving no will or testament and application being made, by John C. Barnes and Thomas J. Childress to have letters of Administration granted them on said Estate and they having entered into bond given security and qualified according to law, the Court therefore order that they have letters accordingly.

Pg. 630 This day, James B. Crook returned into Court here on oath an inventory of all and Singular the goods and Chattels of William D. Crook, deceased, which said inventory is received and ordered to be recorded.

This day, Isaac Braden, Coroner of this County returned on inquisition held by him on the body of a slave formerly the property of Mrs. Johnson, deceased, which is received and it is ordered that the same be certified to the County Trustee.

Ordered that James H. Chambers be appointed overseer of the road from Mill Creek at Rutherfords Old Mill to the Key Corner, and that he have all the hands, west of Dyersburg road and north east of said road except Matthew Brandon and that he keep the same in repair as a second class road.

Ordered, that Fleming Cheney, be appointed overseer of that portion of the public road leading from Covington to Brownsville lying between the termination of the Big Hatchie Turnpike and Haywood County-line and that he have the hands South east of Sagoon Creek in this County and that he keep said road in repair as a first class road.

Pg. Ordered that Court adjourn until Court in Course.

631 Jas. L. Green, Chairman-
Absalam G. W. Byrn, J. P.-
A. H. Pope, J. P.-

Pg. December Term-1843-

632 State of Tennessee-

Be it remembered, that at a quorum court began and held for the County of Lauderdale in the State aforesaid, on the first Monday in December in the year of our Lord one-thousand, eight-hundred and forty-three, and the Sixty-eighth year of American Independence, it being the 4th day of said month. Present, the worshipful, James L. Green, Esq. Chairman and Absolam G. W. Byrn and A. H. Pope, Esquires legally commissioned and qualified and assigned to hold the quorum courts for said County.

This day the Court here chose and appointed James P. Walker, Guardian of Benjamin R. Walker, a minor orphan whereupon said Walker and David M. Henning and James J. Alison his securities entered into bond in the penal sum of Seven-thousand, five-hundred dollars according to Law and said James P. Walker having been qualified according to Law. It therefore ordered that letters of Guardianship be issued to the said James P. Walker.

Pg. 633 This day, William Deason administrator of all and singular the goods and Chattels, rights, and credits which were of Samuel Deason, Deceased returned into Court here on oath a Sale bill of said estate which is received and ordered to be recorded.

It appearing to the Satisfaction of the Court that the Revenue Commissioner for the 3rd Civil of this County erroneously listed 225 acres of Land to Peter Fitzpatrick the beginning corner of said tract lying in the 1st District and that the same was regularly listed in said 1st. district. It is therefore ordered that said Peter Fitzpatrick be released from the payment of 39¼ cents State Tax and 94⅛ cents County Tax on said tract of land so erroneously listed

Pg. 633 cont. as aforesaid, and the same be certified to the Comptroller of the Treasury and the County Trustee.

This day, Frances J. Murphy produced in open Court a paper writing purporting to be the last Will and testament of Joseph Murphy, Decd.-Whereupon, personally appeared in open court John Watson and Edwin Williams subscribing Witnesses thereto who being first sworn depose and say that they saw Joseph Murphy sign and publish the same as his last Will and testament and that they subscribed the same as witness in his presence and at his request and that said Joseph Murphy was of sound and disposing mind and memory. Whereupon it is ordered that said Will be admitted of record and Francis J. Murphy the Executrix have qualified according to law and being exempt by said will from giving security. It is therefore ordered that she have Letters Testamentary.

Ordered, that Alexander S. Tucker be appointed overseer of the road leading from Durhamville in a Northern direction by Joseph Murphy's place and that he have the hands in the following bounds, (To Wit)- commencing at the forks of the road leading from Brownsville to Ripley and from Brownsville to Fulton running thence west by North west with the Ripley road until it intersects the road from Hurricane Hill to Joseph Taylor's thence with the Hurricane Hill

Pg. 635 road to Watson's Creek on Branch thence down said branch to the Fulton road thence east with said road to the beginning, excluding James E. Street's place and the hands of Mary J. Lee and that he have in addition to the hands in said bounds James C. Lovelace and hands, George W. Tatum and hands, and Jeremiah Penick and hands and that he keep the same in repair as a second class road and that he work from Durhamville to the Ripley and Brownsville road.

It appearing to the satisfaction of the court that Calvin Jones 1960 acre tract of land was listed in the 9th District and that the same was also listed in the 5th District and that the taxes have been paid on said land as listed in said 5th district it is therefore ordered that said Calvin Jones be released from the payment of the State Tax of $1.44 and of the County Tax of $3.40½ on said land as listed in said 9th District and that the same be certified to the Comptroller of the Treasury and the County Trustee.

Pg. 636 It is ordered by the court that Joshua R. Stone be released from the payment of the State Tax amounting to 64 cents and $1.73½ County Tax erroneously assisted to him on 640 acres of land it appearing to the County Court that said Stone did not at the time of testing said land own any such tract and the same be certified to the Comptroller of the Treasury and County Trustee.

This day, James H. Given resigned his commission as constable of the 4th District which is accepted.

This day, James H. Cleawes, Guardian of Alfred Moore returned on oath in open court and account of all the property which has come to his hands by virtue of said appointment which is received and ordered to be recorded.

Ordered that James H. Bates, overseer of the Covington Road from Fullens ferry to Fullens field have in addition to the hands heretofore allowed him, Thos. Boyd and hands, Richard Golding, Wm. Bishop, Jas. M. Barber, Isaac Fullen, Hiram Fullen and James Watson.

Pg. 637 It appearing to the satisfaction of the court that Mary C. Wise has departed this life intestate and John H. Hallaburton having applied for letters of administration and having entered into bond and given security and qualified according to law, it is therefore ordered that he have letters accordingly.

Ordered that the following report and affidavit be received and recorded-(To Wit)-

I, G. L. Rutherford, Sheriff and Collector of Public Tax for the County of Lauderdale and State of Tennessee for the year 1843 hereby report to Court the following insolvent list-(To Wit)-

G. L. Allynes	1 Poll left the County Tax	.50 cents
Pleasant J. Gardner	1 Poll left	.50
Same 2 Slaves valued at $450-		.76
E. C. Lanier	1 Poll left	.50
Wm. Brown	1 " insolvent	.50

Pg.	Andrew Bray½	1 Poll Left	.50
637	John B. Byrn	1 " left	.50
cont.	John Blackwell	1 " left	.50
	Cornelius Durden	1 " left	.50
	Anthony Demory	1 poll	.50
	Elisha Dunnohoe	1 Poll insolvent	.50
	Griffin George	1 " "	.50
	Thomas J. Gardner	1 " left	.50
Pg.	Joseph Glawson	1 " left	.50
638	Demon Millsaps	1 " insolvent	.50
	James M. Pain	1 poll gone	.50
	Allen T. Williams	1 poll left	.50
	Alverson John	1 poll insolvent	.50
	Robert Blackwell	1 poll left	.50
	James Bragden	1 poll	.50
	Joseph Churchwell	1 poll left	.50
	Griffith George	1 poll insolvent	.50
	William T. Holme	1 poll "	.50
	Masten Henry	1 poll left	.50
	Welden Foster	1 poll In.	.50
	John Booth	1 poll left	$1.00
	Burrow A. Neely	1 poll In.	.50
	Samuel Deason	1 poll	.50
	John King	1 poll	.50
	Henry Reynolds	1 poll left	.50
	Isaac Reynolds	1 poll gone	.50
	Benjamin Brown	1 poll died Insolv.	.50
	Abbs. Carnell	1 poll left	.50
	Austin Ward	1 poll Ins.	.50
	Jacob Gingery	1 poll left	1.00
	Dabney P. Hill	1 poll "	1.00
	William Abers	1 " "	.50
	Harry Hooper	1 " "	.50
	Abraham Humble	1 " "	1.00
	Hardy Measles	1 " "	1.00
	Joel D. Mitchell	1 " "	.50
	W. S. Mitchell	1 " "	.50
	J. M. Rucker	1 "m "	.50
	Abner Smith	1 " "	.50
Pg.	J. McHarris	1 "	.50
639	Jacob Linville	1 " Insolvent	.50
		City Tax-	$19.29

I, do solemnly swear that the foregoing list of insolvencies by me exhibited are just and true to the best of my knowledge and that said list fully sets forth the name of each delinquent the amount of Tax he owes and the nature and taxable subjects from which derived and the year for which it accrued and that I have used all legal ways and means in my power to collect the taxes contained in said list from the time I rec'd the Tax Book from the Clerk, This 4th day of Decr. 1843.

Sworn to in open)
Court.)
Test. Isaac M. Steele, Clerk)

G. L. Rutheford, Shff.
and Collector for Lauderdale Cty.

This day, W. A. Simmons resigned his office of Constable of the 5th District which was accepted by the Court.

Ordered, that Thomas G. Rice be appointed Revenue Commissioner to take a list of the Taxable property and polls in the 1st Civil District for the year 1844.

Pg. 640 Ordered that John H. Maxwell be appointed Revenue Commissioner to take a list of Taxable property and polls for the 2nd Civil District for the year 1844.

Pg. 640 cont. Ordered that Abel H. Pope be appointed Revenue Commissioner to take a list of Taxable property and polls for the 3rd Civil District for the year 1844, which said appointment said Pope accepted in open Court.

Ordered that J. M. Alwxander be appointed Revenue Commissioner to take a list of Taxable property and polls for the 4th Civil District for the year 1844.

Ordered that R. C. Campbell be appointed Revenue Commissioner to take a list of taxable property and polls in the 5th Civil District for the year 1844.

Ordered that Elnathan H. Condray be appointed Revenue Commissioner to take a list of taxable property and polls in the 6th Civil District for the year 1844. Which appointment said Condray accepted in open Court.

Pg. 641 Ordered that Edward Fisher be appointed Revenue Commissioner to take a list of Taxable property and Polls for the 7th Civil District for the year 1844.

Ordered that James Soward be appointed Revenue Commissioner to take a list of Taxable property and polls for the 8th Civil District of Lauderdale County for 1844.

Ordered, that A. C. Redding be appointed Revenue Commissioner to take a list of taxable property and polls for the 9th Civil District for the year 1844.

n This day, Isaac M. Steele, Clerk of this court presented to court a settlement made by him with John H. Lanier, Executor of the last Will and testament of Jonathan Jones, Decd. which being examined was approved by the Court and ordered to be recorded.

Pg. 642 Ordered that Court adjourn until Court in Course.

Jas. L. Green, Chairman-
A. H. Pope, J. P. -
A. G. W. Byrn, J. P. -

Pg. 643 January 1844-
State of Tennessee-

Be it remembered that at a County Court, began and held for the County of Lauderdale, in the State aforesaid, in the Court House in the town of Ripley, on the first Monday in January, it being the first day of said Month, in the year of our Lord one-thousand, eight-hundred and forty-four, and the Sixty-eighth year of American Independence, present and holding said Court the Worshipful James L. Green, John H. Maxwell, Elnathan H. Condray, Thomas J. Childress, Abel H. Pope, William R. Ledbetter, Josiah M. Alexander, Thomas G. Rice and Henry S. Peyton, Esquires, Commissioned and qualified according to law, being a majority of all the Justices in said County.

The Court proceeded to elect a chairman for the year 1844 - whereupon James L. Green was duly elected.

The Court appointed James L. Green, John H. Maxwell and Thomas J. Childress, Esquires, three Justices of their own body, to hold the quorum courts for the year 1844.

Pg. 644 This day the Court proceeded to elect an Entry Taker for the County of Lauderdale in the place of James Braden deceased-Whereupon Joseph W. Perkins, Esquire was unanimously elected-Whereupon the said Joseph W. Perkins, Esquire with Joseph Wardlow, James Whitson and Griffith L. Rutherford his securities came into court and entered into bond according to law which said bond is in the words and figures following-(To Wit)-:

State of Tennessee) We, Joseph W. Perkins, Joseph Wardlow, James Whitson
Lauderdale County) and Griffith L. Rutherford all of the State and County aforesaid, acknowledge ourselves indebted to the State of Tennessee, in the penal sum of Twenty-Thousand Dollars, for the payment of which well and truly to be made, we bind ourselves, our heirs, executors and administrators, jointly and severally, firmly by these present, sealed with our seals and dated the 1st day of January , A. D.-1844.

Whereas, the above bound, Joseph M. Perkins, was this day, duly and legally elected

Entry taker of the County of Lauderdale aforesaid. Now the condition of

Pg. this obligation is such, that if the said Joseph W. Perkins shall faithfully
644 /discharge and perform the duties of his office in all things according to law
cont/and shall also account four and pay over according to law, all moneys by him
Pg./ received in payment for all land entered in his office then this obligation to
645/ be void, otherwise to remain in full force and virtue.

Acknowledged in) Joseph W. Perkins-(Seal)
open Court-January) Joseph Wardlow- (Seal)
1st 1844-) James Whitson- m(Seal)
Test. Isaac M. Steele, Clk.) G. L. RutherfordΘ (Seal)

And thereupon the said Joseph W. Perkins, Esq. took the Anti Dueling oath and on oath to support the Constitution of the United States and the State of Tennessee. And also took and subscribed the following oath-(To Wit):-

State of Tennessee) I, Joseph W. Perkins do solemnly swear, that I will
Lauderdale County) faithfully and honestly discharge all the duties appertaining to my office as Entry Taker for Lauderdale County, as directed by law, to the best of my skill and ability; and that I will faithfully and honestly account for all moneys by me received in payment for any land entered in my office, as required by law, So help me God.

Sworn to and subscribed in open)
Court January 1st-1844) Joseph W. Perkins.
Test. Isaac M. Steele, Clerk)

Pg. This day, Isaac M. Steele, Clerk of this Court presented to Court a pro-
646 rata distribution made by him of the Estate of Henderson Jones, Deceased which said distribution was approved by the Court in all things and ordered to be enrolled.

This day, Isaac M. Steele, Clerk of this Court presented to Court a settlement made by him with William D. Lee, Guardian of Malvina A. Marley and Josiah C. Marley and the question being put shall said settlement be confirmed in all things including the fees, Charged by said Clerk, those who voted in the affirmative were Esquires, Alexander, Byrn, Condray, Green, Ledbetter, Maxwell, Peyton and Rice, those who voted in the negative was Esquire Childress, and so said settlement was approved and ordered to be enrolled.

This day, Isaac M. Steele, Clerk of this Court presented to Court, a settlement made by him of the account of Samuel V. Gilliland, Guardian of William A. Wood, Betsy A. Wood, Robert T. Wood, Given R. Wood, Handy Wood, Sabert Wood and Mary E. Wood and the question being put shall said settlement be confirmed
Pg. in all things including the fees charged by said Clerk, those who voted in the
647 affirmative were, Esquires, Alexander, Byrn, Condray, Green, Ledbetter, Maxwell, Peyton and Rice and Esquire, Childress voted in the negative, so said settlement was confirmed and ordered to be enrolled.

This day, Albert W. Posey proved by his own oath the killing of one wolf in the County of Lauderdale over the age of four months there being five Justices present-ordered that the same be certified to the Comptroller of the treasury.

Ordered that the County Trustee pay James L. Green, Esquire, Twelve-dollars for holding the quorum court, Eight days in the year 1843, ayes, Esquires, Alexander, Condray, Childress, Maxwell, Peyton, and Rice, one-third of all the Justices in said County, Noe, Esquire Ledbetter.

Ordered that the County Trustee pay Abel H. Pope, Esquire, Ten-Dollars and 50 cents for holding the quorum Court seven days in the year 1843: Ayes, Esquires, Alexander, Condray, Childress, Maxwell, Peyton and Rice, one-third of all the Justices in said County, Noe, Esquire, Ledbetter.

Pg. Ordered, that the County Trustee pay Absolam C. W. Byrn, Esquire, Twelve-
648 Dollars for holding the quorum court eight days in the year 1843: Ayes, Esquires, Alexander, Condray, Childress, Maxwell, Peyton and Rice one-third of all the Justices of said County, Noe, Esquire, Ledbetter.

Ordered that the County Trustee pay Henry L. Peyton, one-dollar and fifty-cents for holding the quorum court one day in the year 1843; Ayes, Esquires, Alexander, Condray, Childress, Maxwell, Peyton and Rice, one-third of the Justices in said County, Noe, Esquire, Ledbetter.

Pg. 648 cont. Ordered that the County Trustee pay Henry L. Peyton one-Dollar and fifty-cents for holding the quorum court one day in the year 1843: Ayes, Esquires, Alexander, Condray, Childress, Maxwell, Peyton and Rice, one-third of all the Justices in said county, Noe, Esquire, Ledbetter.

Ordered that the County Trustee pay Griffith L. Rutherford, shff and C, fifty-dollars for his ex-officio services in the year 1843: Ayes, Esquires, Alexander, Childress, Green, Ledbetter, Maxwell, Peyton and Rice, one-third of all the Justices of said County.

Ordered, that the County Trustee pay Griffity L. Rutherford, shff and C, twenty-dollars for furnishing wood and water for the Courts and taking care of the Court House, Ayes, Esquires, Alexander, Byrn, Childress, Condray, Green,
Pg. 649 Ledbetter, Maxwell, Peyton, and Rice, one-third of all the Justices in said County.

Ordered, that the County Trustee pay James Whitson one-dollar and fifty cents it being the amount of Tavern expenses incurred by him while guarding Raleigh M. Barber charged with felony-Ayes, Esquires, Alexander, Childress, Green, Ledbetter, Maxwell, Peyton and Rice, one-third of all the Justices of said County.

Ordered that the Commissioners of the town of Ripley proceed again to contract for the ruling in, or inclosing the Court House yard, either at private or public letting to be completed in such time as they may think reasonable- and on such terms as they may think just and equitable-

Ordered, that John H. Maxwell, Elnathan H. Condray and John J. Nelson be appointed commissioners to contract for (on such terms as they may think reasonable) the erection of a bridge on the branch south of Cane Creek on the Dyersburg road, and to take bond and approved security for the completion of the same agreeable to the plan they may draw, on or before the April Session of this court and also to contract for the repair of the bridge on Cane Creek on said road and to take bond for the completion of the same.

It was proposed to lay the following Cty tax to wit:- Jury Tax on each hundred dollars worth of property on which a State Tax is laid 3 cents, Contingent Tax on the same 3 cents, Poor Tax on the same 3 cents, Road and Bridge Tax on the same 3 cents, Jury Tax on each White poll 12½ cents, Contingent Tax on the same 12½ cents, Road and Bridge tax on the same 12½, County Tax on Licenses privileges the same tax as that Levied by the State, those who voted for the above rates were, Esquires, Alexander, Byrn, Childress, Condray, Green, Maxwell, Peyton, and Rice and Esquire Ledbetter present but declined voting making a majority of the Justices of said County-So said tax was laid.

Pg. 651 Ordered that the following good and lawful men of the body of the County of Lauderdale, be summoned by the Sheriff or the law directs to attend at the February term of the Circuit Court of said County, then and there to serve as Grand or Petit Jurors as the case may be-(To Wit)- Samuel Owen, George W. Gause, Thomas T. Tuggle, Edmund Fitzpatrick, Rezin L. Byrn, Robert Walker, William Lunsford, Lance Graves, James B. Crook, David P. Posey, Ellison P. Fuller, David C. Russell, John Fisher, Josiah M. Alexander, John H. Nixon, Lewis Maclin, Dickeson Jennings, Elnathan H. Condray, Jessie Ledbetter, John Wood, Henry Somero, John W. Nearn, Edward Kenly, Benjamin Porter and James M. Lewis and Isaac Moore and Samuel A. Thompson to attend on the Court and Juries as Constables.

Whereas, it appears to the Court, that Furniford McCoy is dead, and having made no will or testament, and application being made by Lance Graves, to have letters of administration granted to him on the estate of the said Furniford McCoy, he having given bond and security, as the by law in such case required, and qualified: the court therefore order that he have letters accordingly.

Whereas, it appears to the Court that Turniford McCoy is dead, and having made no will or testament, and application being made by Lance Graves, to have letters of administration granted to him on the estate of the said Turniford McCoy he having given bond and security, as by law in such case required, and qualified, the Court therefore order that he have letters accordingly.

Pg. 652 Ordered that Court adjourn until 9 o'clock tomorrow morning.

Pg. 652 cont.

Jas. L. Green, Chrm.-
Abs. G. W. Byrn, J. P.-
J. H. Maxwell, J. P.-

Tuesday Morning January 2nd. 1844-

Court met according to adjournment present, James L. Green, John H. Maxwell, Absolam G. W. Byrn and E. H. Condray, T. J. Childress and W. R. Ledbetter, Esquires.

This day, Rezin L. Byrn produced in open court the Certificate of Griffith L. Rutherford, Sheriff and C of his election to the office of constable whereupon the said Rezin L. Byrn entered into bond with security and qualified according to Law.

On motion of Joseph W. Perkins esquire and it appearing to the satisfaction of the Court that Isaac M. Steele a citizen of this County is a man of good moral Character and that he has attained the age of twenty-one years. It is therefore ordered that said facts be certified as a preparatory step to his obtaining licence to practice law in this State.

Pg. 653 This day the following report was received and ordered to be recorded- To Wit:-

State of Tennessee) We, Rezin L. Byrn, John H. Maxwell and Elijah Lake,
Lauderdale County) Commissioners of the Poor House in the County of Lauderdale aforesaid, Respectfully beg leave to report to court, that, our treasurer has received Ninety-two dollars, on the poor tax for the year 1842-that we have paid Joseph Glawson Sixty-dollars, and William D. Lee, Twenty-Seven Dollars, in part payment for the poor house ocupant claim, which we heretofore reported to your worships that we had purchased, and fifty-cents to the Entry taker for recording the transfer to as of said ocupant claim. We rented said Occupant claim for the year 1843, to James McElyea for $13\frac{1}{2}$ barrels of corn. Nine and a half barrels of which has been paid and four barrels are yet due and unpaid. We have rented the said place for the year 1844 to ----- Pierson and sold him the said $9\frac{1}{2}$ barrels of corn, for which he s to make sundry repairs and improvements and to pay 20 barrels of corn next fall.

Pg. 654 We have not had a poor house built according to the order of your workhips for the want of funds.

All which is very respectfully submitted this 2nd day of January 1844.

Rezin L Byrn-
J. H. Maxwell-
Elijah lake-

Ordered that Caleb Miller be appointed overseer of the old Dyersburg road from the South bank of Cane Creek, to where said road intersects the road from Ripley to Dyersburgh and that he have the following hands to work under him- (To Wit)-Brice McElroy, Curtis Ellis, the hands on David Harris old place and the hands on Love's tract of Land, and that he keep the same in repair as a second class road.

The following report is received ordered to be recorded and it is ordered that said road be turned according to said report which report is in the words and figures following to wit:-

The undersigned being appointed and sworn to view and determine on the propriety of turning that part of the public leading from Isaac Moore's to Ripley at the corner of B. F. Boydstengs field over which James P. Ledbetter as

Pg. 655 overseer do report that in our opinion that said road ought to be changed as follows, To Wit:- beginning at a small poplar at the corner of Boydsten's fence, thence to a large black oak on the point of the ridge thence south to the road all which is respectfully submitted to the consideration of the court this Decr. the 29, 1843.

Wm. R. Ledbetter-
Henry Shearer-
Thos. Wilcox-
H. Meadows-
I. Moore-

Pg. 655 cont. Ordered, that Hiram C. Keller, Isaac Braden and James Whitson be appointed Commissioners to let out (either publicly or privately as to them may seem best) the building of a bridge on Cane Creek on the old Ashport road and that they superintend the building of the same and that they have the same completed as soon as practicable and that they report to the April Session of this court.

Griffith L. Rutherford this day presented to Court the following account to wit:-

G. L. Rutherford, Dr.
with Wm. P. Gaines for Goal work

1842-April 29,	To making Goal Key -	$ .75
Sept. 13,	To 1 pr. of Hand cuffs	3.50
Sept. 20,	To making 1 plate for Door	2.50
Pg. 656	To repairing Lock for "	1.00
	To making second pr. of Cuffs	2.00
	To Ironing one foot of Simpson	1.00
	Going to the Goal and taking the Irons off Simpson	.50
	To 1 ball of Iron	1.25
	Water Bucket	.50
		$13.00

It is ordered, that the County Trustee pay G. L. Rutherford the above account of Thirteen Dollars, Ayes, Esquires, Byrn, Condray, Childress, Green, Ledbetter and Maxwell, one-third of all the Justices of said County, Noes, None.

Ordered, that James Gillespie, Thomas Golding and Elijah Lake appointed Commissioners to contract for and Superintend the building a bridge on Goodwin's Creek on the public road leading from Ripley to Fulton on such terms as to them may seem equitable, and that they report to the April Session of this Court.

Ordered, That Samuel V. Gilliland and Rezin L. Byrn, Esquires, be appointed Revenue Commissioner to settle with the County officers for the year 1844.

Pg. 657 Ordered that James M. McClelland be appointed overseer of the old Fulton road and that he work from Ripley to the forks of the road near Wm. P. Gaines's old place, and that he have the following hands to work under him to wit:- James Price, John McCall, the hands on Whitson's place and the hands on Wardlow's plantation and that he keep said road in repair as a second class road.

The following report was received and ordered to be recorded to wit:-

State of Tennessee) I, Rezin L. Byrn, Treasurer of the Commissioners for
Lauderdale County) town of Ripley in the County aforesaid Respectfully beg leave to report to your worships, that the amount of money in my hands at the time of my last report to your worships on the 3rd day of April 1843 was $412.50

Received May 1st 1843 of J. A. Morris	56.00
	$468.52

I have made the following disbursements - To Wit:-

Paid John S. Day for painting the inside of the Court House -	$165.00	
For Lettering three Doors -@ 9/-	4.50	
Pg. 658 For painting dome on the Cupolo- 8 blinds at 12/-----	16.00	
For Ading the base of the Cupolo- finding hinges and hanging blind-	4.50	
For painting and fixing platform-	10.00	
Paid B. F. Fisher for washing window lights and helping to take the window sash-	2.00	
Paid Jordan-(a man of Colour)- for stopping cracks in the Columns and fixing outside door-	2.00	
Paid James M. Hamm for digging up twenty-eight stumps & two gums-	7.50	$211.50
Leaving in my hands the sum of		$257.02

Two-hundred and fifty-seven dollars and two-cents, all which is respectfully

Pg. 658 cont. submitted, this 2nd day of January 1844.

Rezin L. Byrn.

Ordered, that the Commissioner of the town of Ripley, proceed forthwith to collect the money yet due for the sales of Lots in said town.

Pg. 659 It appearing to the satisfaction of the Court that James Braden has died making no will or testament and application being made by James A. Lockey and Milton F. Lake to Letters of Administration granted to them upon said estate and the Court being satisfied with their claim to the administration and they having given bond and security as required by law and been qualified the Court therefore order that they have letters accordingly.

Ordered, by the Court that John H. Maxwell, Hiram C. Keller and Abel H. Pope (freeholder unconnected by affinity or consanganuity with Elizabeth M. Braden, widow of James Braden) be appointed Commissioners to lay off and set apart so much of the crop, stock, provisions, money and other assets on hand or due as may be necessary for the support of the said Elizabeth Braden and her family for one year from the death of her husband and the said James Braden. Ordered that Court adjourn until Court in course.

Pg. 660
Jas. L. Green, Chairman-
Thos. J. Childress, J. P-
A. G. W. Byrn, J. P.-

Pg. 661 February Term-1844

State of Tennessee-

Be it remembered that at a Quorum Court began and held for the County of Lauderdale in the State aforesaid, in the Court House in the town of Ripley on the first Monday being the fifth day of February in the year of our Lord one-thousand, eight-hundred and forty-four and the 68th year of the Independence of the United States of America, Present and holding said Court, the Worshipful James L. Green, Esq., Chairman and Tho. J. Childress, and Henry L. Peyton, Esquires.

This day, William Turner, Administrator of all and singular the goods and chattels, rights, credits which were of Sarah Cook, returned on oath in open Court an Inventory of said estate which is received and ordered to be recorded.

This day, Edwin N. Cook came into Court, (and it appearing to the satisfaction of the Court that the Edwin N. Cook is more than fourteen years of age) and chose William Turner, his Guardian, whereupon, the said William Turner came into court and entered bond and gave security was qualified according to law.

Pg. 662 This day, the court here chose and appointed Thomas J. Childress Revenue Commissioner to take list of Taxable property and polls for the 3rd Civil District of this County for the 1844 and thereupon said Tho. J. Childress accepted of said appointment in open court.

This day, Pleasant G. Davenport and John L. Pope produced in open court the last will and testament of Abel A. Pope and thereupon appeared in court, James A. Lackey and David M. Henning subscribing witnesses there to who being first sworn depose and say that they saw him (the said Abel H. Pope) sign, seal and publish the same as his last will and testament and that they subscribed the same in his presence and at his request and that they believe that he was of sound and disposing mind and memory. It is therefore ordered that said will be admitted of Record. And the said Pleasant G. Davenport and John L. Pope having given bond and security and qualified according to law the court therefore order that they have letters Testamentary accordingly.

This day, James B. Crook, Administrator and C of W. D. Crook, deceased, returned on oath in open court an account of sales of said estate which is received and ordered to be recorded.

Pg. 663 This day, John C. Barnes and Tho. J. Childress, administrators and C. of Nancy Childress, Dec'd. returned on oath an inventory of said estate which is received and ordered to be recorded.

This day, Henry Willard and Isaac M. Steele produced in open court commissions from James C. Jones, Governor of the State of Tennessee appointing them

Pg. Justices of the peace for the County of Lauderdale. Whereupon, the said Wil-
663 lard and Steele took the Several oath prescribed by law for Justices of the
cont.peace.

Ordered that Julius L. Gause be appointed overseer of that part of the public road leading from Tho. G. Rice's Gin to Brownsville lying between Tho. G. Rice's and Haywood County-line and that he have Moreau P. Estes and hands, Shadrick Rice and hands, Samuel L. Gause and hands and his own hands and that he keep the same in repair as a second class road.

This day, Isaac M. Steele, Clerk of this Court presented to Court settlements made by him with Robert C. West, Guardian of Frances Marian Millen
Pg. and Rachael Caroline Millen, and with David Williams,Admr. and C. of George
664 Williams, De'd. and also with John Thompson, Guardian of John W. Rudder which said settlement after being fully and thoroughly examined by the Court are in all things confirmed and ordered to be recorded.

This day, R. C. West, Guardian of Francis M. Millen and Rachael Caroline Millen came in open Court and renued his Guardian bond according to law.

This day, Samuel V. Gilliland, Guardian of Robert T. Wood, Rezin L. Wood, Handy Wood, Sabert Woods and Mary Ellen Wood came in court and resigned said appointment whereupon the court here chose and appointed William A. Wood, Guardian of said Robert T. Wood, Rezin L. Wood, Handy Wood, Sabert Wood and Mary Ellen Wood in the room and stead of Samuel V. Gilliland whereupon said William A. Wood came into court and entered into bond and gave security and was qualified according to law.

Pg. This day, Guilford Jones, Trustee of Lauderdale made the following report
665 to court on oath which ordered to be recorded.

Receipts by the Trustee of Lauderdale County For the year 1843-

To aggregate Tax List	$ 1148.19
Proceeds of land sold in 1842	49.17
Supplementary report	3.55
Amt. paid by Jas. B. Hucheson for Stray	6.00
John Fletcher - " "	10.00
Amt. paid Dickerson Jennings- " "	2.25
" " Samuel Lusk - " "	2.50
" " Jas. H. Hogsette- " "	13.00
" " Jas. A. Morris- " "	21.25
" " S. Maxwell- " "	6.25
" " F. C. Dial- " "	.75
" " Saml. Strickland- " "	15.00
" " Shadrick Rice- " "	3.50
" " Revenue from Clerk Circt Court	31.66¼
" " " " Clerk of Cty Court	69.68 3/4
" " Proceeds of lands in 1843	76.67 ¼
" " Stray said on $12-Sub-60	11.40
	$ 1470.83¼

Disbursements in the year 1843-

To Amt. Credit due Sheriff on reported lands-	$ 276.46
" " " " for insolvents-	30.38
" " Commissions due Sheriff for collecting-	56.64½
" " Pd. Commissioners 66 poor house	126.45
" " Pd. Joseph Currie Jury Ticket	3.00
" " Pd. Ezekiel Wakefield- Jury Ticket	3.00
Pg. " " George W. Young- " "	3.00
666 " " Sugar T. Evans- " "	3.00
" " Jas. H. Hogsette- " "	3.00
" " Jno. H. Nixon- " "	3.00
	$ 504.91½
" " E. S. Campbell- " "	3.00
" " Robert Meadows- " "	3.00
" " Richard Parr- " "	3.00
" " Drury Massey- " "	3.00
" " E. H. Hinton- " "	3.00

Pg.	To	Amt.	Edmond Wright-Jury Ticket-	$ 3.00
666	"	"	" " " " -	3.00
cont.	"	"	Jas. Salesbury- " " -	4.00
	"	"	Henry Willard - " " -	4.00
	"	"	Benjamin Brown- " " -	4.00
	"	"	Jas. Shearman - " " -	4.00
	"	"	William Turner- " " -	4.00
	"	"	Saml. L. Gause- " " -	4.00
	"	"	Calvin F. Ledbetter" " -	4.00
	"	"	Monroe P. Estes-" " -	4.00
	"	"	Wm. McClelland- " " -	4.00
	"	"	Isaac D. Maxwell" " -	4.00
	"	"	Moses B. Chism- " " -	2.00
	"	"	Henry Crichfield, Jr." -	2.00
	"	"	Henry Pitts- " " -	2.00
	"	"	Saml. Given- " " -	2.00
	"	"	John F. Jett- " " -	2.00
	"	"	A. G. Byrn - " " -	2.00
	"	"	Dickerson Jennings- " -	2.00
	"	"	Wm. Hafford - " " -	2.00
Pg.	"	"	George R. Williams- " -	2.00
669	"	"	Wm. B. Sawyer- " " -	2.00
	"	"	Lance Graves - " " -	2.00
	"	"	Elijah Lake- " " -	2.00
	"	"	Saml. Deason- " " -	4.00
	"	"	A. H. Pope, R. Boswell Pauper-	20.00
	"	"	G. L. Rutherford, Order Wood-	21.12$\frac{1}{2}$
	"	"	G. L. Rutherford, ex-officio services-	50.00
	"	"	Isaac Braden for Inquest-	5.00
	"	"	Jno. H. Maxwell, holding 2 Court-	12.00
	"	"	J. H. Maxwell for N. Grant, pauper-	10.00
	"	"	Geo. Chipman - Jury Ticket-	4.00
	"	"	Jesse Ledbetter- " " -	4.00
	"	"	Jno. W. Nearn- " " -	4.00
	"	"	James Hubbard- " " -	4.00
	"	"	Joseph Churchwell-" " -	4.00
	"	"	Smith Kent- " " -	3.00
	"	"	Tho. J. Childress" " -	3.00
	"	"	Zachariah Mitchell" " -	3.00
	"	"	P. G. Davenport- " " -	2.00
	"	"	R. C. Campbell- " " -	2.00
	"	"	Benjamin Nearn- " " -	2.00
	"	"	Wm. Williams- " " -	2.00
	"	"	Jas. Gillespie- " " -	4.00
	"	"	Jno. W. Hamil for coffin R. Boswell-	5.00
	"	"	J. M. Alexander, Revenue Com.-	10.00
	"	"	Daniel Williams- Jury Ticket-	2.00
	"	"	Bill of costs-State vs. Wm. P. Gaines-	18.31$\frac{1}{4}$
	"	"	Bill of costs- P. G. Davenport-	11.75
	"	"	" " " - Jas. Shearman-	18.68 3/4
Pg.	"	"	" " " -James B. Crook-	15.81
670	"	"	" " " -Jno. Blackwell-	32.85
	"	"	" " " -E. S. Wakefield-	7.87$\frac{1}{2}$
	"	"	" " " -W. D. Wakefield-	9.50
	"	"	" " " -Albert Posey-	11.50
	"	"	William B."Sawyer-Rec. Com.	10.00
	"	"	Isaac Braden, order for burial Expenses-R. Boswell-	6.50
	"	"	G. L. Rutherford, Ct. order-	4.12
	"	"	C. G. Fisher for Entry Takers papers-	5.00

Pg.	To	Amt.					
Pg.	To	Amt.	E. H. Condray-hold 2 Courts				$ 12.00
670	"	"	J. L. Hearring- 2 Desks & Co.				12.50
cont.	"	"	I. M. Steele-Order				24.78¼
	"	"	I. M. Steele-Order				26.93 3/4
	"	"	E. H. Condray-Rev. Coms.				10.00
	"	"	Henry Willard holding Quo Court				3.00
	"	"	A. Vickory for Bridges				45.00
	"	"	Lee H. Rucker-Rev. Com.				10.00
	"	"	I. M. Steele-order				2.37½
	"	"	A. G. W. Byrn-Quorum Court				3.00
	"	"	A. H. Pope-	"	"		3.00
	"	"	G. W. Tatum-Witness Ticket-				.75
	"	"	" " " -				3.00
	"	"	Edmund Fitzpatrick-Jury Ticket-				2.00
	"	"	" " -	"	"	-	2.00
	"	"	Walter Glawson-	"	"	-	2.00
	"	"	Saml. Hooper-	"	"	-	2.00
	"	"	H. R. Chambers-	"	"	-	2.00
	"	"	Robt. Crihfield-	"	"	-	4.00
	"	"	Henry Shearer-	"	"	-	4.00
	"	"	Isaac Thompson-	"	"	-	2.00
Pg.	M	"	Mark Watson-	"	"	-	2.00
671	"	"	Jas. B. Crook-	"	"	-	2.00
	"	"	Jno. Chapman-	"	"	-	2.00
	"	"	Wm. Jennings-	"	"	-	4.00
	"	"	Joseph Currie-	"	"	-	4.00
	"	"	Wm. B. Sawyer-	"	"	-	4.00
	"	"	Rezin L. Byrn-	"	"	-	4.00
	"	"	Wm. A. Wood -	"	"	m-	3.00
	"	"	M. A. Posey-	"	"	-	3.00
	"	"	Chas. G. Manning-	"	"	-	3.00
	"	"	John Wood-	"	"	-	3.00
	"	"	Hugh Super-	"	"	-	3.00
	"	"	Wm. Hafford-	"	"	-	3.00
	"	"	Wm. Boydston-	"	"	-	3.00
	"	"	Green Baker-	"	"	-	3.00
	"	"	Jas. Whitson-	"	"	-	3.00
	"	"	S. A. Thompson-	"	"	m -	3.00
	"	"	Jas. H. Given-	"	"	-	3.00
	"	"	R. L. Byrn-	"	"	-	3.00
	"	"	Abner Pitts-	"	"	-	3.00
	"	"	Hiram Meadows-	"	"	-	3.00
	"	"	Jno. C. Barnes-	"	"	-	3.00
	"	"	Arch Phillips-	"	"	-	3.00
	"	"	Jno. T. Smith-	"	"	-	3.00
	"	"	Josiah Blankenship-	"	"	-	3.00
	"	"	Cyrus Webb-	"	"	-	3.00
	"	"	R. P. Russell-	"	"	-	3.00
	"	"	E. P. Fuller-	"	"	-	3.00
	"	"	D. C. Russell-	"	"	-	3.00
	"	"	Asa Pate-	"	"	-	3.00
	"	"	John Arnold-	2	"	Q	3.00
Pg.	"	"	Claiborne Rounsaville"		"	-	3.00
672	"	"	Saml. Lusk-	"	"	-	3.00
	"	"	S. D. Maxwell-	"	"	-	3.00
	"	"	A. S. Tucker-	"	"	-	3.00
	"	"	Geo. R. Williams-	"	"	-	3.00
	"	"	Henry Willard-	"	"	-	3.00
	"	"	Andrew Coplinger-	"	"	-	3.00

Pg.	To Amt.	Benjamin M. Flippin-	Jury Ticket-	$ 3.00
672	" "	Wm. Lunsford-	" " -	3.00
cont.	" "	Jas. T. Robinson-	" " -	1.00
	" "	Jno. A. Clark-	" " -	3.00
	" "	Geo. Thum-	" " -	3.00
	" "	Bill of Costs-State Vs. Posey-		12.50
	" "	Jno. A. Clark-	Jury Ticket-	3.00
	" "	Geo. Thum-	" " -	3.00
	" "	Bill of Costs-State Vs. J. P. Silvertooth-		12.06¼
	" "	H. S. Peyton for C. Smoot-pauper-		15.00
	" "	" " " for Revenue book-		7.50
	" "	A. H. Pope-bufial of R. Boswell-		7.76
	" "	Thos. G. Rice-Revenue Comsr.		10.00
	" "	A. G. W. Byrn-	" " -	10.00
	" "	Jno. S. Robbins-	" " -	10.00
	" "	I. M. Steele-Cty. Court order-		21.50
	" "	Isaac Braden-Inquest-		5.00
	" "	E. S. Campbell-Revenue Coms.		10.00
	" "	R. H. Hamil, Coffin for Blackwell-		5.00
	" "	Wm. I. Crocker, Jury Ticket-		3.00
	" "	Leonard Dunavant-	" " -	3.00
	" "	Wm. McClelland-	" " -	3.00
	" "	Wm. Curtis-	" " -	3.00
Pg.	" "	Isaac Moore-	" " -	3.00
673	" "	Jno. Oliver-	" " -	3.00
	" "	Jno. Thompson-	" " -	3.00
	" "	Bennett Griffith-m"	" -	3.00
	" "	Samuel A. Given-	" " -	3.00
	" "	Jno. Watson-	" " -	3.00
	" "	J. L. Hearring-	" " -	3.00
	" "	James B. Hutcheson-"	" -	3.00
	" "	Joseph Currie-	" " -	3.00
	" "	Jas. J. Robinson-	" " -	3.00
	" "	Archer Phillips-	" " 2	3.00
	" "	Fred Barfield-	" " -	3.00
	" "	Jno. D. Edney-	" " -	3.00
	" "	W. G. Hogsette-	" " -	1.00
	" "	R. L. Byrn-	" " -	2.00
		Trustee's Commissions-		56.70
			Amount-	$1471.32
			Due-	1470.83
			in favor of Trustee-	.49

this Feb. 5, 1844. Guilford Jones, Trustee of L. County.

Ordered, that John Hodges be appointed overseer of the road leading from Bolling Fishers to Ashport Commencing at Bolling Fisher's lane and working to where said road intersects the Bucks ferry road and that he have the following hands to work said road to wit:- Nicholas Reynolds, William Read,
Pg. Armstead B. Mily, Philip Crihfield and Ancel Reynolds and that they keep the
674 same in repair as a second Class road.

Ordered that court adjourn until tomorrow morning at 9 o'clock.

Jas. L. Green, Chairman-
Thos. J. Childress, J. P.-
Henry L. Peyton, J. P.-

February 6th-A.D.-1844.
Court met according to adjournment.

Present the worshipful James L. Green, Esq. Chairman and Henry L. Peyton and Thomas J. Childress, Esquires.

Ordered, that the following men be appointed Judges and Clerks to hold the popular elections on the first Saturday in March next-(To Wit)-. For the first District Archer Philles, Geo. W. Young and Edmund Fitzpatrick, Judges

Pg. 674 cont. Tho. J. Cain and Geo. W. Gause, Clerks For the 2nd District, Rezin L. Byrn, Joseph Wardlow and Wm. P. Gaines-Judges, J. L. Hearring and J. A. Lackey, Clerks-For the 3rd District Hiram C. Keller, Thos. Golden and Elijah Lake, Judges, Fred Barfield and Milton F. Lake, Clerks. For the 4th District, Saml. A. Given, Josiah M. Alexander and Jesse Hutcheson, Judges, Jas. P. Anderson and J. J. Roberson, Clerk For the 5th District-Jas. Hubbard, E. S. Campbell, and R. C. Campbell, Judges, John H. Nixon- and Lewis Maclin, Clerks-For the
Pg. 675 6th District, Elnathan H. Condray, Jesse Ledbetter and Saml. Lusk, Judges and Wm. Boydston and C. F. Ledbetter, Clerks. For the 7th District, Edward Fisher, Stith Richardson and Edmund Wright, Judges and J. W. Richardson and Wm. Wright, Clerks. For the 8th District, Richard Parr, Benj. Porter, and Wm. B. Sawyer, Judges and B. T. Porter and Wm. Owen, Clerks. For the 9th District ----- Pearson, Lee H. Rucker and A. H. Redding, Judges and Jas. M. Rucker and Jas. McLewis, Clerks.

Ordered that Court adjourn until Court in course.

Jas. L. Green, Chairman-
Henry L. Peyton, J. P.-
Thos. J. Childress, J. P.-

Pg. 676 State of Tennessee-

Be it remembered, that at a quorum Court began and held in the Court House in the town of Ripley for the County of Lauderdale in the State of Tennessee aforesaid, on the first Monday being the fourth day of March in the year of our Lord one-thousand, eight-hundred and forty-four, and the Sixty-eight year of American Independence. Present and holding said court the Worshipful James L. Green, Esq. Chairman and Thomas J. Childress and Wm. R. Ledbetter, Esquires Commissioned and sworn according to law when the following proceedings were had and done-To Wit:-

This day, Isaac M. Steele, Clerk of this court presented settlements made by him with Jas. H. Cleaves, Guardian of Alfred Moore, also a settlement made by him with David A. Bradford, Guardian of Mary J. Burke, Eleanor A. Burke, Robert A. Burke and Caledonia T. Burke, also a settlement made by him with Isaac Braden as former Guardian of Martha Braden and Mahala Braden and as Guardian of John Braden, Elizabeth Braden, Reuben Braden, Willie Braden, and Sarah
Pg. 677 Jane Braden and also a settlement made by him with Mrs. Gilly Braden formerly Mrs. Gilly Hunter, Guardian of William Hunter which said settlement being severally examined and approved by the Court are ordered to be recorded.

This day, Thomas G. Rice, resigned his office of Justice of the Peace for the County of Lauderdale.

Ordered that William B. Chisholm be appointed overseer of the road leading from Isaac Moore's to Ripley and that he have the following hands to work under him-(To Wit)- John B. Moore, B. F. Boydston, Wm. Boydston, John Lockard, Roland Ledbetter, John Meadows, Moses B. Chism, Drury Massey and Hiram Meadows and that he keep the same in repair as a second Class road.

Ordered that Banks M. Burrow be released from the payment of Double Tax on 364 acres of land lying in the 6th District erronously listed as 368 acres.

Pg. 678 Ordered that James M. Lewis, Esq. be appointed Revenue Commissioner to take a list of taxable property and polls in the 9 Civil District for the year 1844 in the place of C. A. Reading who has failed to a list according to law. Whereupon said Jas. L. Lewis came into open Court and accepted said appointment.

Ordered that Josiah Blankenship be appointed overseer of the road from Hurricane Hill, to the Ripley road East of Wm. P. Gaines old place on the same road, and that he have the following hands to work said road-(To Wit)- William Boyd, Wm. Spence, Samuel Davenport, John Fullen, John Alverson, James Blankenship and Leabern Rhea and that he keep the same in repair as a second class road.

Ordered that William Guy be released from the payment Double Tax on one-hundred and thirty acres of land in the 8th Civil District listed for Double Tax and that Henry Rutherford be released from the payment of Double Tax on 80 acres of land in said district.

Pg. 679 Ordered that the Court adjourn until Court in Course.

Pg. 679 cont.

Jas. L. Green, Chairman-
Thos. J. Childress, J. P.-
Wm. R. Ledbetter, J. P.-

Pg. 680

State of Tennessee)
Lauderdale County)

Be it remembered that at a County Court began and held for the County and State aforesaid in the Court House in the Town of Ripley on the First Monday in April in the year of our Lord, one-thousand eight-hundred and forty-four, it being the first day of said month and the sixty-eighth year of the Independence of the United States of America. Present, J. M. Alexander, A. G. W. Byrn, E. S. Campbell, R. C. Campbell, Thomas J. Childress, E. H. Condray, Edwin Fisher, J. M. Green, James Gillespie, E. H. Hinton, Edward Kennelly, Wm. R. Ledbetter, H. S. Peyton, James Soward, and Isaac M. Steele, Esquires, Commissioned and sworn according to law holding the quarterly Court, Isaac M. Steele, Clerk and Griffith L. Rutherford, Sheriff.

Proclamation being made the Court proceeded to business.

This day, Lysander M. Campbell, presented in open Court a certified from Isaac Braden, Coroner of said County of his having been duly elected by the qualified voters of Lauderdale County to the office of County Court Clerk for said County who took the several oaths prescribed by law and entered into bond according to law which are in the words and figures following-(To Wit):-

Know all men by these presents that we Lysander M. Campbell, Griffith L. Rutherford, William R. Ledbetter, Joseph Taylor and J. F. Jett all of the

Pg. 681

County of Lauderdale and State of Tennessee are held and firmly bound to James C. Jones, Governor of the State of Tennessee for the time being and his successors in office in the penal sum of five-thousand dollars; for which payment well and truly to be made, we bind ourselves, our heirs, executors and administrators, Jointly and severally, firmly by these presents, sealed with our seals, and date the 1st day of April A. D. 1844.

The condition of the above obligation is such that whereas, the above bounden Lysander M. Campbell was on the 2nd day of March 1844 duly and legally elected, Clerk of the County Court of Lauderdale County as appears from the certificate of Isaac Braden, Cornner of said County: Now if the above bounden Lysander M. Campbell shall safely keep the records of said Court and in all things well and truly discharge and perform the duties of Clerk of said Court according to law so long as he may continue in said office, then this obligation to be null and void, otherwise to remain in full force and virtue.

Acknowledged in open	Lysander M. Campbell -(Seal)
Court and approved by the same	J. F. Jett - (Seal)
April 1st, 1844	Wm. R. Ledbetter- (Seal)
Test- James L. Green	his
Chairman of the County Court	Joseph(X)Taylor- (Seal)
of the County aforesaid	mark
	G. L. Rutherford- (Seal)

Pg. 682

Know all men by these presents, that, we Lysander M. Campbell, Griffith L. Rutherford, Wm. R. Ledbetter, Joseph Taylor and J. F. Jett all of the County of Lauderdale and State of Tennessee are held and firmly bound unto James L. Green, Chairman of the County Court of the County aforesaid for the time being and his successors in office in the penal Sum of two-thousand Dollars; for the payment of which well and truly to be made, bind ourselves, our heirs, executors and administrators jointly and severally, firmly by these presents, sealed with our seals and dated the 1st day of April, A.D.1844.

The condition of the above obligation is such, that whenas the above bounden Lysander M. Campbell was on the 2nd day of March A.D.1844 duly and legally elected clerk of the County Court of the County of Lauderdale aforesaid. Now if the said Lysander M. Campbell shall well and truly pay the Trustee of Lauderdale County all County revenue by him Collected or which ought to have been collected on or before the first day of October in each and every year during his continuance in the said office of Clerk, then the above obligation to be void, otherwide to remain in full force and virtue.

Pg. Acknowledged in open) Lysander M. Campbell-(Seal)
682 Court and approved by the Court) J. F. Jett- (Seal)
cont. April 1st. 1844) Wm. R. Ledbetter- (Seal)
Test. James L. Green) his
Chairman of the County Court of) Joseph(X)Taylor - (Seal)
the County aforesaid-) mark
G. L. Rutherford- (Seal)

Pg. Know all men by these presents, that we, Lysander M. Campbell, Griffith L.
683 Rutherford, William R. Ledbetter, Joseph Taylor, and J. F. Jett all of the County of Lauderdale and State of Tennessee are held and firmly bound unto James C. Jones, Governor of the State of Tennessee for the time being and his successors in office in the penal sum of two-thousand Dollars; for the payment of which, well and truly to be made we bind ourselves, our heirs, executors and administrators jointly and severally, firmly by these presents sealed with our seals and dated the 1st day of April A.D.1844.

The condition of the above obligation is such that whereas the above bounden, Lysander M. Campbell was on the 2nd day of March 1844 duly and legally elected clerk of the County Court of Lauderdale County;

Now if the said L. M. Campbell shall well and truly pay the Treasurer of the State of Tennessee all revenue by him collected, or which ought to have been collected on or before the first of November in each and every year during his continuance in the said office of clerk then the above obligation to be null and void, otherwise to remain in full force and virtue.

Acknowledged in open) Lysander M. Campbell-(Seal)
Court and approved by the) J. F. Jett- (Seal)
Same April 1st.1844) Wm. R. Ledbetter- (Seal)
Test. Jas. L. Green) his
Chairman of the County Court) Joseph(X)Taylor- (Seal)
of the County aforesaid) mark
G. L. Rutherford- (Seal)

Pg. This day, Griffith L. Rutherford, came into Court and presented a certi-
684 ficate from the Coroner of Lauderdale County certifying that he was duly and legally elected sheriff of Lauderdale County on the 2nd day of March-A.D.1844. Whereupon the said Griffith L. Rutherford entered into bond and was qualified according to Law which said bonds are in the words and figures following- (To Wit):-

Know all men by these presents that we, Griffith L. Rutherford, Henry F. Rutherford, William P. Gaines and James L. Green all of the County of Lauderdale and State of Tennessee are held and firmly bound unto James C. Jones, Governor of the State of Tennessee aforesaid for the time being and his successors in office in the Penal Sum of Three-Thousand dollars for the payment of which well and truly to be made we bind ourselves, our heirs, executors and administrators jointly and severally firmly by these presents sealed with our seals and dated the first day of April A.D.1844.

The condition of the above obligation is such that whereas the above bounden Griffith L. Rutherford was on the 2nd day of March A.D.1844 duly and legally elected sheriff of Lauderdale County, as appears from the Certificate of Isaac Braden, Coroner of said County if Therefore the said Griffith L. Rutherford shall well and truly execute and due return make of process and precepts to him directed and pay and satisfy all fees and all sums of money by him received, or levied by virtue of any process into the proper office, by which the same by the
Pg. tenor thereof ought to be paid or to the person or persons to whom the same shall
685 be due, his, her or their executors, administratos, attorneys or agents and in all things well, truly and faithfully execute the said office of sheriff, during his continuance therein, then above obligation to be void, otherwise to remain in full force and effect.

Acknowledged in open) G. L. Rutherford- (Seal)
Court and approved by) H. F. Rutherford- (Seal)
them April 1st day 1844) Wm. P. Gaines - (Seal)
Test. L. M. Campbell9) Jas. L. Green- (Seal)

Pg. 685 cont. Clerks of the County Court of said County-

Know all men by these presents, that we, Griffith L. Rutherford, Henry F. Rutherford, William P. Gaines and James L. Green all of the County of Lauderdale and State of Tennessee, are held and firmly bound unto James C. Jones, Governor of the State of Tennessee for the time being, and his successors in office in the penal sum of twelve-thousand dollars, for which payment of which will and truly to be made, we bind ourselves, our heirs, executors and administrators, jointly and severally, firmly by these presents; sealed with our seals and dated the 1st. day of April A.D.1844.

Pg. 686 Whereas, Griffith L. Rutherford, was elected sheriff and collector of the public Taxes for the County aforesaid, on the 2nd day of March A.D.1844, as appears from the Certificate of Isaac Braden, Coroner of said county-Now if the said Griffith L. Rutherford, Shall, well and truly collect and pay to the Treasurer of the State Tennessee, all taxes by him collected, or which ought to have been collected, on or before the last day of December in each and every year in which he shall collect the taxes, then the above obligation to be void, otherwise to remain in full force and virtue.

Acknowledged in open Court and approved by them April 1st 1844) Test. L. M. Campbell, Clerk of the County Court of said County-)

G. L. Rutherford - (Seal)
H. F. Rutherford - (Seal)
Wm. P. Gaines - (Seal)
Jas. L. Green - (Seal)

Know all men by these presents that, we, Griffith L. Rutherford, Henry F. Rutherford, William P. Gaines, James L. Green, all of the County of Lauderdale and State of Tennessee, are held and firmly bound unto James L. Green, Chairman of the County of Lauderdale aforesaid and his successors in office, in the penal
Pg. sum of Four-thousand Dollars; for the payment of which well and truly to made,
687 we bind ourselves, our heirs, executors and administrators, jointly and severally firmly by these presents; sealed with our seals and dated the 1st day of April A.D.1844.

Whereas, Griffith L. Rutherford was the 2nd day of March A.D.1844, elected Sheriff and collector of the State and County Taxes for the County aforesaid, as appears from the certificate of Isaac Braden, Coroner of the County aforesaid. Now if the said Griffith L. Rutherford shall, well and truly collect and pay to the County Trustee of the County aforesaid, all County taxes by him collected or which ought to have been collected, on or before the last day of December in each and every year in which he shall collect the taxes, then the above obligation to be void otherwise to remain in full force and virtue.

Acknowledged in open Court and approved by the same April 1st 1844. Test. L. M. Campbell, Clerk of the County Court of said County)

G. L. Rutherford-(Seal)
H. F. Rutherford-(Seal)
Wm. P. Gaines- (Seal)
Jas. L. Green- (Seal)

Pg. 688 At the request of L. M. Campbell, Isaac M. Steele was duly and legally qualified Deputy Clerk of this Court.

This day, Guilford Jones produced in open Court the Certificate of Isaac Braden, Coroner of Lauderdale County-Certifying that he was on Saturday the 2nd day of March last duly and legally elected Trustee of the County aforesaid. Whereupon, said Jones entered into bond and was duly qualified according to law which said Bond is in the words and figures following-(To Wit)

Know all men by these presents, that we, Guilford Jones, David P. Posey and S. A. Thompson all of the County of Lauderdale and State of Tennessee are held and firmly bound unto James L. Green, Chairman of the County Court of the County of Lauderdale aforesaid and his successors in office, in the penal sum of four-thousand Dollars, for the payment of which well and truly to be made, we bind ourselves, our heirs, executors and administrators, jointly and severally, firmly by these presents, sealed with our seals and dated the 1st. day of April A.D.1844.

Pg. 688 cont/ Pg./ 691/ The condition of the above obligation is such, that whereas the above bounden Guilford Jones was on the 2nd day of March A.D.1844, duly and legally elected Trustee of the County of Lauderdale aforesaid as appears from the Certificate of Isaac Braden, Coroner of said County. Now if the said Guilford Jones shall safely keep and faithfully pay out all county moneys which shall be deposited in his hands, agreeably to the orders of the County Court of said County and faithfully discharge and perform all duties incumbent on him by law as such trustee; then the above obligation to be null and void, otherwide to remain in full force and virtue.

Acknowledged in open) Guilford Jones- (Seal)
Court and approved) David P. Posey- (Seal)
by the same April 1st 1844.) S. A. Thompson- (Seal)
Test. Jas. L. Green,)
Chairman of the County Court)
of said County-)

This day, Ivey Chandler came into Court here and produced the Certificate of Isaac Braden, Coroner of this County Certifying that he was on Saturday the 2nd day of March last duly and legally elected to serve as Constable in the 1st Civil District of this County.

Pg. 692 Whereupon the said Ivey Chandler entered into bond and was qualified according to law.

This day, Joseph Balderson and Daniel McLeod came into Court here and produced the Certificate of Isaac Braden, Coroner of this County Certifying that they were duly and legally elected on Saturday the 2nd day of March last to serve as Constable in the 2nd District Civil of this county. Whereupon the said Joseph Balderson and Daniel McLeod, entered into bond and were qualified as the Law directs.

This day Robertson Meadows came into court here and produced the Certificate of Isaac Braden, Coroner of this County certifying that on Saturday the 2nd day of March last, he was duly and legally elected to serve as Constable in the 6th Civil District of this county whereupon the said Robertson Meadows entered into bond and was qualified as the Law directs.

This day, Alex M. Dunavant came into court here and produced the Certificate of Isaac Braden, Coroner of this County, certifying that on Saturday the 2nd day of March last he was duly and legally elected to serve as Constable in the 7th Civil District of this County-Whereupon the said Alex M. Dunavant entered into bond with security and was qualified according to law.

Pg. 693 This day, William J. Pitts came into court here and presented the certificate of Isaac Braden, Coroner of this county certifying that on the 2nd day of March last he was duly and legally elected to serve as Constable in the 8th Civil District of this County-Whereupon the said William J. Pitts entered into bond with security and was qualified according to law.

This day, the Court proceeded to elect a County Surveyor for Lauderdale County. Whereupon Jonathan L. Hearring was duly and legally elected Surveyor as aforesaid. Thereupon the said Johnathan L. Hearring came into Court and entered into bond with security and was duly qualified according to law.

This day, Isaac D. Maxwell tendered to the Court here his resignation of the office of Ranger of this County which resignation was accepted. Whereupon the Court proceeded to elect a Ranger for Lauderdale County. William Boydston having been duly and legally elected Ranger as aforesaid entered into bond and was duly qualified according to Law.

This day, James Gillespie and Edward Kennelly presented their commissions from James C. Jones, Governor of the State of Tennessee appointing them Justices of the Peace for Lauderdale County-whereupon they were duly qualified according to law.

Pg. 694 Ordered that Right Koonce, overseer of the road from Durhamville to the West end of James Anthony's land have the following hands to work said road to wit:- Caleb Arnold, Miles Arnold, James Brown, James Cleaves, William Cleaves, Samuel Pitman, Joseph Hayes, John Holmes, Thos. Holmes, Wm. Matthews, Saml. Thompson's hands, William Thompson, Wm. Holmes, John Cleaves, S. S. Koonce,

Pg. 694 cont. C. T. Walker and that he continue to keep said road in repair as a first class road.

Ordered, that Thomas Hazlewood be appointed overseer of the Turnpike road from Haywood County-line to the road leading from Durhamville To Ripley and that he have the following hands to keep said road in repair-(To Wit)- Thomas Blackwell and Hands, Benjamin Watkins and Robt. Walker and hands and Walter Glosson and that he keep the same in repair as a second class.

Ordered that Robert C. West be appointed overseer of the public road leading from Ripley to Brownsville by the way of Champ C. Conners and that he work
Pg. 695 from Ripley to the County-Line, and that he have all hands in the following bounds to work on said road to wit:- Beginning at the forks of the road near James Prices' running with Prices branch or down to Cane Creek thence up the same to the mouth of Matthews Creek, thence up said Creek to where Champ C. Conner's road crosses the same then east with said road to Haywood County-line, thence South with said line to the south boundary line of Lance Graves tract of land thence west with said last mentioned line to Matthews Creek, thence down said creek to R. L. Byrn bridge, thence West to Paynes Spring branch, thence up the North fork of the same so as to intersect the Brownsville road west of Wm. T. Morehead's grass lot, Thence West with the Brownsville road to the beginning, and that he keep said road in repair as a second class road.

Ordered that Thomas Aug. Anthony be appointed overseer of the public road from Durhamville Spring to the road leading from Brownsville to Ripley and that he have the hands of Mary J. Lee and Artham Williams and that he keep the same
Pg. 696 in repair as a first class road.

Ordered that Smith Kent be appointed overseer of the public Brownsville road leading from Brownsville to Ripley from Haywood County-line and that he work to the North end of Mary J. Lee's field and that he have his own hands Peter R. Wenningham and hands and Thomas Tuggle and hands and that he keep the same in repair as a first class road.

Ordered that John F. Jett be appointed overseer of the road leading from Ripley to Brownsville commencing at the four mile post from Ripley and working to the North Corner of Mary J. Lee's fence and that he have his own hands, P. C. Dial's and hands and G. W. Tatum and hands and that he keep the same in repair as a first class road.

This day, L. M. Campbell, Clerk of this Court presented to Court settlement made by Isaac M. Steele, late Clerk of this Court with Wm. P. Gaines, Guardian to Juretta G. Neiswanger, with D. P. Posey, Guardian to Virginia H. Keller and Benj. S. Tyus, Administrator of the estate of J. D. Coachman and
Pg. 697 also a settlement made by him with Joseph Hays, Guardian to the heirs of Jesse Moore, which settlement after being examined by the Court are confirmed in all things and ordered to be recorded.

On motion of Isaac M. Steele, Esq. and it appearing to the satisfaction of the Court, James L. Green a citizen of this County is a man of good moral character and that he has attained the age of Twenty-one years: It is therefore ordered that said facts be certified as a preparatory step to his obtaining License to practice law in this State.

Ordered, that the following good and lawful men of the body of this County be summoned by the Sheriff as the law directs to appear before Honorable the Circuit Court to be held for this County in the Court House in Ripley on the third Monday in June next, then and there to serve as Grand or Petit Jurors as the case may be-(To Wit):- George W. Young, David A. Bradford, David Gilliland, Christopher Watson, A. G. W. Byrn, John F. Jett, Gordon M. Stone, James L. Green, Elijah Lake, Wm. Allen, Jas. Gillespie, Tho. J. Childress,
Pg. 698 Henry Willard, James H. Given, E. S. Campbell, Levi Gardner, Drury Massey, Wm. R. Ledbetter, ----- Simmons, Wm. J. Connelly, E. H. Hinton, John T. Smith, James Soward, Samuel Hooper, -----Pierson and N. B. Jackson, and Ivey Chandler, and Daniel McLeod constables to attend said court and Jury.

This day, Lance Graves, Administrator of all and singular the goods and chattels, rights, and credits which were of F. McCoy, deceased returned in open court

Pg. 698 cont. here on oath, an inventory and Sale bill of said estate which is received and ordered to be recorded.

This day, James A. Lackey and Milton F. Lake, Administrators of all singular the goods and chattels, rights and credits which were of James Brandon renturned here in open court on oath an inventory and Sale Bill of said estate which was received and ordered to be recorded.

Ordered the County Trustee pay John F. Jett, Forty-Dollars to be expended for the support and maintainance of Charles Smoot for and during the year 1844 to be paid Quarterly, Ayes, Alexander, E. S. Campbell, Childress, R. C.
Pg. 699 Campbell, Fisher, Green, Gillespie, Kennelly, Peyton, Soward, Steele, a majority of all the Justices in this County, Noes, Byrn and Condray.

Ordered that the County Trustee pay James Gillespie the sum of Thirty-dollars to be expended for the support and maintainance of Nancy Grant a pauper for and during the year 1844 to be paid Quarterly, Ayes, E. S. Campbell, R. C. Campbell, Childress, Fisher, Green, Gillespie, Hinton, Kennelly, Peyton, Soward and Steele, Esquires, a majority of the Justices of this County, Noes, Condray, Byrn and Ledbetter.

Ordered, that Isaac Braden, Coroner of this County be paid by the County Trustee the sum of Eleven-Dollars for holding the popular election in March 1844, that is to say three-Dollars to himself and one-dollar for each of his eight Deputies, Ayes, Esquires, Byrn, Condray, Childress, Fisher, Green, Gillespie, Kennelly, Ledbetter, Peyton, Soward and Steele a majority of the Justices in this County.

Ordered, that the County Trustee pay Wm. W. Lea the sum of Five-Dollars
Pg. 700 for coffin and other funeral expences for Charles Catrell in May 1843, Ayes, Alexander, E. S. Campbell, R. C. Campbell, Childress, Condray, Fisher, Gillespie, Ledbetter, Peyton, Steele, a majority of all the Justices in this County, Noes, Green, Kennelly and Soward.

It is ordered, by the Court that the County Trustee pay William A. Simmons, Eight-Dollars for making coffin and intering a drowned man, Ayes, Alexander, E. S. Campbell, R. C. Campbell, Childress, Fisher, Green, Peyton and Steele, Noes, Condray, Gillespie, Kennelly, Ledbetter and Soward.

It is ordered by the Court that the County Trustee pay to Thos. Hazlewood five-dollars for making coffin for Cooper a free negro, Ayes, E. S. Campbell, R. C. Campbell, Childress, Fisher, Green, Gillespie, Ledbetter, Peyton, Soward and Steele, Noes, Kennelly.

It is ordered by the Court that the County Trustee pay to Elnathan H. Condray, the sum of Twenty-six Dollars for repairing a bridge on the Dyersburg road, Ayes, Alexander, Byrn, E. S. Campbell, R. C. Campbell, Childress, Condray, Fisher, Green, Gillespie, Kennelly, Ledbetter, Peyton and Steele.

Ordered that the County Trustee pay Isaac M. Steele the sum of Twenty-
Pg. 701 Dollars for Money sent to Nashville on the 9th day of March last to purchase a minute book for this Court and a book for the Clerk of the Circuit Court to record License in, Ayes, Esq. Byrn, Condray, Childress, R. C. Campbell, E. S. Campbell and Green, one-third of all the Justices in this County.

Ordered that the Cty. Trustee pay Elnathan H. Condray, Ten-Dollars for taking in a list of taxable property and polls for the 6th Civil District of Lauderdale County for the year 1844, Ayes, Esquires, Byrn, Condray, Green, Gillespie, Ledbetter, Peyton and Steele, one-third of all the Justices of this County.

Ordered, that the County Trustee pay Isaac M. Steele, Twenty-four Dollars and Seventy-five cents for recording the returns of the Revenue Commissioners for the years 1840, 1841, 1842 and 1843, Ayes, Esquires, Byrn, Condray, Childress, Fisher, Green, Gillespie, Hinton, Kennelly, Ledbetter, Peyton and Soward, a majority of all the Justices in said County.

Ordered, that the County Trustee pay Isaac M. Steele, Clerk, Two-Dollars, for a Witness Docket for the office of Clerk of the Circuit Court, Ayes, Esquires,
Pg. 702 Alexander, Byrn, E. S. Campbell, R. C. Campbell, Childress, Condray, Fisher, Green, Gillespie, Kennelly, Peyton and Soward, a majority of all the Justices of said County.

Pg. Ordered, that the County Trustee pay Isaac M. Steele nine-Dollars for
702 Road orders, Juries of view Jury Tickets, Venire Facias and postage since the
cont. October Term of this Court-Ayes, Esquires, Alexander, Byrn, E. S. Campbell, R.
C. Campbell, Childress, Condray, Fisher, Green, Gillespie, Hinton, Kennelly,
Ledbetter, Peyton, and Soward, a majority of all the Justices in this county.

Ordered that the County Trustee pay to W. Bevins nine-dollars for expences in burying A. Q. Barnes, Ayes, Alexander, E. S. Campbell, R. C. Campbell,
Childress, Fisher, Green, Kennelly, Soward, Noes, Byrn, Condray, Gillespie,
Ledbetter, Peyton, Steele, one-third of all the Justices voting in the affirmative.

Ordered that the County Trustee pay to Rezin L. Byrn, Two-dollars and fifty cents for settling with the County Trustee as revenue commissioner, Ayes,
Alexander, Byrn, E. S. Campbell, R. C. Campbell, Childress, Condray, Fisher,
Green, Gillespie, Kennelly, Ledbetter, Payton, Soward, Steele, a majority of
all the Justices in this county.

Ordered that the County Trustee pay to Saml. V. Gilliland, Two+Dollars
Pg. and Fifty cents for settling with County Trustee as Commissioner of Revenue,
703 Ayes, Alexander, Byrn, E. S. Campbell, R. C. Campbell, Childress, Condray,
Fisher, Green, Gillespie, Kennelly, Ledbetter, Peyton, Soward and Steele.

Ordered that the County Trustee pay Isaac Braden, Coroner of Lauderdale
County, Five-Dollars for holding an inquest on the body of A. G. Barnes.

Ordered that the County Trustee pay Isaac Braden, Coroner of Lauderdale
County, Five-Dollars for holding an inquest on the body of a man drowned,
name unknown.

Ordered that the County Trustee pay Caleb Miller - forty-five dollars for
building a bridge on the Dyersburg road-Ayes, Alexander, Byrn, E. S. Campbell,
R. C. Campbell, Childress, Condray, Fisher, Green, Gillespie, Kennelly, Ledbetter, Peyton, Steele a majority of all the Justices in this County.

Ordered that the County Trustee pay Thomas G. Rice, Ten-Dollars for taking
in a list of taxable property and polls for the 1st District of this County for
the year 1844. Ayes, Esquires, Byrn, Condray, Green, Gillespie, Ledbetter,
Peyton and Steele, one9third of all the Justices of this County.

Pg. Ordered that the County Trustee pay John H. Maxwell, Ten-Dollars for tak-
704 ing a list of Taxable property and polls for the 2nd district of this county
for the year 1844. Ayes, Esquire, Byrn, Condray, Green, Gillespie, Ledbetter,
Peyton and Steele, one-third of all the Justices of this County.

Ordered that the County Trustee pay R. C. Campbell, Ten-Dollars for taking a list of Taxable property and Polls for the 5th District in this County
for the year 1844. Ayes, Esquires, Byrn, Condray, Green, Gillespie, Ledbetter,
Peyton and Steele, one-third of all the Justices of this County.

Ordered that the County Trustee pay Edward Fisher, Ten-Dollars for taking
a list of Taxable property and palls in the 7th District of Lauderdale County
for the year 1844. Ayes, Esquires, Byrn, Condray, Green, Gillespie, Ledbetter,
Peyton, and Steele, one-third of all the Justices of this County.

Ordered that the County Trustee pay Thos. J. Childress, Ten-dollars for
taking a list of Taxable property and polls in the 3rd district of Lauderdale
County for the year 1844, Ayes, Esquires, Byrn, Condray, Green, Gillespie, Ledbetter, Peyton and Steele, one-third of all the Justices of this County.

Ordered that the County Trustee pay to J. M. Alexander Ten-Dollars for
taking a list of Taxable property and polls for the year 1844 in the 4th District of Lauderdale County, Ayes, Esquires, Byrn, Condray, Green, Gillespie,
Ledbetter, Peyton, and Steele, one-third of all the Justices of this County.

Pg. Ordered that the County Trustee pay to James Soward, Ten-Dollars for tak-
705 ing a list of Taxable property and polls in the 8th district of Lauderdale
County for the year 1844, Ayes, Esquires, Byrn, Condray, Childress, Green, Gillespie, Ledbetter, Peyton and Steele, one-third of all the Justices of this
County.

Ordered that the County Trustee pay to James M. Lewis-Ten-dollars for taking a list of Taxable property and polls in the 9th district of Lauderdale County for the year 1844. Ayes, Esquires, Byrn, Condray, Green, Gillespie, Ledbetter,

Pg. Peyton and Steele, one-third of all the Justices of this County.
705 Ordered that the County Trustee pay David Williams, Twenty-seven dollars
cont. and twenty-five cents for building a Bridge across Goodwin Creek on the road leading from Ripley to Fulton, Ayes, Byrn, Condray, Green, Gillespie, Ledbetter, Peyton, E. S. Campbell and Steele, one-third of all the Justices of this county.

Ordered that the County Trustee pay Isaac Braden the sum of seventy-dollars for building a bridge across Cane Creek on the Old Ashport Road. Ayes, Byrn, Childress, Condray, E. S. Campbell, R. C. Campbell, Green, Gillespie, Peyton, Steele, Esquires. A majority of all the Justices of this County. The clerk is required not to issue the above claim until the commissioners appointed to let out said bridge shall report to him that said Bridge is completed and the said Braden shall enter into bond with security for keeping the said bridge in repair for five years from the time of its completion.

Pg. Henry F. Rutherford came into open court and was duly qualified as deputy
706 sheriff of this County according to law.

Isaac M. Steele came into court here and was duly qualified as deputy Ranger of this County according to law.

This day, Rezin L. Byrn and Samuel V. Gilliland presented to court a settlement with the County Trustee made by them as Revenue Commissioner of Lauderdale County which was ordered to be recorded.

It is ordered by the Court that it be the special duty of the County Court Clerk to attend to the prevention of the Court House from Injury, in keeping the Blind-doors and windows closed.

Whereupon Court adjourned until ten o'clock tomorrow morning.

Jas. L. Green, Chairman-
Thos. J. Childress, J. P.-
E. H. Condray, J. P.-
James Gillespie, J. P.-
Isaac M. Steele, J. P.-

Pg. April 2nd, 1844.-
707 Court met according to adjournment. Present the worshipful James L. Green, Chairman and Justices, Condray, E. S. Campbell, R. C. Campbell, Childress, Gillespie and Steele.

Ordered that John Donalson be released from payment of Double Tax on twenty-five hundred acres of Land in the 3rd Civil District valued at $2500.

Ordered that Walter Carooth, Wm. Carooth and Richard Hill be attached to that part of the old Dyersburg road being north of Cane Creek to the conjunction of the said road and the Ripley road and Wm. Carooth be appointed overseer in the place of Calep Miller and that the following hands be attached to that road Brice M. McLeroy and Curtis Ellis and to be kept as a second class road.

It appearing to the satisfaction of the Court that the bond of G. L. Rutherford, sheriff of this County given yesterday for the ddscharge his duties is defecient in the amount of the penal sum. It is therefore ordered that he be notified to come into Court at its May session and give bond with secutity as the law directs.

This day, Gilly H. Braden came into Court here and renewed her bond with security as Guardian of William Hunter according to law which was ordered to be recorded.

Ordered that Court adjourn until Court in Course.

Jas. L. Green, Chairman-
Thos. J. Childress, J. P.-
Isaac M. Steele, J. P.-

Pg. May 1844-
708 State of Tennessee-

Be it Remembered that at a Quorum Court began and held for the County of Lauderdale in the State aforesaid, in the Court House in the town of Ripley on the first Monday it being the sixth day of May A.D.1844 and the 68th year of the independence of the United States of America-Present and holding said Court

Pg. 708 cont. the worshipful Elmathan R. Condray, Henry S. Peyton and A. G. W. Byrn, Esquires.

This day, David Fitzpatrick and N. B. Jackson presented their Commissions from James C. Jones, Governor of the State of Tennessee appointing them Justices of the Peace in and for Lauderdale County-Whereupon they were duly qualified according to law.

Whereas, it appears to the Court that Robert Critchfield has departed this life intestate and application being made by E. H. Hinton to have letters of administration granted to him on the estate of the said Robert Critchfield, deceased, he having given bond and security and qualified as the Law in such cases direct; it is therefore ordered by the Court that he have letters accordingly.

Ordered that Thomas Blythe be appointed overseer of that part of public
Pg. road leading from Ripley to Dyersburg lying between the North bank of Caruths
709 Creek and the North end of Boling Fishers field and that he have the following hands, Onesimus Fudge, John A. Pewit, Abram Hamel, and Marian Parker, and that he keep the same in repair as a first class road, also Boling Fishers hands-(To Wit)-

Ordered by the Court that B. M. Flippin be appointed overseer of the road leading from Ripley to Canton Commencing at the forks just beyond Henry Somerow's and continuing on that road to the bridge across Mill Creek and that he have the same hands that were given to Robert Critchfield, deceased, and that he keep the same in repair as a Second class road.

Ordered by the Court that Thomas R. Tuggle be appointed overseer of the public road leading from Brownsville to Ripley from the Haywood County-line and that he work to the North end of Mary J. Lees field and that he have Smith Kent and hands, Peter R. Winningham and hand and JohnHawkins and hands and Thomas H. Hawkins and hands and his own hands and that he keep the same in repair as a first class road.

This day, L. M. Campbell presented to the Court a pro rata distribution of the estate of Robert Ford deceased which being by the Court fully examined and understood is in all things confirmed.

This day, William A. Wood, Guardian to Robert T. Wood, Rezin L. Wood,
Pg. Handy Wood, Sabert Wood and Moses E. Wood returned here into open Court on oath
710 a report of all the claims due him and by him or guardian aforesaid which was received and ordered to be recorded.

This day, John Floyd came into Court and presented the Certificate of the Coroner of Lauderdale County certifying that on the 2nd day of March 1844 he was duly and legally elected a Constable in and for the 3rd Civil District of this County, Whereupon the said Floyd gave bond with security and was qualified according to law.

This day, James M. Rucker came into court and presented the Certificate of the Coroner of Lauderdale County, certifying that on the 2nd March 1844 he was duly and legally elected a Constable in and for the 9th district of this county-whereupon the said Rucker entered into bond with security and was qualified according to law.

This day, Griffith L. Rutherford in obedience to an order made at last court came into Court here and renewed his bond for the discharge of his duties as sheriff of this County which bond is in the words and figures following-(To Wit)- Know all men by these presents that we, Griffith L. Rutherford, Henry F. Rutherford, Joseph Wardlow and William P. Gaines, all of the County of Lauderdale and State of Tennessee, are held and firmly bound unto James C. Jones,
Pg. Governor of the State aforesaid for the time being and his successors in of-
711 fice in the penal sum of Twelve-Thousand dollars; for the payment of which well and truly to be made, we bind ourselves, our heirs, executors, and administrators, jointly and severally, firmly by the presents, sealed with our seals and dated the 6 day of May, A.D.-1844.

The condition of the above obligation is such that whereas the above bounden, Griffith L. Rutherford was on the 2nd day of March, A.D.1844 duly and legally elected sheriff of Lauderdale County as appears from the Certificate of Isaac Braden, Coroner of said County, if therefore the said Griffith L. Rutherford shall, well and trully execute and due return make of all process and

Pg. precepts to him directed and pay and satisfy all fees and sums of money by him
711 received or levied by virtue of any process into the proper office by which
cont. the same by the tenor thereof ought to be paid or to the person or persons to whom the same shall be due his, her or their executors, administrators, attorneys, or agents, and in all things well and truly and faithfully execute the said office of sheriff during his continuance therein then the above obligation to be void otherwise to remain in full force and effect.

Acknowledged in open court and) G. L. Rutherford, -(Seal)
approved by the same 6th May 1844) H. F. Rutherford, -(Seal)
Elnathan H. Condray, Chr. protem-) Joseph Wardlow, -(Seal)
Wm. P. Gaines, -(Seal)

Ordered by the Court that Court adjourn until Court in Course.

E. H. Condray,(J.P.)-Chairman Protem
H. L. Peyton, J. P.
A. G. W. Byrn, J. P.

www.ingramcontent.com/pod-product-compliance
Lightning Source LLC
Chambersburg PA
CBHW080610270326
41928CB00016B/2993

* 9 7 8 0 7 8 8 4 9 0 7 7 4 *